MILITARY EDUCATION AND THE EMERGING MIDDLE CLASS IN THE OLD SOUTH

This book argues that military education was an important institution in the development of the southern middle class as a regional group and as part of the national middle class in the late antebellum years. It explores class formation, professionalization, and social mobility in the 1840s and 1850s, using these data to define the middle class on a national level, while also identifying regionally specific characteristics of the emerging southern middle class. Green argues that antebellum military education illuminates the emerging southern middle class, a group difficult to locate and differentiate; that it offered social stability or mobility; and that it explicitly linked middle-class stability or mobility to the ongoing national professionalization of teachers. Ultimately, these schools demonstrate that educational opportunity and reform took place in the antebellum South and that schooling aided southerners in social mobility.

Jennifer R. Green is associate professor of history at Central Michigan University. Her dissertation, completed at Boston University, won the Claude A. Eggertsen Best Dissertation Prize from the History of Education Society. She has published articles in the *Journal of Southern History, Journal of the Historical Society*, and the collection *Southern Manhood* and presented at major conferences. She was the recipient of a Teaching American History Grant for 2004–2007.

T0370556

Military Education and the Emerging Middle Class in the Old South

Jennifer R. Green
Central Michigan University

CAMBRIDGE UNIVERSITY PRESS
Cambridge, New York, Melbourne, Madrid, Cape Town, Singapore,
São Paulo, Delhi, Dubai, Tokyo, Mexico City

Cambridge University Press
The Edinburgh Building, Cambridge CB2 8RU, UK

Published in the United States of America by Cambridge University Press, New York

www.cambridge.org
Information on this title: www.cambridge.org/9780521201285

First published 2008
First paperback edition 2011

A catalogue record for this publication is available from the British Library

Library of Congress Cataloguing in Publication Data

Green, Jennifer R.,
Military education and the emerging middle class in the Old South / Jennifer R. Green.
    p. cm.
Includes bibliographical references and index.
ISBN 978-0-521-89493-7 (hbk.)
1. Military education – Southern States – History – 19th century.   2. Middle class –
Southern States – History – 19th century.   3. Southern States – Social conditions –
19th century.   4. Southern States – Economic conditions – 19th century.   I. Title.
U409.S9G73   2008
305′.55097509034–dc22   2008004826

ISBN 978-0-521-89493-7 Hardback
ISBN 978-0-521-20128-5 Paperback

Contents

List of Illustrations and Tables

Illustrations

Illustrations follow page 150

9.   John Joseph Chadick demonstrates the cadets' literary flare in this poem.
10. An invitation to the Western Military Institute's 1852 Military Ball sent by W. M. Johnson to Miss Nannie E. Marshall.

Tables

Appendix Tables

List of Abbreviations

AAS	American Antiquarian Society
ALSMA	American Literary, Scientific and Military Academy
CIT	The Citadel Archives and Museum
Duke	Refers to the Rare Book, Manuscript, and Special Collections Library, Duke University
Emory	Refers to the Department of Special Collections, Richard Woodruff Library, Emory University
FHS	Francis H. Smith
GMI	Georgia Military Institute
HMA	Hillsboro Military Academy
KMI	Kentucky Military Institute
KMMA	Kings Mountain Military Academy
NCMI	North Carolina Military Institute
NCSA	North Carolina State Archives
SCDAH	South Carolina Division of Archives and History
SCHS	South Carolina Historical Society
SCL	The South Caroliniana Library, University of South Carolina
SCMA	South Carolina Military Academy
SHC	Southern Historical Collection, Wilson Library, University of North Carolina at Chapel Hill
UNC	University of North Carolina
USMA	United States Military Academy
Vanderbilt	Refers to the Jean and Alexander Heard Library, Vanderbilt University Archives

VHS	Virginia Historical Society
VMI	Virginia Military Institute
WKU	Western Kentucky University
WMI	Western Military Institute

Acknowledgments

The years that this project evolved from a graduate school seminar paper to a book have changed me even more than the project has changed. Over the course of those ten years, I have become a stronger person and more nuanced critic, and I clearly see how the book has benefited from my own development. It has a more significant and compelling argument than it could have had a decade ago. I know both my life and the text have improved with the assistance of so many people with whom I have come into contact. Let me express my gratitude to the many people who helped me in small and great ways. I hope you know who you are.

I would not be where I am without Lou Ferleger's assistance and contributions as reader, mentor, and friend. He has been a thorough and constant supporter of my work; even when I disagreed with his advice – I took *many* additional research trips rather than sitting down and writing – he encouraged the project and my career. I am indebted for his time, phone calls, emails, and advice that have made me a better historian, helped me in the profession, and encouraged me to lead the best life I can. My dissertation advisor, Nina Silber, led me into southern history and for that I thank her. Her penetrating questions made this a better work and improved my historical skills. Ken Greenberg, Mary Steedly, and Bruce Schulman also served on my dissertation board those years ago.

I have enjoyed many thought-provoking comments and support from scholars at conferences and in correspondence. I greatly appreciate the generosity of those people. Thank you. In particular, the intellectual and warm atmosphere of the St. George Tucker Society of southern scholars made me think more critically, and most recently dialogue with Jon Wells helped me focus my interests in the history of education and social class even as my ideas about them expanded. The Cambridge University Press editors and reviewers offered excellent suggestions that improved the final version of this book; any omissions or imprecision are my fault alone.

As a dissertation, the manuscript received financial assistance from a Mellon Research Fellowship at the Virginia Historical Society and an Edmund N. Snyder Graduate Fellowship from the Stonewall Jackson House. Lexington, Virginia has become a home away from home with excellent friends. At later stages, the work also benefited from a Filson Fellowship at The Filson Historical Society in Louisville, Kentucky; the College of Humanities & Social and Behavioral Sciences and a Faculty Research and Creative Endeavors Research Grant from Central Michigan University provided support. I appreciate the assistance of the CMU History Department's office staff, especially Executive Secretary Annette Davis, and former graduate student Paul Yancho who helped me with a summer of number crunching.

Archivists and librarians have assisted me to locate invaluable resources. I must make special note of Diane Jacob and Mary Laura Kludy at the Virginia Military Institute Archives; their knowledge, provided with good humor, saved me a great deal of time in my repeated visits, phone calls, and emails. Jane Yates at the Citadel Archives and Museum also provided assistance from afar. In addition, I benefited from the collections and expertise of the staffs at the Rare Book, Manuscript, and Special Collections Library, Duke University; Department of Special Collections, Richard Woodruff Library, Emory University; Georgia Department of Archives and History; The Library of Virginia; Department of Archives and History, North Carolina State Archives; South Carolina Department of Archives and History; South Carolina Historical Society; The South Caroliniana Library, University of South Carolina; Southern Historical Collection, Wilson Library, University of North Carolina at Chapel Hill; Tennessee State Library and Archives; Special Collections, University of Kentucky; University of Texas at Austin; Jean and Alexander Heard Library, Vanderbilt University; and Department of Library Special Collections, Manuscripts, Western Kentucky University.

Versions of this work have appeared in *Journal of Southern History*, 73 (2007), *The Journal of The Historical Society*, 5 (2005), and *Southern*

Manhood: Perspectives on Masculinity in the Old South (University of Georgia Press, 2004), edited by Craig Thompson Friend and Lorri Glover. The editors and reviewers of these articles assisted in refining my writing and ideas.

As we all know, being a historian can be a solitary business, whether long hours in archives or coffee shops, but a community of the most wonderful kind sustains me. My network stretches from Portland, Oregon, to the community in Mt. Pleasant, to Boston, with many highlights in between. Many of my friends are as excited by the completion of this book as I am. I hope the people I love know how much their presence in my life has supported me personally and allowed me to pursue this work. Exchanging chapters and advice with Amy Hay provided important deadlines and comments. Finally, I'm happy to be able to offer my family a physical tome to show for the work and thought that they have followed over these years. I dedicate this book to my grandmother Inez G. Green (1910–1996).

Illustrations

Figure 1. The Kentucky Military Institute's barracks, cadet corps, and healthful location are highlighted in this etching, circa 1850. Courtesy of the Kentucky Historical Society.

Figure 2. Henry K. Burgwyn (front row, center) poses with classmates William Bray, Emmett Morrison, William Smith, and Richard Williams at the Virginia Military Institute (VMI) in 1861. These young men, as members of the Class of 1861, went to Richmond as drillmasters the April before their graduation. Courtesy of the VMI Archives.

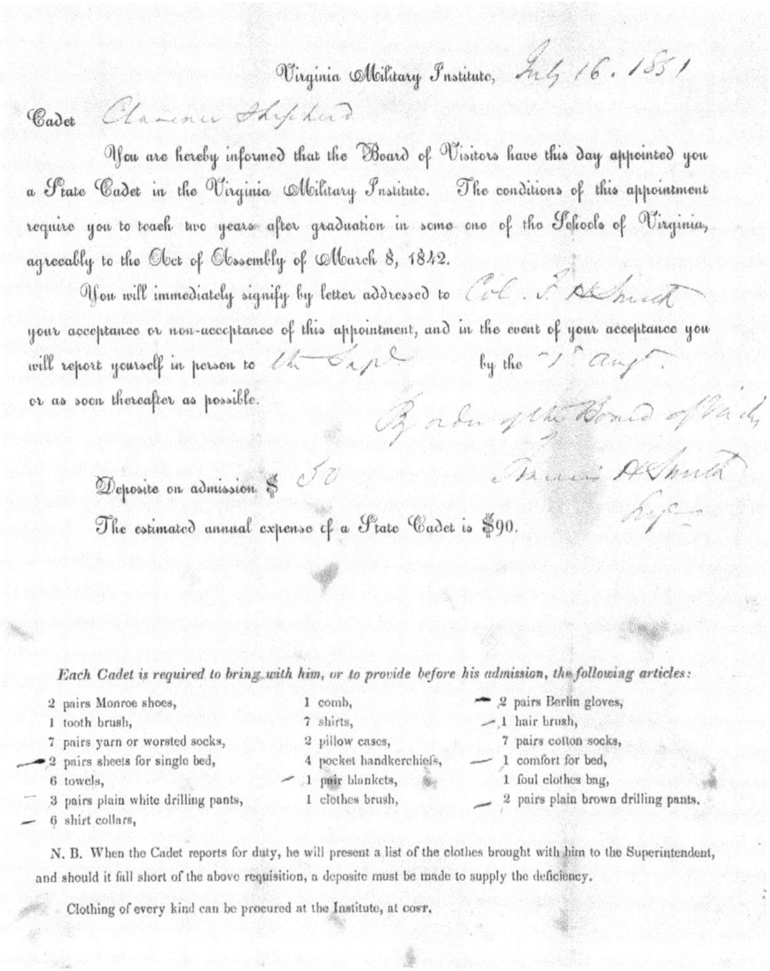

Virginia Military Institute, July 16. 1851

Cadet *Clarence Shepherd*

You are hereby informed that the Board of Visitors have this day appointed you a State Cadet in the Virginia Military Institute. The conditions of this appointment require you to teach two years after graduation in some one of the Schools of Virginia, agreeably to the Act of Assembly of March 8, 1842.

You will immediately signify by letter addressed to *Col. F. Smith* your acceptance or non-acceptance of this appointment, and in the event of your acceptance you will report yourself in person to *the Supt* by the *1st Augt.* or as soon thereafter as possible.

By order of the Board of Visitors

Francis H. Smith
Supt.

Deposite on admission $ 50

The estimated annual expense of a State Cadet is $90.

Each Cadet is required to bring with him, or to provide before his admission, the following articles:

2 pairs Monroe shoes,
1 tooth brush,
7 pairs yarn or worsted socks,
2 pairs sheets for single bed,
6 towels,
3 pairs plain white drilling pants,
6 shirt collars,

1 comb,
7 shirts,
2 pillow cases,
4 pocket handkerchiefs,
1 pair blankets,
1 clothes brush,

2 pairs Berlin gloves,
1 hair brush,
7 pairs cotton socks,
1 comfort for bed,
1 foul clothes bag,
2 pairs plain brown drilling pants.

N. B. When the Cadet reports for duty, he will present a list of the clothes brought with him to the Superintendent, and should it fall short of the above requisition, a deposite must be made to supply the deficiency.

Clothing of every kind can be procured at the Institute, at cost.

Figure 3. Edward Clarence Shepherd's 1851 admission letter from the Virginia Military Institute (VMI) lists precisely the clothing and supplies with which a student should arrive. It also indicates his costs as a state-funded cadet at $90 per annum and the obligation to teach in Virginia for two years after graduation to repay that funding. Courtesy of the VMI Archives.

Figure 4. Edward Clarence Shepherd, Virginia Military Institute (VMI) Class of 1855, in uniform with stripes and shako. Coming from Shepherdstown (now West Virginia), this young man was a middle son with an older sister teaching school and a mother who wanted him prepared for "usefullness." He was one of many military school alumni who worked in the profession of teaching. Courtesy of the VMI Archives.

Figure 5. One of a series of drawings of the residents of Virginia Military Institute (VMI) Barracks Rooms 12 and 14, 2nd stoop, done by Cadet James Waddell in 1855, the year he graduated. Dressed in the same uniforms shown in the daguerreotype from 1854, this drawing appears to represent cadet life; Waddell defies the regulations by smoking as his friends sit by, a shako rests on the wardrobe, and bedrolls are stacked on the right. His companions are Edward Magruder, Thomas Barksdale, Edward C. Shepherd, John Wilson, and probably Davidson Penn, who graduated in 1856. As they look to be the typical cadets of the 1850s, five of them also represent alumni antebellum career trends: a future military educator in Georgia, an orphan who became a teacher and lawyer, another teacher, a man who worked as a lawyer and in a cotton press business, and one of the few elites, a tobacco planter. Courtesy of the VMI Archives.

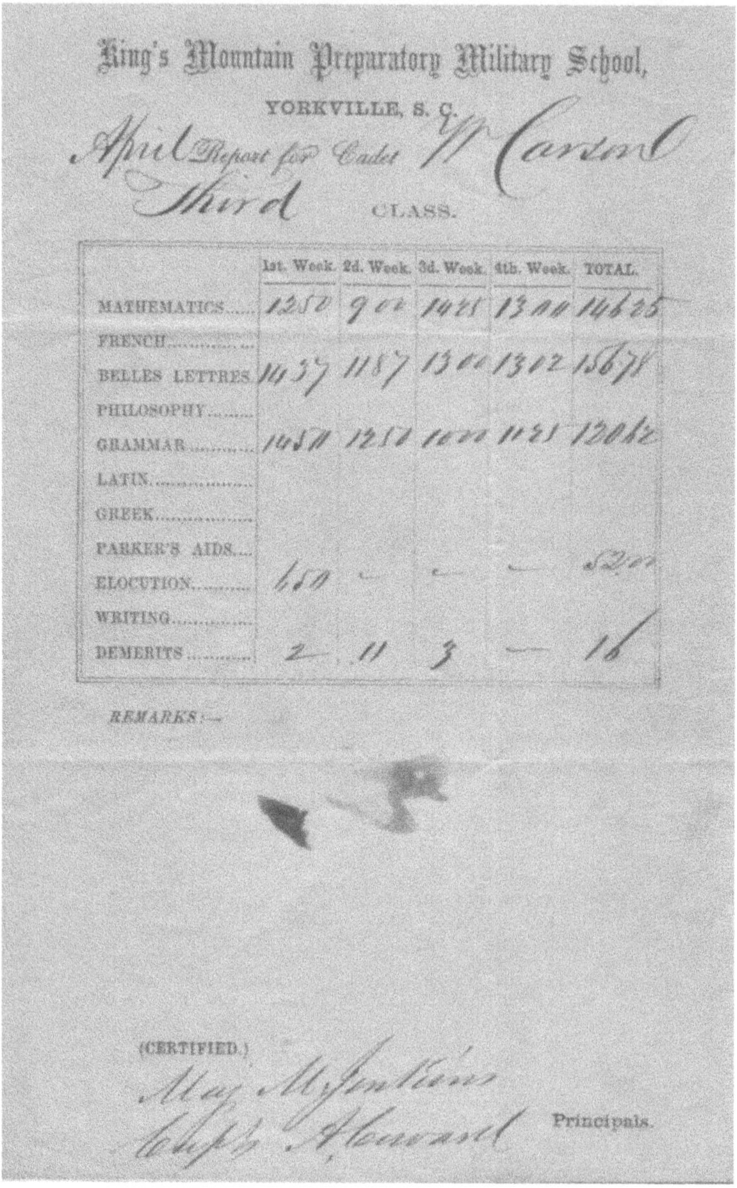

King's Mountain Preparatory Military School,

YORKVILLE, S. C.

April Report for Cadet W Carson

Third CLASS.

	1st. Week.	2d. Week.	3d. Week.	4th. Week.	TOTAL.
MATHEMATICS	1250	900	1425	1300	14625
FRENCH					
BELLES LETTRES	1437	1187	1300	1312	15678
PHILOSOPHY					
GRAMMAR	1450	1250	1000	1125	12062
LATIN					
GREEK					
PARKER'S AIDS					
ELOCUTION	650	—	—	—	520
WRITING					
DEMERITS	2	11	3	—	16

REMARKS:—

(CERTIFIED.)

Maj. M. Jenkins

Capt. A. Coward

Principals.

Figure 6. Graduates Micah Jenkins and Asbury Coward (South Carolina Military Academy, 1854) ran Kings Mountain Military Academy before the Civil War. This grade report shows Cadet William Carson's standing in April 1857, nearly a year before his dismissal for extreme disobedience. Notice that the list of subjects includes Greek, which indicates the school trying to act as a preparatory academy for the classical curriculum at colleges. Neither Jenkins nor Coward learned Greek at the South Carolina Military Academy, but their former professor C. C. Tew advised them to add a classical course in 1855. From the Collections of the South Carolina Historical Society.

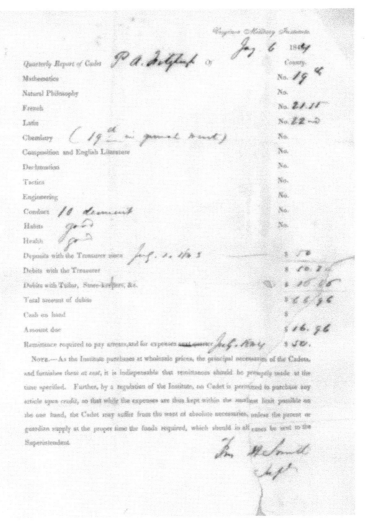

Figure 7. Quarterly reports such as this one informed families of their son's ranking in courses, general merit, and conduct. Philip A. Fitzhugh's mediocre standing and debts are listed for his brother, who acted as a guardian for this orphan. In January 1844, his second term at the Virginia Military Institute (VMI), Fitzhugh took mathematics, French, Latin, and chemistry. Notice that VMI does not offer Greek, and the military aspects of the curriculum received little attention; the only military subject is Tactics and Fitzhugh has no grade in it. The report reminds guardians that money should be sent directly to the school administration. After graduating in the bottom quarter of his class, Fitzhugh became a doctor. Courtesy of the VMI Archives.

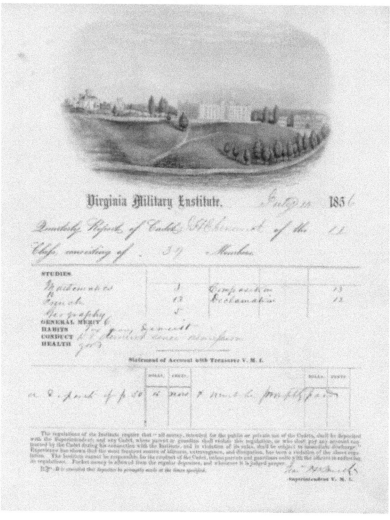

Figure 8. Compared to Fitzhugh's 1844 report, Joseph Chenoweth's July 1856 grade report illustrates the improvement in both circulars sent to parents and the construction of barracks at the Virginia Military Institute (VMI) in Lexington. Like the Kentucky Military Institute image from 1850, the bucolic setting is meant to suggest health, yet it is dominated by the school buildings. The "Too many demerit" Chenoweth received were listed on the back of the report; he received and accepted a similar report to the one that had precipitated the Gordon-Thompson 1852 courts-martial. The bottom third of the report again concerns finances, here requesting the prompt payment of a $50 deposit. The report is signed by Superintendent Francis Henney Smith. Courtesy of the VMI Archives.

Figure 9. John Joseph Chadick demonstrates the cadets' literary flare in this poem. He extols the everlasting nature of Christian love over tender human love, expressing a religiosity common to many antebellum cadets. The North Carolina Military Institute buildings shown on this stationary would reopen as the Mecklenburg Female College after the Civil War. Courtesy of Duke University Rare Book, Manuscript, and Special Collections Library.

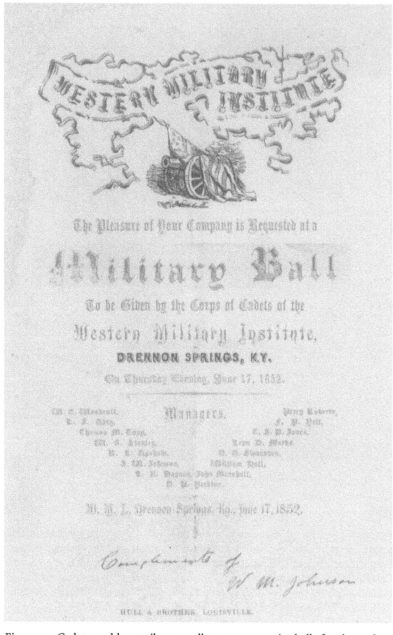

Figure 10. Cadets could contribute small sums to organize balls for themselves and members of the local communities. Of course, many young men especially wanted to encourage the presence of young women. This invitation to the Western Military Institute's 1852 Military Ball was sent by W. M. Johnson to Miss Nannie E. Marshall. Courtesy of The Filson Historical Society, Louisville, Kentucky.

Introduction

The year 1839 witnessed the founding of the Virginia Military Institute (VMI), the first state military school in the U.S. South. By the outbreak of the Civil War in 1861, there were twelve state military academies in the South, as well as more than seventy private ones. Together, these institutions educated more than 11,000 young men – a generation, or possibly two, of the growing southern middle class.[1] The rise of southern military education occurred in the context of increasing sectional tensions preceding the Civil War, and this timing certainly contributed to the institutions' success and informed the students who passed through their gates. Yet military schools also participated in the modernization of the Old South; they were more culturally and socially significant and progressive than their current image as institutions of retrograde, militaristic extremists would suggest. Indeed, the study of southern military education provides an excellent window into the makeup and priorities of the southern middle class that emerged in the late antebellum years. This book emphasizes military education as one location for the development of the middle class as both a regional and a national group.

---

[1] Bruce Allardice, "West Points of the Confederacy: Southern Military Schools and the Confederate Army," *Civil War History*, 43 (December 1997), 321, counts ninety-six southern military academies and computes that 12,000 alumni entered the Confederate army. My calculations confirm only 11,000 matriculates, but Allardice's figure suggests a larger number as not all alumni served in the Confederate army. Lester Austin Webb, "The Origin of Military Schools in the United States Founded in the Nineteenth Century" (Ph.D. diss., University of North Carolina, 1958), 207, discovers thirty military academies in Virginia, 1840–1860, which may suggest a higher total number of schools than both Allardice and I have evidence for. Given the records and transitory nature of nineteenth-century schools, a higher figure would be unsurprising. Appendix 1 lists the military schools I have confirmed by evidence.

It explores class formation, professionalization, and social mobility in the 1840s and 1850s through military education. Military schools, which educated non-elite young men in the Old South, were used to advantage (and for their advantage) by the families who sent their sons off to be cadets. Middle-class southerners mirrored their northern counterparts in leveraging education to develop professional occupations, social stability, and what are often identified as bourgeois values; as they accomplished these things, they attempted to redefine the southern criteria for upward mobility to make those criteria attainable for men of their standing.

The complex work of defining the emerging southern middle class – were they small planters? were they yeomen? – has begun but is far from complete. Perhaps the best definition of that class, and one supported by this research, comes from Jonathan Daniel Wells, who identifies it as made up of nonagricultural professionals. Wells estimates that the middle class of nonagricultural professionals encompassed 10 percent of the urban population in the South. My analysis of military education suggests that the group includes rural professionals and thus the figure may be even higher, perhaps reaching 15 or 20 percent of the southern population.[2] This small but growing constituency of doctors, merchants, teachers, and other white-collar workers in southern society often remains absent from or underrepresented in historical texts.[3] Defining the socioeconomic characteristics of this class sheds light on the group, as well as on the structure and processes of class in the South and across the nation. For this reason, the first chapter of this study outlines the emerging southern middle class and indicates how military school patrons fit into that rank.

All military schools modeled themselves on the United States Military Academy at West Point. In addition to offering education free of

---

[2] On the difficulties of defining the middle class, see Peter N. Stearns, "The Middle Class: Toward a Precise Definition," *Comparative Studies of Society and History*, 21 (July 1979), 377–96. Wells, *The Origins of the Southern Middle Class, 1800–1861* (Chapel Hill: University of North Carolina Press, 2004), 8. Wells employs the term "middling class" for before 1850 and "middle class" for post-1850. This text focuses on the formation of the southern middle class during the antebellum years; thus, the term "emerging" or "developing" is implicit herein even when not printed.

[3] An exception is Alden B. Pearson Jr., "A Middle-Class, Border-State Family During the Civil War" in *The Southern Common People*, ed. Edward Magdol and Jon L. Wakelyn (Westport, CT: Greenwood Press, 1980), 151–74. Southern scholars have turned attention to these groups since 2000; see especially work by Jonathan Daniel Wells, Frank Byrne, Scott Marler, and Beth Barton Schweiger.

the cost of tuition, fees, or living expenses, West Point and Annapolis guaranteed employment in the armed services upon graduation. As the federal military academy, West Point possessed a special prestige. Unlike the national academies, southern military schools offered no connection to the U.S. military; cadets at state and private schools received no preferential entrance to the armed forces, and 95 percent of them chose civilian careers. The twelve southern state legislatures that established military institutes did so not to train soldiers so much as to employ cadets as guards for state arms and to procure teachers by requiring scholarship recipients to teach in the state for two years after graduation. Private military education, likewise, fell into a category of educational experimentation and expansion commonplace throughout the nation in the early nineteenth century, adopting West Point's science-based curriculum and disciplinary program without its military mission.

This study focuses on southern private and state institutes, not the U.S. service academies. I do not analyze education at northern military institutions, though southern boys certainly enrolled in Alden Partridge's American Literary, Scientific and Military Academy, the first private military school, before southern schools took root.[4] Only 12 percent of military schools were located in the North. These schools exhibited the same curriculum and disciplinary structure as southern schools, and they probably attracted northerners for similar reasons as the southern schools attracted southerners. Northern military education did not aid non-elites in the same way as it did in the Old South, however, because northerners had more options for practical, low-cost, and public education available to them. Perhaps for this reason, there is little evidence that many northern military academies remained open beyond the 1840s.

This study of military schools helps to redress gaps in the neglected history of education in the antebellum South and its connection to the emerging middle class. The northern experience has become the historiographic model for the history of education, with the South relegated to an exception. Canonical texts in the field, such as Lawrence Cremin's *American Education* and Carl Kaestle's *Pillars of the Republic*, correctly highlight developments in northern education and society but make only

[4] See, for example, John Ball in Lorri Glover, *Southern Sons: Becoming Men in the New Nation* (Baltimore: The Johns Hopkins University Press, 2007).

passing references to the schooling of southern children. Despite calls to redress this imbalance by historians in every generation from Charles William Dabney in 1936 to Wayne Urban in 1981 and John Hardin Best in 1996, educational history's focus on New England, its so-called Massachusetts Myopia, has persisted.[5] Although classic works in educational history describe the enlargement of educational opportunity throughout the antebellum North, especially with public systems educating non-elite youths, those works and, equally as surprising, those by southern historians have yet to investigate the applicability of their descriptions to the southern context.

What scholarship there is on antebellum southern education has usually focused on public (common) schools, which achieved only limited success, or on higher education, which appears to have benefited

[5] It is historiographically clear why: (1) the Progressive school did it because they connected education to industrialization (thus omitting the Old South); (2) the next wave described public education (absent in the Old South); (3) revisionists focused particularly on Massachusetts and public education as social control in the industrializing era (not the Old South); and (4) the newest trend is the inclusion of previously excluded groups (not southern white men). As a new generation reworks Theodore Sizer's *The Age of Academies*, Edgar Knight's 1919 and Dale Robinson's 1977 works on the Academy Movement in the South are passed over. Similarly, only in 2004 did Robert F. Pace revise E. Merton Coulter's work on southern colleges, whereas northern texts from the early twentieth century, such as Donald Tewksburg's *Founding of American Colleges*, have been much revised. Pace's *Halls of Honor* brought attention to southern college students in a broad synthesis; my data contraindicate Pace's categorization of VMI as a college. Pace, *Halls of Honor: College Men in the Old South* (Baton Rouge: Louisiana State University Press, 2004); Coulter, *College Life in the Old South* (1928; reprint, Athens: University of Georgia Press, 1951); Natalie A. Naylor, "The Antebellum College Movement: A Reappraisal of Tewksbury's *Founding of American Colleges and Universities*," *History of Education Quarterly*, 13 (Fall 1973), 261–74; Carl L. Kaestle, *Pillars of the Republic: Common Schools and American Society, 1780–1860* (New York: Hill and Wang, 1983); Lawrence A. Cremin, *American Education: The National Experience, 1783–1876* (New York: Harper and Row, 1980); Colin B. Burke, *American Collegiate Populations: A Test of the Traditional View* (New York: New York University Press, 1982), 94, 114, 125, analyzes the South but notes the lack of sources for the region, which limits many of his conclusions; Charles William Dabney, *Universal Education in the South* (1936; reprint: New York: Arno Press and the New York Times, 1969), 1:60–1; John Hardin Best, "Education in the Forming of the American South," *History of Education Quarterly*, 36 (Spring 1996), esp. 44, 48; Wayne J. Urban, "History of Education: A Southern Exposure," *History of Education Quarterly*, 21 (Summer 1981), 133–36; "Symposium: Reappraisals of the Academy Movement," *History of Education Quarterly*, 41 (Summer 2001), 216–70. Only four articles on antebellum southern education appeared in 2003, and the number was down to two in 2006; "Southern History in Periodicals, 2003: A Selected Bibliography," *Journal of Southern History*, 70 (May 2004), 351–402; "Southern History in Periodicals, 2006: A Selected Bibliography," *Journal of Southern History*, 73 (May 2007), 363–412.

primarily the elite.[6] Southern military schools, as postprimary but not collegiate institutions, fall into a third category, which has been recently labeled "higher schooling." That terminology, offered by Nancy Beadie and Kim Tolley, usefully distinguishes from colleges and universities the numerous academies that offered education beyond common schools but did not confer bachelor's degrees. As scholars of the nineteenth century are well aware, antebellum academies and colleges did not display the more distinct definitional clarity that they began to assume in the latter half of the century.[7] What are now different types of institutions – academies, institutes, seminaries, and schools – might in the Old South have had the same curriculum, structure, type of students, and meaning in the students' lives as a culminating school experience. Some military institutions became preparatory academies; others added military programs to existing colleges and occasionally granted bachelor's degrees. The larger military institutions compared themselves to colleges (even without granting B.A.s), but they also competed with nonmilitary academies for students. Any young man attending VMI, for example, chose it over Washington College, which was located mere yards

[6] On southern education, see: Bruce W. Eelman, "'An Educated and Intelligent People Cannot Be Enslaved': The Struggle for Common Schools in Antebellum Spartanburg, South Carolina," *History of Education Quarterly*, 44 (Summer 2004), 250–70; Kathryn A. Pippin, "The Common School Movement in the South, 1840–1860" (Ph.D. dissertation, University of North Carolina, 1977); J. Mills Thornton III, "Fiscal Policy and the Failure of Radical Reconstruction in the Lower South," in *Region, Race, and Reconstruction*, ed. J. Morgan Kousser and James M. McPherson (New York: Oxford University Press, 1982), 378–84; Christie Ann Farnham, *The Education of the Southern Belle: Higher Education and Student Socialization in the Antebellum South* (New York: New York University Press, 1994); L. Ray Drinkwater, "Honor and Student Misconduct in Southern Antebellum Colleges," *Southern Humanities Review*, 27 (Fall 1993), 323–44; Robert F. Pace and Christopher A. Bjornsen, "Adolescent Honor and College Student Behavior in the Old South," *Southern Cultures*, 6 (Fall 2000), 9–28; Jan Price Greenough, "Forgive Us Our Transgressions: Rule and Misrule in Antebellum Southern Schools," *Southern Historian*, 21 (2000), 5–24; Pace, *Halls of Honor*.

[7] Nancy Beadie and Kim Tolley, eds., *Chartered Schools: Two-Hundred Years of Independent Academies in the United States, 1727–1925* (New York: RoutledgeFalmer, 2002), 3, 21. Using "higher schooling" generally connects more closely to the historiography of academies but, in the South, military higher schools had roles similar that of colleges; thus, scholarship on "higher schooling" needs to bridge the separate histories of academies and colleges that do not always reflect the realities of the antebellum period. Linguistic difficulties are noted in Roger Geiger, "The Rise and Fall of Useful Knowledge: Higher Education for Science, Agriculture and the Mechanics Arts, 1850–1875," *History of Higher Education Annual*, 18 (1998), 52. Because of this difficulty using nineteenth-century terminology with twenty-first century meaning, the words school, academy, institution, and institute are used interchangeably throughout this work.

away. Indeed, many cadets thought of themselves as college students and equated the two types of institutions, as one father did in 1841 when he described military schooling as providing "a collegiate education." The majority of military institutions, however, were higher schools, not colleges.[8]

Institutions of higher schooling proliferated in the Old South, and this study of military schools provides support for Beadie and Tolley's argument that higher schools were significant institutions in their communities, educating the majority of southern men who received secondary schooling. If they had been enumerated as colleges in the 1850 census, military higher schools would have represented 9.2 percent of the colleges in the same states. For example, the 1850 census enumerated twelve colleges with 1,343 students in Virginia, and VMI served 12 percent of that number.[9] The study of military education also confirms post-1970s revisionist conclusions that non-elites pursued collegiate educations: Just as it did in the North, the reform of curricula away from the classics and toward scientific pursuits in some southern schools encouraged middle-rank southerners, and others below the planter class, to enroll.[10] Across

---

[8] Recommendation letter, [1841] (quotation), Carlton Munford student file, Preston Library, Virginia Military Institute Archives. For clarity, the term "college" as used in this work denotes bachelor's degree–granting colleges and universities. Rather than B.A.s, most military academies gave certificates granting a "Degree" of graduate. Throughout the antebellum years, state legislatures began permitting military institutes, especially colleges with military programs added, such as the University of Alabama, or programs offering Latin, such as the Kentucky Military Institute, to bestow bachelor's degrees. The North Carolina Legislature began conferring the "degree of bachelor of science" in its state military institute in 1859 – the B.S. had been first granted eight years earlier at Harvard – and three years later stipulated that the Hillsboro Military Academy could offer the same degree as "other institutions of learning." Generally, the degrees from military academies and colleges differed, but they fulfilled similar functions as statements of a completed education within a nonstandardized education system. "Report on the Governor's Message," Committee on the Military and Petitions, 6 December 1849, South Carolina Division of Archives and History; Chapter 284, 1859, Chapter 54, 20 February 1862, North Carolina Legislature; William Couper, "The V.M.I. Diploma," *The VMI Alumni News*, 6(3) (June 1930), 4.

[9] Beadie and Tolley, *Chartered Schools*, 3–6. Census data available online at http://fisher.lib. virginia.edu/collections/stats/histcensus/php/state.php, accessed 8 February 2005; public schools excluded. The 1850 census categorized schools either as "colleges" or "academies and other schools," whereas the 1860 census did not.

[10] David F. Allmendinger's pioneering study of northern colleges finds that poor young men attended them in *Paupers and Scholars: The Transformation of Student Life in Nineteenth-Century New England* (New York: St. Martin's Press, 1975); Burke, *American Collegiate*

nineteenth-century America, education played a significant role in the formation of the middle class, the development of professionalization, and the definition of social mobility. Filling the void of research on southern education helps illuminate the middle social position in the South during the early and mid-nineteenth century and makes apparent that the formation of the middle class proceeded in similar – though not identical – ways in the North and South.

The absence of research into military schooling in the South is not the result of an absence of source material. The biographies and correspondence of 1,057 cadets, consisting of approximately 10 percent of the total military school matriculates and including all VMI matriculates from 1839 through 1859, provide the source base for this study. I attempted to locate demographic information on all antebellum military school matriculates and have compiled information on nearly 1,100 young men. All extant personal and institutional records relating to these individuals, available at twenty-two archives and in publication, enable the creation of a detailed picture of military education and its primarily middle-class constituency.

The amount of information available per cadet varies greatly by person, and more records and data exist on men who succeeded in (or after) the Civil War than on their peers. Overall, however, the amount of primary source material available for the study of military education exceeds what is often available for analysis of southern youths and middling groups. For example, occupational data exist on 855 cadets (including 704 from archival research and 151 published in the 1860 South Carolina Military Academy catalogue), 368 of their fathers, and 174 of their kin. This data set compares favorably to smaller ones, such as Beth Barton Schweiger's set of 123 antebellum ministers and Peter

Populations; more recently, Beadie and Tolley's *Chartered Schools* expands "higher schooling" research into women's and African Americans' schooling; it details how private academies allowed women to pay to attend in situations in which they otherwise would have been excluded; the same analysis needs to be applied to southern men in a class-based study. Frederick Rudolph asserts that southern universities clung to classical curriculum (which inherently privileged the elite) longer than northern schools. Rudolph, *Curriculum: A History of the American Undergraduate Course of Study since 1636* (San Francisco: Jossey-Bass Publishers, 1977), ch. 3, esp. 71–75; likewise, Pace, *Hall of Honor*.

Carmichael's set of 110 young Virginians.[11] In addition to demographic data, middle-class southerners' expectations, goals, concerns, and views also come to life in correspondence, speeches, legislation, newspaper and magazine accounts, and institutional records.

Military schools had three distinctive characteristics – funding, discipline, and curriculum – that attracted and benefited the southern middle class. Four chapters of this study analyze these characteristics and their relationship to middle-class formation. Chapter 2 describes the advantages that funding offered southerners with sufficient resources. Legislatures funded military higher schools in Virginia, South Carolina, Georgia, Kentucky, and most southern states, which provided an education at reduced cost for at least one young man per senatorial district. The South Carolina Military Academy (SCMA) opened in 1842 with two locations: the Arsenal Academy in Columbia (for first-year cadets) and Citadel Academy in Charleston. Each year at SCMA, half the cadets could receive scholarships, as compared to only one student per year at South Carolina College. Thus, state military schools offered expanded educational opportunity. This opportunity was not available to just anyone, however: Some schools charged cadets fees of up to $200 per year, which meant that no destitute student would have been able to attend. By providing many students with tuition remission, military schools offered men with limited but sufficient resources places to educate their sons.

In addition to funding, military discipline defined the schools. Military regulation may now be the most recognizable trait of a military education, but it probably was less significant for many antebellum patrons than was the availability of funding or the content of the curriculum. To consider antebellum military schools, we need to put aside common twentieth- (or twenty-first-) century perceptions of them. Court battles of the 1990s about sexual discrimination and images of Citadel men cheering the departure of the school's first female candidate brought with them a spate of critiques that military schools promoted oppressive

---

[11] Beth Barton Schweiger, *The Gospel Working Up: Progress and Pulpit in Nineteenth-Century Virginia* (New York: Oxford University Press, 2000); Peter S. Carmichael, *The Last Generation: Young Virginians in Peace, War and Reunion* (Chapel Hill: University of North Carolina Press, 2005); *Official Register of the South Carolina Military Academy* (Charleston: R. W. Gibbes, 1860), 21–24. Burke, *American Collegiate Populations*, has an extraordinary sample size over 10,000, although also privileging northern sources.

and outdated southern ideals.[12] Such interpretations often rest on a misrepresentation of the history of nineteenth-century military education. Prewar military schools represented educational reform and the concerns of an emerging middle class that employed them to promote social stability and mobility. The discipline system reflected an appreciation of militarism and southern regionalism, of course, but it did far more than just affirm regional culture. Southern military schools, in other words, did not simply reflect the predominant values of the "militant South," as John Hope Franklin proposed in 1956.[13] Cadets, to be sure, faced a strict discipline system, drill requirements, and guard duty as they received their education. Chapter 3 describes the disciplinary program at southern military schools and shows how these schools, more than other southern institutions, encouraged young men to adopt self-regulation. The self-discipline that military education expounded dovetailed with traits advocated by the northern middle class that were increasingly accepted in the South in the late antebellum years, but the emerging southern middle class did not adopt northern middle-class traits wholesale; rather, cadets adapted self-discipline to traditional southern values, such as hierarchy and mastery.

The self-discipline that cadets learned from their military programs influenced the values these young men adopted, which borrowed but remained distinct from those of both the Old South elite and the northern middle class. Entering adulthood, young men grappled with different

[12] Susan Faludi, "The Naked Citadel," *New Yorker* (5 September 1994), 62–81; Faludi, *Stiffed: The Betrayal of the American Man* (New York: William Morrow and Company, 1999), esp. 115, 136; Catherine S. Manegold, *In Glory's Shadow: Shannon Faulkner, the Citadel, and a Changing America* (New York: Alfred A. Knopf, 1999), 37–38. On women at VMI, see: Laura Fairchild Brodie, *Breaking Out: VMI and the Coming of Women* (New York: Pantheon Books, 2000); Elizabeth Fox-Genovese, "Strict Scrutiny, VMI, and Women's Lives," *Seton Hall Law School Constitutional Law Journal*, 6 (Summer 1996), 987–90; Barbara Long, *United States v. Virginia: The Virginia Military Institute Accepts Women* (Berkeley Heights, NJ: Enslow Publishers, 2000); Philippa Strum, *Women in the Barracks: The VMI Case and Equal Rights* (Lawrence: University of Kansas Press, 2002). The negative perceptions of military schools that some of these authors exhibit arose out of the Vietnam era and more recent issues. Twentieth and twenty-first century military education lie far outside the scope of this study.
[13] John Hope Franklin, *The Militant South, 1800–1860* (Boston: Beacon Press, 1956), ch. 8. Marcus Cunliffe questions Franklin's assertion of southern militancy at West Point, *Soldiers and Civilians: The Martial Spirit in America, 1776–1865* (Boston: Little, Brown and Company, 1968). Rod Andrew Jr., *Long Gray Lines: The Southern Military School Tradition, 1839–1915* (Chapel Hill: University of North Carolina Press, 2001).

models of manhood in the nation. Cadets most appreciated a restrained model that northerners, especially evangelicals, also embraced. This
model – inconsistently adopted even in the North – promoted the ideal
man as a self-restrained, moral, and industrious individual.[14] Chapter
4 illuminates the traits military cadets connected to manhood, many of
which were identical to professional, national middle-class values. Cadets
also refined the southern ideal of honor and developed a vision of manhood based on the competing drives for independence and submission.

The final unique characteristic of military education, investigated in
Chapter 5, was its scientific and vocational nature, which significantly
attracted the emerging middle class and also reinforced the values it
was developing. Military education was a successful product of national
curricular reform, which reduced educational costs. Colleges and universities that required advanced knowledge of Latin and Greek texts for
admission necessitated years of tutoring and remained primarily the bas-
tion of the elite; the intensive study of classics was especially prevalent
at southern state universities. Mirroring trends in national educational
reform, however, some small colleges and academies, including most military schools, rejected the study of classical languages, thereby obviating
the need for extensive primary education and training in these languages.
Even the few military academies the curricula of which included classics
maintained less stringent admission requirements in this regard than
did colleges; most military institutes tested only for basic arithmetic and
reading skills. In the classroom, military school curricula emphasized
scientific and mathematical studies, specifically catering to young men's
career expectations.

Historians most commonly describe the only goal of young men in the
antebellum South to have been entry to the plantation elite.[15] Yet men of
the emerging middle class who entered military education forged their
own institutions and beliefs and attempted to alter cultural expectations
so that their institutions and values were validated. As they prepared for

---

[14] Amy S. Greenberg, *Manifest Manhood and the Antebellum American Empire* (New York:
Cambridge University Press, 2005).

[15] For example, Michele Gillespie, *Free Labor in an Unfree World: White Artisans in the Slave-
holding Georgia, 1789–1860* (Athens: University of Georgia Press, 2000), 33; Drew Gilpin
Faust, *James Henry Hammond and the Old South: A Design for Mastery* (Baton Rouge:
Louisiana State University Press, 1982).

careers, those young men promoted and then moved into nonagricultural and professional occupations. Like members of the northern middle class, the emerging southern middle class turned to education to foster upward mobility. Military schooling not only offered less expensive educational options to middle-class southerners, it also fostered professionalization and enhanced social stability. Given their professional values and occupations, young men in the emerging middle class selected careers that would allow them to match or even to improve upon the professional status of their fathers.

The next two chapters detail the struggle of the southern middle class for social stability in the planter-dominated Old South and the hopes of its members for social mobility – that presumed northern trait. The study of military school alumni demonstrates the social mobility of the generation that came of age in the 1840s and 1850s as compared to their parents' generation; it also reveals the extent to which these alumni actively networked to enhance their individual success and professionalization in the region. Chapter 6 analyzes alumni occupations and intergenerational social mobility. Many military school alumni became teachers, attorneys, and doctors. Similar to their male relatives, they were far more likely to enter professional occupations than were southerners generally, and they were even more likely than their fathers to do nonagricultural work. Military education and the professions it propagated, in other words, offered an avenue of mobility outside slave owning. Of course, education aided social mobility nationally, but this fact has been repeatedly overlooked in the study of the South, where, as this investigation of middle-class formation in the Old South shows, the criteria for mobility were changing in the late antebellum years.

Military school alumni established social networks through their alumni connections – and even their marriages – that also fostered social stability and promoted upward mobility. The best example of these networks developed among military educators, who created teaching positions for men analogous to themselves. Chapter 7 details these networks, in which school administrators, especially Francis Henney Smith at VMI, acted almost as employment agents for their graduates, who in turn secured positions and enrolled their own students. As the period advanced, military school alumni founded other military schools, which graduated an ever-greater number of southern men who were similarly educated and perpetuated the alumni's ideals. These young men actively engaged in networking to further their careers and also succeeded in professionalizing their most chosen career, teaching. Professionalization began to facilitate social mobility and encouraged the growth of the southern middle class.

Alumni networks and the professionalization of teaching mirrored nationwide trends, providing evidence of the start of modern bureaucratic and professional developments in the Old South. The South changed significantly during the late antebellum years, as did the entire nation. The market economy and industry infiltrated the region with increasing acceptance.[16] Middle-class formation occurred alongside the articulation of social, cultural, political, and economic institutions, as well as the maturing of military education and professionalization; these processes resulted in quasi-bureaucratic processes developing more in some locations and less in others. This study focuses on the Old South rather than on intraregional distinctiveness. The decreasing significance and percentage of slave ownership in the Upper South, for example, may have made Virginians even more susceptible to the advantages of military education. Despite the abundance of sources from Virginia, however, comprehensive data from all extant correspondence in major archives in Tennessee, Georgia, North Carolina, South Carolina, Alabama, Mississippi, and Kentucky, as well as supplemental information from Texas and Florida, confirm that middle-class men in the Deep South also embraced military schools by 1860. Westward migration advanced education and carried military schools into the southwest in the 1850s, following the first wave of the movement (VMI in 1839 and SCMA in 1842). The middle class emerged slowly, and military cadets and educators aided its formation.

Comparisons of the southern to the northern middle class can at times cause us to identify the emerging southern middle class too closely with its more established northern counterpart. Those southerners continued to hold beliefs and values that were typically southern, valuing community, hierarchy, and honor, and favoring slavery. The emerging middle class did not reject elite southern culture. Thus, some of the group's core values coincided with those of the northern middle class, whereas

[16] Recent works detail the market economy and culture in the South. See, for example, the work of Jonathan Daniel Wells, Peter S. Carmichael, Tom Downey, and Chad Morgan.

others were distinctly southern. This study highlights national similarities while recognizing regional differences, such as the persistence with which honor was valued in the South.[17] The promotion of schooling, for example, was a national trait, but its significance in promoting professional, nonagricultural careers was distinctly connected to southern hierarchy, mobility, and education. The final chapter considers the antebellum American middle class by presenting characteristics that define the national class and acknowledging how the emerging southern middle class was regionally distinct.

The study of military education, a significant form of higher schooling in the Old South, is in and of itself important to the history of education and social institutions. Moreover, because military schools and their alumni demonstrated many trends of the era, including modernization and professionalization, the study of antebellum military education in the South also allows us to analyze the emerging southern middle class, especially its education, mobility, and professionalization. The possibilities of southern middle-class development could not be realized in the few decades that southern military schools remained in operation. The study of military education thus both illuminates the emerging middle class and illustrates the increasingly important role education played in southern social structure.

---

[17] Much work has defined and explored the northern middle class, including that of historians Burton J. Bledstein, Stuart M. Blumin, Paul E. Johnson, Mary P. Ryan, and Richard L. Bushman. On the northern working class, scholars include Ira Katznelson, Bruce Laurie, and Sean Wilentz.

1

Introducing the Emerging Southern Middle Class

Nineteenth-century thinkers noted the rise of a middle class but had trouble defining it. Modern scholars have had more success refining an interpretation of the definition, composition, and beliefs of the northern middle class over the last thirty years. With detailed studies of northerners completed, the emerging southern middle class needs to be more fully articulated, and that analysis can in turn foster a more inclusive picture of the national middle class (a group that includes both regions). This work has begun in earnest for the southern context, but similar difficulties arise. Not only is a southern middle class hard to locate in historical sources and difficult to differentiate, but using accurate terminology and definitions has proven extremely problematic; unsurprisingly, terms now in use can be anachronistic when applied to the nineteenth century (and nineteenth-century terms now carry different meanings, if they carry any meaning at all).[1] This chapter begins by articulating the theoretical

---

[1] Peter N. Stearns, "The Middle Class: Toward a Precise Definition," *Comparative Studies in Society and History*, 21 (July 1979), 377–96. Stearns's work reflects the depth of scholarship on the northern middle class. The extensive historiography on the North often omits the southern middle class; for example, Burton J. Bledstein, *The Culture of Professionalism: The Middle Class and the Development of Higher Education in America* (New York: W. W. Norton and Company, 1976), 28–29, essentially accepts the nineteenth-century assertions that southerners did not develop a middle class; Stuart M. Blumin, *The Emergence of the Middle Class: Social Experience in the American City, 1760–1900* (New York: Cambridge University Press, 1989), 14, clearly omits southern cities; Blumin, "The Hypothesis of the Middle-Class Formation in Nineteenth-Century America: A Critique and Some Proposals," *American Historical Review*, 90 (1985), 299–338; Paul E. Johnson, *A Shopkeeper's Millennium: Society and Revivals in Rochester, New York, 1815–1837* (New York: Hill and Wang, 1978); Mary P. Ryan, *Cradle of the Middle Class: The Family in Oneida County, New York, 1790–1865* (New York: Cambridge University Press, 1981); and Richard L. Bushman, *The Refinement of America: Persons, Houses, Cities* (New York: Alfred A. Knopf, 1992). Howard P. Chudacoff, "Success

concept of class used for this study and then presents a basic outline of the middle class that was forming in the Old South, along with its generally accepted characteristics.

Class as Process

In his monumental work, *The Making of the English Working Class*, E. P. Thompson famously maintained that societies and cultures form as processes that occur in specific, identifiable historical periods: "We observe patterns in [humans'] relationships, their ideas, and their institutions. Class is defined by men as they live their own history, and, in the end, this is its only definition." Thompson leads me to describe class in a particular time and place in the process of class formation. Indeed, examining class forces us to make a static group out of one constantly in flux. A historian's understanding of class is one that represents "averages," as Peter N. Stearns explains; definitions of a class must allow for variations among individuals and between subgroups, but it must also strive to capture as complete a picture of the group as possible. Individuals have agency to make changes (to be, as it were, individuals), but they are also constrained by their social context.[2] Thus, delineating the boundaries of a class matters – the groupings of "middle class," "working class," and "southern middle class" should contain the same people regardless of which scholar analyzes them.

Given the fluid nature of class, how then can we define it? Karl Marx began with the relationship of the individuals within a class to the means of production, defining the middle class (the bourgeoisie) as owners, whereas Max Weber defined class as a group of people whose similar

and Security: The Meaning of Social Mobility in America," *Reviews in American History*, 10 (December 1982), 105, describes the difficulty of using census reports of occupational titles to identify social position.

[2] E. P. Thompson, *The Making of the English Working Class* (New York: Vintage Press, 1963), 11 (quotation); Stearns, "The Middle Class: Toward a Precise Definition," 380; Lenore O'Boyle, "The Classless Society: Comment on Stearns," *Comparative Studies of Society and History*, 21 (July 1979), 397–413; Ira Katznelson, "Working-Class Formation: Constructing Cases and Comparison," in *Working-Class Formation: Nineteenth-Century Patterns in Western Europe and the United States*, ed. Ira Katznelson and Aristide R. Zolberg (Princeton: Princeton University Press, 1986). Jonathan Daniel Wells, *The Origins of the Southern Middle Class, 1800–1861* (Chapel Hill: University of North Carolina Press, 2004), 9–12, describes his definition of the class and its formation.

"situation" represents a possible basis for communal action. "Class situation," as Weber describes it, includes "the typical chance for a supply of goods, external living conditions, and personal life experiences, in so far as this chance is determined by the amount and kind of power, or lack of such, to dispose of goods or skills for the sake of income in a given economic order." Class is thus, for Weber, primarily economically based, connected to access to goods, to the status (power) bestowed by that access, to wealth, and to life experiences. Class equals the relationship of a group of individuals to the production or acquisition of goods, whereas status reflects the goods that the group is able to consume or the power such ownership conveys in the society. Economic differentiation – indeed class relationships – creates social differences and values, goals, access to goods, and lifestyles. This study focuses on the formation of a specific class, and as the major theorists indicate, class development is based on economic and occupational structure.[3]

The splintering of historical study in the twentieth century led scholars in a variety of subfields to explore class formation and, often independently, to develop different classifications and models of it. Historians investigating the middle class or working class in the United States (both relying on primarily northern evidence) or in European nations have developed their own categories and definitions. One method that has emerged to distinguish how a class developed and where it was in the process of formation at a given time distinguishes whether a particular social group was a class "in itself" or "for itself." A class "in itself" has recognizable similarities, whereas a class "for itself" has recognizable similarities *and* shares identity or consciousness. Members of a class "in itself" can exhibit an awareness of themselves as a group and can share similar characteristics, but they do not possess class consciousness. This study relies on the concept of class "awareness" rather than consciousness, supported by Stuart Blumin and Anthony Giddens' theory of structuration; it allows researchers to observe the nineteenth-century middle class in both regions as possessing similar behavior and characteristics,

---

[3] Max Weber, *From Max Weber: Essays in Sociology*, ed. H. H. Gerth and C. Wright Mills (New York: Oxford University Press, 1958), 181 (quotation), 182–84, 193–94. Andrew C. Holman, *A Sense of Their Duty: Middle-Class Formation in Victorian Ontario Towns* (Montreal: McGill-Queen's University Press, 2000).

although the class lacked consciousness of itself as such.[4] As we shall see, the emerging southern middle class belongs to this category and formed in a dynamic and ongoing process throughout the late antebellum years.

A Preliminary Definition of the Emerging Southern Middle Class

What do we mean by the "southern middle class"? Because the terminology "middle class" has only rarely been used in southern history, it may bring to mind the small planters or rural yeomen of the Old South. Neither group, however, had much in common with the middle class found in the North around the same period. Indeed, the emerging southern middle class was most definitely not a class made up solely of rural yeomen or small planters; those groups have their own location in the social hierarchy. Other possibilities come to mind: Perhaps the southern middle class encompassed agriculturalists in the upper stratum of yeomen or the lower stratum of planters, or perhaps it was made up of artisans, proprietors, or professionals.

Historians have described certain segments of the South's middling social groups without yet finally conceptualizing the middle class. As early as 1949, Frank Owsley called attention to the "plain folk," those whites near the bottom of the social hierarchy, and, as recently as 2005, Samuel Hyde strove to solidify the definition of that group. By the 1980s, historians' research on persons below the elite planters in the southern social hierarchy was thriving. For the most part, however, each middling group of the antebellum South has been studied separately. James Oakes argued for the significance of middling planters in southern society and for their social mobility; Steven Hahn and Stephanie McCurry, among others, detailed yeomen life; and Michele Gillespie explored white artisans. Most recently, Jonathan Daniel Wells articulated a definition of the southern middle class, populating it with urban professionals.[5] Rates

---

[4] See Arno J. Mayer, "The Lower Middle Class as Historical Problem," *Journal of Modern History*, 47 (September 1975), 409–36; Blumin, *Emergence of the Middle Class*, 6–12. A study of the southern working class is Ira Berlin and Herbert Gutman, "Natives and Immigrants, Free Men and Slaves," *American Historical Review*, 88 (1983), 1175–1200.

[5] Frank L. Owsley, *Plain Folk of the Old South* (1949; reprint, Baton Rouge: Louisiana State University Press, 1982); Samuel C. Hyde Jr., "*Plain Folk* Reconsidered: Historiographical Ambiguity in Search of Definition," *Journal of Southern History*, 71 (November 2005); James Oakes, *The Ruling Race: A History of American Slaveowners* (New York: Vantage Books, 1982);

of land and slave ownership separated Oakes's planters with professional employment from Gillespie's artisans cum manufacturers or merchants, but many members of both groups may have had similar work lives. Among all these groups, whiteness and maleness were prerequisites to social opportunity, and ethnicity was held constant by the general homogeneity of the white southern population.[6] How the groups fit into or differed from the emerging southern middle class still requires explicit study.

Some historians remain skeptical about the southern middle class's existence. Critics of the term have suggested that the word "middle" creates a problem, as it is not clear what the class was in the "middle" of. That is, in the absence of the explicit existence of southern classes, how can a group concretely be said to have existed between other unformed "classes"?[7] Whereas class boundaries are fluid by definition, in the antebellum years, this fluidity reflected the early stages of class formation. In the Old South, however, it is possible to identify a middle group with its own characteristics that was distinct from what scholars define as the social extremes of elite planters and laborers. Though the exact location and meaning of the "middle" fluctuated in more than one way, groups nonetheless coalesced, a class began to form, and individuals rose and fell in the social hierarchy.

Steven Hahn, *The Roots of Southern Populism: Yeoman Farmers and the Transformation of the Georgia Upcountry, 1850–1890* (New York: Oxford University Press, 1983); Stephanie McCurry, *Masters of Small Worlds: Yeoman Households, Gender Relations, and the Political Culture of the Antebellum South Carolina Low Country* (New York: Oxford University Press, 1995); Michele Gillespie, *Free Labor in an Unfree World: White Artisans in the Slaveholding Georgia, 1789–1860* (Athens: University of Georgia Press, 2000); Wells, *Origins of the Southern Middle Class*; Frank J. Byrne, *Becoming Bourgeois: Merchant Culture in the South, 1820–1865* (Lexington: University of Kentucky Press, 2006).

[6] See Maris A. Vinovskis, "Quantification and the Analysis of American Antebellum Education," *Journal of Interdisciplinary History*, 13 (Spring 1983), 761–86; Amy Bridges, "Becoming American: The Working Classes in the United States before the Civil War," in *Working-Class Formation: Nineteenth-Century Patterns in Western Europe and the United States*, ed. Ira Katznelson and Aristide R. Zolberg (Princeton: Princeton University Press, 1986), 193; Berlin and Gutman, "Natives and Immigrants, Free Men and Slaves."

[7] See, for example, Elizabeth Fox-Genovese, *Within the Plantation Household: Black and White Women in the Old South* (Chapel Hill: University of North Carolina Press, 1988); Scott P. Marler, "Stuck in the Middle (Class) with You (*The Origins of the Southern Middle Class, 1800–1861*)," *History: Review of New Books*, 35 (Spring 2007), 92(5).

In the last generations before the Civil War, a somewhat fluid con-
tinuum among white workers – from lower-class unskilled laborers to
middle-class professionals – blurred the edges of the various groups
between them. White artisans, for example, who made up 15 to 17 percent
of the adult male population in Georgia, "could parley their knowledge
and ability into comfortable livelihoods," according to Daniel Hundley,
writing in 1860. Thus, some artisans or their children rose into the middle
class, whereas others dropped into skilled or unskilled labor. Small proprietors, likewise, existed in a middle space; they and their progeny struggled to maintain their middling status and not fall, all the while hoping
for greater success.[8] Downward mobility was common, and even planters
could lose their land and slaves. There was a range of social positions
among white men in the social spectrum of the Old South. Founded on
both occupation and the accompanying status, those groups performing
manual, unskilled labor certainly lacked the resources and privileges of
the middle social position and those positions above them. Just as the
lowest ranks were often clear, planters' wealth and prestige would have
been visible to contemporaries and historians now define them by their
land and slave ownership.

The development of a middle class can be most easily identified among
the professional group that coalesced in the late antebellum years. This
is the approach that Wells has taken. Future scholarship will continue to
explore different segments of the southern middle class, including urban
professionals, rural professionals, downwardly mobile planters' younger
sons, professionally minded small planters' sons, artisans cum entre-
preneurs, and small proprietors. Such works will better reckon the number and location of the middle class throughout the Old South, the members of which were the progenitors of the postbellum southern middle
class.

The emerging southern middle class as a whole differed from other
groups by its economic situation and in some, but not all, of the values its

[8] Gillespie, *Free Labor in an Unfree World*, xviii, 101–03, 111 (quotation). Bruce Laurie, "'We Are
Not Afraid to Work': Master Mechanics and the Market, Revolution in Antebellum North"
in *The Middling Sorts: Explorations in the History of the American Middle Class*, ed. Burton J.
Bledstein and Robert D. Johnson (New York: Routledge, 2001); Dudley S. Johnson, "William
Harris Garland: Mechanic of the Old South," *Georgia Historical Quarterly*, 53 (1969).

members cherished. Thus, the rank reflected its members' middle economic and occupational status and their wish to perpetuate or improve upon it, often by means of education. This is the basic definition. Different subdivisions of the class probably had their own interests. This book focuses on nonagricultural and professional men, the largest portion of the class, and their attraction to military education. Focusing on educational institutions allows for consideration of upwardly mobile working-class men, downwardly mobile planter kin, and stability-minded professionals. This study begins the work of delineating how inclusions in (or exclusions from) the southern middle class can be determined.

This study balances a focus on economic position (occupational structure, status, and multigenerational mobility) with consideration of culture. It furthers Wells's analysis of the emerging middle class by defining the group more specifically and analyzing its social mobility; it investigates the meaning of status, professionalism, and the results of education in a new way. Wells frames his study of the middle class broadly, whereas this study uses a control group as a proxy. Clearly, the number of professionals and the status they accrued increased in the Old South. Those men began to work toward a society in which they could augment their status and, surely, their incomes. The study of military education demonstrates that middle-class southerners neither adopted nor duplicated northern patterns of class formation and mobility.

The emergence of the southern middle class resulted from the social changes of the antebellum era, especially the modernization of slave society. Modern ideas had filtered into the plantation society, and a number of planters and other southerners had accepted some of them by the 1840s and 1850s; for obvious reasons, however, free labor – an important aspect of modern capitalism – was not among the ideologies that became widely accepted. One of the central debates in southern history centers on the prevalence or absence of capitalism and profit-driven slavery in the Old South. As scholars provide more evidence regarding the adoption of industry in areas of the antebellum South, the historiographic discussion about the meanings of that industry continues. Eugene Genovese's *The Slaveholders' Dilemma*, for example, integrates a concept of progress into its description of planters' prebourgeois ideology, whereas William Scarborough broadens the definition of capitalists to assert that planters were "Capitalists All!"[9] The maturity of southern industry and the increasing acceptance of ideas about progress and commerce allowed the southern middle class to grow. By 1860, nonetheless, this class was the group most accepting of these changes in the Old South, but it had not become a threat to planter rule or the existing power structure. This study does, however, challenge the latent idea that planters alone drove economic change.[10] Middle-class southerners, I argue, acted in ways that promoted economic modernization.

The emerging southern middle class developed some social, demographic, and cultural distinctions from other social groups. The historians and theorists who have written on the northern middle class suggest that membership can be first identified by occupation, which was largely professional. In the antebellum years across America, those occupations and their status placed men in the middle position in the social hierarchy. Moreover, as professions generally necessitated some type of schooling – requiring reading ability but not necessarily a degree – many professionals educated their sons (to ensure social stability). A closer examination of the fathers of cadets suggests some additional criteria for identifying the emerging southern middle class.

Occupation and Status of Cadets' Fathers

Occupation and economic position were the primary criteria that defined the middle class in the social hierarchy, regardless of region. Within the basic parameters of the definition of the southern middle class, men who

---

[9] Genovese, *The Slaveholders' Dilemma: Freedom and Progress in Southern Conservative Thought, 1820–1860* (Columbia: University of South Carolina Press, 1992); Scarborough, *Masters of the Big House: Elite Slaveholders of the Mid-Nineteenth-Century South* (Baton Rouge: Louisiana State University Press, 2003); Mark M. Smith, *Mastered by the Clock: Time, Slavery and Freedom in the American South* (Chapel Hill: University of North Carolina Press, 1997). Recent studies on southern industry include Tom Downey, *Planting a Capitalist South: Masters, Merchants, and Manufacturers in the Southern Interior, 1790–1860* (Baton Rouge: Louisiana State University Press, 2006); Chad Morgan, *Planters' Progress: Modernizing Confederate Georgia* (Gainesville: University Press of Florida, 2005).

[10] In a review essay, James Oakes addresses this idea in the historiography; Oakes, "The Politics of Economic Development in the Antebellum South," *Journal of Interdisciplinary History*, 15 (Autumn 1984), 310. Wells, *Origins of the Southern Middle Class*, 67, places the emerging middle class at the forefront of southern industrialization.

enrolled their sons for military education were members of that class. Middle social position and nonmanual, professional careers created a particular status for men in the emerging middle class and separated them from the majority of southern society. Cadets' fathers exhibited the traits of that rank, while demonstrating less, but similar patterns of, southern land and slave ownership. The values that their rank encouraged – and, reciprocally, the same values that encouraged the formation of the class – centered on education to achieve and maintain that social status.

The families of cadets tended to be nonagricultural, white-collar workers and employers. Seventy percent of fathers who sent their sons for military schooling did not find their primary employment on the land. Of course, variations existed between institutions and states. Attendees of South Carolina's Citadel had a slightly higher percentage of agricultural backgrounds, especially as planters. The fathers of cadets at the Kentucky Military Institute (KMI) were more likely to be in public service than were the fathers of cadets at other schools.[11] The emerging southern middle class was concentrated in nonmanual occupations, particularly those careers that provided sufficient status and wealth to maintain a middle social position. Cadets' fathers were men so positioned. Less than 6 percent of them never rose above the lowest levels of nonagricultural occupations, as Table 1.1 indicates. Skilled laborers rarely afforded or chose military education (only 1.6 percent). In total, however, only one-fourth of fathers who worked in one career in their lifetime, and less than one-third (28.5 percent) overall, worked in agriculture. Only 23.4 percent of all fathers achieved their highest status in agriculture (reflecting fathers mixing agricultural and professional careers).

In contrast to families using military education, the majority of antebellum southerners remained in agriculture. In upcountry Georgia and North Carolina, at least 75 percent of the male population worked agriculturally, as contrasted with the less than 3 percent who worked

---

[11] This result could be a consequence of the records maintained rather than any actual difference between schools. KMI enrolled the son of a Kentucky governor, although the politician may have risen out of a middle economic position. See James Darwin Stephens, *Reflections: A Portrait – Biography of the Kentucky Military Institute, 1845–1971* (Georgetown, KY: Kentucky Military Institute, 1991).

Table 1.1. *Cadets' fathers' occupations: highest-achieved occupational status*

Occupation	Number of alumni	Percentage
Professional	193	52.5
Agriculturalists	86	23.4
Proprietors	41	11.1
Public Service	27	7.3
White-collar Employees	15	4.1
Skilled Trades	6	1.6

$N = 368$ individuals

Note: The data of this study represent the highest-achieved status based on the observed rates of occupations among alumni's fathers. It combines men with single and multiple occupations. See Appendix 2, Table 1, for the occupations in each category.[12]

Source: See Appendix 2, Table 1.

professionally.[13] The nonagricultural occupational tendency among military school families resonates with James Morrison's conclusions that West Point cadets were members of the middle class and that their fathers were 19 percent less likely to be farmers and 10 percent more likely to be attorneys than the general 1850 population. Morrison puts West Point cadets' fathers' nonagricultural involvement at 71 percent, and Peter Karsten calculates this same figure at 66 percent for slightly different years.[14] The similarity in class background of West Point students and

[12] This and other tables employ Michael Katz's occupational classifications, with slight modifications for southern regionalism. Specifically, Katz identifies engineers as machinists, although the civil engineer of the military school was certainly a professional, relying on advanced schooling and earning a solid salary. This study also locates teachers in the professional category rather than that of white-collar employees because, as will be demonstrated, one reason for the mobility of southern middle-class alumni was the professionalization of educational careers. I have followed Katz's directive to separate occupational structure from occupational mobility; analysts should delineate the structure of a society before trying to examine members' success at mobility. Thus, Table 1.1 presents the occupational structure of cadets' fathers (and Chapter 6 will do the same for alumni). Michael B. Katz, "Occupational Classification in History," *Journal of Interdisciplinary History*, 3 (Summer 1972), 67, 80. Katznelson, "Working-Class Formation," 14.

[13] Hahn, *The Roots of Southern Populism*, 21, 295; Robert C. Kenzer, *Kinship and Neighborhood in a Southern Community: Orange County, North Carolina, 1849–1881* (Knoxville: University of Tennessee Press, 1987), 166.

[14] The Army Corps of Engineers interviewed each cadet entering in the 1840s and 1850s. James L. Morrison, *"The Best School in the World": West Point, the Pre-Civil War Years, 1833–1866*

the students at southern military academies followed from the unique attractions of military schooling for middle-class families, particularly due to its emphasis on professional training.

The professional tendency of cadets' families set them apart within southern society. It also reflected changes in the region in the 1850s, including a rise in the number of nonagricultural workers. Southern rates of farming decreased according to the 1850 and 1860 censuses, suggesting that whites were beginning to move out of farming and into industrial and professional work in the decade when military education reached its apex.[15] That some white southerners were choosing nonagricultural occupations reflected patterns of national modernization and the creation of new avenues of social mobility. By 1850, merchant, doctor, minister, and attorney were the most common professional occupations in the country; the number of clerks and teachers rivaled the number of men in the "learned professions."[16] White-collar jobs could serve as launching pads for professional careers (or so men in those occupations generally hoped). These groups reflected the growth (and growing acceptance) of the emerging middle class in the Old South.

The sons of professionals were heavily represented at military schools. Cadets' fathers displayed a broad diversity in their occupations, including "large proprietors," doctors, ministers, teachers, a hatter, and a shoemaker.[17] In general, however, most cadets' fathers worked in professional

(Kent: Kent State University Press, 1986), 62, 155–59, used data from 1842 through 1857. Peter Karsten, *The Military in America*, 2nd Ed. (New York: Free Press, 1986), 110, used data from 1845 through 1860.

[15] T. Lloyd Benson, "The Plain Folk of Orange: Land, Work, and Society on the Eve of the Civil War" in *The Edge of the South: Life in Nineteenth-Century Virginia*, ed. Edward L. Ayers and John C. Willis (Charlottesville: University of Virginia Press, 1991), 59. Census data suggest that occupations in Virginia were similar to those of other states.

[16] Morrison, *Best School in the World*, 158. The 1860 census figures for Georgia, North Carolina, South Carolina, Tennessee, and Virginia confirmed this list as the most common occupations. However, the proportion of lawyers was lower in some southern states. Although the number of "civil and military engineers" was low in all states, Virginia reported more "railroad men" than clergy or attorneys; some of these men were probably engineers. J. D. B. DeBow, *Statistical View of the United States . . . The Seventh Census* (1854; reprint, New York: Norman Ross Publishers, 1990), vol. 4, Table 129, 126–28; *Population of the United States in 1860; Eighth Census* (1864; reprint, New York: Norman Ross Publications, 1990), 77, 362–63, 454–55, 471, 524–25.

[17] Charles Mason Sr. to Francis H. Smith, 10 June 1852, Preston Library, Virginia Military Institute Archives (hereafter VMI Archives); Thomas Huguenin, "A Sketch of the life of Thomas Abram Huguenin," unpublished memoir; Victor Manget, unpublished memoir;

occupations: They were attorneys, physicians, and ministers, in order of frequency. Close to three-quarters (72.5 percent) of military fathers who maintained one occupation held white-collar positions or above, and slightly less than half (45.8 percent) were solely professional men. Here, the dominance of nonmanual occupations and concentration in professions show in the group as whole. Numerous individual examples could further illustrate the professions and generational development of military school men; for example, Cadet Robert Archer's grandfather was a merchant who suffered losses during the Revolutionary War, whereas his father succeeded in the War of 1812 as a surgeon, remaining in the army for twenty-five years before apparently purchasing a farm and then running (or aiding the development of) the Armory Rolling Mill.[18] Cadets' fathers – just under three-quarters in nonmanual positions and half in professions – found employment in similar types of occupations. By comparison, less than one-third of all cadets' fathers were employed in agriculture; this is true of both single- and multiple-career men.

More than 50 percent of military fathers achieved professional standing, as Table 1.1 and the careers of men like Dr. Archer indicate. Others, such as the 22.5 percent in proprietorships, public service, and white-collar occupations, labored in the less lucrative portion of the middle class. White-collar jobs and professional careers offered different status, and the latter certainly conferred more status – a lawyer received more prestige than a clerk – and more income. The nonmanual and nonagricultural nature of both jobs, however, set men who had them apart from the rest of southern society. It is to be hoped that later studies will answer whether these 22.5 percent of men should be considered "lower middle class" and if that group differed significantly from the entire middle class (nationally and regionally). In addition, a substantial percentage of cadets' fathers (17 percent) held positions as legislators either before

Henry D. Moore, unpublished memoir, [1900], The Citadel Archives and Museum (hereafter CIT); William P. DuBose, "Soldier, Philosopher, Friend Awakener of the Undying Good in Men," typescript 1946, The South Caroliniana Library, University of South Carolina, (hereafter SCL); Recommendation letter, John Moomau student file; Charles Derby to Father, 4 April 1846, VMI Archives. Unless otherwise noted, VMI cadet correspondence comes from the VMI Archives' individual student files or Superintendent's Correspondence.
[18] Robert S. Archer, unpublished memoir, Watson Family Papers, Virginia Historical Society.

or after their sons attended higher schools; legislators were usually not wealthy or elite when elected.[19]

In the diversifying southern economy, men could mix agriculture and nonagricultural careers or own land and slaves while working professionally. The amount of land and slaves individuals owned helps us to distinguish between members of the emerging middle class and planters (especially small or middling planters) with professions. Agricultural men in military schools would generally have been classified as farmers and occasionally as small planters. Cadets described their families' property in a variety of ways. They recorded knowledge of their fathers' crops: More than one cadet speculated on how the weather at school was affecting the corn at home.[20] Land ownership would not have been exceptional among rural professionals, land being a valuable commodity that could also convey status; it can be confirmed in the families of only one hundred cadets.[21] Although most fathers possessed no land, the majority of those men with agricultural property controlled homesteads or sufficient holdings rather than plantations. Men of the emerging southern middle class relied on income from their nonagricultural occupations, even though a limited number of them owned land.

Following the norm in the South, more cadets' families owned land than owned slaves. Owning a few slaves was certainly compatible with

---

[19] Eugene D. Genovese, "Yeomen Farmers in a Slaveholders' Democracy," *Agricultural History*, 49 (April 1975), 339. Fathers with unspecified "public service" have been included in the 17 percent. See Appendix 2, Table 1, for fathers' occupations.

[20] Claudius Fike to G. A. Fike, 6 July 1862, Claudius Lucian Fike papers; Lafayette Strait to Mother, 27 July 1853, Papers of the Gaston, Strait, Wylie and Baskin Families, SCL.

[21] The difficulty in presenting a comprehensive picture of holdings comes from the data: The mean amount of property known to be owned by military education families was eight hundred acres (probably including unimproved tracts) ranging from one to one hundred. This high figure is influenced, however, by the fact that eleven of the military school fathers I studied were clearly in the category of rich landholders. These few very rich planters, including Edmund Ruffin, who sent his seventh child to the Virginia Military Institute, skewed the figures to make ownership amounts appear higher than the actual average. This is unsurprising, as the historical record privileges larger owners like Ruffin – the fame of and attention paid to them increased the visibility of men with wealthier estates over poorer men. Cadets who wrote memoirs and therein described their fathers' estates tended to have large land holdings. (See, for example, DuBose, "Soldier, Philosopher, Friend Awakener of the Undying Good in Men," SCL.) Furthermore, records of land ownership from wartime, often occasioned by death or debt, reflected wealth accumulated over the lifetime of an alumnus or his father (or a combination of both).

middle-class status. Oakes presents "middle-class slaveowners" as educated dual-career professionals and argues that the middling planter, the "typical slaveholder," had an important place in – and influence on – southern culture. As Oakes does not describe the emerging professional middle class, or middling planters' connection to it, the subject remains ripe for exploration. Some men of the middle social position may have been sons of small or middling planters, Oakes's typical slaveowners; the sons of such men would have had reasons to try to attain upward mobility through a professional career, and younger sons in particular would have needed to look beyond their fathers' lands for an occupation.[22] Ownership of a few slaves placed a man below the elite (by the definition of a planter) but could easily put him in the middle economic position, whether he was an artisan on the rise or an agriculturalist moving into a profession.

Slave ownership patterns indicate that some professionals could certainly afford to purchase slaves. In Orange County, Virginia, professional men were more likely than men in other occupations to own land or more than one slave, and they were equally as likely to own land and slaves as were men recorded as "farmers." Gillespie and others have found that more than three-quarters of urban master artisans each owned approximately five slaves.[23] Still, just as the majority of white men in the antebellum South did not own slaves, few cadets indicated that their families did. Cadet letters occasionally revealed that there were slaves at home in messages to greet the "Negroes" or to punish a particular servant.[24] Thus, a few cadets' fathers appear to have been slaveholders, and these men, like the typical southerner, possessed considerably fewer than twenty slaves.

---

[22] Oakes, *Ruling Race*, argues for social fluidity and capitalism in southern society; some of what he attributes to a man's capitalistic mobility, however, could have been accumulated through marriage and with age. Oakes, *Ruling Race*, 58–59.

[23] Benson, "The Plain Folk of Orange," 64. Gillespie, *Free Labor in an Unfree World*, esp. ch. 4.

[24] Cadets recording their fathers owned slaves include Robert W. Williams Jr. and Ralph A. Wooster, ed., "A Cadet at Bastrop Military Institute: The Letters of Isaac Dunbar Affleck," *Texas Military History*, 6 (Spring 1967), 89–106; Lafayette Strait to Aunt, 28 January 1853, Lafayette Strait to Father, [February 1853]; R. O. Sams to Mother, 17 November 1861, Sams Family Papers, SCL; and John Gittings to Joseph R. Anderson, 23–27 November 1903, VMI Archives. Micah Jenkins to John Jenkins, 7 January 1860, SCL, and Benjamin Perry, account book, South Carolina Historical Society, indicated that the cadets owned slaves, which were held by guardians.

In total, slave ownership can be confirmed for 6.1 percent of cadets' families; the sixty-four cadets' families who held slaves possessed fewer than five slaves on average. Although the number of slaves owned falls within the average for southern society, the 6 percent figure is much lower than ownership rates in southern society at large. Cadets' families' slaveholding fits the profile of the middle class, as did their primarily nonagricultural focus.

Cadets' kin were even more significantly removed from agriculture than were cadets' fathers. Almost half of the cadets' maternal kin (whose occupations were recorded) were doctors or lawyers. Paternal relatives showed a high proclivity to have been attorneys or legislators. In all, 58 percent of cadets' relatives were professionals, and those who were not were rarely in agriculture (12 percent of the 147 for whom data are available).[25] A few explanations for this professional preponderance exist. Kin may have influenced a young man's choice of school, encouraging him to seek a profession and professional training, or a young man with professionals in his family tree may have been more likely to lean that way. In addition, cadets may have been the poorer professional relations of successful families; Citadel cadet John Wylie's father, a doctor with planter relations, certainly fits in that category. The large number of youths whose guardians or relatives paid for their schooling is also informative: A kinsman may also have helped a young man secure a tuition-free position at a state school or at West Point after he attended a military preparatory school. In all, cadets' fathers and their extended kin worked in the nonagricultural, professional occupations that defined the emerging southern middle class.

Education as a Middle-class Vehicle for Social Stability and Mobility

In addition to possessing a specific occupational standing and status, the antebellum middle class, in similar ways across regions, valued education and sought to improve their sons' careers through schooling. The early nineteenth century saw the expansion of public schools, academies, and colleges nationwide, and the middle class in both regions drove these changes. In the antebellum years, the South mirrored northern reform

[25] See Appendix 2, Table 3.

movements. Despite being less successful, southern education was, indeed, increasingly legislated and routinized. By mid-century, the proliferation of schools at all levels provided a new infrastructure for the South.

Educational development proceeded in the South more rapidly than in the North in at least two ways. The number of schools grew in the South and West more quickly than the North in the early nineteenth century; furthermore, state universities opened in the South before equivalent universities opened in the North (so, in this instance, educational change moved north, not vice versa). Whereas most southern attempts at public school systems failed, efforts to gain public financing of military institutions were successful in twelve southern states before 1861. Middle-class southerners joined in the national reforms that promoted public, scientific, and nonclassical higher schooling, and they built military education. The increasing number of academies and the specific characteristics of military higher schools allowed more southerners to enter education after the third decade of the nineteenth century than had previously.[26]

By the 1840s and 1850s, colleges and academies grew alongside regional tensions. As many southerners began to worry that sending their sons to the North to be educated would infect the boys with faulty northern views, southern educators increasingly created schools in the South, answering James DeBow's plea for "southern education for Southrons."[27]

---

[26] As Wells states, "the importance of publicly funded education became a key element of southern middle-class ideology"; Wells, *Origins of the Southern Middle Class*, 135. Colin B. Burke, *American Collegiate Populations: A Test of the Traditional View* (New York: New York University Press, 1982); Edgar W. Knight, *The Academy Movement* (Chapel Hill: N.p., 1919), 40–48; *Chartered Schools: Two-Hundred Years of Independent Academies in the United States, 1727–1925*, ed. Nancy Beadie and Kim Tolley (New York: RoutledgeFalmer, 2002). Developments in common schools have been well documented by historians of education. Carl Kaestle, *Pillars of the Republic: Common Schools and American Society, 1780–1860* (New York: Hill and Wang, 1983); Lawrence A. Cremin, *American Education: The National Experience, 1783–1876* (New York: Harper and Row, 1980); Frederick Rudolph, *The American College and University: A History* (Athens: University of Georgia Press, 1990); Bruce W. Eelman, "'An Educated and Intelligent People Cannot Be Enslaved': The Struggle for Common Schools in Antebellum Spartanburg, South Carolina," *History of Education Quarterly*, 44 (Summer 2004), 250–70. On southerners attending northern colleges, see John Hope Franklin, *A Southern Odyssey* (Baton Rouge: Louisiana State University, 1976), ch. 2; Lorri Glover, *Southern Sons: Becoming Men in the New Nation* (Baltimore: The Johns Hopkins University Press, 2007), 40–1.

[27] Southern universities also rivaled the size of northern ones. In 1860 Yale was the largest university in the United States with 502 students; the University of Virginia, at the same time, enrolled 417 and University of North Carolina taught 450. David Madsen, *Early National Education, 1776–1830* (New York: John Wiley & Sons, Inc., 1974), 110; Donald G. Tewksbury, *The*

Many men worried about their sons' being influenced by northerners, or, as they might have said, "abolitionists." Thus, the growth in military education was certainly connected to the historical context: The development of both the middle class and sectional tensions drove interest in the schools. Military higher schools must have appealed as sites that would teach southern boys how to become southern men. "It surely becomes us to preserve our children from any influence that might mislead their judgment or weaken their patriotism," declared the Jefferson College Charter as early as 1840, continuing, "WE MUST KEEP THEM AT HOME."[28] Indeed, the number of military institutions and their attendance increased in step with sectional hostility.

That many military alumni served in the Civil War does not mean, however, that militarism was the defining characteristic of military schools' antebellum clientele. The growth of military schooling in the South also resulted from the flow of military graduates becoming educators. Middle-class youths attended military higher schools because these institutions held specific attractions for them: The advantage of education suited their families' financial standing and professional identities. Consequently, the number of military schools increased dramatically, doubling in the 1840s and 1850s at the same time that the number of new colleges doubled.[29]

The historiographic neglect of southern education, especially non-elite schooling, has caused it to be generally accepted that southern culture

Founding of American Colleges and Universities Before the Civil War, With Particular Reference to the Religious Influences Bearing Upon the College Movement (1932; reprint, Hamden, CT: Archon Books, 1965), 144, 157, 169–70; Burke, *American Collegiate Populations*. On southerners promoting southern education because of regional politics, see Michael Sugrue, "South Carolina College; The Education of an Antebellum Elite" (Ph.D. diss., Columbia University, 1992); Wayne Flynt, "Southern Higher Education and the Civil War," *Civil War History*, 14 (June 1968), 211–25. The terms *college* and *university* are used interchangeably throughout this text, except that "university" reflected the larger schools that retained classical curricula whereas colleges showed more diversity.

[28] *The Charter and Statutes of Jefferson College, Washington Mississippi, as Revised and Amended* (Natchez: Book and Job Office, 1840), 10 (emphasis in original). *Report by the Board of Visitors of the Georgia Military Institute* (1853), 13; also see John Hope Franklin, *The Militant South, 1800–1860* (Boston: Beacon Press, 1956), 135–37; Rod Andrew Jr., *Long Gray Lines: The Southern Military School Tradition, 1839–1915* (Chapel Hill: University of North Carolina Press, 2001); and Bruce Allardice, "West Points of the Confederacy: Southern Military Schools and the Confederate Army," *Civil War History*, 43 (December 1997), 310–31.

[29] Tewksbury, *Founding of American Colleges*, 16. Burke, *American Collegiate Populations*.

played a more significant role in young men's careers than did education. Focusing on militarism, for example, can deemphasize the importance of education in the Old South and for the emerging middle class. Influential educational historian Lawrence Cremin moreover presents southern career training as involving the "three significant educative relationships" of kin, role model, and employer. Cremin's figuration of the southern path to professional success, despite his primarily northern evidence, offers valuable insight: Southerners may indeed have relied on personal relationships and community connections longer than did northerners.[30] His tripartite model, however, obscures the struggles of individuals who lacked those resources to succeed, and it also ignores the significant role that schooling played in social mobility. By the 1840s and 1850s, the emerging southern middle class entered formal education, in part via military schools, and used those institutions as the basis for social stability in the master-class–dominated world.

Elite Exceptions in Military Education

Although more than two-thirds of cadets' fathers were in nonagricultural professions, a few elites did enroll their sons at military academies. These young men were the exception to the general composition of cadets in the emerging middle class. The largest planters in the Old South rarely sent their children to military school, instead pursuing university education for them. Wealth allowed men to enroll sons in universities and classical academies or to opt not to educate them at all, because plantation management required no degree. "I wish to take advantage of the Instruction he may receive," one father explained when he decided to forego sending his son to Princeton in favor of the Virginia Military Institute (VMI), as he wanted the boy to become an engineer.[31] Yet such decisions were

---

[30] Cremin, *American Education*, 465 (quotation). Bertram Wyatt-Brown, *Southern Honor: Ethics and Behavior in the Old South* (New York: Oxford University Press, 1982). As she deftly presents James Henry Hammond, Drew Gilpin Faust follows him from South Carolina College as a first step into the elite. The fact that formal education's role in his success receives little attention suggests the ongoing historiographic omission of the significance of schooling as an agent for mobility in the antebellum South. Faust, *James Henry Hammond and the Old South: A Design for Mastery* (Baton Rouge: Louisiana State University Press, 1982), ch. 1.

[31] Robert M. Marshall to Col. Charles Dorman, 5 October 1839, John Marshall student file, VMI Archives.

clearly quite rare: Of the more than 300 elite planters who lived in the South in 1850 and 1860, only one of them sent his son to a military school. More commonly, cadets were kin to elite families or members of those families' circle of influence. Some prominent southerners gained entrance into military schools for their relatives. The governor of Virginia who oversaw the creation of VMI in 1839, for instance, "procured appointments" for two of his nephews but not for any of his sons.[32]

When we look closely at the few elite young men who were educated at military schools, some trends become clear. Because higher schools acting as preparatory or collegiate schools were entirely privately funded, they needed to have wealthier members of society in their student bodies. Evidence of their success in attracting such young men can be found in attendance rosters; for example, the Hillsboro Military Academy in North Carolina educated three sons of probable planters and a state senator's son.[33] Those planters' sons who did attend military academies, moreover, were generally younger sons. Famed agriculturist Edmund Ruffin sent only his third son and ninth child, Charles, to a military institution.[34]

[32] I compared my 1,057-person database to the comprehensive list of elite planters compiled in Scarborough, *Masters of the Big House*, Appendices C and D. Philip St. George Cocke, a member of the VMI Board of Visitors, sent his son John to that school. In at least four cases, cadets may have come from the same families as elite planters; Ruffin was not included in the Appendices. C. O. Bailey entered the Western Military Institute in 1861 with a planter father, but was not the son of William Bailey with 330 slaves who also resided in Florida. Robert Carter's grandson appears to have attended VMI, and by his own accounts was one of the wealthiest youths there. Gov. David Campbell to General Caruthers, 14 October 1844 (quotation), Rare Book, Manuscript and Special Collections Library, Duke University. The second son of a subsequent Virginia governor attended VMI for a few months in 1851.

[33] The occupations of only seven HMA cadets' fathers can be determined. Stephen A. Ross, "Hillsboro Military Academy," *Bennett Place Quarterly* (Summer 1999), 1–2, stresses the elite nature of HMA cadets, but offers insufficient evidence to support that view; he describes the cadets as "hailing from wealthy and middle-class families" in "To 'Prepare our Sons for all the Duties that may Lie before Them': The Hillsborough Military Academy and Military Education in Antebellum North Carolina," *North Carolina Historical Review*, 79 (January 2002), 16. Louisiana and the newer southern states contained the highest per capita income in the United States between 1840 and 1860. Richard A. Easterlin, "Regional Income Trends, 1840–1950," in *The Reinterpretation of American Economic History*, ed. Robert William Fogel and Stanley L. Engerman (New York: Harper and Row, 1971), 40–41; R. W. Fogel and S. L. Engerman, *Time on the Cross* (Boston: Little, Brown and Company, 1974), 248.

[34] Ruffin to Francis H. Smith, 8 February 1851, 25 April 1851, Charles Ruffin student file, VMI Archives. William Kauffman Scarborough, ed., *The Diary of Edmund Ruffin*, vol. 1 (Baton Rouge: Louisiana State University Press, 1972), xvi–xx, 114–15 (18 October 1857).

Birth order determined the extent of a young man's inheritance, as well as the proportion of funds that could be spent on his education. Younger sons were likely to be educated or trained inexpensively compared to eldest sons – if they could be educated at all. Philip Winn, a fourth son, resigned from VMI in 1841 when his father, a small planter and attorney, could not pay his fees; not only had his three elder bothers sapped family resources, but he had eleven younger siblings waiting to receive an education, and the cost of their maintenance limited the cash available for his schooling.[35] The majority of the students at VMI were younger sons. In the larger sample of southern military schools, only 21 percent of 281 cadets for whom family position could be determined were the oldest or only sons. Of the remaining cadets, a clear 50 percent were younger sons.

Younger sons had to work their way up, though they might receive help from their older brothers. They lived in various family situations: One cadet was seventh of nine brothers in a family of sixteen children, another the fourth son and ninth child of eleven. A fourth son and seventh child, John H. Weller, graduated from KMI in 1860 and then clerked for one older brother in his liquor store and bourbon distillery. Weller was given a small amount of land by his eldest brother, Jacob, who possessed 600 acres of timber and kept 60 acres for John and their third youngest brother.[36] Clerking gave Weller an entrée to a professional career. Among the nine cadets studied who were second-oldest brothers, all but one had a family of five or more siblings. The preponderance of younger sons at military schools suggests that these academies were not the first choice of families who could afford better, but that they were perceived as having practical value as means of vocational training for young men in need of it. Thus, the large number of younger sons at military schools indicates the importance to cadets' families of these institutions.

At the same time, some middle-class families sent their elder sons to military institutes (and elsewhere, of course) to help spread financial

---

[35] Winn student file, VMI Archives.

[36] Jacob F. Weller Papers, The Filson Historical Society. Kenzer, *Kinship and Neighborhood in a Southern Community*, 218, indicates that the men in his study had an average of 1.81 sons; compare this figure to the large family size of many cadets. Younger sons usually inherited half as much as the eldest son and perhaps money rather than land.

responsibility so the earnings of alumni could help provide for younger siblings. "His Father is a poor man with large family," a recommendation stated, "Alonzo is particularly desirous to get the place [with state funding] to qualify himself to teach school that he may support his Mother and [her] eight children." Large families recognized the monetary burden that education placed on them and the worry that burden created. "I have a large family to educate and provide for," one father wrote in explaining why he sent his son to a military school, "and am particularly solicitous that this my oldest may receive such an education moral, intellectual, and physical as would enable him to advance the interests of the rest in case of my loss to them."[37] Of the cadets who were oldest sons and whose family size is known, 77 percent had at least four younger siblings; five men had more than ten younger brothers and sisters.

Perhaps the most interesting aspect of the elite who were attracted to military education is that they exhibited characteristics that made them similar to the middle class. P. G. T. Beauregard, for example, who graduated from West Point and sent two sons to the Louisiana state military academy, practiced a professional career rather than defining himself as a planter. That an elite and members of the developing middle class could share institutions and views in such a way reflects the changing situation in the South, especially evident after 1850.

Conclusion

The families who used military education serve as a study of the developing southern middle class. Attempting to identify that class means analyzing it in the process of its formation. Families, individuals, and locations did not move consistently or coherently toward one ideal of "middle class." As we examine people in the middle social position, historians can start to identify the emerging southern middle class with economic distinction, especially occupation and status. Its members were nonagricultural and often professional, and sought education to ensure and enhance status. Specifically, southern middle-class families

---

[37] S. Godwin recommendation, 7 May 1847, Alonzo Jordan student file (first and second quotations); Henry Garnett to Francis H. Smith, 25 February 1841 (third and fourth quotations), Thomas Garnett student file; William Wheelwright to Francis H. Smith, 31 August 1853; James Bryan to Francis H. Smith, 23 January 1841, VMI Archives.

sent their sons to military schools as part of that trend. It is unsurprising that state-funded education attracted men who were economically in the middle ranks. Middle-class men sought education for their sons across the nation, and men so located in the antebellum South sent their sons to military higher schools (and other schools they could afford). Two-thirds of military fathers were not in agriculture, and approximately half attained professional status; these qualities suggest membership in the emerging middle class of the Old South. The modernizing trends of the 1840s and 1850s encouraged a few elites to enroll their sons or, more often, kin in the scientific and vocational military institutes. Those younger sons often entered professions, the same as their middle-class compatriots. Those middle-class sons' development and choices illustrate the formation of their class. The rest of this book analyzes their sons' education, values, beliefs, occupations, rank, status, and mobility.

2

"The advantage of a collegiate education"
Military Education Funding

"I am fully aware of the importance of my maintaining my situation here as a [state-funded] cadet," Joseph Chenoweth wrote his father. "I will never be able to repay you for your kindness, in allowing me to take advantage of this opportunity of obtaining a good education." In addition to parental benevolence, Chenoweth implied that his state scholarship allowed him to attend school, something he found valuable. "I cannot attend any Institution whereby my attendance I would incur less expense than at this," another cadet at Virginia Military Institute (VMI) wrote his guardian and brother, "although my expense since I have been here has been much more than I had anticipated; they will be much less next year, and each year after the first."[1] These young men realized that the subsidized tuition at VMI allowed them to secure secondary education.

Other than a few letters about his VMI experience from the 1850s, Joseph Chenoweth has faded into the list of Confederate casualties. His correspondence home to Randolph County, now West Virginia, described experiences typical to cadets: hazing (which he denied was serious), being caught playing cards, grieving over a brother's death, and explaining his courses and military drills. The quarterly report of his school performance is reproduced as Figure 8. As he recognized the advantage of a good education, in fact, he described "obtain[ing] as good a mathematical education here as at any place in the United States." Chenoweth complained when he felt that the school administrators, as

---

[1] Joseph Chenoweth to Father, 18 February 1856 (first and second quotations), 21 November 1858, Preston Library, Virginia Military Institute Archives (hereafter VMI Archives). Philip Fitzhugh to Patrick Fitzhugh, 22 May 1844 (third and fourth quotations), Virginia Historical Society (hereafter VHS).

representatives of the state, took advantage of cadets. His worries may
have come from his father's social position; the cadet's letters suggested
that his father worked in the building trades because he mentioned con-
tracts for building a bridge and two academies. This twenty-one-year-old,
who graduated from VMI in 1859, however, clearly explained the advantage he received from his state scholarship: the opportunity to get an
education and prepare himself for a career.[2]

Middle-class young men in similar situations benefited from the practical curriculum of military schools and secured education through the
funding arrangements at state military institutes. The scholarships, in
conjunction with the nonclassical curriculum, allowed young men with
limited resources to enter higher education. This chapter describes the
funding at state military schools, how it represented the ad hoc nature of
public education in the Old South, and how it contrasted with the funding in public universities. It then explores the cadets' resources: Their
families had sufficient wealth to send the sons to partially funded (and
academically reduced) military programs but also demonstrated that
they were not wealthy. Their limited resources meant that cadets exhibited a moderate standard of living even as their parents complained about
spending. Finally, the parents' concerns over funding and their use of debt
to ensure education show the lengths they went to achieve the benefits of
military education.

The Advantage of Funding

Young southerners such as the Virginian Chenoweth and his family
described military education as an "advantage." Their terminology reflected the antebellum belief in the opportunity and benefit that education
offered an "advantage" specifically noted in Webster's 1828 dictionary.[3]
Southern parents perceived the most important aspect of a military
institution's advantage to be the opportunity to receive an education; the

[2] Joseph Chenoweth to Father, 18 February 1856 (quotation), 21 November 1858, VMI Archives. Chenoweth student file, VMI Archives, and Joseph Hart Chenoweth Papers, VHS.
[3] The 1828 dictionary listed the third definition of advantage as "Means to an end; opportunity; convenience for obtaining benefit; as, students enjoy great *advantages* for improvement"; Noah Webster, *An American Dictionary of the English Language* (1828; reprint, New York: Johnson Reprint Corporation, 1970) (italics in original).

primary result of the military school was education where few options for one existed. The number of examples of parents, sons, and speakers using advantage in this manner is too numerous to list. Use of the term spanned the years from the first VMI class in 1839 to the young men entering military schools on the verge of the war in 1860; the use increased in frequency, however, in the 1850s as the emerging middle class grew and sought schooling. Middle-class southern parents and cadets asserted that education was a special opportunity, something valuable yet difficult to obtain. One father described his state-funded son as "determined to make the best use of the advantages which he now enjoys," perhaps thinking of his advantage in comparison to the cadet's brother who was employed as clergy. "You have advantages that so many would be thankful for (and I hope you are)," a mother reminded her son. Advantage represented education with state money.[4]

For cadets like Chenoweth, military schools both joined the larger southern system for educating the destitute and increased the educational opportunity for those not destitute. Poor children in New England began attending public schools by the early nineteenth century. At the elementary level, antebellum northern states developed free public systems, and some southern states similarly started programs, including unregulated common school systems, for poor whites without resources.[5] In the

---

[4] William N. Page to Francis H. Smith, 20 July 1852 (first quotation), Philip Page student file, VMI Archives. Mother to Walter Clark, 21 January 1860 (second quotation), R. H. Graves to David Clark, [1860], in *The Papers of Walter Clark*, ed. Aubrey Lee Brooks and Hugh Talmage Lefler (Chapel Hill: University of North Carolina Press, 1948). For the use of the term "advantage," see, among others, Robert M. Marshall to Col. Chas. Dorman, John Marshall student file, 5 October 1839; Francis Suddoth to Francis H. Smith, 18 July 1856; Joseph Chenoweth to Father, 18 February 1856; Briscoe Baldwin to Francis H. Smith, 30 May 1849, VMI Archives; Thomas Affleck to Isaac D. Affleck, 24 April 1861, in Robert W. Williams Jr. and Ralph A. Wooster, eds., "A Cadet at Bastrop Military Institute," *Texas Military History*, 6 (Spring 1967); Charles Duffy to S. J. Sedgwick, 6 February 1859, Charles Duffy Papers, Rare Book, Manuscript and Special Collections Library, Duke University (hereafter Duke); Robert Preston Carson, unpublished memoir, VHS; Richard Yeadon, *Address, on the Necessity of Subordination, in our Academies and Colleges, Civil and Military* (Charleston: Walker and James, 1854), 14–15.

[5] Bruce W. Eelman states that attempts to start common schools were ineffectual in most southern states and completely unsuccessful in antebellum South Carolina; at the same time as South Carolina legislators studied common schools, however, they followed Virginia's model, creating a state-funded, scholarship-rich military academy for teacher education (the South Carolina Military Academy [SCMA], opened in 1842). Common schools provided elementary education whereas SCMA was a higher school; Eelman, "'An Educated and Intelligent People Cannot Be Enslaved': The Struggle for Common Schools in Antebellum

South, however, most schools operated with private funding. Some non-elite southerners received education at schools funded by their wealthier neighbors. Others found benefactors who paid for their primary schooling. Finally, some boys applied to the state for primary education. Southern states funded basic education for students whose parents claimed poverty and increased the number of charity schools throughout the antebellum period; lotteries, literary funds, or charity funds augmented southern legislatures' small capital expenditures on education. A certain stigma surrounded the schools, but attendance at one did not necessarily indicate destitution. Young Thomas Jackson, for example, received his early education at state expense after his father died, despite having relatives who could have paid for it. Jackson continued on to West Point and went on to teach at VMI.[6]

Beyond primary education, southern states had programs that offered secondary education to a very small number of youths who went through several rounds of elimination. After each school year, the state system demanded that the number of boys funded be reduced by half until only one graduated from the state college.[7] Following this system, the legislatures of South Carolina and Virginia granted scholarships to the state universities, but after annual reductions usually only one youth was funded completely through graduation. In contrast, legislatures in twelve southern states funded the entire tuition for a dozen or more young men annually through military higher schools.

All state military institutes funded young men's entire education rather than selectively reducing the number of recipients. State military schools in the antebellum South put systems in place that financed at least one student per senatorial district; Virginia did so for VMI, as did South

Spartanburg, South Carolina," *History of Education Quarterly*, 44 (Summer 2004), 250–70. David F. Allmendinger Jr., *Paupers and Scholars: The Transformation of Student Life in Nineteenth-Century New England* (New York: St. Martin's Press, 1975), ch. 3. Educational history on public high schools clearly excludes the antebellum South as that specific institution did not develop in the prewar period. See Maris Vinovskis, "Have We Underestimated the Extent of Antebellum High School Attendance?" *History of Education Quarterly*, 28 (Winter 1988), 551–68.
[6] James I. Robertson Jr., *Stonewall Jackson: The Man, the Soldier, the Legend* (New York: Macmillan, 1997), ch. 1.
[7] For example, Edgar W. Knight, *Public School Education in North Carolina* (Boston: Houghton Mifflin Co., 1916), 74.

Carolina, Georgia, North Carolina, and Louisiana, among others.[8] Each year, dozens of cadets at the state-funded institutes and often a majority of cadets at VMI received free tuition in exchange for guarding state arms during their cadetship and for teaching for two years in the state after graduation. This arrangement offered the best public funding for southern higher schools at a time when no southern state maintained a functional public school system.

This arrangement still meant that a military school could be considered a "noble charity," as the South Carolina Legislature dubbed its South Carolina Military Academy (SCMA), which opened in 1842.[9] In that way, state military institutes could claim to answer calls for public schooling and for the education of the disadvantaged. In contrast, parents and cadets resisted any attempt to equivocate military academies with charity schools. They used the West Point model, which (despite federal funding) enjoined no comparisons to charity schools. Like those at West Point, cadets served their country modeling the citizen–soldier ideal during their enrollment and in their required two-year teaching duty.[10]

Fathers who had trouble providing for a young man to receive a classical education but who could finance a rudimentary English education – including modern subjects and sparing the expense of extensive classical tutoring – found the advantage that students received at military schools particularly attractive.[11] Furthermore, the funded positions at state military academies (called "state cadets") allowed between five and thirty young men per state to have their tuition paid by the legislatures. This

[8] See, for example, Georgia Legislature, Bill No. 3, "An Act to provide for the education of a certain number of State Cadets in the Georgia Military Institute," 21 January 1852; North Carolina General Assembly, House Doc. No. 32, "A Bill to Create a Scientific and Military School and a State Arsenal" (Raleigh: W. W. Holden, 1854), 296–97; North Carolina Senate, Bill No. 25, "A Bill to Provide for the Education of State Cadets at the NCMI, and for Other Purposes," 1860–61 Session.

[9] Committee on the Military, "Report on the petition of sundry citizens of Richland District praying for the abolishment of the Military Academy in Columbia," c. 1844, South Carolina Division of Archives and History (hereafter SCDAH).

[10] Rod Andrew Jr., *Long Gray Lines: The Southern Military School Tradition, 1839–1915* (Chapel Hill: University of North Carolina Press, 2001); Stephen A. Ross, "To 'Prepare Our Sons for all the Duties that May Lie before Them': The Hillsborough Military Academy and Military Education in Antebellum North Carolina," *North Carolina Historical Review*, 79 (January 2002), 1–27.

[11] Curriculum discussed in detail in Chapter 5.

opportunity saved parents at least 100 dollars per year, and in some cases, like at SCMA, offered a fully funded higher schooling or collegiate education. This tuition-free or subsidized education created the advantage of education among the developing middle class able to finance some, but not an extensive, education for their sons.

As part of nineteenth-century American educational reforms, funding reflected concerns with increasing educational opportunity. In 1839, VMI founders certainly capitalized on the idea of educating poor and middle-income southerners and ensured the social usefulness of the institution by making it a normal (teacher-training) school. The demand for teachers, as the appeal of education rose nationwide, also increased in southern states, which lacked the social and bureaucratic institutions to provide such professionals. The existence of the state military institutes as sites for teacher training promised their viability. Throughout the 1840s and 1850s, those schools sent a steady stream of alumni across the South as teachers.

The funding arrangement of the state military academies and military schools' role as teacher-training schools were distinctly southern. These military institutions acted similarly to public schools in the developing northern system. Indeed, when state military schools started to open, they reinvigorated military education, causing it to develop as a primarily southern institution. Before 1839, most military schools were located in the North, including American Classical and Military Lyceum, Mantua Classical and Military Academy, and Unity Scientific and Military Academy. In all, twelve northern schools existed before 1860. The movement started with Alden Partridge opening the first private military school, American Literary, Scientific and Military Academy (ALSMA), after leaving West Point in 1819; half a dozen graduates of that school become military educators and founded schools on both sides of the Mason–Dixon line. Partridge disciples and native southerners founded a few schools in the 1820s and 1830s, such as Rice Creek Spring Military Academy and North Carolina Literary, Scientific and Military Academy. After the state funding of southern military institutes, however, the numerical balance shifted regions. As the first schools expanded – for a variety of reasons – their alumni established new schools and produced more graduates. The use of military education as public or common schools, development of state funding (not done in the North), and improvement of teacher training expanded opportunity and created social significance in the Old South.

In addition to the largest and most significant schools – the state military institutes – educators opened private academies. Whether for the first generation of founders (often northerners coming south, a standard pattern in education and teaching in the early nineteenth century) or for the later generation of military graduates becoming teachers, the prestige of private schools increased, and these schools often acted as feeders for the larger schools. Their relationship to state funding is therefore distinct, but parents found some of the same advantages in them. The available evidence indicates that only one military academy, Portsmouth Academy in Virginia, had scholarship processes similar to that of the states. After graduating from ALSMA, William Collins ran the Portsmouth Academy as a military program with his former superintendent's assistance in the mid-1840s. The proceedings of the academy trustees stated that the school's "benefits have not been confined to the rich, for several youths unable to educate themselves have enjoyed its advantages without charge to them." Five young men gained free education at the school over the same number of years that Collins directed it.[12] This one-a-year rate correlated to schools that received appropriations through the state lottery. The Portsmouth program suggests that private schools may have had separate funding arrangements and, given that states routinely provided them armaments, some legislatures may have contributed to school funding, particularly to promote teacher training.

Men who paid tuition at military schools (called "pay cadets" at the state institutions) represented the wealthier segment of the cadets. All cadets, however, performed the same duties and work whether they were state funded or paid their own tuition. The emerging middle class grasped the lower cost and lack of classical education requirements for their sons, as indicated by the expenses remaining close to the maximum

---

[12] *Journal of the Proceedings of the Board of Trustees of Portsmouth Academy*, 10 December 1845 (quotation), Duke. The Portsmouth Academy may have formally been the Virginia Literary, Scientific and Military Academy. See Virginia Literary, Scientific and Military Academy, broadside (n.p., January 1841), American Antiquarian Society. VMI graduate Robert H. Simpson described the situation of the Portsmouth school in 1845, Simpson to Francis H. Smith, 23 December 1845, VMI Archives.

of what they could afford. They could also rely on other resources, such as patronage or kin connections.

The Sufficient Resources of the Middle Class

Other advantages of military education that the middle class described were occasionally intangible but often monetary, specifically hopes for the young men's future careers. Thus, thinking about advantage occurred in the context of monetary resources. The advantages were especially prescient for the emerging professional middle class, who self-identified as having a moderate income or who were men on the fringe of society, including orphans.

When examining cadet resources, it is apparent that middle-class families with sons in military schools had sufficient resources to seize the advantages of education. Free tuition reduced the amount of wealth that a family had to possess in order to send a son to a higher school. Cadets' fathers had sufficient assets, then, to afford secondary education at reduced costs. Although state cadets received free tuition, the fees required were often substantial. At VMI, state cadets paid out of their pockets for room, board, uniforms, and other incidentals; an 1842 VMI acceptance letter stated that, per year, a cadet funding his own education would spend $261.50 and a state cadet, $122; the Edward Shepherd acceptance letter reproduced here indicates a lower state cadet fee of $90/year (Figure 3). Meanwhile, at the SCMA, parents had to supply only uniforms, room supplies, and spending money. These costs compare favorably to antebellum southern colleges: University of Georgia cost between $178 and $213.50; South Carolina College charged approximately $160, not including housing and summer expenses; and the private and less prestigious College of Charleston demanded $50 to $80 in tuition alone.[13] Although the tuition appears to have been higher at VMI than

---

[13] Appointment letter, 6 July 1842, Philip A. Fitzhugh student file, VMI Archives. E. Merton Coulter, *College Life in the Old South* (1928; reprint, Athens: University of Georgia Press, 1951), 56; Daniel Walker Hollis, *South Carolina College*, vol. 1 (Columbia: University of South Carolina Press, 1951), 129, 153; J. H. Easterby, *College of Charleston* (Charleston: College of Charleston, 1935), 102. During the Civil War, military academies became more expensive for state cadets as funds were cut; Claudius Fike to Parents, 7 January 1862, Claudius Lucian Fike papers, The South Caroliniana Library, University of South Carolina (hereinafter SCL), and Burwell to Father, 5 July [1861], The Citadel Archives and Museum (hereafter CIT).

at some small colleges, the total cost for pay cadets was comparable. Reduced costs opened education to the young man of the emerging middle class but left almost no opportunity for the destitute. One scholar found that increasing costs made college education "less accessible" by 1860 for skilled laborers.[14] Access to higher education required sufficient resources, a sign of living above a plain folk or yeoman's subsistence level.

Some southern fathers accepted paying for their son's futures, especially because they valued education so much. "I hope you will not entertain the least idea of leaving school and thereby neglect your education which is the most important part of your fortune, to be low in idiocy and in company with ignorance. I wish you to soar above such notions and move on in pursuit of knowledge which is power and wealth," wrote a man to his son at the Kentucky Military Institute. "As to the expense of education, I spend no money with such much pleasure and I think no prize so easily acquired worth so much."[15]

The young men's standard of living while at school indicated that they had both cash and limits on their spending. Whereas some youths spent more than average, most cadets received more censures against extravagance than they did cash. The money that young men obtained and spent while away at school reflected their economic situation. One cadet recorded paying $483.50 for four years at VMI, which virtually equaled the estimated state cadet expenses. Another young man found that, at graduation, he still could not pay the $150 in excess of his state-funded tuition that he owed the school.[16] Receiving presents and money from home indicated that a family had sufficient resources to provide for more than their sons' rudimentary expenses.

Because such a large number of young men wrote home to describe their activities, it is evident that most controlled some cash. Whether they received funds from their fathers in increments of one, five, or ten dollars or their guardians sent them an allowance, many cadets circumvented the institutions' control of their spending. Military school regulations

---

[14] Colin B. Burke, *American Collegiate Population: A Test of the Traditional View* (New York: New York University Press, 1982), 49 (quotation).

[15] M. Cartwright to Americus Cartwright, 6 January 1856, Cartwright Papers, The Center for American History, University of Texas at Austin.

[16] Examples from, in order: Edward C. Shepherd, unpublished diary; Daniel R. Flowerree to Francis H. Smith, 22 June 1858, VMI Archives.

stipulated that all cash should be sent to the superintendent rather than to the cadet, and schools disallowed merchants from contracting with cadets (see the image of Fitzhugh's quarterly report; Figure 7). Over decades as VMI superintendent, Francis H. Smith wrote to parents that he monitored boys' spending because otherwise they spent too much.[17] His oversight was obviously not absolute because some cadets purchased expensive clothes or listed parties and dinners, travels to nearby towns, and goods that they purchased.

Some families of low-to-middle economic status could barely afford to enroll a son in higher schooling and could not send that son a great deal of additional funds or supplies. Most cadets did not spend freely and asked only for small amounts. Many of the cadets repeatedly asked for small sums of money and received them, either for necessary expenses or minor luxuries.[18] Requests for a few dollars were often paid as fees for the debating societies or as stamps to write home. Students wanted cash to purchase school supplies, even books. Their requests for items and funds indicated that many families could provide their sons with slightly more than a basic standard of living. The cadets had spending money, some young men more than others, but most of them had enough to keep them happy though not in luxury.

In addition to spending money, cadets most commonly asked for food. The desire for a home-cooked meal or specific treat was probably intrinsic to students away from home. Concerns about food could also have illustrated high expectations based on the standards to which they were accustomed at home.[19] Few letters home, however, contained outright condemnations of the food; cadets occasionally listed their fare

[17] For example, Francis H. Smith to John Winn, Philip Winn student file, 29 February 1840, VMI Archives.

[18] See, for example, exchanges between Hillsboro Military Academy (HMA) cadet Walter Clark and his parents, *The Papers of Walter Clark*, esp. 23 August 1860, 25 August 1860, 31 August 1860; VMI cadet Charles Derby and his father, 4 April 1846, 26 February 1847, 27 December 1847, VMI Archives; Citadel cadet Lafayette Strait and family members, 25 January 1853, 10 March [1853], 29 March 1853, Papers of the Gaston, Strait, Wylie and Baskin Families, SCL; John Weller to Jacob Weller, n.d. May 1857, 11 May 1858, Jacob Weller Papers, The Filson Historical Society.

[19] Allmendinger, *Paupers and Scholars*, 84, interprets the evaluation of food in this way. Pierce M. B. Young to Mother, 25 April 1854, P. M. B. Young Papers; Seaborn Montgomery to Julia Montgomery, 28 July 1863, 7 May 1864, S. Montgomery Jr. Papers, Duke; Lafayette Strait to Mother, 15 February 1853; Strait to Father, [February 1853]; Claudius Fike to Parents, 7 January 1862, SCL; C. O. Bailey to James Bailey, 10 March 1861, James B. Bailey Papers,

but more often simply remarked on its adequacy. Close to the same number of cadets complimented or accepted the victuals as complained about them.[20] The general tolerance of school fare implies that it did not sharply contrast with their experience at home; thus, cadets did not have the expectations of superior food and accommodations of wealthy students. Overall, the cadets' purchases, spending, and standard of living placed them in a middle economic position (neither rich nor poor), generally within the emerging middle class.

Cadets' anxiety over money sometimes reflected their knowledge of their families' financial circumstances. While his father worked and obtained state money, VMI cadet Joseph Chenoweth questioned the entire state funding system: "How much good will accrue to young Virginians, who are in moderate circumstances – even from an Institution, in which the State proposes to educate them for a mere trifle," he exhorted in 1858, "while the men charged with the government of this Institution make these young men pay almost as much as their education would cost them at other Institutions where they would have to pay for every item in the list of College expenses." More specific worries gnawed at cadets. "Knowing the extreme shortness of the crops, and the bad Prospect of there being a number of Boarders," another cadet wrote his father, "I shall I assure you be as frugal as possible, and go to as little unnecessary expense as I can."[21]

Frugality was a common theme among cadets, and they appeared to need to be thrifty because their families' situations forced them to

Southern Historical Collection, Wilson Library, University of North Carolina at Chapel Hill (hereafter SHC).

[20] Seaborn Montgomery to Julia Montgomery, 28 July 1863, 7 May 1864, Duke; Lafayette Strait to Mother, 15 February 1853; Claudius Fike to Parents, 7 January 1862, SCL; C. O. Bailey to James Bailey, 29 February 1861, SHC. Some exceptions are: William Ervin to James Ervin, 25 August 1850, James Ervin Papers, Duke; Affleck, "Cadet at Bastrop Military Institute"; E. G. B. Russell to Robert Y. Russell, 2 February 1854, SCL. During the Civil War, different cadets lamented the HMA food, describing the meat as too fatty. Gratz Cohen to Parents, 23 June [1862], SCL; J. P. Cromartie to Grandmother, c. 1863, North Carolina State Archives (hereafter NCSA); John E. Dodson to Harriet Cogbill, 8 May 1863, VHS, wrote his mother that the HMA's poor food caused repeated fights. Before the war, Egbert Ross to Emma Ross, 18 June 1860, Egbert A. Ross Papers, SHC, said that HMA's food was worse than that of his previous school, North Carolina Military Institute, but it appeared to be acceptable.

[21] Joseph H. Chenoweth to Father, 21 November 1858 (first and second quotations), VMI Archives. Robert E. Johnson to General Robert R. Johnson, 1 September 1826 (third and fourth quotations); another boy declared his economy at HMA, Frederick Bryan to Mother, 25 February 1861, John Heritage Bryan Collection, NCSA.

be so. Parents exhibited concern over students' spending, because they both wanted their children to learn moderation and worried about the financial obligations. The monetary concerns showed the parents' fear of losing their sons' educational advantage. The older generation worried that they would be unable to afford the debts their sons incurred at school. Resources were tight for these families, and any expenses in excess of the costs outlined in the school circulars proved difficult. "My son's expenses have been much more than I expected or was led to expect from your advertisement. It was stated that from $250 to $275 would be the expenses of a Cadet, but his expenses will go over $300," father J. R. Bridges explained. "I mention this because I am not in a situation to incur a large expenditure, as I am really dependant [*sic*] upon my daily labour for a support." Five months later, Bridges again complained about expenses, "I am a poor man and have a large family to support and educate." The disagreement escalated as the superintendent blamed the extra costs on the cadet's not arriving with proper clothing (clearly outlined in the acceptance letter shown in Figure 3) and the youth's carelessness with clothing. "You seem to labour under an erroneous impression as to the expenses of a Cadet," the superintendent explained. "The Institution has no pecuniary interest in any Cadets expenditures beyond his tuition fee & this is fixed for each year. We endeavor to act as the guardian of the Cadet, purchase for him all of his necessary supplies, and issue them at cost."[22] Bridges apparently refused to pay the expenses, and the case went to an attorney the following year after young Bridges had graduated from the state military school.

Like Mr. Bridges, parents most often claimed poverty after they received a bill from their sons' schools, particularly one with demands for more cash than they had expected. One father, like many unfortunate others, shared his shock with the VMI superintendent upon receiving a bill for $485, more than $200 in excess of the listed yearly expenses. Parents blamed their sons and the schools for excessive costs, but even when they received bills more than double their expectations, most paid, if in installments.[23] Parents presented the typical paradox, claiming to be too

---

[22] J. R. Bridges to Francis H. Smith, 3 March 1849, 28 August 1849; Francis H. Smith to J. R. Bridges, 4 September 1849, 31 August 1850, Edward Bridges student file, VMI Archives.

[23] Henry Garnett to Francis H. Smith, 18 June 1841, Thomas Garnett student file, VMI Archives. Other examples include Francis H. Smith to John Winn, 29 February 1840, Duke; Edmund Ruffin to Francis H. Smith, 5 December 1852, Charles Ruffin student file, VMI Archives.

poor to finance schooling and expenses, yet in fact paying for tuition and items above the base amount.

Some families did pay the tuition when young men failed to get state money. Indeed, a few families enrolled one son in an academy as a state cadet and another as a pay cadet at the same time. After New Orleans engineer P. G. T. Beauregard refused the position of superintendent at the Louisiana State Seminary and Military Academy, he arranged for his older son Rene to be a state cadet and paid for his younger son.[24] These cases illustrate, first, the range of wealth among middle-class southerners (and the few elite at the schools), and second, the possession of sufficient resources by men attracted to military higher schools.

The situation of Philip Winn differed greatly from that of Chenoweth, yet some of the same patterns can be seen. Winn's father was a small planter working also as a lawyer, tobacco assessor, and postmaster. Although the family obviously had money, they were constantly short of cash. "Knowing my situation as you do, you will no doubt, use as much economy as possible," the father cautioned his son. "What is absolutely necessary will be supplied."[25] After three months at VMI in 1840, Philip accounted that he had spent $125.

After a year paying tuition, Mr. Winn declared that his son must receive state funding or resign: "In my former application it was not deemed necessary or desirable that my friends should represent me as entirely unable to educate my children, nor will I now plead poverty, yet I am frank to acknowledge that my limited means will not afford to all of them, even a tolerable English education." Mr. Winn decried that the size of his family (fifteen children of which Philip was the fourth son) made it difficult to ensure them even basic education; there was evidently no possibility of classical, college education. "I had already extended my means in the education of the present applicant, as far as my ability would justify, with due regard to the residue of my children, but from his great anxiety to go through a regular course in your institution, and obtain an education, was induced to exert myself still further in aid of his laudable views," Winn stressed the importance of his son's educational advantage. He expected,

---

[24]Philip Winn to John Winn, 1 May 1840, Duke. George Mason Graham to Robert Wickliffe, 2 November 1859; George Mason Graham to G. T. Beauregard, 1 November 1859, Graham Family Papers, VHS.

[25]John Winn to Philip Winn, 16 November 1840, Duke.

however, "this extra expenditure is to be refunded, or accounted for by" his son, presumably from the alumnus' future salary. Over the course of 1840, Winn's economic situation worsened, causing him to remove his son from school: "from the state of my pecuniary affairs, and the expense and education of a very large family of younger children, I shall be unable to supply my son Philip James with the necessary means of remaining at your Institution."[26]

Same as Philip Winn found, familial cash shortages forced other cadets to resign, as was the case for Cadet Piggott who resigned at his mother's "inability to defray his expenses as a pay Cadet." Parents explained that they had large families and small incomes or that their own income was low, in many cases due to illness; whatever the circumstance, young men's educations were sacrificed either because they could no longer afford even reduced expenditures or they could not pay the actual expenses in excess of the advertised rates.[27] "From letters which I have lately received from home, I have learned that, the expenses of an irregular [pay] Cadet, are greater than my father imagined, when he got me the appointment. And moreover, unless I am appointed a regular [state] Cadet, that I must resign," Cadet James Bryan worried. "My father is fast approaching the end of the short period allotted to man below, he has also a large family of young children dependant [sic] on him for their daily bread, and I being his eldest child would dislike to clog his efforts for the support and education of my little brothers and sisters." Birth order and family size influenced middle-class men's ability to obtain education, as Philip Winn's fourteen siblings limited the funds for his schooling. Indeed, when sons left a military school, fathers often wrote the young men that their education had ended and, for more than two-thirds of dropouts, schooling did cease.[28]

As the Winn family situation suggested, reversals of fortune afflicted a number of families who sent their sons to military schools. "He is the son

[26] Philip Winn to John Winn, 18 January 1840, 5 September 1840; John Winn to Board of Visitors, 4 May 1840 (first to third quotations); John Winn to Francis H. Smith, 25 December 1840 (fourth quotation), Duke.
[27] Order #36, 26 May 1856 (quotation), *Order Book 1852–1857*, VMI Archives. Also, Burwell B. Wilkes to Francis H. Smith, 24 February 1841, Samuel Pryor student file, VMI Archives.
[28] James Bryan to Francis H. Smith, 23 January 1841 (quotation); William Meredith to Francis H. Smith, David and Thomas Meredith student files, 10 January 1844, 6 June 1844, VMI Archives; Father to E. Montague Grimke, [July 1852], Edward Montague Grimke Correspondence, SCL.

of a gentleman of high standing of large family," one recommendation letter specifically described the applicant, "who lost his property in the cala-
mitous times of [18]42 & [18]43." In addition to downturns in the market
or volatile business cycles, reversals often came with the death or disability
of a father. A widow complained that she did not have enough resources
to pay her son's school bills, describing the situation, "Our property is
too small to admit of one indulgence beyond our [modest] income, the
most scrupulous economy alone can enable us to meet honestly all our
engagements."[29] Her son's guardian, a paternal relative, would pay the
debts. Many parents accessed education as this mother did; they desired
the available education and its advantages but were unable (or refused)
to spend beyond a certain amount for it.

Dual desires of economy and social maintenance suggest the middle-
class nature of military school matriculates. "I cannot assume any debts he
may contract at the Institute, beyond the legal sum for State Cadets," one
mother wrote, "yet I wouldn't mortify him by preventing his uniting with
fellow Cadets in any improving or usual custom requiring small sums
of money." Although this mother passed authority of her son's spending
onto the military academy administration, she maintained the ability to
fund important extra expenses in the same breath that she forbade them.
Similarly, after complaining about the costs of VMI, Joseph Chenoweth
asked his father for a new furlough coat at forty dollars. With a nice
explanation that he did not need the coat, he ended with the subtle
manipulation of "the Cadets generally buy one."[30] Even the parents who
claimed to be nearly destitute did not want their children to feel, or more
importantly, to appear poor. Monetary reality encouraged economy at
the same time as the desire for refinement and social status sent the
opposite message to the emerging middle class.[31]

Of course, even parents and students who had sufficient resources
for education and luxuries complained about costs. Most young men,

[29] T. Carrington to Board of Visitors, 1 June 1850 (first quotation); Mary Lee to Francis H.
Smith, 4 December 1852 (second quotation), William Lee student file, VMI Archives.

[30] Mary Lee to Francis H. Smith, 4 December 1852 (first quotation), William Lee student file;
Joseph Chenoweth to Father, 21 February 1857 (second quotation), VMI Archives.

[31] On refinement and its middle-class connections, see Richard L. Bushman, *The Refinement
of America* (New York: Alfred A. Knopf, 1992); Daniel Kilbride, "Southern Medical Students
in Philadelphia, 1800–1860: Science and Sociability in the 'Republic of Medicine,'" *Journal
of Southern History*, 65 (November 1999), 697–732.

including pay cadets, told their parents that school was expensive. Henry Burgwyn, future Boy General of the Confederacy, attended a West Point preparatory school for a year but failed to get appointed to the United States Military Academy. After attending the University of North Carolina (UNC) for a year and taking a few more off, he enrolled in VMI immediately before the Civil War started. In a representative letter, Burgwyn wrote,

> This is a very expensive school for pay cadets; especially for those who come from out of state. The tuition fee alone is $100. That at [UNC in] Ch. Hill was only $56. A great many minor charges for items is [*sic*] made and for whatever you break no matter how valuable in reality to have to pay the original cost with 20% addition. The final expenses for class ring, diplomas &c amount up pretty high.[32]

Burgwyn accurately noted that tuition for out-of-state students could be higher than for state residents, as with many state schools today. As evident in his earlier education experience and his out-of-state costs, the young North Carolinian was well off. Despite listing these expenses at VMI, Burgwyn clearly spent in a free manner. In the same letter, he described purchasing ambrotypes of his friends for fifty dollars, certainly a luxury a poor student would not have considered.[33] (See Figure 2.)

Some cadets like Burgwyn recorded spending more than a poor cadet would have been able. Wealthier cadets could expend more money for the higher standards of living they expected than could the majority of their peers. Indeed, a few young men had standing orders at home for monthly boxes and asked for goods in virtually every letter. The young men applied for a number of things, particularly additional food and clothing. For example, a few cadets wanted their parents to send personal guns and horses (despite the fact that military schools forbade the possession of them). One planter's son at the Bastrop Military Institute in Texas requested many items from home and, on his own, spent money for a bed

---

[32] Henry Burgwyn to Anna Burgwyn, 3 March 1861, Burgwyn Family Papers, SHC. Also, Affleck, "Cadet at Bastrop Military Institute."

[33] Indeed, Burgwyn recorded that he spent $119.75 (more than a year's tuition at VMI) in a little less than two months during the middle of UNC's spring term. Henry Burgwyn to Anna Burgwyn, 3 March 1861; Burgwyn, unpublished expense record, 3 April 1859, SHC.

and curtains.[34] Such largesse was in contrast to the other cadets' letters
and concerns with limited resources.

Most students worried about expenses and reflected the sufficient
but limited resources their families possessed. Cadet Lafayette Strait,
for example, spent thirty dollars in excess of tuition each semester. His
parents continued expressing their poverty while funding their son's
expenses while he attended the state military institute in South Carolina.
Like other parents who claimed to be poor, Strait's parents initially stated
that one dollar was all they could afford to send him and then three weeks
later enclosed five dollars in another letter. Strait's sister also enjoined
him that their father could not send money.[35]

On the whole, cadets expressed middle-class resources and access to
goods. They received and spent allowances but had to curb their purchases because of the limits on those family resources. Even young men
who could not purchase their own luxuries partook of their wealthier
roommates' boxes from home and could hope for their own treats.[36]
These families possessed sufficient resources to afford schooling, either
with cash or access to other resources such as patronage and loans.

Accepting Patronage and Debt

Whatever their circumstances, men with limited wealth and families in
the emerging middle class tried to find advantage for the next generation.
They used their resources, perhaps turning to the southern system of
patronage, to enter nonclassical and reduced-cost military education.

A patronage system existed in the South to benefit respectable orphans
or deserving young men of the emerging middle class. Patronage meant

[34] See, for example, Gratz Cohen to Miriam Cohen, 2 November 1861, 7 July 1862, SHC; Affleck,
"Cadet at Bastrop Military Institute"; Seaborn Montgomery to Julia Montgomery, 28 July
1863, 1 May 1864; Henry Hendrick to John Hendrick, 24 December 1860, Duke; Micah Jenkins
to Mother, 6 August 1853, 23 April 1854, SCL; C. Irvine Walker, "Reminiscences of days in
the Citadel," unpublished memoir, CIT; Robert Scott to Joel Scott, 27 September 1853, 31
October 1853, Department of Library Special Collections, Manuscripts, Western Kentucky
University.

[35] Sallie Strait to Lafayette Strait, 18 March 1853, 2 April 1853; Lafayette Strait to Father, 27 April
1853, SCL.

[36] Many boys described sharing boxes and food received, especially among roommates: Walker,
"Reminiscences of days in the Citadel"; Philip C. Gibbs, unpublished diary; Charles Derby
to Father, 27 December 1847, VMI Archives.

that a family accepted money to send a son to school, including using the advantage of a reduced-cost military institute.[37] Parents could similarly employ the reputation of influential patrons to write recommendations to obtain state-funded cadetships. Cadets' families apparently possessed respectability and status in their communities to access these types of patronage. At the same time, however, they lacked the monetary freedom that came with landed stability.[38] Their situation and use of patronage suggests a connection between the growing southern middle class and the elite. Whereas elite planters controlled large land holdings and large incomes, the majority of military school fathers, generally men of the growing middle class, maintained professional careers. Cadets' fathers accepted patronage for their sons' secondary education, which highlighted their middle economic status.

Recommendation letters and the financial situation of some cadets provide direct examples of patronage. A father might write a board of visitors' member asking for his son's entry into a school, as Harrold Smyth did. Others asserted their ability to pay with the assistance of "friends," as in the case of a cadet unable to continue schooling "unless his friends advance the funds necessary to complete his course." Young men were also sponsored to attend military schools. In the same year that his son quit VMI, Edmund Ruffin funded another cadet and complained when the costs exceeded the amount indicated in the catalog. Similarly an Edisto Island planter financed a cadet from the island for two years at Kings Mountain Military Academy.[39]

Young men also accepted loans under the southern patronage system. In his memoir, for example, former cadet Robert P. Carson remembered that his father "made strenuous efforts to have all his children educated, and by borrowing money, succeeded pretty well." He was one of many fathers and sons who took out loans from family friends for schooling. In a similar fashion, another cadet borrowed money from neighbors to

---

[37] For example, James Shepherd to Francis H. Smith, 13 August 1849, Edward Shepherd student file; Robert H. Simpson to Francis H. Smith, 24 June 1853, VMI Archives.

[38] Robert Tracy McKenzie, *One South or Many?: Plantation Belt and Upcountry in Civil War-Era Tennessee* (New York: Cambridge University Press, 1994), 125 n. 2.

[39] Smyth to Judge Brockenbrough, 14 July 1846, Alexander Smyth student file; Robert Simpson to Francis H. Smith, 24 June 1853 (quotation); Edmund Ruffin to Francis H. Smith, 5 December 1852, Charles Ruffin student file, VMI Archives; John Jenkins Estate entry, 1856, 1857, Legare and Colcock Account Books, South Carolina Historical Society.

continue at the Citadel. When VMI cadet Edwin Edmonds's father died, a family friend with a son attending the same school loaned him the substantial sum of $100.[40] Gaining patronage reflected the middle status and resources of the families making applications.

These families went into debt to attain education. The significance and meaning of personal debt in the antebellum South needs more exploration. Colonial historian T. H. Breen argues that it became part of the mentalité of the Revolutionary generation, and its public exposure led to revolutionary ideology. After its increased prevalence and awareness (especially following the Panic of 1837), personal debt may have been more acceptable in the antebellum era. The cadets never described mortification or social disgrace in conjunction with their debt, which suggests that owing money to a school was not viewed negatively. Parents who had trouble paying for their sons' expenses generally informed the schools of that fact unapologetically. Even an alumnus who explained his father's business debt did so not to erase the debt but to explain its justifiable cause.[41] These cadets accepted debt as they did patronage.

Cadets at state military institutes received an almost free collegiate education as only students at the U.S. service academy and the very few state university scholarship recipients did and similarly appeared to do so without any stigma. Citadel regulations stated, "No difference shall be made in the treatment, or in the duties required, between the [tuition paying and scholarship] Cadets; nor shall any distinction between Cadets be known in the Academy, other than that arising from merit."[42] States monitored to whom they gave funds, attempting to benefit families who could not otherwise afford education.

In general, however, the funding system depersonalized patronage. Rather than owing deference to an elite neighbor or relative, cadets in the developing middle class contracted with their states. In addition to their

[40] Carson, memoir, VHS. W. M. Mobley to Susan Wylie, [10 March 1854], Papers of the Gaston, Strait, Wylie and Baskin Families, SCL; William Fowle to Francis H. Smith, 10 August 1855, 7 August 1856, Edward Edmonds student file, VMI Archives.

[41] Breen, *Tobacco Culture* (Princeton: Princeton University Press, 1985). Charles Denby to Francis H. Smith, 1 August 1849, VMI Archives; Thomas Huguenin, "A Sketch of the Life of Thomas Abram Huguenin," unpublished memoir, CIT.

[42] *Regulations of the Military Academies of South Carolina* (Columbia: R. W. Gibbes, 1858), 14 (quotation).

practical obligations – generally two years teaching after graduation – they also internalized the duty they owed the state. Their responsibility, however, ended upon repayment of debt. Accepting patronage from the government reflected a separation between the emerging middle class and the elite and a bureaucratic replacement of traditional community relationships.

The state payments could most benefit young men with the greatest need for patronage. Military school rolls evidenced many orphans and even more students with only one parent living. Fatherless cadets and younger sons represented men on the margin of society who frequently enrolled in military schools. The attendance of these men meant, first, that they had less access to community-based patronage systems and, second, that they came from households seeking to establish their sons without land. A father's death left his son to provide for his own education or to rely on a guardian for one. Superintendent Smith of VMI took pride in accepting orphans or fatherless children to spread educational opportunity. Similarly, the South Carolina Military Academy was so attractive that the orphan house petitioned the legislature to guarantee entry to its charges.[43] Although some orphans paid their tuitions with family wealth, the system of state funding offered schooling to those youths unable to bear the expense on their own.

Orphans' position on the margin gave them little financial security. Many of those cadets relied on guardians who expended funds on education in order to reap that advantage. Some guardians paid for their wards' education; others pulled a young man from his school when the cadet's inheritance dwindled. The guardians who obtained entrance for their dependents were certainly the ones concerned with the advantages of an education. One such man represented the expected behavior. "I as a Relative have taken Thomas [Barksdale], and wish to educate him for a Teacher," Thomas Hamner described his responsibility to his nephew. "I do not feel able to give him a complete education unless I can avail myself of the liberality of the State and get him in as a State student, a Cadet at the V.M. Institute." He could have mentioned that he educated his nephew to

[43]"Orphan house petitioning...," 16 December 1854, Committee on Military, South Carolina Legislature, SCDAH.

honor the memory of his sister or for the benefit of his relatives, as other kin did.[44] Hamner, instead, presented the practical reasons for entering a ward in a military higher school; he felt that the military institute would give him the ability to educate his orphaned nephew and train the young man for a career. Hamner obviously had enough resources to pay for his nephew's expenses at school. His nephew, however, had to rely on the liberality and patronage of both the uncle and the state to achieve an education. That education, in turn, placed the nephew into professional careers (teaching and law) and the emerging middle class. Tom Barksdale is shown with a pipe in a cadet drawing from 1855 (Figure 5).

In quite a few cases, older brothers acted as guardians or helped to finance their younger brothers' education.[45] "He is too poor to educate himself and in my presence a brother has agreed to furnish the necessary means to pay his expenses if he should be appointed [a state-funded cadet]," said one recommendation letter, "and I know the funds so generously offered was [*sic*] the proceeds of that brother's labor." The letter specifically described the funds as coming from "labor," not interest or other passive income. Orphan John Weller's older brother, his guardian, received a bill from the Kentucky Military Institute that included $186 overdue from the previous semester; the brother's six-month lack of payment of tuition suggests financial strain. Another cadet portrayed his ability to attend a state military school, "I feel that I am under great obligations to my Father and Brothers for the advantage which I have enjoyed."[46]

Because guardians were generally less involved with their wards at school than were parents, the occupations of only a few guardians can

---

[44]Thomas F. Hamner to Francis H. Smith, 10 December 1850, Thomas Barksdale student file, VMI Archives. Other men recorded as orphans, J. Campbell to Francis H. Smith, 1 February 1851, John Lightner student file; Archd. Atkinson to Board of Visitors, 1 June 1840, John C. Wills student file; Mary A. Williams to Francis H. Smith, 4 September 1856, Titus Williams student file, VMI Archives; Charles R. Brewster to Walter Brewster, 1 October 1847, CIT. For another guardian, see Benjamin Perry, unpublished account book, South Carolina Historical Society.

[45]There are at least sixteen such cases at VMI: P. Bouldin, B. Elliott, B. Ficklin, P. Fitzhugh, A. Gooch, T. Harman, A. Harrison, R. Harrison, J. Hunter, E. and H. Ker, W. Mayre, J. Mays, J. McBridge, B. Nalle, and P. Winn.

[46]Recommendation letter, Jonathan F. Mays student file (first quotation); Quarterly Report, 16 June 1860, Jacob Weller Papers, The Filson Historical Society; Francis M. Suddoth to Francis H. Smith, 18 July 1856 (second quotation), VMI Archives.

be determined. Of the few guardians with discernable occupations, a significant majority (64 percent) worked as physicians.[47] This fact reinforces the predominance of professionals and the middle-class nature of the families and associates. It also may suggest that, as a part of patronage, wealthier men in the family took responsibility for the less fortunate members, as did Mr. Hamner. Family members most often shouldered the burdens of guardianship. Men without stable families or financial situations had more need of patronage, including that from the state.

Sufficient resources included relying on wealthier relatives. "The boy's grandmother has a small sum of money which she is willing to appropriate to his education provided the interest is paid to her during her life," another letter explained the monetary situation that would finance a cadet's education. "This [interest payment] some friend has agreed to be responsible for."[48] This youth relied on his grandmother's money and a friend's payments for his education. Certainly, accepting any such patronage tied a cadet and his family to the elite 'patrons' in a subordinate position. Middle-class young men, especially orphans, found patronage where they could – with family, local elites, or outright loans.

With or without loans, some young men made up their own mind to become cadets. These independent students were either old enough to be separate from their parents' purview or, more often, were orphans. Many of these self-sufficient young men or youths with guardians lived closer to the poverty level than the cadets whose families sent them to military schools. Consider the cadet who hoped for a state-funded position, but if one were not available, would borrow money to enroll in VMI. "I dread to start in life with a debt hanging over me yet to complete my education I will as a last resort incur the debt," the student stated his resolution. He would accept debt, however, because graduates of the Virginia institution successfully entered careers, particularly teaching. His teacher at Fleetwood Academy, a VMI alumnus himself, endorsed the young man's credentials.[49] This young man expressed his belief that military education led to a profession, so much so that he would accept patronage or debt for the chance; perhaps to avoid debt, he never enrolled.

[47] See Appendix 2, Table 3.
[48] James Shepherd to Francis H. Smith, 9 June 1851 (quotation), Edward Shepherd student file, VMI Archives.
[49] R. S. Smith to Francis H. Smith, 21 February 1851, VMI Archives.

The advantage sought with state funding provided benefits, and middle-class southerners saw beyond the economic ones that military education provided. "By your example encourage those who either through modesty or idleness fail to take advantage of the many opportunities here presented to them," a cadet speaker at a literary society instructed his peers.[50] He described the advantages that accrued to young men who gave speeches and debated, thus improving their minds. Their education offered them advantage in southern society and they gained the value of education through public funding. Men in the middle economic position possessed sufficient resources for schooling, including the resources of access to patronage or loans. This economic position reflected the emerging middle class and indicates one reason why military education in particular attracted the group; they would have similarly sought advantage in other low-cost colleges and higher schools. Thus, military education's funding aided the development of the middle class. Middle-class southerners promoted public education, and their success in state military school funding furthered the depersonalization of patronage, even as many cadets with limited resources relied on community or family patronage. Another distinctive characteristic of military schools – their discipline – begins to describe the uniqueness growing in the values among the emerging southern middle class.

[50] Gibbs, diary, 1 March 1851, VMI Archives.

3

"Your duty as citizens and soldiers"
Military Education Discipline and Duty

Twenty-one-year-old William Gordon, a senior at the Virginia Military Institute (VMI), was not well liked among his peers. By his senior year in 1851, at least three cadets had gotten into fights with him. Gordon's apparently contentious nature did not make his first three and a half years at VMI extraordinary, but, in his final term, the young man found himself the center of a series of courts-martial. The controversy started with a simple report in January 1852. Functioning as the cadet captain, the highest-ranking student officer at a military school, Gordon wrote up Cadet John A. Thompson for "not keeping eyes to the front at Dinner Roll Call." The report itself, a routine part of the military academy disciplinary system, would have disappeared into institutional records had Thompson accepted the punishment it entailed. Instead, Thompson sent Gordon a letter that declared, "I want this to be the last time that ever I shall be reported by so mean a villainous scape-gallows as William Gordon."[1] With this letter, Thompson resisted what he chose to interpret as a public insult and reacted as the dictates of southern honor prescribed. Gordon, in response, obeyed his military duty and carried the letter to VMI's authorities.

At least seventeen of the twenty-five VMI seniors interpreted Thompson's behavior as legitimate and branded Gordon a coward. Rather than revolt en masse, as southern college students often did when they

---

[1] For the details of the Gordon–Thompson affair, see 21 January 1852, *Order Book*; 20 January 1852 (quotation), *Courts Martial 1848–1854 Book*; Walter Wheeler Williams, unpublished diary, 15 January to 25 February 1852; and Thomas Munford to Joseph Anderson, 23 August 1912, Preston Library, Virginia Military Institute Archives (hereafter VMI Archives).

disagreed with administrators, VMI cadets petitioned school authorities on behalf of Thompson. When VMI officials treated the petition as an illegal student collusion, the cadets withdrew it and instead ostracized Gordon, denying him their "kindly <u>feelings</u> and . . . mutual <u>confidence</u> and <u>esteem</u>."[2]

The conflict between Gordon and Thompson highlights how complex the matter of obedience to duty could be for antebellum cadets in the South. This chapter argues that cadets encountered, and most of them negotiated, a tension between their duty to the military school and their duty to the standards of southern honor. It details the regulations and disciplinary expectations of military education in the antebellum period and examines how cadets responded to them. As parents' influence in their sons' lives decreased, cadets combined military and southern values, often acting as adolescents do – in their own best interests. Middle-class cadets learned to embody duty, obedience, and self-regulation in order to successfully complete their education. They did so within self-regulated peer groups that were as strong as those of other youths of the era; these groups accepted minor rule breaking but consistently reinforced obedience to the regulations and self-discipline – values that dovetailed with their middle-class position. Indeed, the cadets' negotiation of discipline, duty, and honor suggests the ongoing formation of the emerging southern middle class.

Cultivating Moral Discipline

Classroom style and ideology reinforced the fundamental goal of all nineteenth-century education: moral and mental discipline. The pedagogical structure of antebellum colleges, higher schools, and military academies alike promoted mental discipline above all else and emphasized training over acquiring knowledge. "Knowledge is not the principal end of college instruction, but habits," said the South Carolina College president in 1853. The nineteenth-century recitation method required memorization and obviated creative thinking. Obedience in and out of the classroom was thought to build character; young men had to fit into schools, not vice versa. As child-centered learning was not yet prevalent,

---

[2] William O. Yager, unpublished diary, VMI Archives (emphasis in original).

teachers expected students to motivate themselves.[3] Most educators, parents, and teachers explicitly stressed the importance of the moral component of education.

Young cadets would have found many aspects of life in military school comparable to those in other higher schools; colleges, non-military schools, and military academies maintained similar teaching methods and schedules, and they placed like emphasis on discipline. "However intellectually gifted the teacher may be the mass of parents regard strict disciplinarianism as the loftiest test of qualification [of teachers]," described a speaker. Military schools were simply stricter and more systematic. As early as 1823, critics responded to the privations of military schools by calling the first private military institution (a northern academy) a "reformatory." These detractors were in the minority, however, and their characterization contradicted the perceptions of the school's educators, students' parents, and most newspaper reports. Military schools' regulations were designed to cultivate moral discipline, not reform bad behavior. The *Nashville Union and American* promoted the Western Military Institute (WMI) by writing, "It combines physical with mental development. It teaches obedience, subordination and deference to authority, which constitute a sound basis for good citizenship, and elevated morals."[4] Indeed, military school discipline and admission requirements reflected the era's standards. Students submitted references that attested primarily to their moral character and proper behavior and only secondarily to their academic suitability for secondary education. No military schools, and few colleges, would have accepted a young man who exhibited discipline problems.[5]

[3] Quotation in Michael Sugrue, "South Carolina College; The Education of an Antebellum Elite" (Ph. D. diss., Columbia University, 1992), 33. George P. Schmidt, *The Liberal Arts College: A Chapter in American Cultural History* (New Brunswick: Rutgers University Press, 1957), 13–19; Frederick Rudolph, *The American College and University* (Athens: University of Georgia Press, 1990), 119–20. After the 1860s, the theories of Johann Heinrich Pestalozzi filtered into the United States. Pestalozzi's ideas based teaching on oral instruction and student interaction.

[4] Edwin Heriot, *The Polytechnic School, the Best System of Practical Education. An Address Delivered before the Cadet Polytechnic Society, State Military Academy. June 14, 1850* (Charleston: Walker and James, 1850), 14 (first quotation). "Western Military Academy," *Nashville Union and American* (14 February 1855), 2 (second quotation).

[5] William G. Smith to Francis H. Smith, 10 May 1849, Isaac Robins student file, VMI Archives, refused to recommend his ward's reinstatement at school because of the youth's behavior. Also, see *Regulations of the Kentucky Military Institute* (Frankfort: A.G. Hodges & Co., 1851), 2;

Nonetheless, discipline was a major problem for many parents of school-age children in both the North and the South. College administrators worried about misbehaving youth and reported major disturbances – from riots and shootings to fights and swearing. In particular, southern boys had the reputation of being ungovernable; although many no doubt deserved this reputation, their behavior was often no worse than that of their northern counterparts. Across the nation, collegiate young men acted out adolescent rebellion by testing the rules, rioting, shooting into buildings, and striking professors. Many people in the antebellum era had negative feelings about universities and the cities that housed them, believing that colleges bred temptation.[6] Even students expressed fear about the atmosphere: A Washington College student, for example, worried that he would start drinking and card playing if he attended the University of Virginia, and while the VMI constructed its barracks, cadet Joel Scott wished to move to the country because he believed he spent too much time surrounded by the transgressions of town life. The lack of discipline among college students may have become progressively worse in the early nineteenth century as colleges loosened their regulations – a trend that military schools countered.[7]

Thus, academy discipline proved attractive to middle-class parents. Parents interested in sending their sons to military higher schools tended to be southerners who sought antidotes to college temptations and valued discipline, restrained manhood, and professional traits. One mother believed the discipline at her son's military school averted the temptations found in cities. She expressed the common view that the military regimen,

Dean Paul Baker, "The Partridge Connection: Alden Partridge and Southern Military Education" (Ph. D. diss., University of North Carolina, 1986), 194–95, 260.

[6] For discussions of disobedience at nonmilitary schools, see Baker, "Partridge Connection," ch. 7, esp. 251–52, 288; Rudolph, *American College and University*, 97–99, 104–07; Schmidt, *Liberal Arts College*, 13–19, ch. 4; Robert F. Pace and Christopher A. Bjornsen, "Adolescent Honor and College Student Behavior in the Old South," *Southern Cultures*, 6 (Fall 2000), 9–28.

[7] Alexander Brown to Fanny Brown, 7 September 1848, VMI Archives; Joel Scott to Robert Scott, 24 October 1853, Special Collections, Western Kentucky University (hereafter WKU). Robert F. Pace, *Halls of Honor: College Men in the Old South* (Baton Rouge: Louisiana State University Press, 2004). Most New England schools had strict codes originating at Yale in 1745. David Allmendinger Jr., *Paupers and Scholars: The Transformation of Student Life in Nineteenth-Century New England* (New York: St. Martin's Press, 1975); Rudolph, *American College and University*, 106–07.

which kept boys in a confined location and prescribed a detailed schedule, produced a better moral environment. Parents of military school cadets tended to express a general desire to eradicate their sons' idleness or profligacy while hastening to affirm the generally good moral character of their boys. In some instances, they suggested that their sons needed guidance in curbing their extravagance or indolence.[8]

In order to arrest behavior problems, most antebellum colleges and higher schools imposed stringent regulations on students' time and actions. Students followed schedules that instructed them to rise at 5:00 A.M. and regimented their time throughout the day. A student at Emory and Henry College in southwest Virginia rose with the 5:00 A.M. bell and studied from 6:00 to 7:00 A.M., 8:00 A.M. to 1:00 P.M., 2:00 to 4:00 P.M., and 6:00 to 7:00 P.M. Students at the elite South Carolina College studied from 6:00 A.M. to 12:00 P.M. and from 1:00 to 5:00 P.M. unless reciting; they were free after chapel at 9:00 P.M.

Military institutes, too, scheduled their students' days, but they went even further than colleges by instituting twenty-four-hour schedules, in which every half-hour was assigned a purpose. "No cadet can, with impunity, absent himself for a single hour without the consent of some member of the Faculty," stated the Kentucky Military Institute Board of Visitors in 1856.[9] From reveille to tattoo, cadets attended recitations, drills, parades, meetings, and study time; between study and recitation hours, academies also assigned and monitored students' time. Recitations usually lasted from 8:00 A.M. to 4:00 P.M., with an hour for lunch, and cadets took part in daily drills and parades (except on Sundays). Between tattoo and reveille, the regulations scheduled the cadets' sleep hours. A second-year cadet at VMI would have met with his math class daily from 8:00 to 9:00 A.M., taken Latin from 11:00 A.M. to 12:00 P.M., had lunch from 12:00 to 1:00 P.M., and taken French from 2:00 to 3:00 P.M. He would have had drawing lessons and drill each three times a week, and

[8] Cadet Walter Clark's mother stressed equally the importance of good deportment and morality through Bible reading; Aubrey Lee Brooks and Hugh Talmage Lefler, eds., *The Papers of Walter Clark* (Chapel Hill: University of North Carolina Press, 1948), 15 September 1860, 25 October 1860. Also, Amelia Shepherd to Francis H. Smith, 20 June [1851], Edward Shepherd student file; E. C. Finney to Francis H. Smith, 8 May 1847, William Finney student file, VMI Archives.
[9] *Catalogue of the Officers and Cadets of the Kentucky Military Institute* (Cincinnati: Moore, Wilstach, Keys and Co., 1856), 20.

he would have studied during the remaining available daytime hours.[10] After Jefferson College attached a military component and disciplinary system to its classical curriculum, it planned every minute of the cadets' time from dawn until 10:00 P.M. The schedule demanded four hours of study per day and allowed one hour of recreation – the only undirected time. Rappahannock Military Institute and the state military institutes of Georgia, South Carolina, and Tennessee had nearly duplicate timetables. As many as five daily roll calls recorded attendance and assured that cadets followed the prescribed expectations. WMI even issued a regulation that any cadet "absent from his lodgings, except for attending drills for recitations, or who shall employ the time otherwise than in study" would be arrested.[11]

Young Eugene Cordell explained his routine in the cadet corps at the preparatory academy Episcopal High School in detail:

> At six in the morning we are aroused by the ringing of the bell, which is the signal of everything. We have to be dressed and in the lower lavatory in 10 minutes. In the lavatory we wash for 10 or 15 min. and then the bell is rung and we go to the Chapel for prayers. Which finished we study in the school room for an hour, and then have a few minutes recess. Then the bell rings and in go to the lavatory and clear our teeth brush and comb our hair &c and then fall into ranks and go into the Refectory for breakfast. Afterwards we play until 9 ock and go to the school room until 12 or half after. The bell rings at a quarter past one and we wash and have dinner. From 2 until 5 we are in school. From

[10] See, among others, Order #3, 10 January 1856, Order #42, 15 January 1858, Order #144, 14 January 1859, *Order Book*, VMI Archives.
[11] WMI *Order Book*, vol. 5, 21 April 1848 (quotation), Jean and Alexander Heard Library, Vanderbilt University Archives (hereafter Vanderbilt); *The Charter and Statutes of Jefferson College* (Natchez: Book and Job Office, 1840), 54–55; *Regulations of the Kentucky Military Institute*, 8, §82; *Regulations of the Georgia Military Institute, Marietta, Georgia* (n.p., January, 1853); *Register of Cadets and Regulations of the Western Military Institute at Georgetown Kentucky* (Georgetown: n.p., 1849), American Antiquarian Society, 15; *Regulations of the Citadel Academy at Charleston, and Arsenal Academy at Columbia* (Columbia: A. S. Johnston, 1849), 25–26, 37. Institutional publications made the scheduling clear: the northern American Classical and Military Lyceum broadside, [1828], American Antiquarian Society, described a dawn-to-9:30 P.M. timeline for boys as young as ten years old; *Catalogue of the Officers and Students of the Rappahannock Academy and Military Institute, Caroline County, Virginia* (Baltimore: John Murphy and Co., 1851) in Virginia regulated from 5:30 A.M. in summer or 6:30 A.M. in winter until 10 P.M.

5 to six intermission. After supper an intermission of 1/2 or 3/4 of an hour. Then to the Chapel for prayers. Then study our lessons for an hour. A few minutes recess and then return to bed.

"The rules," he concluded, "are very strict."[12] Cordell found a comparable routine at VMI when he entered a few years later. Another VMI cadet told his father that the cadets had to rise by six in the morning, but that he was usually up at four in order to have additional study time. Likewise, a different young man described a daily timetable lasting from five in the morning to eleven at night. "Everything goes on like clock work, everything is conducted so regularly that I know today exactly what I'll have to do in a month hence," wrote Theodore Fogle from the Georgia Military Institute (GMI).[13] Moreover, the year-round schedule of military schools, including encampment in the summer, kept cadets in the control of institutional regulations longer than did the short terms of other schools.

One historian states that antebellum colleges' routines "resembled nothing so much as a benevolent parental despotism with overtones of a military barracks."[14] But young college men could find reprieve from such restriction by boarding off-campus, where they had more freedom. Colleges varied in their housing arrangements, and whereas some boarding houses regulated behavior closely, others gave students freer rein. At military schools, in contrast, all cadets lived in barracks under the constant supervision of their peers, while professors routinely patrolled rooms

[12] Eugene F. Cordell, unpublished diary, 19 September 1859, Rare Book, Manuscript, and Special Collections Library, Duke University (hereafter Duke). Another cadet described the same school as "the most rigid school you can imagine to be in existence" despite having attended another military academy; William Waller Govan to B. H. Goodloe, 16 September 1854, Jones Family Papers, Virginia Historical Society (hereafter VHS).

[13] Philip James Winn to John Winn, 18 January 1840, Duke; Dabney Overton Atherton to Parents, 23 September 1852, VMI Archives. Henry K. Burgwyn Jr. described being in recitations from 7:00 A.M. to 4:00 P.M.; Burgwyn to Anna Burgwyn, 8 September 1860, Burgwyn Family Papers, Southern Historical Collection, Wilson Library, University of North Carolina at Chapel Hill (hereafter SHC). Also, see Williams, diary, 13 April 1852, VMI Archives. Theodore Fogle to Father and Mother, 2 July 1852 (quotation), Theodore F. Fogle Papers, Department of Special Collections, Richard Woodruff Library, Emory University (hereafter Emory).

[14] Schmidt, *Liberal Arts College*, 79 (quotation); Edgar W. Knight, *The Academy Movement* (Chapel Hill: 1919), 45; Sugrue, "South Carolina College," 62–63. Jennings L. Wagoner Jr., "Honor and Dishonor at Mr. Jefferson's University: The Antebellum Years," *History of Education Quarterly*, 26 (Summer 1986), 166–71.

and imposed discipline. As military institutions increased the number of regulations to which students were subject, they also reversed the trend of allowing students to board and eat off campus or independently. Whereas many universities came to see dormitories as a breeding ground for student vice, military education returned to an eighteenth-century ideal of boarding large numbers of students in self-contained buildings.[15] On their campuses, cadets were much more closely supervised by professors and by their peers than were students at nonmilitary educational institutions.

Military schools not only increased the regulation of students through more extensive scheduling and housing, they also implemented comprehensive lists of regulations and a system of demerit points for breaking them, copying the program at West Point, where commandant Sylvanus Thayer had instituted a disciplinary system based on demerits in 1825.[16] When cadets disobeyed the regulations, the authorities assigned penalties for minor offenses, such as being late at roll call, and for more serious ones, such as leaving campus without permission. VMI cadet Gordon's original report on Thompson for failing to keep his eyes front during dinner roll call, mentioned in this chapter's introduction, would have resulted in demerits had Thompson not escalated the incident.

Most academies gave fewer demerits for academic than for disciplinary problems; skipping class earned a cadet five demerits at VMI, for example, whereas being out of the barracks after lights out earned him eight, plus five more for every additional half-hour that he did not appear. Administrations counted a cadet's demerits throughout the term and deducted them from his overall class ranking. Reports of cadets' demerits are reproduced in the image section (Figures 6–8). An excellent student with disciplinary problems, then, might rank below a mediocre but obedient cadet. Excessive demerits could even push a cadet's ranking so low that he could not graduate, despite his having attended and

---

[15] From 1820 to 1860, northern colleges including Yale did away with collegewide commons and housing in part because they had admitted a greater number of non-elite students who could not afford those amenities; Allmendinger, *Paupers and Scholars*, 81–83; Rudolph, *American College and University*, 96–101.

[16] There are many histories of West Point; see, for example, George S. Pappas, *To the Point: The United States Military Academy, 1802–1902* (Westport, CT: Praeger Publishers, 1993), 159.

passed his courses. The most serious infractions would result in the commandant of cadets, the supervisory faculty member, initiating a court-martial.[17] Courts-martial brought cadets before a faculty judiciary board with the power to dismiss them. Many trials, however, resulted in cadets' confinement to room or campus, extra hours of guard duty, or walking tours of the parade ground.[18]

The complex set of regulations instituted at southern military schools, following the West Point standard, specified where cadets had to be for all but a few hours a day, how they had to behave, and what they had to wear. Indeed, academy educators' concern with absolute discipline led many of them to want to keep cadets under supervision at all times. In 1852, the VMI Court Martial Board suggested that the institute ring a bell to call cadets back to post for roll call, even on Sundays; this test, the board argued, would accustom the students to obeying rules and encourage them to stay close to campus. Schools took nearly complete control over cadets' lives, whether the students were on or off duty, on or off post. In doing so, they imposed the regulation of modern time.[19] They required adherence to the schedule with roll calls and greater vigilance than did nonmilitary schools.

Regulations also stipulated what possessions cadets could keep in their rooms and what clothes they could own. One Citadel cadet described his room's furnishings to his parents as including a mirror, two small tables, a washstand, bucket, cup, washpan, foot tub, wardrobe, four chairs, and a cot and mattress for each cadet. Other cadets described sleeping on mattresses laid on the floor. All military schools disallowed specific

---

[17] See, for example, *Regulations of the Kentucky Military Institute*, 11–12, 124; Order #64, 15 May 1858, *Order Book 1852–1857*, VMI Archives; University of Nashville, Collegiate Department, and Western Military Institute, *The Official Register of Officers and Cadets for the Collegiate Year 1854–5, and Rules and Regulations, with Annual Announcement of Faculty and Officers for 1855–6* (Nashville: Cameron and Fall and Book and Job Printers, 1855), 31–32. The Georgia Military Institute had a unique regulation to increase academic standards; it required professors to report cadets who performed below certain grades on their daily recitations; *Regulations of the Georgia Military Institute* (1853), 38.

[18] Cordell, diary, 19 September 1859, Duke, described having to copy pages out of the dictionary as a minor punishment.

[19] *Courts Martial Book*; Order #43, 29 December 1852, Order #64, 28 June 1852, 15 May 1858, *Order Book*, VMI Archives, includes a revised list of demerits. See Mark M. Smith, *Mastered by the Clock: Time, Slavery and Freedom in the American South* (Chapel Hill: University of North Carolina Press, 1997).

personal possessions, including weapons, animals, and servants. Some excluded any belongings beyond the prescribed ones. Superintendent Alden Partridge, the founder of the first private military academy, felt that living a "Spartan life" bonded the cadets and erased external social distinctions.[20]

Cadets all wore the same uniforms (though student officers were assigned stripes). Figures 2 and 4 show cadet and cadet officer uniforms. They displayed their uniforms, modeled after those of West Point, and their military aspect when the public attended drills or cadets appeared at public events. Both the students' and the public's appreciation for the uniform reflected militarism in the Old South. Historians have portrayed the region as prone toward violence and a martial spirit, which it exhibited specifically in military schools, yet uniforms and physical activities outwardly manifested the educational and disciplinary benefits of military education as much as they did its martial content. Likewise, different values could have motivated a student to enter a military school or a young man to join a militia, including the individual's (or his parents') militarism or appreciation for the citizen–soldier ideal, masculinity, or respectability. Militarism also reflected the cultural values of mastery and self-discpline. As one historian explained, military academies "probably did not . . . have any special appeal in the South."[21] They did, however, offer educational opportunity to middle-class southerners in ways that northern schools did not.

Military institutions extended their disciplinary control over students by requiring cadets to act as guards and officers of the cadet corps. Cadets

[20] Claudius L. Fike to Parents, 4 January 1862, Claudius Lucian Fike papers, The South Caroliniana Library, University of South Carolina (hereafter SCL). Baker, "Partridge Connection," 137 (quotation).

[21] At the center of this debate are John Hope Franklin, *The Militant South, 1800–1861* (Boston: Beacon Press, 1956), and Marcus Cunliffe, *Soldiers and Civilians: The Martial Spirit in America, 1775–1865* (Boston: Little, Brown and Company, 1968), esp. ch. 10; Dickson D. Bruce Jr., *Violence and Crime in the Antebellum South* (Austin: University of Texas Press, 1979), ch. 7, 171 (quotation); Rod Andrew Jr., *Long Gray Lines: The Southern Military School Tradition, 1839–1915* (Chapel Hill: University of North Carolina Press, 2001); Amy S, Greenberg, *Manifest Manhood in the Antebellum American Empire* (New York: Cambridge University Press, 2005), 271–72; Harry S. Laver, "Refuge of Manhood: Masculinity and the Militia Experience in Kentucky," in *Southern Manhood: Perspectives on Masculinity in the Old South*, ed. Craig Thompson Friend and Lorri Glover (Athens: University of Georgia Press, 2004), 1–21.

supervised one another within a hierarchy of officers that copied the military ranking system. Assigned to their positions by school administrations, cadets found prestige in being the cadet captain, an officer of the day, or a corporal of the guards who commanded others or led maneuvers. Commissions such as William Gordon's captaincy were awarded on a combination of academic merit and good conduct; bad behavior could cause them to be taken away.

In the real military, soldiers obeyed commanders because they accepted the authority that rank granted. Likewise, a cadet had to accept the legitimacy of the hierarchy of rank. Military schools (re)trained young men to react in a self-regulated way; cadets were to abide by military protocol, supervising themselves as they supervised others. In contrast, the only antebellum plan to allow college students self-governance, proposed by Thomas Jefferson at the University of Virginia, failed.[22] Military academies' regulations dictated that student officers, or any cadet assigned guard duty, had to report their peers' disobedience. The entire disciplinary system functioned because cadets performed their duties. Cadets could find acting as an authority figure difficult, as Gordon apparently did, but perform those duties they did. Gordon's problems with Thompson originated from Gordon's performing his duties as cadet captain – essentially the head of the school police.

Regulations and Parents

Military schools also worked to break cadets of their lingering ties to parental authority. In *College Reform*, VMI superintendent Francis H. Smith explicitly compared the discipline at nonmilitary schools to that at his institute. Implementing military discipline would eliminate the chaos at colleges, he argued. Smith criticized colleges for giving parents too much control in the regulation of students: "The discipline of the [nonmilitary] college consists in circular reports to parents or guardians, exhibiting the number of absences from appointed duties, and the general diligence of the student." Many colleges gave parents the final authority to discipline their children; as one college insisted, bad behavior earned

[22]Wagoner, "Honor and Dishonor at Mr. Jefferson's University."

a student "*what he merits* – a rebuke from home."[23] In contrast, military schools acted in loco parentis and enacted their own judgments and punishments on cadets. In doing so, they removed discipline from the family setting and replaced parents as the arbiters of good behavior. Cadets obeyed school regulations in order to avoid institutional censure rather than parental punishment.

Upon entering a military school, cadets took an oath to obey its regulations, even if those regulations conflicted with parental directions. "When a cadet enters the Institute," the state military academy of Virginia explicitly ordered, "he enters the service of the State under the military command of those appointed to govern it and . . . he is not subject to the independent controll [*sic*] of his parent except in subordination to the law and authority of the Institute." In the state-funded institutions, this pledge reminded young men of their responsibility to guard the state armories housed therein.[24] Entering a workforce outside of the family home distanced cadets from their parents in a more than physical way: It moved cadets' responsibilities and experiences beyond their parents' domain and associated them with the military institutions where they studied.

Parents seem often to have acknowledged that their sons had moved out of the sphere of their control; they gave advice to their cadet sons more often than they gave directives. Homesick sixteen-year-old Leeland Hathaway, for example, ran away from WMI and returned home. His father, although disappointed with his son's action, gave the cadet shelter. Beyond expressing disapprobation, however, the father demanded nothing from his son, which forced Hathaway to make his own decision regarding whether to return to school. Indeed, parents exerted limited influence over cadets' day-to-day behavior. "I only regretted that while

[23] Francis H. Smith, *College Reform* (Philadelphia: Thomas, Cowperthwait and Co., 1851), 17 (quotation); Monthly Report of Moses A. Curtis Jr. at the College of St. James, 29 December 1860, SHC (italics in original); Baker, "Partridge Connection," 251. Colleges and academies discussed the benefits of acting in loco parentis; University of Virginia, for example, was founded with that model; military schools, however, adopted parental authority more than most nonmilitary schools. Of course, there were individual variations because of the lack of educational standards. See Wagoner, "Honor and Dishonor at Mr. Jefferson's University," 166.

[24] Order #14, 27 January 1860 (quotation), *Order Book July 31, 1858-December 31, 1860*, VMI Archives. Even young men who paid their own tuition worked as guards and accepted the duties and responsibilities that came with the job.

you was [*sic*] so near having a perfect record," a father of another WMI cadet told his son, "you was not quite able to have it completely unexceptionable."[25] The father lamented the situation but refrained from criticizing the poor performance of his son or ordering better behavior.

Parents encouraged their sons to develop the values that military schools encouraged – self-discipline, obedience, and morality – and focused more on those qualities than on academic performance. "I do not know that I care about your getting first distinction," wrote Walter Clark's father to his son, "but should like for you to deserve it which you will do if you do your duty." Walter's mother described what should be the focus of her son's life on his fourteenth birthday: "establish[ing] firm moral and religious principles . . . that will render you useful in the service of God and your fellow man." In the same letter, she also requested that he send her his weekly marks.[26] Walter's parents followed their son's ranking at school but paid less attention to his academic performance than to his behavior: They expected him to be obedient and of service, values central to military discipline and, probably, their social position.

Like the Clarks, most parents focused on the benefits of doing one's duty in advising their sons. Father Daniel Flowerree explained, "I have written to [my son] admonishing him to the discharge of his duties as a matter of duty to the state, to the faculty of the Institute, to the kind friends who interested themselves in his behalf, when applicant for the appointment as State[-funded] cadet, and lastly but not least, the importance to himself of graduating, which I hope he will well consider

[25] Robert Scott to Joel Scott, 31 October 1853 (quotation), WKU. Leeland Hathaway, unpublished memoir, c. 1890, SHC. Michael Zuckerman, "Penmanship Exercises for Saucy Sons: Some Thoughts on the Colonial Southern Family," *South Carolina Historical Magazine*, 84 (1983), 152–66, concludes that elite parents in the colonial South ignored their sons until the boys were young adults and unaccustomed to authority. The elite, as a class, was assured of good fortune; in contrast, parents of cadets sought to instill self-restraint in their sons. On the decreased role parents played, also see Stephen M. Frank, *Life with Father: Parenthood and Masculinity in the Nineteenth-Century American North* (Baltimore: The Johns Hopkins University Press, 1998), esp. ch. 2; E. Anthony Rotundo, *American Manhood: Transformation in Masculinity from the Revolution to the Modern Era* (New York: Basic Books, 1993), esp. 62–71; Shawn Johansen, *Family Men: Middle-Class Fatherhood in Early Industrializing America* (New York: Routledge, 2001), esp. 133–36; Lorri Glover, *Southern Sons: Becoming Men in the New Nation* (Baltimore: The Johns Hopkins University Press, 2007), esp. 32.

[26] David Clark to Walter Clark, 2 November 1860; Mother to Walter Clark, 20 August 1860, *The Papers of Walter Clark*, 41, 29.

and profit thereby."[27] Flowerree was concerned with the community appraisal of his family, with the patronage he received that allowed him to send his son to school, and with his son's future aspirations. He clearly had an idea of the advantages with which military education provided his son and, additionally, of the responsibilities that they engendered. This father wanted his son to improve his course but had little influence over the young man (who graduated in the bottom half of his class and worked as a merchant).

Even when reacting to their sons' misbehavior, parents most commonly conveyed disappointment rather than gave a lecture. Some parents with disobedient children described their personal mortification at their sons' actions. "I feel it my duty to state that I have no unfriendly feelings towards you," one parent wrote to Superintendent Smith, trying to save face, "but feel mortified, as things have turned out."[28] Another father worried for his son's honor. "I could bear his death," Philip Harrison lamented, "with much more philosophy than I should his disgrace." Three months later, Harrison continued this theme as his son continued to behave badly: "His death would not be much more grievous to me than his dismissal." When young Walter Harrison was dismissed for excessive demerits, however, his father, failing to manifest the mortification he had predicted, petitioned the Board of Visitors to reinstate the young man.[29] Mr. Harrison's reaction represented the fear of southern dishonor – that his son's irresponsible conduct would become public – but it also reflected the middle-class fear of losing his son's educational advantage.

---

[27] Daniel R. Flowerree to Francis H. Smith, 6 February 1857, VHS. Similarly, a mother appeared to be stating something out of the ordinary when she said she would guide her son: "I will write to him, and I firmly believe that his affection for me is such, that I may be still able by my influence to arrest his present course of conduct"; E. C. Finney to Francis H. Smith, 8 May 1847, William Finney student file, VMI Archives.

[28] William Meredith to Francis H. Smith, 12 January 1844 (quotation), David Meredith student file, VMI Archives. Other examples include: William G. Smith to Francis H. Smith, 28 October 1846, Charles Smith student file; Gabriel Jordan to Francis H. Smith, 13 November 1851, VMI Archives; Robert Scott to Joel Scott, 30 April 1854, WKU; John Winn to Philip Winn, 8 January 1841, Duke; Mother to William M. Tennent, [1856], William Tennent Correspondence, SCL.

[29] P. Harrison to Francis H. Smith, 10 January 1844, 11 April 1845, Walter Harrison student file, VMI Archives. The Board complied, and Walter promised to behave. In the end, he did not receive his diploma because too many demerits dropped his class standing too low in his senior year.

The Tension between Military Discipline and Southern Honor

Young men, in the process of moving away from their parents and sub-
merged in a strict institutional setting, had to reconcile a tension between
the dictates of traditional southern honor and military schools' discipline.
In doing so, they embraced duty and self-regulation. Duty – important
to southerners across the social spectrum – took on a great deal of significance within the military school context, where it also reflected the
developing middle class's views. The imposition of military structure
served to emphasize duty and to highlight the emerging class's adherence
to and modification of the values of southern honor.

Again, the Gordon–Thompson case at VMI helps to focus this point.
By January 1852, Thompson was not unfamiliar with his classmate
Gordon. Thompson's former roommate, Hiram Strickler, had resigned
two months earlier after a run-in with Gordon. Strickler had challenged
Gordon to a duel when the cadet captain reported him. Strickler's challenge necessitated his departure from VMI. Thompson, like his former
roommate, interpreted a report by Gordon as a personal attack and
responded with a vicious note, in which he called Gordon "a low, mean,
cowardly, contemptible scoundrel."[30] Gordon, as we have seen, turned
the letter over to the school authorities. A court-martial against Thompson ensued. Before the school tribunal, Thompson defended his actions
as wholly consistent with what was expected of him as a southern gentleman. Reflecting a reliance on southern honor, Thompson asked the
faculty and student jury: "Gentlemen I put it to you as men of honor, as
freemen, as men who have been brought up to love honor and justice,
is there [anything] more repugnant to the feelings of a free-born man
than such an imputation, than such an affection of superiority?"[31] In
asking this question, Thompson rejected the idea that the standards of
the military hierarchy, in which Gordon was his superior officer, should
apply to his dispute with Gordon. Here, he applied the standards of
southern honor. He concurrently employed the principles of military
honor as well; Thompson described Gordon's authority as illegitimate,
because Gordon had violated school (and thus military) regulations by

[30] John Thompson letter, 20 January 1852, *Courts Martial Book*, VMI Archives.
[31] *Ibid.*

carrying a gun. Thompson's defense showed how the two ideological systems that informed cadets' sense of duty – southern honor and military discipline – overlapped. Sometimes, the systems produced similar directives and judgments; in other situations, however, they demanded contradictory behavior.

Honor, a basic feature of any culture, defines the behavior and expectations of a community that organizes social relations around its preservation. Bertram Wyatt-Brown adroitly describes the basic concept of honor: "Honor is essentially the cluster of ethical rules, most readily found in societies of small communities, by which judgments of behavior are ratified by community consensus. Family integrity, clearly understood hierarchies of leaders and subordinates, and ascriptive features of individuals and groups are guides for those evaluations." On the basis of this description, historians have identified the shared concepts of hierarchy, community judgment, and family-directed behavior that governed elites in the antebellum South. Planters moved in a world structured by male fraternal relationships. Honor, as it connected these men, was the "language" that elite southern men shared. Traditional southern honor rested on the public face shown to one's community, especially as it exhibited mastery and informed manhood. Scholars have found echoes of this concept of honor among other groups, specifically yeomen and backcountry whites.[32]

As middle-class southerners at military schools expressed it, however, honor balanced southern and national middle-class ideals. Although cadets felt the demands of duty – especially in the form of military discipline – more than did other members of the emerging southern middle class, these young men reflected the larger group's increasing acceptance of those traits and those southerners' adaptation of traditional southern

---

[32] Southern honor will be more directly addressed in Chapter 4. Major works include Bertram Wyatt-Brown, *Southern Honor: Ethics and Behavior in the Old South* (New York: Oxford University Press, 1982), xv (first quotation), ch. 3; Kenneth S. Greenberg, *Honor and Slavery* (Princeton: Princeton University Press, 1996), xiii (second quotation); Edward L. Ayers, *Vengeance and Justice: Crime and Punishment in the Nineteenth-Century American South* (New York: Oxford University Press, 1994); Pace, *Halls of Honor*; Stephanie McCurry, *Masters of Small Worlds: Yeoman Households, Gender Relations, and the Political Culture of the Antebellum South Carolina Low Country* (New York: Oxford University Press, 1995); Elliott J. Gorn, "'Gouge and Bite, Pull Hair and Scratch': The Social Significance of Fighting in the Southern Backcountry," *American Historical Review*, 90 (February 1985), 18–43.

honor. The formation of the class reflected similar adaptation throughout the society, most clearly seen in the lower social ranks translating
the meaning and behaviors of southern honor. Cadets in particular tem-
pered traditional southern honor with military honor, both of which
demanded duty, obedience to rules, and (most importantly) peer-group
arbitration of the standards. They adopted attention to duty as defined
by regulations, not by culture. The young men at military schools obeyed
authority on a daily basis. They performed specific required tasks (such
as guard duty or the mess-hall monitoring that precipitated Gordon's
report against Thompson).

Although most cadets interpreted being reported by their peers as a
form of school discipline (not as a personal attack, in keeping with the
military academy system of honor), others maintained southern concepts
of honor and behaved more like their college peers. A report such as
Gordon's could therefore elicit opposite reactions: Most students would
accept demerits under the regulations, whereas a few chose to challenge
the reporter. Thompson, like his former roommate Strickler, responded
to Gordon's decision to report him in the language of southern honor:
Strickler issued Gordon a challenge to duel, and Thompson wrote a letter
to him in which he, like his former roommate, interpreted Gordon's
actions as a personal affront.

Institutional hierarchy and regulations were supposed to replace community judgment at military institutions. Professors and administrators
judged cadets and expected them to act according to institutional rules,
not cultural dictates. School hierarchies were not based on property, slave
ownership, occupation, family, rank, or privilege outside the school walls.
Instead, middle-class southern adolescents found at military schools a
hierarchy based on military rank in which they could excel. The lifestyle
of elite southern honor – the life of the rugged man who dueled, drank,
gambled, and possessed property (including guns, servants, horses, dogs,
and expensive clothing) – was outlawed, and schools attempted to replace
it with regulations. The assembly of the middle social ranks in this way
characterized military education, with its regulations, schedules, and barracks, in a way that it did not characterize colleges, though certain private
academies and other types of higher schooling may have performed a
similar social role. The peer groups at military schools contained a majority of cadets from the emerging middle class; thus, a cadet from that social

position spent his formative school years among a community primarily made up of his social peers.

Self-regulation: Reconciling Military Duty with Southern Honor

Unlike Strickler and Thompson, cadets who succeeded at military schools accepted the military concept of duty and integrated it with southern honor in a way that resolved any contradictions between the two. Most young southerners combined their parents' expectations with school regulations; at military institutions, cadets did so by fulfilling their duty and, more notably, by regulating themselves. Soon after arriving at WMI, Leeland Hathaway fought with another cadet over an insult about his clothing. He eventually became friends with his opponent, because the fight stayed among the cadets and did not become known to the administration. His memoir described his preenrollment concept of honor as that of a traditional gentleman who was unable to accept a slight: "I had been taught the good creed of the gentleman to do to others only what you would be willing to take from them and to never give, or suffer an insult," he remembered; "this had involved me in the usual catalogue of troubles with my country playmates and I had bound to give and take in play ground battle."[33] Hathaway's successful attendance at two military institutes demonstrated a change in this attitude, a retreat from the aggressive defense of his reputation. Cadets like Hathaway came to accept the self-discipline that military schools, their parents, and national middle-class culture encouraged.

Indeed, the fact that cadets did not duel as often as college students (if at all) is further evidence of this point. Whereas no cadet diary or letter recorded a duel (and common knowledge was necessary for restoring public face), at least one duel at South Carolina College killed a student and a University of Virginia student shot a professor. North Carolina Military Institute (NCMI) founder Daniel Harvey Hill asserted that "the moral tone imparted by a Military Education" resulted in few armed confrontations and that no cadet had been stabbed or shot at West Point. "Contrast this with the state of our Colleges," he continued; "in how many of them have there not been outrageous and cold-blooded

---

[33] Hathaway, memoir, SHC.

murders? And in some of them, shootings and stabbings are almost of annual recurrence." The *Yorkville Enquirer* in South Carolina forwarded the same comparison that praised Kings Mountain Military Academy in January 1860.[34]

Scuffles between boys, in contrast, were probably as commonplace at military schools as at others; the causes of some tussles exhibit cadets' blending of duty with the southern and military traditions. In December 1844, a VMI student described the "disagreeable necessity" of getting into two fights. Cadet Philip Fitzhugh related that Richard Sinton would not follow the orders Fitzhugh gave as officer of the day, so Fitzhugh decided to watch him closely. Sinton took offense at this intrusion and demanded to know why Fitzhugh watched him. Fitzhugh replied that it was his "duty" to do so. Of course, in one sense, he was correct. As officer of the day, he was responsible for maintaining discipline among the guards, including Sinton. Sinton clearly took Fitzhugh's surveillance as a personal affront, however, and his response was to insult Fitzhugh. Fitzhugh responded by striking his fellow cadet, and a fight began. Sinton had his underclothes torn, but both cadets escaped unharmed and unreported. The next day, Sinton sought satisfaction, which obligated Fitzhugh to fight him a second time. Honor was restored, and Fitzhugh told his brother and guardian that he had now befriended Sinton.[35] Fitzhugh's sense of the "disagreeable necessity" of fighting stemmed from his notions of duty and honor. Like Gordon eight years later, Fitzhugh asserted his right to command other cadets in the military hierarchy of the academy. Fitzhugh fought Sinton, at least in part, to assert the legitimacy of his military rank, which stood in for social status as the basis for

[34]Stephen A. Ross, "Hillsboro Military Academy," *Bennett Place Quarterly* (Summer 1999), 2, writes that Cadet W. L. Torrance was expelled from HMA for challenging the local constable to a duel, but does not state that the duel went through. J. Marion Sims, *The Story of My Life* (1884; reprint, New York: Da Capo Press, 1968), 88–92; Wagoner, "Honor and Dishonor at Mr. Jefferson's University"; Rudolph, *American College and University*, 97; Greenberg, *Manifest Manhood and the Antebellum American Empire*, 10; D. H. Hill, *Essay on Military Education, delivered at Wilmington NC, November 14, 1860 Before the State Educational Convention* (Charlotte: Daily Bulletin Office, 1860), 9–10 (quotation); John Donald Duncan, "Pages from Froissart: The Ante-Bellum Career of Micah Jenkins" (M.A. thesis, University of South Carolina, 1961), 76.

[35]Philip Fitzhugh to Patrick Fitzhugh, 28 December 1844, VMI Archives. In addition, the fact that no institutional record of the fight existed supports that students maintained their own discipline.

his action: He fought to defend the legitimacy of military duty. Fitzhugh's report card recording "good" habits earlier that same year can be seen in Figure 7. Thus, some behavior that appeared at first glance to be in keeping with the traditional defense of southern honor actually represented a departure from it.

Throughout the antebellum years, contests of this sort arose in different ways at different institutions. Some young men remained unreconciled to the self-discipline of military academies and of the middle class. At the Citadel, Montague Grimke felt he had "acted right" when he resigned due to another student's treatment of him. He placed the necessity of maintaining his honor above that of maintaining his connection with the school, thus disobeying his father's wishes and his pledge to the institution. "I am sorry this thing has occurred," Grimke wrote his father upon his resignation, "for as I had entered the Citadel, I should have preferred remaining to graduate, but I am conscious that I have acted right."[36] Grimke's letter indicates his independence from parental authority and the high value he placed on the southern code of honor. Apparently, the South Carolinian expected his father to agree with his ethical choice, but regardless of his father's feelings, Grimke, like other cadets who rejected military duty – or self-discipline – could not remain in school.

Cadets used their self-regulation to modify military educators' unyielding expectations. D. H. Hill of NCMI wrote in *College Discipline* that cadets should inform the authorities about one another's misbehavior. Indeed, this idea was central to the cadet corps report and guard system. Military honor stressed the acceptance of regulations and the hierarchy of rank. Hill added that a guilty cadet should come forward before his peers were forced to rat him out to the authorities.[37] Administrators' strict interpretation of military honor, of which Hill provides an example, was not the interpretation of a majority of students, however.

Given cadets' position in southern society, it is unsurprising that their concept of honor and propriety did not completely coincide with either

---

[36] E. Montague Grimke to Father, 1 July 1852, The Citadel Archives and Museum (hereafter CIT).

[37] D. H. Hill, *College Discipline* (Salisbury, NC: Watchman Office, 1855), 15.

institutional rules or traditional southern honor. Cadets more often followed expectations about duty that blended the two cultural directives. "While true honor forbids the violation of confidence or the betrayal of an associate, even at the Professor's bidding, and calls, in such case, for the martyr-spirit of suffering and self-sacrifice," an orator told cadets at the Citadel in 1853, "it also demands undeviating truth, submission to law and constituted authority, patriotism to country and obedience to parents."[38] At the same time as he acknowledged the possible contradictions in this view, the speaker clearly supported the tenets of traditional southern honor, although significantly omitting the importance of mastery and presenting an honorable public face. He denied Hill's and other educators' assertion that the cadet community should be entirely subordinate to the regulations; however, he emphasized also the importance of the rule of law and submission to authority valued at the schools. Military education was supreme within its community of honor, which was the school society. Military schools placed little emphasis on the maintenance of public face, on which southern honor depended. The central fear in traditional southern honor was of being socially unmasked, shown to be a coward, a liar, or dishonorable, whereas these young men learned obedience to internal conscience as honorable. Cadets, according to this speaker, had to adopt "true honor," which included many principles of southern honor but stressed self-discipline and obedience as well.

As they created their own balance, cadets rarely described the qualities of which they perceived honor and duty to consist. Only occasionally do essays and orations clearly indicate their constructions. Most of all, cadets at military schools embodied duty by obeying the regulations (and they obeyed rules more than did their elite counterparts at South Carolina College, for example). They took their duties seriously, and their general obedience to the rules suggests that they accepted the value of self-discipline. Even in almost empty diaries, cadets recorded the demerits they handed down as officers of the day or those that they received.[39] These lists of daily demerits sometimes included a majority of one

[38] Richard Yeadon, *Address, on the Necessity of Subordination, in our Academies and Colleges, Civil and Military* (Charleston: Walker and James, 1854), 20.
[39] William Calder, unpublished diary, Duke; Edward S. Hutter, unpublished diary; Edward Shepherd, unpublished diary, VMI Archives; John Boinst, unpublished diary, CIT.

barracks or class, illustrating that students routinely accepted demerit points for minor offenses. Most cadets accepted reports such as the one Gordon recorded against Thompson at dinner roll call. Joseph Chenoweth, for example, accepted a similar report for "Not casting eyes to the right" on 3 June 1856, which was recorded on the reverse side of his quarterly report (Figure 8). Institutional records indicated that, overall, few courts-martial occurred. Indeed, most cadets accused of offenses or court-martialed prior to the Civil War affirmed the justice of the punishment, even dismissal, resulting from their actions. Indeed, they demonstrated duty and their desire for education by going through the court-martial process rather than resigning from school.[40]

The average cadet felt an obligation to perform his duty, no doubt, but he was also motivated by both altruistic and practical reasons. Primarily, performing one's duty made punishment less likely. A cadet who conformed received few demerits; his school superiors, not to mention his parents, would have had few complaints. Other young men honestly wanted to fulfill their expected duties. Doing one's duty, and more importantly, being perceived as having done so, was a requisite component of a cadet's honor. A VMI cadet explained to his father, for example, that he would never be caught violating regulations again: "I feel my duty as your son to follow your directions," he professed.[41] This young man reinterpreted his duty to his father as duty to his school. The responsibilities of honor with which he started the academy filtered into new expectations. Indeed, with his entry pledge, a cadet was held to both southern and military honor to obey the school's regulations and to work for his state. His oath transferred his existing honor to the duties that military honor fostered (and that prepared him for work).

Young men also obeyed because they desired the approval of their families. While at the Citadel, cadet Micah Jenkins was concerned for his reputation and future success. He wished to have a high class standing, he told his parents, "not only for the pleasure it would give you all, but also for my own private satisfaction." Jenkins listed his family's pleasure ahead of his own gratification and made no mention of his reputation.

[40] At VMI, the most courts-martial in one year was twenty-six in 1855; *Courts Martial Book*, VMI Archives.
[41] Joseph Chenoweth to Father, 18 February 1856, VMI Archives.

A young man at VMI in 1847 said that he would "resist temptations" and do his duty for his family's sake.[42] Finally, and perhaps most importantly, cadets' duties often coincided with what young men themselves wanted to do, so that they acted in accordance with their own desire in fulfilling their duties. Like other children who appeased their parents to get what they wanted or to avoid punishment, cadets often wrote letters home in which they combined updates regarding their good behavior with requests for money. Perhaps they said they would do their duty to placate their parents and thereby get what they wanted.[43]

Whatever their motivation, most cadets performed their duties and thereby exhibited self-discipline. Fulfilling military duty required them to exhibit good discipline by developing and following internal rules – that is, to exhibit self-regulation. Discipline was most prevalent at military schools because of the middle-class student body. Although they surely did not recognize it, cadets of the late antebellum years were part of a transitional generation, the first to fully encounter the market economy. They learned to adopt self-discipline as they matured and as it increased as a culturally prevalent value. Having entered military higher schools to attain the advantage of their practical education, cadets appeared ready to accept most duties and hierarchies of military honor and professional values. The traits they learned were advantageous to middle-class men entering the market, and absorbing those qualities aided their professional development.[44]

Back at VMI in 1852, the cadets' reaction to the courts-martial of Thompson and Gordon illustrated how they practiced the self-discipline they had learned. At the court-martial, Thompson met the same fate as his former roommate: The court upheld the regulations of the institute and

---

[42] Micah Jenkins to John Jenkins, 23 September 1853 (first quotation), SCL; Samuel Garland to Samuel Garland, 23 January 1847 (second quotation), Garland Family Papers, VHS.

[43] Zuckerman, "Penmanship Exercises for Saucy Sons," connects boys' behavior – "playing" a part to get what they wanted – to southern parenting style.

[44] I do not want to argue that the schools consciously inculcated market values, although that has been asserted in northern history of education scholarship; see Stanley K. Schultz, *The Culture Factory: Boston Public Schools, 1789–1860* (New York: Oxford University Press, 1973). Scholars have well portrayed nineteenth-century market values and recently described a growing professional group as increasingly accepting those values in the 1840s and 1850s in the Old South; self-discipline is accepted as a central tenet of northern market culture.

dismissed Thompson for disrespect to a superior officer.[45] The following day, Gordon, too, was expelled, in his case for carrying a concealed weapon and for striking Thompson in a scuffle over the original report. The VMI superintendent saved Gordon from a dishonorable discharge, however, and reinstated him based on his prior good behavior. Gordon received a reprimand but kept his office.

The affair created a huge outcry among the more than 100 cadets at VMI in 1852. The student body was not upset over Gordon's dismissal for striking a fellow cadet and carrying a concealed gun, nor did they oppose his reinstatement through the clemency of Superintendent Smith. Rather, the students protested the dismissal of Cadet Thompson and Gordon's carrying of Thompson's private letter to the authorities. They portrayed Thompson as having acted correctly in the whole situation – after all, he was the one who informed the authorities about Gordon's gun. Cadet diaries recorded surprise at Thompson's dismissal. The cadets' anger and shock are interesting, because everyone knew that Thompson had defied a superior officer's orders, issued a challenge, and fought with another cadet – each a dismissible offense. The cadet response indicates the rift between the students' views of duty and the institution's formal, written regulations.

Seventeen seniors gathered and drafted a petition asking for the reinstatement of Thompson and condemning Gordon's actions. The meeting's secretary, Cadet William Yager, wrote it up and submitted it to the Board of Visitors. Yager recorded the letter in his diary. "But there is a higher law. It is justice – the law of God," a portion of the petition pled, "– and in the name of justice we appeal for the reinstatement of Mr. Thompson."[46] The Board responded negatively to the petition, classifying it as an inappropriate student challenge to school authority. Rather than stand behind their convictions, as a southern gentleman must do, the cadets withdrew the petition. Indeed, they said that they had displayed poor judgment in submitting it. In doing so, they bowed to the authority of the administration and agreed to obey its rules. At the same time, however, they struck at Gordon, refusing to speak to him

---

[45] Alexander C. Jones to Francis H. Smith, 5 May 1852, VMI Archives, noted that Thompson returned home "imbittered" about his dismissal.

[46] Diarists Williams and Yager, VMI Archives, recorded the student meetings about the Gordon–Thompson affair.

and exiling him emotionally from the group. Even as they struggled with military authority and rejected it as the sole arbiter of their personal relationships with one another, these cadets reinforced it in their public lives and internalized the self-discipline that it required.

Gordon's peers' retreat from revolt was a typical response of military school cadets to an assertion of authority by the administration: one of acceptance rather than rebellion. At most antebellum nonmilitary schools, by contrast, student independence led to mass resignations or revolts. Most major colleges had at least one student rebellion in the antebellum years; Princeton suffered six between 1800 and 1830. In comparison, no group riots occurred at military schools. The largest examples of mass disobedience at military academies, by contrast, involved little physical violence. In cases like the VMI students' intervention on behalf of Thompson, cadets joined together to inform the administration when they disagreed with a disciplinary action. In another VMI disciplinary situation, all the members of a class signed oaths not to drink in order to earn readmittance for an offender. Administrations occasionally interpreted such actions as an undesirable form of student collusion and dismissed or punished entire classes. VMI suspended twenty-four cadets for attending a murder trial after being explicitly forbidden to do so. (The young men had rejected the interdiction to show respect for the victim, who had been a classmate.) After nearly an entire class at the Citadel rejected a school disciplinary decision and were expelled, a speaker told the remaining cadets: "false or mistaken honor is generally at the root of college combinations and rebellions."[47] What the speaker saw as "false honor" was the disjunction between school and cadet expectations.

Cadets' negotiation of the meaning of duty and honor, then, could include protest as a legitimate and honorable act. The significance of such large- and small-scale rejections of discipline, however, is that they were the exceptions to the rule, and they occurred less frequently at military

[47] Order #12, 2 September 1857, *Order Book 1852–1857*, VMI Archives. Gibbs, diary, VMI Archives, discussed the murder of Cadet Blackburn by a Washington College student. Other disciplinary actions against large numbers of students include Lafayette Strait to Father, 12 July 1854, SCL, in which twenty-two cadets boycotted a professor's class; W. R. Wiggins to Theodore Kingsbury, 23 December 1846, SHC, forty-two suspended at Jefferson College after they protested a professor reproving a student; William P. DuBose, "Soldier, Philosopher, Friend Awakener of the Undying Good in Men," typescript 1946, SCL, noted the expulsion of an entire class at South Carolina College. Yeadon, *Address*, 19 (quotation).

academies than they did at nonmilitary schools. Unlike elite students who followed the traditional southern code of honor, cadets rarely issued challenges to one another or behaved disobediently in their daily lives. Thompson and Strickler were among the rare few who did. Even cadets who resigned usually showed that they accepted the school's authority over them, choosing to submit written statements of resignation rather than simply to leave the school without making a statement. Most cadets worked within the system to affect change. Daily obedience inured young men to duty and self-restraint.

On occasion, some cadets refused to learn self-discipline and demanded autonomy, even leaving school. One cadet hated his military school so much that he wrote his grandfather that he would leave "either honorably, or dishonorably." If he threatened his family's reputation in the hope of extorting a release from school, it did not work. Cadet William Carson had been a fine student according to his report card from April 1857, Figure 6, at Kings Mountain Military Academy in upcountry South Carolina. Almost a year after that report, however, the superintendents dismissed him for stealing, breaking arrest (implying that he had already been a discipline problem), and instigating others to break discipline.[48] The cadet achieved his original goal of leaving the institution, but he did so by unquestionably dishonorable means. The superintendents indicated that the cadet was sorry for his actions after being caught and dismissed. This young man, one of the minority, neglected his duty at the cost of his education.

Indeed, even young men who whined about discipline regularly continued to obey. Although many cadets praised the military component of their schooling, many others complained about the boredom of military and school life (as have young men throughout history).[49] One Hillsboro Military Academy (HMA) diarist, for example, commented on

---

[48] William Carson to Jas. L. Pettigru, 10 November 1857; Micah Jenkins and Asbury Coward to Jas. L. Pettigru, 23 March 1858, William Carson Papers, South Carolina Historical Society (hereafter SCHS).

[49] Positive reviews of military life include John P. Thomas, *On the Profession of Arms* (Charleston: Walker, Evans, and Company, 1859); John D. Wylie to G. Lafayette Strait, 27 April 1855, SCL; Gratz Cohen to Solomon Cohen, 10 June 1862, SHC; William Terrill to Francis H. Smith, 3 December 1857, George Porterfield student file, VMI Archives.

his "manifold duties" and "the regular routine of barracks life" throughout the month that he kept his journal. "To day's diary is the self same
monotony of the every day life at the V.M.I.," recorded another cadet.[50]
Both young men must not have hated military life too much because the
VMI student graduated and his compatriot resigned from HMA to join
the Confederate Army in 1861. Of course, a few cadets strongly disliked
the component of their schooling, but only in rare circumstances did
dislike lead to disobedience.

Cadets could translate their sense of duty to their state because they,
like other southern men, also felt an obligation to their homeland. One
graduation speaker in 1847, for example, used the metaphor of filial duty
to characterize the cadets' duty to the state: As children of the state, he
argued, students had to fulfill their duty to it. The 1857 Citadel valedictorian declared that he and his fellow alumni would guard South Carolina's
"good name and honor." More important than the state's prosperity or
residents was its amorphous reputation. "Every breath is burdened with
its bidding," the cadet continued, "and every minute bears its mission."[51]
Speakers' and cadets' emphasis of duty to the state remained constant
throughout the antebellum years, without any appreciable increase as
sectional fervor rose. During the period of their studies, cadets possessed
specific responsibilities to their states that students at nonmilitary schools
did not. Cadets' duty, then, had a component of reciprocity: They were
responsible for guarding state arms on behalf of the citizens of the state,
and those with state scholarships also had to perform two years of service teaching. Acting for the state thus reflected both the obligation of

[50] Calder, diary, 25–26 March 1861, 4 April 1861 (first and second quotations), Duke. Hutter,
diary, 24 March 1858 (third quotation), VMI Archives. Other cadets wrote about their boring
lives: George Penn to Thomas Penn, 15 November [1842], SHC; Williams, diary, 26 March, 29
March [1852]; James D. Saunders to Johnny, 24 November 1842, VMI Archives; John Pressley
to Thomas, 6 November 1849, CIT; Beverly Stanard, *Letters of a New Market Cadet*, ed. John
G. Barrett and Robert K. Turner Jr. (Chapel Hill: University of North Carolina Press, 1961),
1, 28, 40; Thomas Hart Law, *Citadel Cadets: The Journal of Cadet Tom Law* (Clinton, SC:
PC Press, 1941), passim, esp. 26 March 1859; Carey Thomas, unpublished diary, 13 May 1863,
SCL.
[51] S. W. Trotti, *An Address Delivered before the Calliopean and Polytechnic Societies of the
State Military Academy* (Charleston: Burges, James and Paxton, 1847), 7; William Tennent,
"Valedictory," unpublished speech, [1857] (quotations), SCL. Yeadon, *Address*, 15, made a
similar construction.

military duty and the demands of southern honor. Cadets surely believed in being citizen–soldiers.[52]

Peer-group Enforcement

Removed from the control of their parents and negotiating the strict regulations of military schools, students formed intense friendships. Like boarding school and college students, they developed unwritten codes of behavior.[53] At military higher schools, cadets' concepts of honor and proper conduct were influenced not only by institutional rules but also by their peer group, which acted as the final arbiter of behavior. Thus, that important southern trait of community judgment rested with the cadets, not with the school or even the family. All students expressed loyalty to their compatriots, but the institutional regulations of the military schools demanded that the cadets incorporate this bond within the disciplinary system and their concept of duty.

It seems clear that another significant component of the young men's concepts of duty and honor was maintaining loyalty. Although students at all schools probably valued peer loyalty above the duty to inform teachers and administrators of transgressions, cadets had a more express duty to their school regulations, their professors, and the student guards, as educator D. H. Hill emphasized. Gordon's decision to convey Thompson's letter up the chain of command suggested that he prized military hierarchy above all else; his classmates, however, reacted against him, proving they valued peer loyalty more.

Peers acted as the social and moral police; thus, cadets at VMI in 1852 felt Gordon should have kept Thompson's challenge between them. In another notable incident, a group of Citadel cadets found a classmate drunk in downtown Charleston. They informed Superintendent F. W. Capers about him, but they refused to name him to the administration. The cadets decided that this student was no longer worthy of being their compatriot and resolved to strip off his uniform. The administration admonished them that it was not their place to punish another student.

---

[52] See Andrew, *Long Gray Lines.* Cadets' actions at the time of secession are discussed in this study's Conclusion.

[53] Pace, *Halls of Honor*, 83, states this clearly about college students.

The resolution to this impasse came when the Charleston police caught the wayward youth. With the pressure of police intervention, the cadet was dismissed. Not only did the Citadel cadets in this example clearly reject D. H. Hill's argument that students should inform on each other, they showed their unity and their belief that they were an internally regulated group capable of enforcing its own concept of the regulations.[54] Students bonded at military academies, as they did at all schools, but cadets strictly enforced their moral codes through the power given them by their institution. The content and coercion of their peer pressure went beyond that at any nonmilitary school and was, indeed, sanctioned by the military system.

VMI cadets' reaction to Gordon and to the administration reflected a conflict between cadets' peer-regulated codes and administrative regulations that was shared at other military schools. Claudius Fike described a nearly identical episode and result at the Arsenal Academy: Cadet Cannon reported another cadet, who responded by calling him "a liar, cursed him, and even struck him in in [*sic*] the face with a stone." Like Gordon, Cannon reported the attack, and then the "rowdy sort of cadets" labeled Cannon a coward but did nothing. Fike concluded, "I suppose [they] will not [do anything]. Several Cadets were arrested for making ungentlemanly demonstrations to Cannon about it."[55] Just as VMI cadets rejected Gordon's decision to report his peer to the administration, Arsenal cadets reacted against Cannon for doing the same thing. It is significant that only "several" cadets took personal action against Cannon, however; most students accepted the outcome of the military procedure.

Cadet agreements and group behavior demonstrated that cadets internalized the military schools' imposition of peer-group regulation; they banded together in their moral and social expectations. VMI cadets' attitude toward an awkward new professor provide an illustration: Thomas

[54] C. Irvine Walker, "Reminiscences of Days in the Citadel, 1858–1861," unpublished memoir, CIT. In this case, the drunk could embarrass the school so the cadets reacted both to his violation of military regulations and to his threat to the Citadel's public reputation.

[55] Claudius Fike to G. A. Fike, 15 May 1862, SCL. Other cases are in Lafayette Strait to Mother, 16 March 1853; John D. Wylie to Grandmother [Annie Wylie], 25 March 1853, Papers of the Gaston, Strait, Wylie and Baskin Families, SCL; Henry Carrington to William Carrington, 1 December 1849, VMI Archives.

Jackson, who later became known as "Stonewall" during his Civil War career, arrived at VMI in 1851 and became the butt of many cadet jokes. Cadets threw rocks and other missiles at him; they also repeatedly unhitched the artillery he used during drill. The courts-martial in which Jackson was involved left a clear record of students, over the course of a decade, acting against the professor. One cadet refused to "write upon the Black Board, certain parts of the Regular lesson" and was confined to the post for two months. The court acquitted another cadet of throwing rocks at Jackson during an artillery drill in 1854 (though clearly at least one cadet was guilty) and dismissed another cadet for a practical joke indirectly involving Jackson. Jackson also charged two cadets with talking back to him in the classroom. In an example that indicated the similar treatment of professors at another military school, Walter Clark wrote that Lieutenant Hamilton, drawing professor at HMA, "is made the butt for everyone to vent their spleen upon (as in Academies they do to the Assistants and in College the Tutors) they do him bad I tell you." Though their collusion may have been unspoken, cadets definitely agreed about which professors they respected and which they did not.[56] Their resistance to authority, even at this individual level, illustrates the existence of a cadet community and suggests how it differed from the institutional military ideal.

A cadet's experience at school depended to a great extent upon his classmates, who acted as the judge of appropriate conduct. For example, a GMI cadet explained to his parents why a local youth returned home. The cadet refused to study and, besides, was "a continual pest." He "flew into a passion" with one schoolmate and then threw the author's copy of the Bible at him. The young country boy obviously rejected any attempts by the school or by his classmates to rein him in. The letter writer indicated that the local young man received no help remaining at GMI because he alienated the other cadets. In a similar case at another

---

[56] 7 May 1852, 24 January 1853, 21 June 1854, 7 April 1856 (first quotation), *Courts Martial Book*, VMI Archives. For more on Jackson and antebellum education, see Jennifer R. Green, "From West Point to the Virginia Military Institute," *Virginia Cavalcade*, 49 (Summer 2000), 134–43; Edward D. C. Campbell Jr., "Major Thomas J. Jackson and the Trial of Cadet Walker," *Virginia Military Institute Alumni Review* (Winter 1976), 19–21. Clark to Mother, 15 August 1860, *Papers of Walter Clark*, 26–27 (second quotation). John Custis to [?], 17 May 1861, SHC, also described cadets throwing bread at (most likely) Lt. Hamilton.

academy, a youth thought that cadets had ganged up on his cousin to get the young man expelled.[57]

Students frequently acted together outside of the regulations, and they could in some cases also use school authorities to enforce their decisions. Despite the interdiction against cheating, cadets recorded using cheat sheets and whispering answers at VMI, and it is reasonable to infer that the same behaviors occurred at other schools. According to an alumnus's memoir about the Citadel, only a cadet in the running for one of the top standings received no help from his peers, who discouraged any single cadet's receipt of undue prestige but were otherwise happy to band together to succeed as a class. Remembering this situation as an adult, the alumnus questioned "the ethics, whether right or wrong," of such behavior. Among cadets, however, the only form of cheating that drew censure was stealing the work of others. In a Citadel case involving stolen homework, the cadets went to the superintendent, who rejected their approach as a form of student collusion. Following a negotiation between the faculty and student body, the guilty cadet confessed to the crime in public but was honorably discharged. "The indignation was great," an HMA diarist commented regarding another cadet who stole, "and had [the thief] not been expelled, he would have been compelled to leave by the Cadets."[58] Cadets, then, clearly regulated each other, in some cases using their institutions and institutional position to enforce their decisions.

As a self-regulated group, cadets accepted some rule breaking when it occurred among the corps. Common infractions occurred when cadets returned to sleep after morning roll call rather than studying or cleaning their rooms as the regulations stipulated. All sorts of infractions against the more social or parental rules were hidden from authorities, often including drinking, card playing, and hazing. The cadets used their own judgment about which regulations could be flouted rather than adopt

[57] Theodore Fogle to Father and Mother, 16 August 1852 (quotation), Emory. John D. Wylie to Aunt, 19 July 1854, 28 July 1853, SCL.

[58] Edward McConnell Sr. to Francis H. Smith, 20 November 1853, VMI Archives. Walker, "Reminiscences," 2 (first quotation). Calder, diary, 27 March 1861 (second quotation), Duke. Pace, *Halls of Honor*, esp. ch. 3 and 4, notes the contradictory actions honor spurred among elite college students. Pace's excellent descriptions of stealing and cheating in southern antebellum colleges can be compared to the evidence throughout this section.

their parents' and schools' views. Throughout the period, for example, teachers and strict parents rallied against smoking and card playing. Both acts indicated bad moral character and were considered to be the first step down a path toward dissolution. One VMI cadet noted in his diary, however, that although smoking was against the regulations, it was a necessity the students "could not have done without." The VMI cadet drawing that shows one young man violating the rule against smoking indicates that the practice continued (Figure 5). Likewise, the recurrence of courts-martial for card playing at VMI indicated that cadets widely disobeyed the regulation forbidding it, as well.[59] The difference in perception was obvious: Adults felt that card playing was a sin, whereas the students enjoyed the pastime (especially given the tedium of military academy life).

Some cadets were even known to steal from their institutions. While at GMI, a cadet told his mother that another youth had raided the quartermaster's cellar. Similarly, a cadet at Kings Mountain Military Academy was dismissed for breaking arrest to steal molasses. Cadet Charles Smith stole sugar. Charles's father explained to the VMI superintendent that other cadets had told his son that drinking a mixture of sugar and vinegar would help the young man's cold. Thus, Charles chose to steal sugar from the VMI stores.[60] Both the cadets and this father put the student's well-being above what they considered to be a minor violation of the rules.

Nor was college drinking unheard of. While at the University of North Carolina (UNC), future VMI cadet Henry Burgwyn wrote home that the authorities caught twenty students drinking. He said nothing of their expulsions; presumably, they were not harshly disciplined. Likewise, a VMI diarist recorded some cadets drinking off-post in town.[61]

[59] Gibbs, diary, 1850, VMI Archives. Card-playing courts-martial included 24 January 1853, 8 November 1853, 5 February 1856, 13 March 1856, 7 September 1859, 7 July 1860, 21 December 1860, *Courts Martial Book, Order Book*, VMI Archives.

[60] Seaborn Montgomery to Julia Montgomery, 1 May 1864, Duke; Micah Jenkins and Asbury Coward to Jas. L. Pettigru, 23 March 1858, SCHS. Mr. Smith had none of the same compassion when his ward misbehaved; William G. Smith to Francis H. Smith, 9 December 1847, 10 May 1849, Isaac Robins student file, VMI Archives.

[61] Henry Burgwyn to Anna Burgwyn, 17 February 1857, SHC; Philip James to John Winn, 20 March 1840, Duke; Stanard, *Letters of a New Market Cadet*, 25; Early, diary, 23 December 1849; Shepherd, diary; Edmund Pendleton to Philip Winn, 20 March 1842; Robert H. Simpson to Francis H. Smith, 24 February 1852; Henry Williamson to Francis H. Smith, 25 April 1845, VMI Archives; Claudius Fike to G. A. Fike, 23 August 1862, SCL.

Although drinking was a common adult behavior, schools strenuously enforced their prohibition of alcohol, widely perceived to be a negative moral influence. Cadets, in contrast, seem to have considered drinking a permissible behavior by the standards of southern honor and rugged manhood, especially as these standards were exhibited by southern elite college students, including those at UNC. The cadets who drank disregarded their duty, but because carousing stayed within the student body, they agreed to flout rules that impeded their fun. Although peer groups condoned drinking, the number of temperance society supporters at military schools also suggests many cadets' resistance to southern wildness.

William Gordon's case, similarly, showed that cadets carried weapons, despite the rules against it.[62] Military administrators rarely ignored the presence of weapons when they found out about them, just as they were unlikely to turn a blind eye to student drinking, but cadets usually kept their knowledge of weapons possession to themselves. When it was revealed that Gordon carried a pistol, other cadets acknowledged that they had known about it but did not report him because they judged his decision to carry a gun to be a reasonable response to his situation. Only after the senior class as a whole revolted against Thompson's expulsion did its members inform on Gordon and declare his violation of the regulations inappropriate. They maintained the supremacy of peer-group regulation, especially about social interactions.

Young men at military schools found hazing, too, to be an acceptable violation of the rules. This behavior bonded young men together – first-years endured harassment, survived it, and moved on to harass the new class. The most common types of hazing were physical assaults, practical jokes, and mock trials of the new cadets. In a typical joke on an unsuspecting first-year cadet, upperclassmen lured the newcomer into a room and tied him to a chair. They then leaned the chair against a

---

[62] Few boys specifically noted owning guns or hunting at home, which may indicate that it was not a noteworthy part of their lives or that these generally middle-class cadets were not connected to that agricultural activity. Those who mentioned guns include Henry Hendrick to John Hendrick, 24 December 1860, Duke; Benjamin Perry, account book, SCHS; James Saunders to Johnny, 24 November 1842, VMI Archives; Walter Clark to Mother, 26 September 1860, *Papers of Walter Clark*; John D. Wylie to Aunt, 29 February 1852, SCL. On guns and hunting, see Nicolas W. Proctor, *Bathed in Blood: Hunting and Mastery in the Old South* (Charlottesville: University of Virginia Press, 2002).

professor's door and knocked; when the professor opened the door, the cadet fell helplessly into the room. VMI dismissed one cadet for directing such a hazing incident, but the practice was so widespread that a senior wrote to his nephew's roommates not to "caution my protege against the usual ceremonies of the initiation," because he found no disadvantage to them, though he asked his roommates to spare the plebe the worst.[63] Cadets accepted hazing, stealing, and drinking, then, because the acts benefited them and remained within the school community. In this way, they engaged in some of the behaviors that they witnessed in elite southern culture, but they also moderated that behavior with obedience to the majority of regulations. More significantly, cadets did not tolerate all rule breaking and united as a peer group to enforce their concept of duty.

Disobeying regulations did not worry most cadets; instead, they cited the institutional or parental discovery of their transgressions as their real fear. This idea reflected typical adolescent thought and, in addition, mirrored the external focus of southern honor, with cadet peers as the new (if temporary) community.[64] For the cadets who felt that only being caught violated their honor code, reports became personal affronts. If a cadet could get away with most of his infractions, it took on special meaning when one cadet reported another. This was the context within which Thompson called Gordon dishonorable.

On the few occasions when young men contested reports and courts-martial, for instance, they declared that they had legitimate reasons to break the rules. Thompson explained that Gordon had acted worse than he had. An extreme case was Henry Williamson, who was court-martialed for drunk and disorderly behavior. "I violated no article of the Regulations on Saturday last," Williamson began his defense, "for I have drank on the Institute Hill before the Professors once or twice which was as much a violation of the regulations as I did on Saturday last."[65]

---

[63] 24 January 1853, *Courts Martial Book*, VMI Archives. Henry T. Lee to Fellows, 15 July 1844 (quotation), Daniel Powell student file; Joseph Chenoweth to Father, 28 September 1855, VMI Archives, said hazing was commonplace in camp.

[64] Examples at different schools include Philip Winn to John Winn, 14 December 1839, VMI Archives; Thomas Casey to Marien Passage, 8 September 1834, Thomas Casey Correspondence, SHC.

[65] Henry Williamson to Francis H. Smith, 25 April 1845, VMI Archives; Order #58, 14 April 1845; Order #81, 22 April 1845, *Order Book*, VMI Archives. The court was, not surprisingly, unconvinced by Williamson's argument. His confession of previous bad acts and guilt of

Williamson suggested that professors having condoned his previous defiance of the rules meant that the written regulations no longer applied to him. Cadets evidently defined duty, only partially, as school expectations.

Though disobedience was rarely so blatant, cadets frequently refused to follow rules that they believed were unfairly applied. The young men's peer-based understanding of duty reflected their demand for consistency, as Williamson's remarks implied. A cadet at Rappahannock Military Institute echoed this idea when he wrote that he no longer wanted to respect the regulations after being unjustly accused of an infraction. Similarly, a young man in the cadet corps at Episcopal High School declared that rules were foolish, but he would try to conform.[66] These comments and the examples given above suggest that some cadets judged the regulations and adapted to them as they saw fit. Whereas military schools stressed the importance of discipline and obedience, cadets obeyed within limits determined by their peers and their own goals. They set their own expectations, reflective of youth culture and their social position.

Despite calls for consistency, regulations, and tough rhetoric, military school discipline varied by professor, school, and year. Consider the case of one WMI cadet caught with liquor, an extremely serious offense. He went before the court-martial board and received two weeks' confinement to quarters and two months' probation. The court attributed the lightness of the sentence to the cadet's remorse and youth. In another example, an 1853 court expelled Cadet William Page for having a pack of cards (strictly prohibited by the regulations and considered "one of the most serious evils" by Superintendent Smith). Three years later, three cadets convicted of having cards in their room received a sentence of two extra tours of duty and six weeks' confinement to campus. Smith recalled the previous case in his condemnation of the court's sentence, but the verdict stood. Falling short of the strict morality and discipline that military academies promised, such lenience may have been an attempt to retain students.[67]

intoxication could represent a gentleman's honesty, cadet's duty, or youth's misplaced logic, but it condemned him at trial.

[66] James Burwell to Ann Latane, 22 August 1820; William Govan to B. H. Goodloe, 16 September 1854, VHS.

[67] WMI, 12 December 1850, *Order Book*, Vanderbilt. Another example is in WMI, 23 March 1852, *Order Book*, Vanderbilt. The Board of Visitors upheld the sentence; 24 January 1853, *Courts Martial Book*; Order #9, 25 February 1856, *Order Book*, VMI Archives. Between 1848 and

Even when a court dismissed a cadet, his expulsion was not guaranteed. The superintendents of all academies had the authority to reject the court's sentence recommendation and to grant clemency, as Superintendent Smith did with Gordon. An offender or his parents could also appeal to a school's board of visitors for clemency. At VMI, the Board consistently reinstated cadets throughout the 1850s. Smith often resented the Board's overturning a dismissal, but precedent had been set at West Point.[68] Following West Point procedure, the VMI Board reinstated many cadets who applied to them, regardless of the original charge and the proof of guilt. Thus, a dismissal was often a formality that caused problems but did not necessarily end a young man's educational career. This fact highlights the extent to which cadets' general obedience and the relative rarity of courts-martial were indicative of cadets' practice of self-restraint.

It also makes William Gordon's second appearance before the VMI court-martial board in the winter of his senior year surprising. The second trial was an unprecedented inquiry because Gordon initiated it and because the trial did not investigate infractions of the regulations.[69] Less than one month after his reinstatement, Gordon desired an inquiry to clear his name of dishonor. He remained unsatisfied with simply being reinstated; he wanted his honor restored and the perception that he had acted improperly contradicted. Interestingly, he returned to the VMI court for that vindication. His apparent belief that a court ruling would

---

1853, thirty-five cases resulted in twelve dismissals (34.3 percent) and between 1854 and 1858, sixty-nine cases resulted in nineteen dismissals (27.6 percent), plus three times the number of reinstatements; *Courts Martial Book, Order Book,* VMI Archives. Citadel graduate and Kings Mountain Military Academy founder Micah Jenkins connected maintaining strict discipline to decreasing enrollment. He dismissed ill-behaving students, feeling that discipline was more important than revenue; Micah Jenkins to John Jenkins, 20 October 1856, SCL.

[68] The bylaws of West Point allowed the Secretary of War to return students expelled by the Academic Board. In 1836, the West Point Board attempted to restrict the outside influence of the Secretary. Secretaries of War, however, continued to reinstate cadets intermittently. James L. Morrison, *"The Best School in the World"* (Kent: Kent State University Press, 1988), 43. Colleges had similar inconsistencies holding students to the rules. At Yale, for example, the principal told a father to argue to the Board against his son's dismissal and claim the son was not governed by the college's rules at the time of the infraction. See Jeremiah Day to John Breckenridge, 9 February 1815, VHS.

[69] One other VMI cadet, A. L. Dearing, asked for a court martial in an attempt to have the court vacate his dismissal; the court upheld the punishment. 24 January 1853, *Courts Martial Book,* VMI Archives, 284–92.

alter his peers' opinion evinces his profound misunderstanding of his peers' self-regulation.

In Gordon's second, unique trial, every available cadet at VMI voiced opinions of the situation. Those who were knowledgeable about the Gordon–Thompson affair voiced their disapproval of its outcome. The students testified and affirmed that Gordon did the "ungentlemanly" thing when he shared Thompson's private letter and carried an unauthorized weapon.[70] By not forcing Gordon out, they accepted the superintendent's decision to keep him at VMI. His social standing, however, remained unrepaired after the institutional proceeding.

Conclusion

In the end, William Gordon endured his classmates' ostracism because a diploma helped his prospects more than the respect of his peers did. Gordon's father was described as a blacksmith, one of the few skilled tradesmen who sent a son into military schooling. Without education, young men such as Gordon probably would have had little choice but to remain in a low social position as his father's son. With education, however, cadets like Gordon could merge into and sustain the expanding southern middle class. Military education afforded Gordon the vocational training to enter his first career as a civil engineer and his second as a military educator during the Civil War.[71] He never received the admiration of his peers, however: Classmates related that no one, except a roommate, spoke to Gordon for the rest of the year. In a lasting symbol of this rejection, virtually the entire class purchased class rings with the number twenty-five as the class total – instead of twenty-six, which was the total when Gordon was included.[72] This action suggests the extent to which the cadets had established a code of ethics separate from that

---

[70] 18 February 1852, *Courts Martial Book*, VMI Archives.

[71] Robert Carson to Joseph R. Anderson, 9 August 1912, William Gordon student file, VMI Archives. Gordon's subsequent enrollment at the University of Virginia, however, indicates that his father had also earned sufficient wealth to afford the social mobility of his son.

[72] Thomas Munford to Joseph R. Anderson, 23 August 1912, VMI Archives. Munford reported that he and one other cadet purchased rings with a class number of twenty-six. He also contended that he was the one who turned Thompson's roommate Strickler in to the authorities. Robert Carson described Munford as the only cadet who stood by Gordon; R. P. Carson to J. R. Anderson, 9 August 1912, VMI Archives.

advocated by the school authorities. They ably enforced that code within the social arena of the school in a way that made a lasting impression.

At times, cadets struggled with the striking contrast between the self-restraint they practiced and the code of southern honor with which they were surrounded. Under the southern code, a man had to master his environment. In contrast, a good soldier, even a good commander, had to obey the chain of command. Southern boys who attended military schools transitioned from one set of social expectations to another, but they also remained connected to their home communities and the larger southern society, never fully adopting institutional expectations. Cadets perceived their duty to be distinct from both military regulations and the dictates of southern honor. The youths from the emerging southern middle class who entered military academies demonstrated the values of their class and of their specific educational situation, to which duty, self-discipline, and peer-group loyalty were central. Cadets developed their own views – not simply military school administrators' – and regulated them within their community, which the schools' structure endorsed. Thus, we see the potential development of the emerging middle-class culture that could extend outside military education. Self-discipline was an important trait of the national middle class, and the other beliefs cadets and alumni expressed emphasized the values of restrained manhood and professionalism that were also becoming important to the middle ranks across the nation. The southern setting should introduce variations to the current historiographic middle-class model (which relies upon northern evidence), but in the South, too, we find the characteristics that defined the emerging southern middle class and placed its members in a national middle class.

4

"Honor as a man"

Manhood and the Cultural Values of the Emerging Southern Middle Class

"Your son and my cousin has acted like a MAN," Citadel senior John Wylie reported of his kinsman and fellow South Carolina Military Academy (SCMA) cadet, Lafayette Strait. In July 1854, Wylie wrote to his uncle and aunt that their son Strait, despite his suspension and resignation, had remained true to the ideas about manhood he learned at the military school. The Citadel administration suspended Strait for permitting an unauthorized cadet meeting while on guard duty, but Strait insisted that he had done no wrong and resigned rather than accept censure. The cadet evidently rejected the advice that his cousin gave him two years before his trouble; Wylie urged Strait to maintain "your honor as a man" and use "*Iron-Will*" to adapt to the contradictory impulses of traditional southern male independence and military academy duty.[1] Military school environments required cadets, like these two young men, to balance the submission that discipline required with their desire to act independently. Wylie declared Strait a "MAN" because he embodied the qualities of manhood that cadets accepted.

Strait's departure from the Citadel indicated the difficulty in reconciling the conflicting ideals of manhood within the military school situation. The meanings given to gender fluctuate for the people of any time and varied significantly in the late antebellum era, ranging between southern rugged manhood and a self-restrained, entrepreneurial model, more

---

[1] John D. Wylie to Aunt [Isabella Strait], 14 July 1854 (first quotation), Papers of the Gaston, Strait, Wylie and Baskin Families, The South Caroliniana Library, University of South Carolina (hereafter SCL). For the details of the event, G. Lafayette Strait to Father, 12 July 1854; John D. Wylie to G. Lafayette Strait, 25 December 1852 (second and third quotations), SCL (emphasis in original).

prevalent and commonly described in the North. Young men in military institutes demonstrated that no monolithic concept of manhood existed among southern youth of the period.[2] These southern cadets, maturing from boys to men, strove to achieve a male ideal from a variety of influences – society, peers, parents, and school – as did their peers at nonmilitary schools and colleges. Leaving their parents' advice and homes for military school, young men formed their vision of manhood in a primarily male environment, defining themselves in opposition to women and blacks. The nonplanter origins and the particular setting of the military school led cadets to combine these factors into a gendered worldview that originated in their regional location and class status. Cadets imbibed and refined different models of manhood (rugged and restrained) to create a flexible concept – not fully either of those ideals – but one that reflected and benefited their middle social position.

Male Environment at Military Schools

For most adolescents, young men's values centered in peer-based male groups and, as the previous chapter demonstrated, this was especially true at military schools. Students stepped into the first stage of manhood, developing from boyhood to adolescence and leaving home for a state of

---

[2] Amy S. Greenberg presents that two types of masculinity (restrained and martial) competed for dominance in the antebellum years but that men accepted these and other models; she writes, "there co-existed multiple practices of manhood at mid-century, none of which was hegemonic," *Manifest Manhood and the Antebellum American Empire* (New York: Cambridge University Press, 2005), 10 n. 23 (quotation), 9–14. E. Anthony Rotundo, *American Manhood: Transformations in Masculinity from the Revolution to the Modern Era* (New York: Basic Books, 1993), introduction, ch. 1, 3; Michael Kimmel, *Manhood in America: A Cultural History* (New York: Free Press, 1996), part 1; David D. Gilmore, *Manhood in the Making: Cultural Concepts of Masculinity* (New Haven: Yale University Press, 1990); Mark C. Carnes and Clyde Griffen, eds., *Meanings for Manhood: Constructions of Masculinity in Victorian America* (Chicago: University of Chicago Press, 1990). On developing southern manhood, see Craig Thompson Friend and Lorri Glover, eds., *Southern Manhood: Perspectives on Masculinity in the Old South* (Athens: University of Georgia Press, 2004); John Mayfield, "'The Soul of a Man': William Gilmore Simms and the Myth of Southern Manhood," *Journal of the Early Republic*, 15 (Fall 1995), 477–500; Peter S. Carmichael, *The Last Generation: Young Virginians in Peace, War and Reunion* (Chapel Hill: University of North Carolina Press, 2005). Anya Jabour, "Masculinity and Adolescence in Antebellum America: Robert Wirt at West Point, 1820–1821," *Journal of Family History*, 23 (October 1998), 394, 399, analyzes parental influence on one southern adolescent at West Point and locates a tension between southern honor and the family's residence in a border state.

semidependence in either apprenticeship or schooling.[3] As young men left their parents and parental control behind, socialization occurred in a clearly defined male space. Every military school and almost every college in the nation employed and enrolled men exclusively. Military academies usually removed women from their campuses and limited visits to beyond school walls. The environment was neither uncommon nor unsurprising because secondary schools facilitated male adolescents' entrance into manhood. Regulations kept cadets scheduled twenty-four hours a day so that, other than classroom recitations, cadets spent little time with adults. At military institutions, the young men lived together (often four to a room), ate together, supervised each other, and spent their waking hours primarily with other cadets.[4]

Within this male atmosphere, cadets defined themselves in contrast to what they perceived as the basic nature of women and of blacks. Although they made allowance for the powers that their mothers possessed, cadets' perceptions of females remained consistent with traditional southern views. They conceptualized women, largely because of their dependence on men, as opposite to men. At the Citadel in the 1850s, Lafayette Strait compared marrying a woman to buying a horse. (Given his youth, perhaps it is not surprising that Strait portrayed the horse as a better deal.) Essays by cadets James Morrison and Joseph Carpenter at the Virginia Military Institute (VMI) in the same decade described women as passive, men's first teacher, men's temptation, and chaste mothers. Most cadets believed that a man remained independent after marriage, whereas

---

[3] Studies generally consider adolescence as the ages between 15 and 25, especially while in academies, colleges, and apprenticeships. Joseph F. Kett, *Rites of Passage: Adolescence in America 1790 to the Present* (New York: Basic Books, 1977), 36; Stephen M. Frank, *Life with Father: Parenthood and Masculinity in the Nineteenth-Century American North* (Baltimore: The Johns Hopkins University Press, 1998), 49, 196 n. 75; Rotundo, *American Manhood*, 20–21, 56; Jabour, "Masculinity and Adolescence in Antebellum America," 404; Thomas Augst, *A Clerk's Tale: Young Men and Moral Life in Nineteenth-Century America* (Chicago: University of Chicago Press, 2003), 19. On the increased role of peers, see Rotundo, *American Manhood*, esp. 62–71; Patricia Cline Cohen, "Unregulated Youth: Masculinity and Murder in the 1830s City," *Radical History Review*, 52 (1992), 46; Robert F. Pace, *Halls of Honor: College Men in the Old South* (Baton Rouge: Louisiana State University Press, 2004), 73.

[4] See, for example, *Catalogue and Regulations of the Western Military Institute at Georgetown, Kentucky* (Cincinnati: Herald of Truth Printers, 1848); *Regulations of the Georgia Military Institute, Marietta, Georgia* (n.p., January, 1853); *Regulations of the Military Academies of South Carolina* (Columbia: R. W. Gibbes, 1858).

a woman became a wife and mother. They defined a man by his own character and a woman by her relationship to others.[5]

Cadets' humor and play stressed their opposition to feminine dependence. One Georgia Military Institute (GMI) cadet told his parents that his roommates called him by "the euphonious name of Chloe"; the student considered being labeled a woman so ridiculous that he construed it as a joke rather than an insult to his honor. Further reinforcing the distinction between masculine and feminine, other jests affirmed the more physical and competitive aspects of male youth – for example, hazing and fighting – that reinforced the cadets' manhood. Cadets engaged in physical tussles, threw "missiles," tied other cadets up and dunked them in water, and employed mental challenges, such as putting new cadets on "trial" for nonexistent crimes.[6] Such actions echoed southern trends of male competition and aggression. Still, cadets' behavior was only a faint echo of elite rugged masculinity; they accepted self-discipline and seldom physically challenged their professors.

Even more explicitly than they asserted the independence that women lacked, cadets rejected the dependence with which blacks lived. As with their view of women, young men adopted the master class's view of black inferiority and white superiority as components of southern non-elite manhood. One rare comparison to a black was made when Strait described himself "as well and hearty as any Quarter darkie." Comparison between the cadet and a slave centered on physical condition

[5] James H. Morrison, "Woman's Character," unpublished essay, 3 December 1857; Joseph H. Carpenter, unpublished diary, 1853, Preston Library, Virginia Military Institute Archives (hereafter VMI Archives); G. Lafayette Strait, "The Disappointed Bachelor," unpublished essay, [23 February 1854], SCL. For similar ideas in a speech to cadets, Albert Pike, *An Address Delivered by Albert Pike* (Little Rock: William E. Woodruff, 1852), 8.

[6] Theodore Fogle to Father and Mother, 16 August 1852 (first quotation), Theodore F. Fogle Papers, Richard Woodruff Library, Department of Special Collections, Emory University (hereafter Emory). Charles Derby to Father, 9 May 1846; Philip A. Fitzhugh to Patrick Fitzhugh, 28 December 1844; Joseph Chenoweth to Father, 28 September 1855; Henry T. Lee to Fellows, 15 July 1844, Daniel Powell student file, VMI Archives; Leeland Hathaway Recollections, unpublished memoir, c. 1890; John Henry Custis to [?], 17 May 1861; Henry K. Burgwyn to Anna Burgwyn, 12 August 1860, Burgwyn Family Papers, Southern Historical Collection, Wilson Library, University of North Carolina at Chapel Hill (hereafter SHC); John Edward Dodson to Harriet Cogbill, 8 May 1863, Virginia Historical Society (hereafter VHS); Beverly Stanard, *Letters of a New Market Cadet*, ed. John G. Barrett and Robert K. Turner Jr. (Chapel Hill: University of North Carolina Press, 1961), 43. Jabour, "Masculinity and Adolescence in Antebellum America," 409, describes the 1820's West Point subculture as fraternal and competitive.

and did not imply any other likeness. More often, cadets used racialized rhetoric common in the antebellum South to describe their own sense of dependence. Young men refused to be treated like "slaves." Their complaints targeted a range of situations from inappropriate comments by professors to the requirement that state scholarship recipients teach for two years after graduation. "The Institute should not seek to make slaves of its graduates," one state-funded VMI alumnus protested when he could not find a teaching job at his desired salary.[7] The majority of cadets reconciled their dependence so that they were not subservient as were wives or slaves, at least in the cadets' own minds.

Within the male environment, then, and part of living their lives, youth came to understand what qualities men exhibited. Gender scholars commonly explain antebellum manhood with models; most discussions describe an opposition between restrained (sometimes Christian or evangelical) and rugged (sometimes martial) manhood and a range of beliefs and behaviors within those extremes.[8] Rugged manhood promoted men asserting their independent prerogative, exhibiting aggressiveness, and dominating others around them in an inherently competitive world; in the other extreme, the restrained archetype called for men to model self-discipline, morality, and industry. Southern men, like their northern counterparts, could accept either model. Historian Amy Greenberg states, "restrained manhood was not middle-class manhood, and martial manhood was not working-class manhood. Although economic and social transformations shaped these two masculinities, they did not determine them."[9] The present study finds that the national middle class, whether northern or southern, privileged restrained manhood.

---

[7] G. Lafayette Strait to Jacob F. Strait, 25 January 1853 (first quotation), SCL; William Lee to Francis H. Smith, 23 March 1854 (second quotation), VMI Archives. Similarly, Timothy Thorp to Francis H. Smith, 9 March 1841, VMI Archives; G. Lafayette Strait to Father and Mother, 7 February 1854; G. Lafayette Strait to Aunt Amanda [Wylie], 7 February 1854, SCL.

[8] The terminology here is awkward: Military schools actually promoted restrained manhood more than martial manhood. I use "rugged manhood" for this reason. Clyde Griffen notes that the men and values between the extremes of evangelical and tough manhood have not been explored historiographically, in "Reconstructing Masculinity from the Evangelical Revival to the Waning of Progressivism: A Speculative Synthesis" in *Meanings for Manhood*, 183–204.

[9] Greenberg, *Manifest Manhood in the Antebellum American Empire*, 13 (quotation), 139–40. On the Early Republic, see Lorri Glover, *Southern Sons: Becoming Men in the New Nation* (Baltimore: The Johns Hopkins University Press, 2007), esp. 41.

This chapter highlights the cadets' ideal of manhood that blended southern and national trends. Successful cadets recognized the southern importance of a man's hierarchical status but modified elite male goals of wealth, honor, and mastery, replacing the standards of valuation with ones they could attain, specifically education and character. Military academy settings encouraged them to promote physicality though military spectacle. Their new ideal, overall, mirrored some nineteenth-century national trends, including the promotion of self-discipline, religiosity, temperance, and industry. Furthermore, the cadets' male archetype culminated in professional responsibility and the traits that supported professional lives. Cadets blended these different expectations into a vision of manhood centered on the self-discipline they cultivated.

Rugged and Restrained Manhood

Cadets consciously reacted to the most prescient cultural message they received about male identity in the antebellum South: the issue of honor. The preeminent authority on southern honor, historian Bertram Wyatt-Brown, stated that children had to display "a military submissiveness" to their fathers as "part of the training in honor," but after reaching adolescence "defiance lent stature to the planter's son and gave confidence in leadership."[10] Deference to fathers, however, rarely translated to schoolmasters. From adolescence to adulthood, elite manhood stressed independence.

Historians often use honor as the foundation to describe southerners as exponents of rugged manhood; it should instead be seen as one component of manhood. Greenberg, for example, describes southern manhood, from planters to yeomen, with the martial manhood model and as "ruled by ideas of honor." As an essential feature of southern manhood, honor both dictated behavior and was reinforced by elite principles of masculinity. Slaveholding necessitated the ability to command dependents, and displaying honor demonstrated such mastery. Aggressive physical displays and the refusal to accept (or at least willingness to defend against)

---

[10] Bertram Wyatt-Brown, *Southern Honor: Ethics and Behavior in the Old South* (New York: Oxford University Press, 1982), 157, 163.

insult marked southern honor. Traditional elite manhood required self-presentation illustrating independence and mastery, while maintaining the public face of honor and status in the social hierarchy.[11] Both antebellum writers and present-day historians often described the raucous behavior of elite southern adolescents. This rugged concept of manhood also meant that elite youths drank, gambled, and demanded that others treat them as independent men of honor.[12] Thus, this model has been called *southern* manhood, but should be *elite* manhood. Even in the Old South, there was no hegemonic masculine ideal.

An important component in an elite southern man's honor was mastery. As Drew Gilpin Faust has shown, James Henry Hammond, the South Carolinian who married into the planter class, needed to control his environment and those around him. The rugged southern man had to demonstrate his mastery over the women in his life, his house and land, his servants, his children, and the world of business.[13] Even more than requiring a man to control his environment, southern elite honor

[11] Greenberg, *Manifest Manhood in the Antebellum American Empire*, 10, 271, 272 (quotation); Edward L. Ayers, *Vengeance and Justice: Crime and Punishment in the Nineteenth-Century American South* (New York: Oxford University Press, 1984), esp. 24; Wyatt-Brown, *Southern Honor*; Bertram Wyatt-Brown, *The Shaping of Southern Culture: Honor, Grace, and War, 1760s–1880s* (Chapel Hill: University of North Carolina Press, 2001); Kenneth S. Greenberg, *Honor and Slavery: Lies, Duels, Noses, Masks, Dressing as a Woman, Gifts, Strangers, Humanitarianism, Death, Slave Rebellions, the Proslavery Argument, Baseball, Hunting, and Gambling in the Old South* (Princeton: Princeton University Press, 1996); Elizabeth Fox-Genovese, *Within the Plantation Household: Black and White Women in the Old South* (Chapel Hill: University of North Carolina Press, 1988); Elizabeth Fox-Genovese and Eugene D. Genovese, *The Mind of the Master Class: History and Faith in the Southern Slaveholders' Worldview* (New York: Cambridge University Press, 2005); Steven M. Stowe, *Intimacy and Power in the Old South: Ritual in the Lives of the Planters* (Baltimore: The Johns Hopkins University Press, 1987), ch. 1, 3; Christopher J. Olsen, *Political Culture and Secession in Mississippi: Masculinity, Honor, and the Antiparty Tradition, 1830–1860* (New York: Oxford University Press, 2000); Nicolas W. Proctor, *Bathed in Blood: Hunting and Mastery in the Old South* (Charlottesville: University of Virginia Press, 2002); Mayfield, "'Soul of a Man.'"

[12] Pace, *Halls of Honor*; Jennings L. Wagoner Jr., "Honor and Dishonor at Mr. Jefferson's University: The Antebellum Years," *History of Education Quarterly*, 26 (Summer 1986), 154–79; Kett, *Rites of Passage*, ch. 1; Robert F. Pace and Christopher A. Bjornsen, "Adolescent Honor and College Student Behavior in the Old South," *Southern Cultures*, 6 (Fall 2000), 9–28; Daniel Kilbride, "Southern Medical Students in Philadelphia, 1800–1860: Science and Sociability in the 'Republic of Medicine,'" *Journal of Southern History*, 65 (November 1999), 697–732.

[13] Drew Gilpin Faust, *James Henry Hammond and the Old South* (Baton Rouge: Louisiana State University Press, 1982).

demanded that he must always appear to do so. An elite man's duty to his public face was primary. Honor demanded that men perform the responsibilities of maintaining it. The external judgment of the community of honor retained primacy over thoughts or actions invisible to the community.

Not only did the individual southern man demand control of his surroundings, but the language of honor of the southern elite defined the boundaries of the group. The southern elite combined an ideology of masculinity, social status, labor, and racism to create the code of honor that maintained their culture.[14] In the 1830s and beyond, the emerging southern middle class started building social institutions partially separate from elite control; military education, for example, offered higher schooling. Cadets mostly from the emerging middle class moved from southern culture into a military educational setting that required them to accept self-regulation. The military hierarchy of military rank and regulation contrasted the southern code of honor, which reflected a hierarchy of class, wealth, and race. Both ethical systems dictated different behaviors, especially as southern honor focused on external judgment and military schools demanded internal decision making. Cadets refined these impulses, and the rugged view offered a foundation for their ideals, but manhood, at least for non-elite cadets, also entailed values connected to self-discipline.

Southern honor, the central component of the ideal southern elite, necessitated hierarchy and mastery. The slow development of middle-class manhood – that which cadets increasingly demonstrated during the late antebellum years – incorporated these qualities with different emphases and specifics. Indeed, just as class formation is a process, cultural change and adaptations in the ideas of honor and manhood occurred at varying rates according to location and individual. Sociability, learning, and piety defined honor among the gentry, and all southerners supported the principle of southern honor that made community central. They certainly maintained the community connections and obligations that cut across class lines. Although elite southerners believed that they presided over the social hierarchy, all ranks of southern white males evinced the hierarchical tendencies of the society. Manhood for cadets

---

[14] Proctor, *Bathed in Blood*, considered this group boundary in respect to the hunt.

built on and modified this traditional southern principle. Furthermore, a fundamental component of manhood in the nineteenth century (and many other eras) was the maintenance of patriarchal privilege. Military school men accepted this prevalent idea of hierarchy. Cadets, however, began to develop distinct qualifications for the ranks within the hierarchy. They could not compete in the established qualities for elite standing: birth/kin, slaves, land, and classical education. Their redefinition developed out of their positions as nonplanters, and reflected a hierarchy of cadet corps military rank, which was assigned without consideration of external variables.[15] When they expressed the specific characteristics that manhood and adulthood entailed, young men expressed the southern elite ideal of hierarchy but modified elite male goals of status, honor, mastery, and wealth, replacing those standards with ones they could accomplish, such as education, self-discipline, and industry. Wylie confirmed his cousin's proper manly behavior because of the cousin's use of will power and fortitude, for example.

By the late antebellum years, portions of the ideal of restrained manhood had found their way into southern culture; for example, Peter Carmichael proposes that what he calls the Christian gentlemen ideal infiltrated *The Last Generation*. The restrained model grew in attraction to the planters' sons, who increasingly entered professions.[16] Especially in the 1850s, both the elite and middle class came into contact with ideas about discipline and industry. Self-discipline was a value prominent among evangelicals in the nineteenth century. Many middle-class northerners accepted religion and the cultural beliefs that mutually reinforced each: self-discipline, self-improvement, industry, and individualism. Southern middle-class cadets entered professional careers more often than did planters' sons, and adopted these values connected to professionalism. It becomes clear from the cadets' attempts to find their ways as men in the Old South that the boundary between southern and

[15] Wagoner, "Honor and Dishonor at Mr. Jefferson's University," 163. The importance of hierarchy existed in other cultures, but cadets received and adapted a specific understanding of it in the Old South; Andrew C. Holman, *A Sense of Their Duty: Middle-Class Formation in Victorian Ontario Towns* (Montreal: McGill-Queen's University Press, 2000), 140. Olsen, *Political Culture and Secession*, 25–26. Wyatt-Brown, *Southern Honor*, also describes hierarchy as a facet of southern honor.

[16] Carmichael, *Last Generation*, ch. 3, leaves the content of Christian manhood and how the southern manifestation of it differed from the northern ideal open for continued exploration.

national trends was fluid. The ideals of manhood suggested the development of a national culture.

Many of the traits that cadets promoted mirrored those of northern
evangelical reformers. This does not mean that the developing middle
class was derivative of the northern middle class. As evidence from cadets'
families shows, members of the emerging southern middle class both
shared motivations with their northern peers (for example, evangelical
directives) *and* acted for southern reasons. Military schools emphasized
a different type of learning, one that men in the middle social position
could obtain (with help from the state, no less) and that increasingly
represented professional modernizing trends across class lines. Middle-
class men in both regions recognized the importance of education and
religiosity, thus confirming that the developing southern middle class
exhibited traits similar to those of the northern middle class. However, in
the southern context, honor and rugged manhood were so prevalent that
traits like hierarchy resonated in cadets' views. Elite southern manhood,
derived from honor and fostered in slaveowning, influenced middle-class
cadets to accept hierarchy and mastery. Combining national trends with
the modernizing South, the young men also appreciated the restrained
manhood ideal and promoted self-discipline.

Cadets adopted the mastering of themselves, reflective of evangelical
trends and helpful to professional, non-elite young men. They also added
the southern traits of hierarchy and mastery (at least in that limited way).
By moderating their standards in this way, non-elite young southerners
did not compete with slaveholders or planters. Theirs was an alternate,
not subversive, ideal; it allowed them to move into traditional elite manhood if they attained plantations and slaves. The same as other groups,
the emerging middle class felt the master class's influence and reacted to
their messages. Yeomen conceptualized their manhood similar to elites
as *Masters of Small Worlds*, according to Stephanie McCurry; similarly,
backwoodsmen fought with a derivative of honor, as Elliott Gorn
detailed.[17] Gender similarities between yeomen and planters reflected
the similarity in goals for the groups; yeomen idealized the planters'

[17] Kate Chavigny, Comment, Organization of American Historians Annual Meeting, Wash-
ington DC, 21 April 2006; Stephanie McCurry, *Masters of Small Worlds: Yeoman Households,
Gender Relations, and the Political Culture of the Antebellum South Carolina Low Country*
(New York: Oxford University Press, 1995); Elliott J. Gorn, "'Gouge and Bite, Pull Hair

goals and were not creating a professional career path. In contrast, the emerging middle class sought to raise its status above yeomen and validate professionalism. Carmichael describes an increase in professional status concurrent to the rise in Christian gentleman traits. Although not a determining factor, the position of the emerging middle class pushed them toward the restrained model of manhood.

Blending Influences

Cousins Strait and Wylie, contemporaries born in the mid-1830s, came from different branches of the same family, but only John Wylie succeeded with a diploma from the SCMA. Wylie better accepted discipline, yet he felt that his cousin adopted the same values of manhood. Wylie, the Citadel graduate, came from the professional side of the family; his father was a doctor, and he would become a lawyer. Despite paying for tuition, he told Strait, "my Parents are not <u>Rich</u>." Wylie followed his family's pro-temperance stand. Of the two cousins, Strait was closer to the planter model. His father was a cotton planter, purchasing 800 acres three years after his son left the Citadel. Strait obviously had more access to resources; while in school, he claimed that he and his roommates shared boxes from home about once a week (with four per room, a family's contribution of once-a-month would be high), and then he attended medical school in the North. Two women in the family (an aunt to both and Strait's sister), however, were teaching school. The young men shared another cousin at SCMA, and a T. M. Wylie enrolled later in the 1850s.[18] Successful cadets and future professionals like John Wylie defined the male hierarchy and the qualities of manhood with education, military bearing, self-discipline (seen in submission, religiosity, and temperance), and professional values (industry, fortitude, and career).

Cadets' non-elite status made their position precarious and necessitated qualities other than land and slave ownership to rank men. Cadets and school speakers defined the most important traits of manhood so that cadets could raise their status in a society where the demarcations of

and Scratch': The Social Significance of Fighting in the Southern Backcountry," *American Historical Review*, 90 (February 1985), 18–43; Friend and Glover, *Southern Manhood*.

[18] John D. Wylie to Lafayette Strait, 19 August 1852 (quotation); Wylie to Aunt Hannah, 11 June 1852; Strait to Sister, 22 March 1853; Hannah Wylie to Strait, 22 February 1854, SCL.

rank were often unclear. "*Indomitable energy* of *purpose,* and *firmness* and *decision of character,*" cadets at the Rappahannock Military Institute were told, "are the qualities which can alone elevate a man above a common level."[19] At the same time as it highlighted energy and decision making, this statement acknowledged that even middle-rank southern men believed in a hierarchy of men, so that VMI cadet Joseph Chenoweth could aspire to be "a man, in the highest, truest, noblest sense of the term!" Citadel cadets learned to become "gentlemen of high tone and the purest sense of honor" through their military education.[20] A cadet would attain the highest rank among men, it appeared, through education and character rather than land and slaves.

As members of the minority of antebellum southerners who achieved secondary education, and reflecting their developing middle-class ideals, cadets unsurprisingly presented their ideal of a true man as a man of letters, a man with knowledge of the world around him, especially of science, which was preeminent in military education curricula. They stressed scientific education more than classical refinement. "My earthly ambition is to be a profoundly learned man," one cadet wrote to his guardian in 1848. Similarly, a decade later, another cadet at the state military institute in Virginia described his "laudable ambition" as gaining intellectual improvement. A Rappahannock cadet wrote that education was a virtual necessity for honor.[21] More specifically, Lafayette Strait praised his education in connection to the medical career for which he hoped: "The day has past when a man, because he had a Diploma, could make a substance by the practice of medicine, though in every sense of the word

---

[19] Rotundo, *American Manhood,* 65–66, 69–70, contends that competition among young men was part of youth culture. He does not suggest that manhood entailed competition among all men for status. This aspect of the cadets' lives derived from the hierarchical nature of southern elite honor. G. W. Lewis, *Address Delivered Before the Literary Society and Students Generally of the Rappahannock Academy and Military Institute* (Washington: Gideon and Co., 1852), 9 (quotation, italics in original).

[20] Joseph H. Chenoweth to Father, 21 February 1857 (first quotation), VMI Archives; Samuel McGowen, *An Address Delivered before the Polytechnic and Calliopean Societies of the State Military Academy* (Charleston: Edward C. Councell, 1851), 20 (second quotation).

[21] Samuel Garland to Samuel Garland, 12 January 1848, Garland Family Papers, VHS; Joseph Chenoweth to Father, 21 February 1857, VMI Archives; Leonard Augustus Slater, unpublished essay book, 1850–51, VHS. Also, see Edwin Heriot, *The Polytechnic School, the Best System of Practical Education* (Charleston: Walker and James, 1850), esp. 21; Pike, *Address,* 5–6.

an ignoramus."[22] Strait echoed the masculine values of his (albeit brief) military school training; education and knowledge formed one basis for attaining status as a man (and would certainly help young men in their professional lives). Thus, performing well at a military school raised cadets' social status (when non-elite young men) and encouraged professional masculine values (even if an elite found himself leaving before graduation, as did Strait and the young men who challenged William Gordon).

More specifically than education, the military system required cadets to maintain proper bearing and demeanor, endorsed in their society as both a man's public honor and a male physicality. The father of Western Military Institute (WMI) cadet Joel Scott, for instance, repeatedly encouraged his son to gain military carriage and good posture. Cadets like Scott had their own reasons for desiring the behavior. They believed that military training brought good health and that upright carriage indicated manners and refinement. In the same year of 1853, although in a different state, drilling made a youth "walk strait so that he looks like somebody," commented one Citadel cadet.[23] The "somebody" epitomized the high male status, military bearing, and appearance of status and manners that cadets associated with manliness. Throughout their discussions of the military component, cadets identified status and refinement as its results. Rank and office provided prestige and respectability; they also reflected national concerns with gentility and manners, as Mr. Scott's

---

[22] Lafayette Strait to Parents, 2 June 1856, SCL (emphasis in original). Interestingly, Steven M. Stowe presents Strait's selection of a medical career as an example of masculine willfulness in *Doctoring the South: Southern Physicians and Everyday Medicine in the Mid-Nineteenth Century* (Chapel Hill: University of North Carolina Press, 2004), 16–7.

[23] G. Lafayette Strait to Aunt [A.S. Wylie], 21 January 1852 [1853] (quotation), SCL; Robert W. Scott to Joel Scott, 27 September 1853, 31 October 1853, Department of Library Special Collections, Manuscripts, Western Kentucky University (hereafter WKU). John P. Thomas, *On the Profession of Arms. The Annual Address Delivered before the Association of Graduates of the State Military Academy of South-Carolina, in Charleston, SC, April 9, 1859*. (Charleston: Walker, Evans, and Company, 1859); Pike, *Address*, 20; Eagleswood Collegiate and Military Institute, *Catalog* (n.p., [1861]), American Antiquarian Society (hereafter AAS). Rod Andrew Jr., *Long Gray Lines: The Southern Military School Tradition, 1839–1915* (Chapel Hill: University of North Carolina Press, 2001); Kilbride, "Southern Medical Students in Philadelphia," describes this drive among elites; Richard L. Bushman, *The Refinement of America: Persons, Houses, Cities* (New York: Alfred A. Knopf, 1992), addresses it primarily for northerners.

concerns indicated. The southern strain of respectability emphasized oration, which cadets practiced, and incorporated gentility as classical learning (or, at least, the appearance of classical knowledge), to which middle-class southerners had little access. Gentility meant exhibiting manners that marked the elite, and military bearing and rank offered a permutation of it.[24] As cadets sought respectability through comportment and rank, they and other middle-class southerners asserted that all education, including nonclassical, reflected refinement.

Cadets proudly wore their assigned uniforms and the associated aura of manliness as the most visible aspects of military education. They showed off these uniforms in photographs such as Figures 2 and 4. The young men received commendation for appearing in uniform as military representatives of their state and station. Uniforms distinguished them from other men, bringing honor and respect. One VMI alumnus working as a teacher, for example, criticized his school's "very stupid ideas on military discipline" in failing to adequately drill and teach tactics; most importantly, he complained, the students "never had a uniform."[25] He stressed that military discipline and its desired result remained incomplete without accompanying appearance and behavior.

Military conduct connected, as noted earlier, to southern trends and to the desire for self-discipline. People incorrectly focused on the "*mere drill and uniform*" of military institutions criticized superintendent Francis W. Capers in 1846, four years after the Citadel's opening. The act of wearing a uniform carried more significance: It represented actual duties and responsibilities. The duties were not those of soldiers because military

---

[24] Glover, *Southern Sons*, 42, states that southern parents in the Early Republic sent their sons to college "to ensure future success as genteel men," a goal pursued at universities or at non-elite schools based on social position.

[25] Charles Denby to Francis H. Smith, 28 January 1851 (quotation), VMI Archives. Also see Stapleton Crutchfield, unpublished speech, 4 July 1855, VHS; W. R. Wiggins to Theodore Kingsbury, 23 December 1846, SHC; William P. DuBose, "Soldier, Philosopher, Friend, Awakener of the Undying Good in Men," unpublished memoir, typescript 1946; Claudius Fike to G. A. Fike, 12 February 1862, 20 April 1862, Claudius Lucian Fike papers, SCL. Catlett Fitzhugh Conway, unpublished "Autobiography," typescript c. 1911, VHS, described in minute detail the uniform and military operations as a cadet at Culpeper Military Academy. On militias and uniforms in the South, James B. Whisker, *The Rise and Decline of the American Militia System* (Cranbury, NJ: Associated University Presses Inc., 1999), ch. 7; John Hope Franklin, *The Militant South, 1800–1861* (Boston: Beacon Press, 1956), 167–68, 176–78, 184–85; Bertram Wyatt-Brown, *Southern Honor*, 10, 418–19.

academies *rarely* produced active soldiers in the United States military. As part of their responsibilities, however, cadets replicated the behavior of militias or of soldiers at drill. Even a traveler passing through Lexington, Virginia, in 1852 noted the "military might" of the VMI cadets, connecting the sight of the school with "war."[26] The cadets would have happily heard this opinion and the status that it gave them.

Accepting Self-discipline and Submission

These physical manifestations reflected something much more important: the development of young men. Cadets became men – educated and self-sufficient – at military schools. The physical self-regulation demonstrated an internalized acceptance of discipline that reflected externally in the cadets' performance. A militaristic appearance represented a part of the cadets' redefinition of manhood – rooted in an inwardly directed sense of duty, discipline, and submission – and the status that these qualities gave young men. It symbolized the industry and fortitude that the cadet maintained during his education. This centrality of self-discipline and submission highlighted a non-elite gender identity – with qualities similar to those of the restrained model – for thousands of young men in the Old South.

VMI superintendent Francis H. Smith, similar to other military administrators, specifically described a goal of military education to instill in young men a sense of self-control. In an 1856 speech, he portrayed the perfect VMI cadet as the man who practiced self-restraint: A cadet must be put "constantly upon his guard – to make him watch against trifling indiscretions." Likewise, "Military institutions educate also through the control and subordination they teach," a speaker told the same cadets in the same year. The message focused on submission to authority particularly through self-monitoring. "I would counsel the governed habitually . . . to hold it more honorable and manly to submit occasionally to individual wrong," an 1854 orator told the Citadel students; "as cadets of a military academy, subordination and submission to discipline

[26] Francis W. Capers, *State Military Academies* (Charleston: Tenhet and Corley, 1846), 8–9 (first quotation, italics in original). Curran Swaim, unpublished diary, 24 August 1852 (second and third quotations), VHS.

are peculiarly your duty." *Regulations of the Georgia Military Institute* asserted that "obedience and subordination are essential to the purposes of this institution."[27] Clearly, submission to duty and authority marked the adolescent's experience at a military academy.

Military education sought to create a different type of man than the elite southern ideal, because military honor required self-discipline. The three significant tenets of military honor included self-control, obedience, and hierarchy.[28] At a military school, cadets learned to internalize the rules and to make self-discipline a duty, as the previous chapter detailed. Military discipline changed the external direction of a cadet's honor from his reputation to the regulations. A cadet must follow his conscience based on his interior values so that he obeyed the rules even if unsupervised. In addition to altering the focus of a man's primary concerns, the military academies replaced the southern social hierarchy with one based on military rank (as William Gordon described in the previous chapter).

A guest lecturer before the cadet literary societies at the Citadel asserted a man's need to learn discipline to command others. "Habits of strict discipline are undoubtedly essential," the speaker told the cadets, "and there are none more capable of commanding, than those who have learned to obey."[29] The speaker implied that boys and men must learn to obey in order to become the ideal man. If this ideal man was a southern man, capable of commanding, the military institute suggested itself as a necessary step to maturity. The military school ideology implied that a man would have been more likely to attain mastery had he been raised with strict discipline and learned obedience. The ability to command

---

[27] Quotations from, in order: Francis H. Smith, *Introductory Address to the Corps of Cadets of the Virginia Military Institute, on the Resumption of Academic Duties* (Richmond: MacFarlane and Fergusson, 1856); Lawrence Massillion Keitt, *Address Before the Two Literary Societies of the Virginia Military Institute* (Richmond: MacFarlane and Fergusson, 1856), 15; *Regulations of the Georgia Military Institute*, 20. Richard Yeadon, *Address, on the Necessity of Subordination, in our Academies and Colleges, Civil and Military* (Charleston: Walker & James, 1854), 17–18, 20.

[28] The military developed expectations of its members that differed from mainstream society. Of course, military schools and the armed forces reflected the society around them. Indeed, the institutions were not static, but dynamic. See William B. Skelton, "The Army in the Age of the Common Man, 1815–1845" in *Against All Enemies*, ed. Kenneth J. Hagan and William R. Roberts (Westport, CT: Greenwood Press, 1986), 98.

[29] Heriot, *The Polytechnic School*, 15.

may have been a common goal of the elite and the middle class, but it was achieved through different means and for different results. The self-regulation and values of this emerging middle class aligned more closely with restrained manhood than with the rugged ideal.

In every school environment, discipline was crucial; too much autonomy led to ungovernable youths, and submission made schools run smoothly. Notwithstanding the operational benefit, though, military educators endorsed the idea that submission could be manly. Military schools promoted a "manly character" of morality and inwardly directed obedience. According to GMI, cadets should obtain "self-reliance, coolness, deliberation and judgement, promptness and subordination which such [a military] education bestows." Representing similar sentiments in his first speech before the literary societies, Citadel superintendent Capers listed the goal of the school to teach cleanliness, regular habits, exercise, and morality (particularly as discipline against bad habits).[30] A decade later in 1857, a speaker at the Citadel told the cadets to "practice the virtues of sobriety, industry and integrity."[31] Military school administrations consistently valued submission and self-discipline, stressing character as a quality that differentiated men.

Part of the military education's message attempted to alleviate concerns in the slaveholding culture. Although many antebellum Americans worried about the temptations that plagued college life, southern students were thought particularly vulnerable. For example, an 1855 article in the *Nashville Union and American* promoted the newly incorporated WMI and lamented that, in the South, blacks performed the labor, which made it "extremely difficult for [white] parents to exercise controlling restraints over youth." A military school remedied this problem: The imposition of military discipline worked as an antidote to lax child rearing. The Trustees at the University of Nashville acknowledged that,

[30] *Report by the Board of Visitors of the Georgia Military Institute, To his Excellency, Howell Cobb, Governor of the State of Georgia For 1853*, Rare Books, Manuscript and Special Collections Library, Duke University (hereafter Duke), 11 (first and second quotations). Capers, *State Military Academies*, 19 (third quotation). Capers moved consecutively from superintendencies at the state military academies in South Carolina, Kentucky, and Georgia between 1843 and 1862.
[31] James D. Tradewell, *Address on the Study of the Federal Constitution Delivered Before the Polytechnic and Calliopean Societies of the Citadel Academy* (Charleston: Walker, Evans and Co., 1857), 33.

because "the Students in our Southern Colleges are as a matter of fact *boys* and not young men," discipline problems resulted. Trustees voted to join with WMI to alleviate this predicament, challenging the more traditional view of students as young men of honor and promoting a military model of men as subordinate to self-discipline.[32]

Reflective of the southernness of the schools, military education was inherently class based. Submission was for the indigent. As Jennings L. Wagoner Jr., pointed out, the University of Virginia could do little to subdue its elite student body, likewise South Carolina College and preparatory academies. The military school constituency was not the future planter (recall that few cadets came from planters' families, and then mostly younger sons). The schools' message was directed by its matriculates: *Non-elite* manhood in the South could be subordinate. Men of the middle social rank accepted some ideals of the restrained model, which the changing environment also brought into the planter class, but for the emerging middle class, manhood could also be subordinate. This outlook reflected their social position, both as students at military schools (rather than at more prestigious universities) and as members of the professions into which they were likely to be placed (in comparison to planters). Class tensions resolved here and in their career choices. WMI promoted this goal in the *Nashville Union and American* article, presenting the qualities of "obedience, subordination and deference to authority, which constitute a sound basis for good citizenship" for southern white men.[33] These youths were not the independent or authoritative men that ruled on plantations. They resisted southern tradition that said that to submit was to act as (or be) a slave.[34] Military schools did not present the rugged model of manhood to them, and the precepts of the men they wanted to become reflected the restrained standard.

[32] "Western Military Academy," *Nashville Union and American* (14 February 1855), 2. Western Military Institute Meeting Minutes, vol. 2, 9 March 1855, Vanderbilt University Archives (hereafter Vanderbilt) (italics in original). Kett, *Rites of Passage*; Pace and Bjornsen, "Adolescent Honor," 13.

[33] Wagoner, "Honor and Dishonor at Mr. Jefferson's University"; *Nashville Union and American*, 2 (quotation). See "Military Institute," *Gleason's Pictorial Drawing-Room Companion* (1 January 1853), 16.

[34] Fox-Genovese, *Within in the Plantation Household*; Steven Kantrowitz, *Ben Tillman and the Reconstruction of White Supremacy* (Chapel Hill: University of North Carolina Press, 2000), 23.

Military schools demanded submission, contrary to rugged manhood, and the cadets' middle-class rank led them to value education and to acquiesce to its requirements. They restrained independence and submitted to the rules if they wanted to remain at their schools. As military education circumscribed the rugged excesses of southern adolescence, the cadets themselves adopted more restrained behavior and accepted limits on their freedom. To earn diplomas, cadets reconciled the southern independent ideal with military submission. They had to "construct [a] code to regulate your actions," as one valedictorian told his peers at the Citadel. This code, he suggested, defined an inviolate self that accepted the authority of others and internalized institutional rules; it echoes the same language that his superintendent used to describe internal restraint. Wylie, in the middle social position compared to his cousin, used "*Iron-Will*" to ensure his graduation. When homesick cadet Leeland Hathaway ran away from WMI, he "had intended to be manly [but] had only played the baby."[35] Because he had not followed the appropriate internal directive, he judged his action as not worthy of a man.

After all, these adolescents aspired to independent manhood even as they negotiated obedience to parents, teachers, and administrators. They were accustomed to the conflict and eager to resolve it. They tried to act independently, but self-discipline forced submission to regulations. At least one educator explored the tension between autonomy and subordination that cadets reconciled. "The young man, who has been taught from his cradle, to reverence parental authority, and to respect Bible truth, and has learned that subordination to government does not involve meanness and cowardice," wrote professor D. H. Hill, "will be distinguished by a manly, upright and an honorable deportment throughout the whole of his College career." He blamed poor training at home as a central cause of poor college discipline.[36] West Point-educated Hill, who started the North Carolina Military Institute (NCMI) five years after this comment, easily combined manhood, physical bearing, and deference.

[35] William M. Tennent, "Valedictory before the Calliopean," unpublished speech, [1857] (first quotation), The Citadel Archives and Museum (hereafter CIT). Hathaway, memoir (second quotation), SHC.
[36] D. H. Hill, *College Discipline* (Salisbury: Watchman Office, 1855), 9 (quotation), 10. On the students' struggle with autonomy in the earlier generation, see Glover, *Southern Sons*, 137–51.

After operating his school, however, Hill stressed that "manliness and independence" were more highly prized than "habits of order and system" taught in military education. In 1860, he declared, "the world is full of timid, time-serving, vacillating men, who never take a decided stand through sheer irresolution. The young men, who receive a Military Education, are in training during their whole collegiate course, to come out boldly, and to come out always on the side of law and order." Daily interactions at the NCMI transformed Hill's views on manhood: It required both submission and independence. The restrained masculine model should not equal weakness or slavery to modern time management, which is interesting given the 24-hour schedule at the institutes. He promoted a view of manhood that relied on submitting to laws, the government, and "authority" in another 1860 speech before the North Carolina Legislature. "The setting up the man's own conscience as superior to his duty of obedience and as superior to his allegiance to Government is a monstrous evil," he explained, "which military schools can in a great measure correct."[37] Cadets internalized military discipline and submission (to regulations and, Hill implies, hopefully to the state); at the same time, they kept the southern man's demand for and their youthful desire for independence.

Even as they retained adolescent desires to leave their semidependent status behind and assume an independent male prerogative, cadets began to balance independence and submission. Cadets, dreaming of independence, named their role models as southern politicians and military leaders. For example, a Citadel graduate speaking before the alumni association on "The Profession of Arms" named Generals George Washington, Winfield Scott, and Andrew Jackson as his role models. Jackson, he felt, was a "true man" because he was "independent, fearless, self-willed," and self-educated. Other archetypes commonly listed were John C. Calhoun, Henry Clay, Patrick Henry, Thomas Jefferson, and James Madison. Cadets appreciated these prominent men for their patriotism, autonomy, energy, and (as sectional tensions intensified), their southernness. Occasionally, Napoleon received credit as a republican and military

---

[37] D. H. Hill, *Essay on Military Education* (Charlotte: Daily Bulletin Office, 1860), 9 (first quotation); Hill, "Remarks of Major D. H. Hill, of the N. C. Military Institute at Charlotte, Before the Committee on Education of the NC Legislature" (n.p., [1860]) (second quotation).

genius.[38] Those who ranked high on the cadets' lists projected precisely what the cadets wanted for themselves: education, independence, social influence, integrity, military competence, and professional success.

Ironically, their autonomy allowed them to *choose* to submit. The central tenet of military discipline necessitated submission to duty and authority. The key to maintaining these rigorous ideals lay in cadets' self-regulation. In general, when institutions or cadets listed the traits that they considered beneficial, they focused on self-control and desired a definition of manhood based on self-restraint. The ideal fit nicely with the military disciplinary system, which regulated every aspect and hour of their lives. The cadets' own ideals dovetailed with Hill's combination of submission and independence as central to manliness. In choosing self-discipline and submission, cadets identified more with the restrained model of manhood that filtered into the Old South and flourished among the northern middle class.

For example, manhood at military schools reflected a religious context that encouraged self-discipline. Christianity played a significant role in the lives of many nineteenth-century southerners, including cadets. Evangelical denominations, especially Methodists and Baptists, increased membership throughout the South after 1800. They influenced southern manhood, and many southern schools saw increases in evangelicalism and religiosity.[39] The evangelicalism of the antebellum era filtered into the South and, in that way, encouraged some national traits. Historian Christine Leigh Heyrman interestingly argues that early nineteenth-century

---

[38] Thomas, *On the Profession of Arms*, 16 (quotation). *Nashville Union and American*, 2, also promoted Andrew Jackson as a role model. Heriot, *The Polytechnic School*, 19–20; George Rumbough, unpublished "Graduating Speech," 4 July 1856; Joseph Chenoweth to Father, 21 February 1857, VMI Archives; John Hankins to Father and Mother, 1855, Hankins Family Papers, VHS.

[39] Christine Leigh Heyrman, *Southern Cross: The Beginnings of the Bible Belt* (New York: Alfred A. Knopf, 1997), esp. ch. 5; Olsen, *Political Culture and Secession*, 23–24; Carmichael, *Last Generation*, ch. 3; Wyatt-Brown, *Southern Honor*, 146, notes that evangelicals often believed in self-discipline in contradistinction to other southerners. On Methodism's challenges to southern manhood in an earlier period, see Cynthia Lynn Lyerly, *Methodism and the Southern Mind, 1770–1810* (New York: Oxford University Press, 1998). Wagoner, "Honor and Dishonor at Mr. Jefferson's University," 178–9, attributes a decrease in student riots in the 1850s at the University of Virginia to this trend. The writing of the only confirmed Jewish cadets in the sample addressed issues in the same manner as their peers. Albert Moses Luria Papers, North Carolina State Archives; Solomon Jacobs student file, VMI Archives; Miriam G. Moses Cohen Papers, SHC.

evangelical ministers strategically adopted the southern elite ideal of mastery, but did so in a distinct way. Elite men displayed their mastery of everything and everyone around them, whereas evangelicals mastered public display and their own behavior in that sphere. Southern evangelicals maintained their strictures against immoderate behavior – drinking, gambling, adultery – but limited their concern to public presentation of (in)appropriate behavior.[40] In this way, the persistent component of elite manhood – mastery – seeped across religious and class lines. It existed in both rugged *and* restrained models in the Old South. Evangelical middle-class southern men could demonstrate mastery over themselves as self-discipline or self-restraint and thus express a national restrained model with southern traits.

Even as cadets expressed religiosity, they did not necessarily subscribe to evangelical denominations. Military cadets and professors appreciated religiosity, though often as Episcopalians or as Presbyterians rather than as evangelical Methodists and Baptists. Some of the same traits that the evangelicals demonstrated were seen in cadets without the same religion or religious concerns. Although military schools often refused to endorse specific denominations, they stressed moral training and required cadets to attend church. At VMI, the senior class had mandatory Bible recitations on Sundays. Reports of church attendance and Bible recitations assuaged concerns about morality and reflected the cadets' acceptance of self-restraint.[41]

Some young men reconsidered the state of their souls and converted or became born again while at an academy. They desired to be religious men and to behave according to religious tenets. "I am much impressed this day with the sinfulness of the life I am leading, and have resolved to try and improve," one Hillsboro Military Academy cadet wrote. "May

[40] Heyrman, *Southern Cross*, ch. 5.
[41] Some alumni became Baptists after the Civil War, but the existent records make it problematic to determine cadets' antebellum denominational affiliations. John Neff claimed that there were no Episcopalians at VMI in 1855, yet cadets identified themselves as such; Neff to Parents, 14 April 1855, VMI Archives; Philip Winn to John Winn, 14 December 1839, Duke; Order #19, 4 November 1844, *Order Book 1839–1852*; William Green to Capt. Duff Green, 10 September 1843, VMI Archives; Claudius Fike to Parents, 20 April 1862; G. Lafayette Strait to Sallie Strait, 9 January 1853, SCL; 28 April 1858, WMI *Order Book*, Vanderbilt; Virginia Literary, Scientific and Military Academy *Catalogue* (January 1841), AAS. Jabour, "Masculinity and Adolescence in Antebellum America," 401–02.

God give me grace to sustain this resolution."[42] Similarly, soon after his VMI graduation, while teaching at a school with a cadet corps, Robert Gatewood's conversion compelled him to give at least 10 percent of his salary to charity. "May I be just, firm, fearless, yet merciful – acting always in love – prompt and decided in action, and my every action be well weighed before acted," Gatewood prayed in 1851; "this can only be done by following the precepts of the word of God and by Prayer to Him for Guidance."[43] Religion became a guiding principle for some cadets, and its prevalence suggests an environment that fostered religious conviction.

Within the barracks, some cadets apparently felt the impact of that religious environment. A cadet at Kentucky Military Institute (KMI) explained the happy conclusion of the conversion of his roommate:

Last Saturday he purchased a small Testament of Col. M[organ, the superintendent] and sit down to read it and Every time he would come to a place where th [*sic*] Lords name was mentioned he would add a large oath to it. I told him kindly that he was endangering himself in so doing. He concluded to pay attention to some of the verses which he was reading and the happy result was that he was led to see how he was standing before Him who reigns supremely and he would ask me to explain certain portions he could not understand and he shed tears over his past conduct and ask me to forgive all he had ever done to offend me which of course I did with pleasure he is now sitting by me reading in his Testament and I hope is pursuing the right path to Everlasting Happiness.[44]

The roommate went from cursing to reading the Bible under his peer's tutelage. In the spring of 1857, these young Kentuckians learned from each other, rather than by instruction of their superintendent or professors, to put religion into their lives. Their values were shaped as they grew into men.

[42] William Calder, unpublished diary, 31 March [1861], Duke. For cadet diaries and letters on church attendance, see Eugene F. Cordell, unpublished diary, 1859, Duke; Carpenter, diary; Robert Gatewood, unpublished diary; Walter W. Williams, unpublished diary, VMI Archives; Gratz Cohen to Parents, 28 July 1862, SHC; Theodore Fogle to Father and Mother, 16 August 1852, Emory.
[43] Gatewood, diary, 14 April 1850, 30 November 1851 (quotation), VMI Archives.
[44] John Weller to Jacob Weller, n.d. March [1857], Jacob Weller Papers, The Filson Historical Society.

Among many cadets, the next logical step was a rejection of sin, in particular the consumption of alcohol. Students from different military schools, including the four largest military academies – the state academies in Virginia, Georgia, South Carolina, and Tennessee's WMI – founded temperance societies. "All the young men here have joined the Temperance Soc but myself," a WMI cadet wrote to his father, "and they have begged me so much to join that I concented [*sic*]."[45] Indeed, entire classes of cadets pledged to abstain from alcohol. At the Rappahannock Military Institute, Leonard Slater turned in a composition on the perils of drinking, condemning it generally as the "worst of evils" and concluding that it could lead wealthy men to crime. Institutional support must have existed for him to feel comfortable handing in that topic to his professor (who, being a graduate of the Virginia state military school, probably agreed). Administrative approval of temperance efforts also existed at the state military academy in South Carolina. Antialcohol pledges at military schools, recorded from 1848 through 1858, distinctly contrasted to the drinking that remained part of traditional southern manhood. Many cadets rejected college "student debauchery," which historian Daniel Kilbride describes "as an important element of upper-class identity."[46]

The religious and temperance mood at the schools led a few cadets to swear off other negative behaviors including cursing or using tobacco. "I Solemnly [*sic*] pledge my honor as a man and Cadet of the Arsenal Academy Columbia That I will neither swear, smoke tobacco, or use it in any of its forms before the thirteenth day of September 1854," pledged Lafayette Strait. This behavior could have been part of why Wylie saw

---

[45] Joel Scott to Robert Scott, 24 October 1853, WKU. Other cadets supporting temperance included: Philip A. Fitzhugh to Patrick Fitzhugh, 28 December 1844, VMI Archives; Theodore Fogle to Mother, 9 July 1852, Emory; John D. Wylie to Aunt Hannah, 11 June 1852; G. Lafayette Strait to Mother, 16 March 1853, SCL; John Scott to Lucinda Henry, 16 July 1850, Ball Family Papers, VHS; Thomas Hart Law, *Citadel Cadets: The Journal of Cadet Tom Law* (Clinton, SC: PC Press, 1941), 7 June 1857. On temperance, see Burton J. Bledstein, *The Culture of Professionalism: The Middle Class and the Development of Higher Education in America* (New York: W. W. Norton and Company, 1976), 153–55; Rotundo, *American Manhood*, 72; Frank, *Life with Father*, 26, 30.

[46] WMI *Order Book*, 1 November 1848, Vanderbilt; Order #12, 5 September 1857, Order #131, November 1858, *Order Book*, VMI Archives. Because abstinence pledges occurred in the only existent order books, many more cadets at other academies probably made similar pledges. Slater, essay book, 18 December 1850, VHS; G. Lafayette Strait to Mother, 16 March 1853, SCL; Kilbride, "Southern Medical Students in Philadelphia," 723.

him as a man. Similarly, at the state military institute in Virginia, a cadet promised not to use tobacco products until the age of twenty-five.[47] Abstinence from tobacco was less recorded than was temperance, but both preferences reflected evangelical impulses in the South and, more specifically, cadets' tendency to restrained manhood. Self-discipline centered in all these traits suggests that the military school environment encouraged young southerners to adopt some characteristics often identified with middle-class northerners. Cadets internalized self-discipline within southern strains of masculinity but embraced beliefs similar to those across antebellum America.

Professional Values of the National Middle Class

Idealizing self-discipline encouraged military academy men to espouse both hierarchy and submission. Southern non-elite manhood echoed "northern" trends and indicated a growing American middle class. For example, accepting hard work reflected growing changes in southern manhood. Often excoriated by planters as being the lot of slaves, industry became a central tenet of cadets' manhood in the 1850s. The success of military education and the broad interest in many of these ideals indicate that cadets probably had their own system for growing into men in the military environment, but that they reflected the larger trends and developments in the emerging middle class both in the South and across the nation. Their religiosity, temperance, and antitobacco pledges can be seen in the same context. Other traits that cadets valued derived from that principle: industry, fortitude, and frugality.

Parents, students, and teachers agreed that life meant strife and that energy, as part of fighting through life, led to success. "Duty calls," the 1857 Citadel valedictorian told his classmates, by which he meant that young men must now enter the larger world and accept its demands.[48] All antebellum schools, particularly military institutes, taught students to do their duty. In the classroom, many schools used the recitation

---

[47] G. Lafayette Strait, n.d., SCL; Henry Burgwyn to Anna Burgwyn, 14 December 1856, SHC; Burgwyn's inclusion of the age implied that he felt that adult men could use tobacco, and twenty-five must have appeared to the be age of majority to the fifteen year old.

[48] Tennent, "Valedictory before the Calliopean." Similarly, the Hon. Willoughby Newton, *Virginia and The Union* (Richmond: MacFarlane and Fergusson, 1858), 31.

method by which students memorized the textbook and recited it back to the teacher. Good grades depended on accurate recitation, not on creativity. At military schools, nineteenth-century pedagogy prepared a young man for the larger duties of life (whether acting as a citizen soldier or succeeding in a career).

The hard mental and physical work of the military school formed the foundation of the cadets' standards. Their belief in their own labor reflected the widespread drive for industry in antebellum America. Cadets accepted national concerns over inactivity and its consequential temptation and dissipation. Industry was the antidote to idleness, and military schools used discipline and schedules to minimize the opportunity for indolence. After a tour of military institutes, University of Mississippi president F. A. P. Barnard reported to the university's Trustees that the schools used "surveillance" to take away "idleness." Likewise, WMI's 1848 *Catalogue* stated that "idleness . . . [was] regarded as contrary to the rules."[49] One of the reasons for military discipline, then, was to promote industry and in turn morality.

Cadets embraced and echoed the rejection of idleness as they thought about manhood. In his inaugural address as the new debating society president, Philip C. Gibbs instructed his peers: "by your example encourage those who either through modesty or idleness fail to take advantage of the many opportunities here presented to them." He called on the community of cadets to assert their power over members and to demand that all young men avoid idleness. Partially, he wanted to encourage cadets to give speeches at society meetings, and he used the tenets of cadet manhood to urge them to do so. Men must possess honor, uphold their oaths (to the society in his case), and overcome timidity.[50] Gibbs, who entered VMI with state funding after two years as a store clerk, surely embodied this industry and meant what he said about using it to create a productive future.

<hr/>

[49] F. A. P. Barnard, *Report on the Organization of Military Academies* (Jackson: Cooper and Kimball, 1861), 14 (first quotation); also see Hill, *College Discipline. Catalogue . . . of the Western Military Institute*, 22 (second quotation). Increasingly throughout the nineteenth century, self-control helped middle-class northerners to promote their ideals and social reforms. Frank, *Life with Father*, 116; Mary Ryan, *Cradle of the Middle Class: The Family in Oneida County, New York, 1790–1865* (New York: Cambridge University Press, 1981), 161; Bushman, *The Refinement of America*. In the southern context, see Mayfield, "'Soul of a Man,'" esp. 481, 497, 499.

[50] Philip C. Gibbs, unpublished diary, 1 March 1851, VMI Archives.

Young men also saw industry and assertiveness as things they would need to cultivate in their future. As Cadet Slater's Rappahannock essay put it, when too successful and wealthy, citizens faced the problem of idleness.[51] "One cannot be responsible for the deficiencies of nature," a Virginia cadet told his father to explain his problems in math. "Yet it is his duty to improve that with which the Lord has blessed him," the young man continued, "application can never create a talent." He indicated, furthermore, that talent might only bring indolence. This southerner's ideas dovetailed with what historian Anthony Rotundo described as nineteenth-century northern masculinity. Apparently, nationwide middle-class men would assert that "talent mattered less than persistence."[52] Cadets extolled the value and virtue of hard work.

Alongside industry, cadets also pursued fortitude. Members of the Strait and Wylie families demonstrate this trait in a few letters. "The military is truly hard," Cadet Lafayette Strait represented a general boast, "but fortunately I am so constituted as to withstand all of its hardships." His aunt had already explained to him that "I feel confident that you can succeed if you will only persevere – energy and perseverance are two traits of character necessary for a man to succeed and which every person ought to cultivate." Here again, southerners perceived life as strife, and cadets unsurprisingly felt it their duty to "struggle on manfully," as John Wylie wrote, through the hardships that a military education brought.[53] In 1855, a VMI cadet considered the importance of the topic in a poem:

> It's all for improvement, these little things come.
> Endurance the lesson we wish to impress
> So let every kind parent keep babies at home
> And send us stout chaps who can bear the distress.[54]

Exhibiting fortitude as "stout chaps," which included describing the hardships they overcame, demonstrated cadets' status.

[51] The Rappahannock cadet's comments also inherently criticized the wealth of the gentry; Slater, essay book, 11 December 1850, VHS. Other examples of promoting industry are in Edmund Ruffin to Francis H. Smith, 8 February 1851, Charles Ruffin student file; Robert H. Simpson to Francis H. Smith, 24 February 1852, VMI Archives.

[52] Charles Derby to Father, 27 December 1847 (first to third quotations), VMI Archives (emphasis in original). Rotundo, *American Manhood*, 175 (fourth quotation).

[53] G. Lafayette Strait to Catharine Baskins, 15 April 1853 (first quotation); Hannah Wylie to Lafayette Strait, 13 February 1853 (second quotation); John D. Wylie to Aunt, 29 February 1852 (third quotation), SCL.

[54] Shepherd, diary, 1855, VMI Archives.

Indeed, enduring the hard work of military discipline gave young men credit for masculine fortitude. WMI cadet Leeland Hathaway described this feeling in his memoir: "The military instruction and discipline were copied rigidly from that maintained at West Point and went far to giving that physical culture which should always go hand in hand with the training of the mind." He further explained that, "Much of [the] manly part rank and I graduated with good credit in all branches of study."[55] By doing well at a military school, Hathaway thought that he outperformed the best young men. He envisioned his status as higher in the male hierarchy through attention to the traits that he and his cadet peers identified as those important to manliness: duty, industry, fortitude, scientific education, and military conduct.

Alumni employed industry to be "useful" in life. One mother listed the qualities necessary for success, describing a successful man as "an earnest, faithful, intellectual, useful man."[56] This drive for usefulness propelled men of the middle class into military education – with its practical curriculum – and into professions after graduation. Some young men felt that, rather than enter any job, they should attain a worthwhile goal. The alumni and their parents focused on the lifelong process of improving themselves and contributing to the world. Just as their parents sought career and personal improvement when sending their sons to military institutes, the sons continued to seek this in their own lives. In the words of a representative VMI graduate, cadets wanted to "secure some position in which [they] might accomplish something worth attaining." This man turned first to the law and, a decade later, to the Office of Coast Survey as the best way to accomplish that goal. To fulfill a similar definition of success, VMI alumnus Robert Simpson promoted the "thankless" job of teaching. A teacher must instruct his charges in "moral, literary, and intellectual" characteristics, and many alumni felt that such instruction was a worthy lifelong pursuit.[57] Success and manhood defined by these qualities would look much the same in the South or North.

---

[55] Hathaway, memoir, SHC. Hathaway attended both Western Military Institute and Kentucky Military Institute.

[56] Mary Lee to Francis H. Smith, 27 December 1852, William Lee file, VMI Archives.

[57] Daniel Trueheart to Francis H. Smith, 10 July 1859 (first quotation); Robert H. Simpson to Francis H. Smith, 24 February 1852 (second and third quotations), VMI Archives. Simpson believed that the firm discipline at VMI encouraged these values.

The focus on industry and perseverance were integral to the goal of military education; enduring military discipline in and of itself benefited the cadet. "To the man who commences life with the firm determination to succeed in whatever pursuit he may select, the world offers a thousand means of arising to distinction, certainly of acquiring a livelihood," Wylie told Strait. "Let 'I Will' be your motto and by the Eternal Heaven! You cannot fail; you must succeed." The goal of a man's life was a constructive process, entailing duty, energy, and industry. He equated success with first perseverance, second with social distinction, next with religion, and lastly with economic security. Here was how Wylie defined manhood for himself and his cousin Strait. Similarly, a father wrote to his son, "Your determination to try to succeed is the best assurance of your success."[58] It was integrally tied to the values of the restrained model, especially self-discipline, and to necessities of middle-class professional life.

By writing home stressing their industry and fortitude, cadets reassured their parents that they imbibed good moral characteristics. Many also described themselves as frugal, a consequence partially of the academies' regulations restricting money usage. Their parents certainly approved of frugality as a reflection of self-discipline against extravagance and a value directly related to the cadets' middle social position. Few cadets enjoyed either a great deal of spending money or access to unlimited resources. Lafayette Strait poked fun at the poor but also at the limits of his resources (after complaints by the family): "I believe I will act like a poor boy [and] not have anything to do with" a ball that cadets hoped to throw.[59] Frugality, same as the other traits that cadets advanced, illustrated self-discipline's central position in the emerging middle-class southerners' manhood.

Part of success, connected to the importance of striving and persevering in life, was entering a professional career. Parents across antebellum America connected manhood to profession, in the same way that parental

---

[58] John D. Wylie to Lafayette Strait, 24 August 1854 (first and second quotations); F. Grimke to Montague Grimke, 10 February 1850 (third quotation), SCL.

[59] Lafayette Strait to Sister, 10 March, [1853], SCL. Also, see Mary Lee to Francis H. Smith, 4 December 1852, William Lee student file; R. D. Powell to Francis H. Smith, 16 August 1845, Augustus Powell student file, VMI Archives; Francis H. Smith to John Winn, 29 February 1840; John Winn to Philip Winn, 16 November 1840, Duke; Frederick Bryan to Mother, 25 February 1861, John Heritage Bryan Papers, North Carolina State Archives; Joel Scott to Robert Scott, 24 October 1853, WKU.

concerns about their sons' future cut across regional and class boundaries. Social position, however, created different goals for those futures and different focuses for those concerns. As one scholar explains, "the idea that what a man did in his working life was an authentic expression of his individuality was one of the most characteristic – and enduring – features of middle-class masculinity."[60] Occupation was a central definitional characteristic of social class and encouraged different traits; as members of the emerging southern middle class entered professional careers, they made the transition to manhood and interpreted that position and those values as manhood. Middle-class southerners sought professional success rather than plantations and focused on self-sufficiency rather than the appearance of it; they entered careers at young ages, could not afford European tours, and did not receive monetary support as elite young men. Beyond hierarchy, submission, self-discipline, and military display, the cadets' transition to adulthood entailed "taking upon ourselves the responsibilities of manhood," as a valedictorian at the Citadel put it. Near the age of twenty-one, apprentices typically came into their own, and society recognized them as men. At the same age, most military graduates entered manhood through the start of a career. "The very beginning of your days of manhood," an uncle described Micah Jenkins, a recent Citadel graduate.[61]

"You know Bro, that you wanted me to make a man of myself which by the help of Divine Providence I intend to do," declared John Weller at KMI in 1857. "No difference what I make of myself just so I have an education placed upon a sound basis that is all I want at present when I

---

[60] John Tosh quoted in Augst, *Clerk's Tale*, 270 n. 8. He was referring to Great Britain, but his analysis is applicable to the northern middle class and the professional strain of the southern middle class. The centrality of occupation, however, was not exclusive to the emerging middle class because planting clearly defined the elite. On career as the transition to manhood, see Kett, *Rites of Passage*; Rotundo, *American Manhood*; and Glover, *Southern Sons*, 149–55.

[61] George G. Wells, unpublished "Valedictory Addresses Delivered by Cadet G. G. Wells," 1862 (first quotation), CIT. This graduate wrote during the Civil War, when most of his graduating class would literally be asserting their manhood by marching off to war. Joseph Jenkins to Micah Jenkins, [1856] (second quotation), SCL. Ages based on Frank, *Life with Father*, 13. Joseph Kett suggests that middle-class or upwardly mobile youth entered manhood when they broke into their professions. Southern men started working in their professions earlier than in other regions; for example, 72 percent of southern doctors started practicing before they were twenty-five (compared to 59 percent for the entire United States), and most lawyers started in their early twenties; Kett, *Rites of Passage*, 35. Rotundo, *American Manhood*, 70.

have grown older I will better able to choose for myself a profession."[62] Education figured as the basis for development into a man, aided by religion and career. The shift to manhood was marked by the move from the physicality of boyhood to the career and intellectual status by which men judged each other. Their adulthood as men entailed a professional role and position. The responsibilities that middle-class men had in adulthood mirrored the duties of cadet life, necessitating the values, including subordination to authority, that they had found in military education.

Not only should the alumni's career exhibit worthwhile values, their success was aided by putting effort into their work. Some parents even felt, for example, that their sons should leave school if they were not doing well, so that the young men might perform adequately at something – if not at school, then at a career. One man specifically suggested that his son should go into "some business at which he might possibly succede [sic]." Advice for other cadets could be even more direct. In 1854, a speaker at VMI told them, "You must seek other roads to wealth and fame than in the walks of overcrowded professions, or along the precarious and slippery paths of politics."[63] Part of this advice sanctioned success through monetary gain, but another part of it called for accomplishing something of value in life. The conclusion of a speaker at a North Carolina military school emphasized the corollary idea of doing good work: "What you do, do well! If you a farmer be a good one. If you are a lawyer be a good one. If you are a physician be a good one. If you are a mechanic be a good one. . . . Unless you are active and persevering you may reach the goal of your ambition too late. To be successful you must be well informed. To be well informed you must read, read, read and observe. Be good and kind, love your mothers, and when you get old enough love the girls."[64] As this speaker suggested, the cadets believed education would help them advance and felt that it would help them reach success. Success,

[62] John Weller to Jacob Weller, May 1857, Jacob Weller Papers, The Filson Historical Society.
[63] Daniel R. Flowerree to Francis H. Smith, 7 January 1855 (first quotation), VMI Archives. Benjamin Johnson Barbour, *Address Delivered Before the Literary Societies of the Virginia Military Institute at Lexington* (Richmond: MacFarlane and Fergusson, 1854), 12 (second quotation).
[64] "Lecture delivered before the Henderson Military and Female Institute," unpublished speech, 25 November 1859, Duke.

as they defined it, was making your best effort, being good at what you did, and was not necessarily dependent on a particular profession; it did entail a profession, however. It also appeared to involve that traditional southern quality of community involvement, as in being a good son and beau. These men were both southerners and members of the emerging middle class.

Conclusion

Of course, the analysis of cadets must take their adolescence into account. When at the academies, boys slowly transitioned into young men, in an era when no strict boundaries between adolescence and manhood existed. These ideas structured their growth as men, but their notions could change when they left school and entered their full independence. While at school, they learned how to balance their drive for independence with submission. Some of the balance represented youth and occurs in youth throughout America even today. They were not fully independent and had to submit, but learned submission appears to have continued into their majority in the forms of accepting their standards of hierarchy and of self-discipline. Their beliefs would be finally embodied in the selection of a profession.

Young men in the 1840s and 1850s worked out the meanings of manhood in a time of changing gender definitions. Cadets modified the hierarchy and honor that southern elites expounded to include the values of evangelicalism, self-discipline, submission, and primarily, military education. Military schools demanded that southern non-elite cadets espouse submission in their lives, and the cadets responded positively. Cadets balanced submission with the impulse of independence, claiming to assert autonomy by internalizing deference. In conjunction with this balance, they adopted the ideal of self-discipline in the forms of industry, fortitude, frugality, religiosity, and temperance. This self-discipline connected them to both southern and national middle-class trends. The developing southern middle class developed ideals separate from the master class in the late antebellum years, a decade or so after the northern middle class, so it is in these cultural ways that the emerging group began to form a class in the Old South, separate from traditional Marxist productionist terms.

As they defined manhood within the military school, they negotiated countervailing forces. The self-regulated manhood that they assumed was both predicated on and reflective of their integration of the military school environment, national values, and southern culture. The emerging southern middle-class ideal of manhood mostly represented a restrained model, as scholars have described in the northern context, which encompassed self-discipline, religiosity, temperance, industry, fortitude, and professional values. It also incorporated aspects of the rugged model, specifically as displayed in the southern elite with hierarchy, mastery (if only over the self), and honor. Finally, the emerging middle class began to express a view of manhood that incorporated these traits into nonclassical education, military bearing, and submission. Military education, then, developed the appropriate self-discipline for career-minded non-elite cadets, the majority of whom went on to work as teachers, lawyers, and doctors before the Civil War.

5

"Practical progress is the watchword"
Military Education Curriculum

"Now practical progress is the watchword. Engineers, Railroads, Surveyors, Inventors &c have succeeded," Virginia Military Institute (VMI) alumnus Robert H. Simpson wrote as he decided to become an engineer. "Great has been the progress of railroads[,] telegraphs &c within the last five years but incredibly great it will be in the next ten."[1] Simpson's point was, of course, that his education had prepared him to succeed in this expansion of "practical progress." The rhetoric of practical education and progress praised military higher schools' encouragement of science and vocations and indicates the social significance of the institutions. Furthermore, both words demonstrate two aspects of military schools that combined to benefit the emerging southern middle class: increases in scientific curricula and vocational education. The combination of these characteristics joined with state military institute funding systems to expand educational opportunity for the developing group in a manner similar to what occurred in the North.

Military education, contrary to its usual portrayal as one facet of a conservative Old South, in fact challenges the notion that southerners were unsuccessful with education and disapproved of science. Instead, these institutions both increased white southerners' access to formal schooling and mirrored northern educational reforms on a smaller scale. Before the Civil War broke out, private and state military schools promoted what they called a practical curriculum, centered on science and on vocational training in engineering and teaching. This program particularly benefited

---

[1] Robert H. Simpson to Francis H. Smith, 12 December 1853, Preston Library, The Virginia Military Institute Archives (hereafter VMI Archives).

the emerging middle class in the Old South because it facilitated careers for young men without landed connections. Military school curricula and state funding at the largest institutions reflected that constituency, as the institutes themselves acknowledged. The schools' encouragement of science and vocations thus dovetailed with a broader (and usually seen as northern) nineteenth-century interest in practical education and progress. Conjoined, the practical curriculum and interest in progress benefited non-elite young men, who saw in the combination a path for their futures. Enrollment in military institutes, then, expanded the opportunity for advanced education to middle-class southerners.

"Practical" and "progress" were words endlessly repeated by people connected with military schools. Both expressions highlight important values for military education and their middle-class constituents: science and professions. "Practical," according to Webster's 1828 dictionary, was something "that may be used in practice; that may be applied to use; as *practical* knowledge . . . [or that was] derived from practice or experience; as *practical* skill or knowledge." Thus, a practical education was first of all connected to science – that which was derived from experience – and, second, was able to be directly applied to a career – that which can be used in practice. Similarly, military school men imbued the word "progress" with two meanings, both more precise than the 1828 definition of an "advance in knowledge [or] intellectual or moral improvement."[2] The first part of their definition detailed progress as the scientific and social advances that frequently occurred in the period. Military institutions actively participated in this progress by educating a different segment of the white population than classical schools and by focusing on scientific inquiry.[3] The second part of the young men's definition of progress was with regard to their personal careers. Specifically, alumni and educators blended the facets of practical progress and posited that the benefits of practical education accrued in professional careers. Both meanings of the words permeated military education, because the

---

[2] Noah Webster, *An American Dictionary of the English Language* (1828; reprint, New York: Johnson Reprint Corporation, 1970) (italics in original).

[3] This idea was clearly presented in William Henry Trescot, *The Annual Address Before the Calliopean and Polytechnic Societies of the Citadel Academy, Charleston SC* (Charleston: Walker and Evans, 1856), 11–15.

schools' curriculum focused on the sciences and on the vocational advantages of scientific fields.

This chapter explores the final distinctive characteristic of military schools – their nonclassical curriculum – and their expansion of educational opportunity to include non-elite southerners as part of national educational development.[4] It then discusses the practical progress vision: Military education fulfilled that vision in science and vocations. The practical curriculum directed middle-class cadets into professional occupations, especially those of a scientific nature.

Practical Education and Antebellum Curriculum

Military school curriculum helped increase non-elite youths' access to higher schooling because it was what nineteenth-century men called "practical." Many schools that were founded in the antebellum years promoted curricula connected to careers and usefulness, such as agriculture (thus, manual labor schools in which boys worked a farm as part of school) or science (thus, military academies). These institutions distinguished the practical or useful curriculum, also called an "English" education, from the classical program, and they replaced Greek and Latin with modern languages (English or French). The practical program of military schools concentrated on science (including mathematics) and deemphasized ancient languages, inherently challenging the classical education prevalent in universities and preparatory academies.

Specifically, southern military schools clearly fit into descriptions of increasing antebellum science education that historians have identified in the North. Because military institutions were higher schools – offering collegiate education according to some and secondary education to others – they dovetail with the conclusions of a new generation of scholars who are showing that useful courses came into both college and academy curricula and that science programs started, even in the South.[5]

---

[4] Because identical education reform did not occur nationwide should not blind us to the expansion of access that did occur. As historian Maris Vinovskis states, expansion need not equal reform; Vinovskis, "Quantification and the Analysis of American Antebellum Education," *Journal of Interdisciplinary History*, 13 (Spring 1983), 763.

[5] Kim Tolley, "Science for Ladies, Classics for Gentlemen: A Comparative Analysis of Scientific Subjects in the Curricula of Boys' and Girls' Secondary Schools in the United States, 1794–1850," *History of Education Quarterly*, 36 (Summer 1996), 129–154, and *The Science*

After 1820, the number of scientific textbooks, courses, equipment, and professors grew continually. Though most colleges accepted the necessity of science, many did not fully embrace its study; instead, they tacked science courses on to their classical programs. For example, the University of Nashville required Latin and Greek for entrance, excluded modern languages from the "regular course," and offered lectures on math and chemistry in addition to the classics course. South Carolina College, likewise, maintained a comparable program and discontinued modern languages after 1817.[6] At elite and southern state universities, and some nonmilitary academies, the classics reigned; they only slowly incorporated science, especially mathematics and engineering, into their curricula.[7] Although small colleges and preparatory academies slowly accepted

Education of American Girls (New York: RoutledgeFalmer, 2003); Roger Geiger, ed., *The American College in the Nineteenth Century* (Nashville: Vanderbilt University Press, 2000). Whereas revisionist works question the conclusion of Tewksbury's *The Founding of American Colleges*, only Robert F. Pace's 2004 *Halls of Honor* has considered Coulter's *College Life in the Old South* as a foundation for analysis; Natalie A. Naylor, "The Antebellum College Movement: A Reappraisal of Tewksbury's *Founding of American Colleges and Universities*," *History of Education Quarterly*, 13 (Fall 1973), 261–74; Albert Fishlow, "The American Common School Revival" in *Industrialization: Two Systems*, ed. Henry Rosovsky (New York: John Wiley, 1966); Stanley M. Guralnick, *Science and the Ante-bellum College* (Philadelphia: American Philosophical Society, 1975); Colin B. Burke, *American Collegiate Populations: A Test of the Traditional View* (New York: New York University Press, 1982); Terry S. Reynolds, "The Education of Engineers in America Before the Morrill Act of 1862," *History of Education Quarterly*, 32 (Winter 1992), 459–82; David B. Potts, "Curriculum and Enrollment" in *The American College in the Nineteenth Century*, ed. Roger Geiger (Nashville: Vanderbilt University Press, 2000).

[6] *Annual Announcement of the Law, Literary, and Medical Departments of the University of Nashville* (Nashville: John T. S. Fall, 1854), 9; the following year, the University of Nashville would adopt the practical curriculum when it annexed the Western Military Institute. Michael Sugrue, "South Carolina College; The Education of an Antebellum Elite" (Ph.D. diss., Columbia University, 1992), 33, 38, 60, 210–11; Frederick Rudolph, *The American College and University: A History* (New York: Alfred A. Knopf, 1962), 113–14, and *Curriculum: A History of the American Undergraduate Course of Study Since 1636* (San Francisco: Jossey-Bass Publishers, 1977), 54, 86; Guralnick, *Science and the Ante-bellum College*; Mary Ann James, "Engineering an Environment for Change: Bigelow, Peirce, and Early-Nineteenth Century Practical Education at Harvard," in *Science at Harvard: Historical Perspectives*, ed. Clark A. Elliott and Margaret W. Rossiter (Bethlehem: Lehigh University Press, 1992), 60–61, 70, explains Harvard's slow adoption of a scientific course auxiliary to its standard degree.

[7] Lawrence A. Cremin, *American Education: The National Experience, 1783–1876* (New York: Harper and Row Publishers, 1980), 404–05; Wayne K. Durrill, "The Power of Ancient Words: Classical Teaching and Social Change at South Carolina College, 1804–1860," *Journal of Southern History*, 65 (August 1999), 469–98; Rudolph, *Curriculum*, ch. 3.

science (and never in a consistent fashion), curricular change occurred more successfully in higher schooling, including military academies.

Whereas southern universities appear to have remained primarily the domain of the elite, higher schools allowed the emerging middle class an advanced education. Entry to higher education with classical curriculum required reading knowledge of foundational ancient texts, after years of study in the languages. Thus, most young men entering such colleges had already taken time away from labor to study at the more expensive academies with classical programs. Revisionist historians such as Colin Burke and David Allmendinger have located middle-class or poor youths who were able to use antebellum curricular reforms and other strategies to attend northern colleges; Nancy Beadie and Kim Tolley conclude that higher schooling provided similar opportunities throughout the nation. Specifically, the curricular move away from classics helped this development, as some poorer students could either enroll after working or work during intersessions to earn tuition. No similar study for the South exists, partly because scholarly work on the southern middle class is seriously lacking, and partly because historians have overlooked the role of southern military education.[8]

Educational reformers and cadets praised this practical curriculum and disagreed with many collegiate educators who preferred to retain classical studies. "I know of no place better for obtaining a practical education," a cadet at the Citadel clarified, "not such as obtained by most young men in the South Carolina College." This young man explicitly preferred the curriculum of military institutes to that of the state university. In South Carolina, President James Henley Thornwell represented traditional, elite college educators and absolutely rejected a practical component of education for his university. "It is not [the College's] office

---

[8] Historians still need to analyze small colleges in the Old South to confirm the northern trend that small private schools turned to nonclassical curricula and other ploys to attract students. Military education can be placed within the context of nonclassical higher schools and colleges. Burke, *American Collegiate Populations*; Fishlow, "American Common School Revival"; Allmendinger, *Paupers and Scholars: The Transformation of Student Life in Nineteenth-Century New England* (New York: St. Martin's Press, 1975); *Chartered Schools: Two Hundred Years of Independent Academies in the United States, 1727–1925*, ed. Beadie and Tolley (New York: RoutledgeFalmer, 2002); Robert F. Pace, *Halls of Honor: College Men in the Old South* (Baton Rouge: Louisiana State University Press, 2004), suggests the elite nature of southern universities.

to make planters, mechanics, lawyers, physicians or divines," Thornwell exhorted; "it has nothing directly to do with the uses of knowledge." The president dismissed vocational content in education, because classical studies were unconnected to it. A student at the same university similarly described the classics as "literary luxury."⁹ Southern universities maintained primarily an elite clientele and a focus on classical literary attainments, whereas military schools proffered education useful for those southerners with practical concerns, particularly their own economic mobility.

From the beginning, military schools adopted a science-centered curriculum, the first meaning of the "practical" label. "I do not desire to send my son to the military institute because it is generally considered a good place for managing boys who can be managed no where else," father J. W. Gantt wrote, "but because . . . it is one of the best schools for a boy to obtain a good practical education . . . [focusing on] sciences." Gantt recognized the unique discipline system – dismissing it somewhat defensively – and chose the school for curricular reasons, privileging the practical curricula. The writing of educators, legislators, fathers, and cadets alike are full of descriptions of military schools as sites of practical education. The examples are too numerous to list; *Harper's Monthly*, for instance, praised the "practical and scientific education" at the South Carolina Military Academy (SCMA). Echoing Gantt, another father of a Virginia state military academy graduate expressed a positive view of the curriculum: "I loose [*sic*] no opportunity that offers, to urge our people to sustain the Institution and send their sons on to get a good practical education, pointing to my own son as an example."¹⁰

⁹John D. Wylie to Lafayette Strait, 19 August 1852 (first and second quotations), Papers of the Gaston, Strait, Wylie and Baskin Families, The South Caroliniana Library, University of South Carolina. Sugrue, "South Carolina College," 33 (third and fourth quotations), 214 (fifth quotation). Similarly, Dartmouth College president Nathan Lord stated that collegiate education was not intended for those planning to "engage in mercantile, mechanical or agricultural operations"; Rudolph, *American College and University*, ch. 11, 135. Thomas Jefferson was one of the earliest proponents of a more applied education, though he did not discourage instruction in the classics. Rossiter Taylor, *Ante-bellum South Carolina* (1942; reprint, New York: Da Capo Press, 1970), 115–16; James, "Engineering an Environment for Change," 60–61.
¹⁰J. W. Gantt to Francis H. Smith, 2 June 1848 (first and second quotations), Henry Gantt student file; Peter Steenbergen to Francis H. Smith, 23 November 1851 (fourth quotation), John Steenbergen student file, VMI Archives. "Charleston," *Harper's New Monthly* (n.d.), Citadel File, South Carolina Historical Society, 11 (third quotation). Other uses of the word

Military schools encouraged young men concerned with the application of knowledge and not belles lettres to seek out their institutions.
Kentucky Military Institute (KMI) succinctly described the primary difference between a military school and a college as based on the classical
languages. Regulation number 139 read: "The course of study adopted
and required for graduation, is that usually taught in the best colleges,
except that but one language is required (Latin or French), the time usually occupied by the second being devoted to a more extended course in
Mathematics, Mechanics, Natural Science, English Literature, and Modern Languages." KMI abandoned Greek and allowed French to replace
Latin. A cadet could completely avoid classical languages, even at a school
that offered them. Instead, his program of mathematics, science, and
modern languages focused on sciences and revealed the practical curriculum. Curricula such as these reflected the trends of educational
reformers, whether northern or southern, who disliked or distrusted
classical schooling. These innovators supported military schools and
sought practical emphasis on science.[11]

Duplicating West Point's structure, most military schools' academic
programs were derived from the national academy's curriculum of the
1830s. In fact, the Tennessee legislature specifically instructed the Western
Military Institute to replicate the West Point program. When not duplicating West Point, antebellum military academies looked to VMI, with
the result that all schools exhibited a great deal of consistency in their core
offerings. Cadets spent some time learning about the branches of the military, of course, but military institute curriculum actually stressed mathematics, natural philosophy (modern-day physics), and engineering. In

"practical" in the manner here analyzed include: *Catalogue of the Officers and Students
of the Rappahannock Academy and Military Institute* (Baltimore: John Murphy and Co.,
1851); *Report of the Board of Visitors of the Virginia Military Institute* (n.p., 1854), American
Antiquarian Society (hereafter AAS), 4; *Catalogue of the Officers and Cadets of the Kentucky
Military Institute* (Frankfort: A. G. Hodges and Co., 1848), 6; *Semi-Annual Register, of the
Officers and Cadets, of the Hillsboro' Military Academy* (Raleigh: Jno. W. Syme Printer, 1860);
John W. Brockenbrough, *On Laying the Corner Stone of the New Barracks of the Virginia
Military Institute* (New York: John Wiley, 1850), 7; Theodore Fogle to Father and Mother, 2
July 1852, Theodore F. Fogle Papers, Department of Special Collections, Richard Woodruff
Library, Emory University.

[11] *Regulations of the Kentucky Military Institute* (n.p., [1855]), AAS, 15. Cremin, *American
Education;* Rudolph, *American College and University,* ch. 6, discusses educational reformers
who promoted science.

the West Point model curriculum, sciences and mathematics took up 71 percent of the classroom hours between 1833 and 1861.[12]

Cadets at southern military institutes studied mathematics, French, and English for at least two years. They took a year each of chemistry, natural philosophy, drawing, geology, geography, and engineering. The Georgia Military Institute (GMI) *Regulations*, with a representative curriculum, stipulated the different courses for the various class years: First-year cadets took math, French, English, and geography; second-year, math, French, English, and drawing (drafting); third-year, math, natural philosophy, chemistry, and drawing; and seniors, engineering and architecture, "Evidences of Christianity," rhetoric, "Moral and Mental Science," and infantry and artillery tactics.[13] Schools often focused on the applied aspects of math; KMI cadets started with algebra and geometry in the first year but moved quickly to trigonometry and analytical geometry, combined with "Mensuration [*sic*] and Surveying," obviously useful for surveying careers; they finished with calculus before taking mechanics and construction.[14]

---

[12] Chapter 73, 24 February 1854, Tennessee Legislature, Tennessee State Library and Archives. Furthermore, when West Point went, unsuccessfully, to a five-year program in the 1850s, some private academies considered the change and VMI did it; like the national academy, all eventually rejected it. *Regulations of the Kentucky Military Institute, Six Miles from Frankfort, Kentucky* (Frankfort: A.G. Hodges & Co., 1851), 2. James L. Morrison Jr., "Educating the Civil War General: West Point, 1833–1861," *Military Affairs*, 38 (October 1974), 108.

[13] *Regulations of the Georgia Military Institute, Marietta, Georgia* (n.p., January, 1853), 4. The SCMA and West Point curricula were virtually identical to that of GMI. *Semi-Annual Register . . . the Hillsboro' Military Academy* (1860); *Rules and Regulations of the Western Military Institute at Tyree Springs, Sumner County, TN, and the Official Register of Officers and Cadets for the Collegiate Year 1853–54* (Nashville: John F. Morgan, 1854), 12; University of Nashville, *The Official Register of Officers and Cadets for the Collegiate Year 1854–5, and Rules and Regulations, with Annual Announcement of Faculty and Officers for 1855–6* (Nashville: Cameron and Fall and Book and Job Printers, 1855), 15–16; *Official Register of the Officers and Cadets at the South Carolina Military Academies* (Charleston: J. B. Nixon, 1850), 9; *Official Register of the Officers and Cadets at the South Carolina Military Academies* (Charleston: J. B. Nixon, 1854), 14; *Official Register of the South Carolina Military Academy* (Charleston: R. W. Gibbes, 1860), 20; *Register of the Officers and Cadets of the Virginia Military Institute* (Philadelphia: Crissy and Markley, 1847); *Register of the Officers and Cadets of the Virginia Military Institute* (Philadelphia: Thomas, Cowperthwait and Co., 1852); *Regulations of the Kentucky Military Institute*; Rappahannock, *Catalogue* (1851); *Catalogue, Course of Study, Address to the Patrons, &c. of Williamsburg Military School* (Richmond: Charles A. Wynne, 1853).

[14] *Regulations of the Kentucky Military Institute* (1851), 3.

In a slight variation on GMI's curriculum, VMI required mathematics, French, and Latin for most of a cadet's four-year stay and a year each of chemistry, English, natural philosophy, drawing, geology, geography, and engineering. VMI cadets learned Latin but did not necessarily enter with exposure to it. Every military school had lower admission requirements than did college preparatory academies and universities so that a young man untrained in Latin and Greek could enroll. Entrance examinations at military schools consisted of tests for literacy, basic mathematical skills, physical fitness, and the ability to perform recitations rather than specific content requirements. SCMA regulation Sec. 17, for example, specified that applicants "must be able to read and write with facility."[15]

This practical curriculum provides evidence that educational expansion did occur in the Old South, but in ways slightly different from the northern patterns. Academies or higher schools provided greater enrollment for non-elites, as in the North; military education was one facet of this southern development. More notably, southern educational opportunity proceeded in the private sector (or in private institutions with public assistance, as were state military institutions), unlike northern common schools. Military academies appealed to the emerging southern middle class because the lower classes could neither afford the fees in excess of the state-paid tuition nor could they employ the technique of working between sessions because of the military program's year-round, four-year structure. The military school student body also consisted of a minority of the elite because those young men had access to and valued the classical curriculum that remained prevalent in universities. This form of education thus installed funding and curricular systems that were particularly attractive to members of the developing middle class, especially those seeking careers dependent on technology and professional training.

Practical Progress: Science

The practical program at military schools tied in neatly with the component of progress equated with advancement in science and technology.

---

[15] *Official Register of the South Carolina Military Academy* (1860), 28.

"This age of progress" described the era both for a speaker at Henderson Military and Female Institute in North Carolina and for a speaker who connected the phrase to both the operation and graduates of the Citadel in South Carolina. GMI promoted science in the "age of physical progress."[16] Such similar usages in different states between 1847 and 1860 suggest analogous notions of science among men connected with military institutions. When the Smithsonian Institution requested permission to place meteorological stations on the two SCMA campuses, the state legislature endorsed the plan, because the schools were meant to teach "practical knowledge." The idea that "the military academy is mostly a scientific institution," as said one speaker at SCMA, was clear.[17] The practical curricula and promotion of progress intertwined.

The flourishing of military education in the Old South indicates that, to a significant degree, concern over technological advancement had indeed taken hold in the region. Echoing Robert Simpson's views that opened this chapter, VMI alumnus Daniel Trueheart clearly expressed the appreciation of science and scientific careers. "After I graduated ten years ago, any other than classical attainment commanded but little respect," he wrote to his former superintendent, "but you have doubtless observed a great revolution in public sentiment in this regard especially in Virginia."[18] Trueheart found employment in the Coast Survey, using his scientific training. By the time of his 1859 letter, it was clear that society accepted a more prominent role for science and the benefits of the military schools' practical curricula. Indeed, what this alumnus, his compatriot Simpson, and the continued expansion and success of

[16] S. W. Trotti, *An Address Delivered before the Calliopean and Polytechnic Societies of the State Military Academy, at the Annual Commencement, November 18, 1847* (Charleston: Burges, James and Paxton, 1847), 9; Anonymous, "Lecture delivered before the Henderson Military and Female Institute," 25 November 1859, Rare Books, Manuscript and Special Collections Library, Duke University (hereafter Duke), connected the "age of progress" to alumni's career prospects. *Report by the Board of Visitors of the Georgia Military Institute, To his Excellency, Howell Cobb, Governor of the State of Georgia For 1853* (n.p., 1853), Duke, 13.

[17] Report on "a communication from the Smithsonian Institution in respect to Meteorological observations," South Carolina Legislature Committee on the Military, 1855, South Carolina Department of Archives and History. There is no indication that the plan was implemented. Trotti, *Address Delivered before the Calliopean and Polytechnic Societies of the State Military Academy*, 19.

[18] Daniel Trueheart to Francis H. Smith, 10 July 1859, VMI Archives.

military education suggest is a developing legitimation of nonclassical, noncollegiate education in the higher schools of the Old South.

Similarly, when mentioning progress, military alumni often empha-sized the important role of scientific and technological developments and even the accompanying social improvements they might bring to the South. An alumnus speaker at the state military academy in Vir-ginia felt that progress would bring forth a government of toleration and decentralization. "Progress is development, enlargement, growth," the 1849 graduate explained, "and in due season, with religious, moral and intellectual power incident to a healthy progress our material pros-perity will move safely forward." Another lecturer at the Citadel in the same year made a similar observation that military institutions sup-ported the "bloodless revolution" of abolishing property qualifications for voting by educating those without property and with less wealth than the elite.[19] Behind these views was an ideology of progress toward modernity, though still inconsistent and dependent on the individual. These military school speakers felt that the South was integrally involved in the movement toward modernity and that military academies were advancing progress as they democratized education.

This view of progress connected to the northern trends of the period, including the nineteenth-century educational concern with morality. Indeed, cadets and professors thought that the scientific advancements stemming from practical education should be directed by faith. "The pur-suit of Science, next to that of Religion," an SCMA speaker declared, "is

---

[19] James W. Massie, *An Address Delivered Before the Society of Alumni of the Virginia Military Institute* (Richmond: MacFarlane and Fergusson, 1857), 34 (first and second quotations), 52; James D. Tradewell, *Address on the Study of the Federal Constitution Delivered Before the Polytechnic and Calliopean Societies of the Citadel Academy* (Charleston: Walker, Evans and Co., 1857), 32 (third quotation). South Carolina was one of the last states to allow universal manhood suffrage, and within this context, these institutions could portray themselves as bringing progress to politically laggard states. A similar example from Virginia was expressed in Brockenbrough, *Corner Stone*, 16. Durrill, "Power of Ancient Words," connects curricular change to modernism. The constituency of military schools primarily remained below the planter elite and appears to have embraced democratization as an opportunity available to their group. On progress also see Laylon W. Jordan, "Schemes of Usefulness," and Jane H. Pease and William H. Pease, "Intellectual Life in the 1830s" in *Intellectual Life in Antebellum Charleston*, ed. Michael O'Brien and David Moltke-Hansen (Knoxville: University of Tennessee Press, 1986), 211–29, 233–45; Dan R. Frost, *Thinking Confederates: Academia and the Idea of Progress in the New South* (Knoxville: University of Tennessee Press, 2000); Rudolph, *Curriculum*, 54.

the highest and most godlike occupation in which man can engage." Military schools believed so strongly in progress and science that they placed their propagation, according to this speaker, second only to religion. "Knowledge is only truly useful when it produces in [a man] a supreme love of Almighty God and perfect Charity to his fellows," a VMI alumnus similarly recorded.[20] Given the prevalence of religious views, this connection is unsurprising. Thus, military institutions offered valuable education with progress and modernization without forsaking morality and faith.

Middle-class men were among the southerners most interested in technology and industry. Recent studies have clearly shown that they were not solely responsible for that development. Planters, such as David Hubbard, invested capital and hoped to establish factories or railroads. Southern lack of success is obvious in comparison to northern manufacturing. As scholars have recently asserted, however, the Old South experienced great growth in industry in this period. Such development encouraged military education with its practical curriculum and vocations.[21]

Practical Progress: Vocations

Certainly the practical progress of military education centered on science, but it also reflected the vocational nature of the schools. Unlike college professors and administrators, military educators felt that a cadet should use his labor profitably and not waste effort on mastering Greek or Latin. "The Dead Languages are rejected under this system, furthermore, because, in view of practical life," the Citadel superintendent declared, "the time and labor bestowed upon them is incommensurate with the results which they accomplish." The "results" of classical studies would not benefit the practical, career-based life of the cadets.

---

[20] Edwin Heriot, *The Polytechnic School, the Best System of Practical Education* (Charleston: Walker and James, 1850), 20 (first and second quotations). Robert Gatewood, unpublished diary (third quotation), VMI Archives.

[21] Robert J. Norrell, *A Promising Field: Engineering at Alabama, 1837–1987* (Tuscaloosa: University of Alabama Press, 1990), 9–10; Geiger, *American College in the Nineteenth Century*; Eugene Genovese, *The Slaveholders' Dilemma* (Columbia: University of South Carolina Press, 1992). Drew Gilpin Faust's *A Sacred Circle* (Baltimore: The Johns Hopkins University Press, 1977) asserts the lack of widespread support for intellectual pursuits but does not significantly pursue the issue of science education. See, for example, the work of Jonathan Daniel Wells, Susanna Delfino, Tom Downey, and Chad Morgan.

Just as this administrator criticized the classics, a father told his son's superintendent, "[My son] has spent most of his time among the dead languages, and I leave it wholly to you to prepare him in the best way you can to move on among the living." Pointing to the goals of practical education, Edwin Heriot, in a speech at the Citadel, promoted "the practical affairs of life," which derived from "a thorough education, and habits of regularity" acquired through the combined curriculum and discipline of the military school; these "qualifications [are] indispensable to success," he argued, "in any calling in life which [a cadet] may engage."[22] Echoing Heriot a full ten years later, North Carolina Military Institute (NCMI) founder D. H. Hill wrote that military education was superior to other pedagogies because the traits it produced translated into alumni success in postgraduate life. The state military institute in Georgia encouragingly concluded that graduates of VMI were *"practical men."*[23] Certainly, all education promoted beneficial traits, but in particular, military training promoted something that contemporaries noted specifically as practical and, hence, as preparation for a career.

Moreover, cadets often considered progress as playing a role in the development of their own futures. Here, the meanings of "practical" and "progress" come together to illustrate the cadets' middle-class status because both terms promised careers for young men who needed them. Because most students would not inherit plantations (or even farms), cadets needed professional occupations. "In your journey through life, let *Progress* be your constant and unchangeable watch-word," a speaker told the Citadel cadets. Given the curriculum, student-run literary societies unsurprisingly used the term and connected it to the promise of their future careers. "'Progress' is our motto – you will find it inscribed on the badges of the Society," Citadel senior Richard Y. Dwight told an entirely different group of young men. "Write it in your minds and let it ever prompt you to push forward to the prize of your high calling." Dwight

---

[22] Quotations, in order, from: F. W. Capers, *State Military Academies* (Charleston: Tenhet and Corley, 1846), 21; Dean Paul Baker, "The Partridge Connection: Alden Partridge and Southern Military Education" (Ph.D. diss., University of North Carolina, 1986), 154; Heriot, *The Polytechnic School*, 11.

[23] D. H. Hill, *Essay on Military Education, delivered at Wilmington NC, November 14, 1860 Before the State Educational Convention* (Charlotte: Daily Bulletin Office, 1860). *Report by the Board of Visitors of the Georgia Military Institute*, 14 (quotation, italics in original).

perpetuated the idea that what young men learned at military schools would help them launch and develop their careers. Cadets thus directly translated learning science in school to the (career) profit it accrued. "The true course of every graduate of the Institute is to pursue the distinctive character of his education," alumnus Trueheart told his former professor; "you can and ought to turn out the best scientific men of the country."[24]

In 1852 and 1853, GMI made it clear that progress included science curriculum for vocational results. The Board of Visitors explained GMI's pool of matriculates: "It must be evident that a large number of our citizens does not design to have their sons enter one of the learned professions. They are able and anxious to educate them; but when educated they expect them to become businessmen, engineers, architects, manufacturers, merchants, planters, &c; To qualify young men for these avocations, in this 'age of physical progress,' a thorough scientific education is obviously the best." GMI intended not to produce college-educated men but to bring employment to men who found that attractive or necessary. The list emphasized white-collar occupations (possibly including planting to avoid alienating any elite matriculates). The exclusion of the learned occupations was by no means universal; even at the same school, speakers alternately promoted and disparaged the professions, particularly law and medicine.[25] This tension, in part, comes from the competing pedagogies of classicists and reformers. The nonclassical and scientific curriculum specifically recommended careers as opposed to South Carolina College and other universities' rejection of vocational training.

Citadel cadets must have been gratified to hear that South Carolina "does want men who, with liberal educations, can undertake the great industrial enterprises which are needed . . . able engineers[,] machinists," and geologists. This speaker contrasted the benefits of practical education to those of "Commerce and the learned professions [that] furnish remunerative employment to but a limited number, and even these, as a general rule, require an advance of capital, or a long and expensive education."

---

[24] Quotations, in order, from: Heriot, *The Polytechnic School*, 22 (italics in original); Richard Yeardon Dwight, "The Noblest Aim of the Student," unpublished speech, 4 July 1856, CIT; Daniel Trueheart to Francis H. Smith, 10 July 1859, VMI Archives.

[25] *Report by the Board of Visitors of the Georgia Military Institute*, 13. Capers, *State Military Academies*, 21.

Three years later in North Carolina, a military educator explained that the state "has now an opportunity afforded her to imitate the example of Virginia and train up a corps of Architects, Surveyors, Engineers, Chemists, Geologists, &c., on the cheapest possible plan." Military institute gradutes eschewed "the crowded professions of Law and Medicine, [and instead] engaged in those duties most needed in the South and the best calculated to promote her interests."[26] Simpson's similar list of careers that opened this chapter reflected the same desires in Virginia. Overall, military schools conceived of their students as men with future "avocations" that would require not the classics but the advantages of scientific knowledge.

Military higher schools' practical curriculum included French, which, as the contemporary language of engineering, reflected the educators' and many cadets' hope for graduates to build engineering careers. Indeed, private and state military academies complemented the nation's main engineering schools, West Point and Rensselaer Polytechnic Institute in New York. GMI made a direct explanation for using the same curriculum as Sylvanus Thayer developed at West Point: "The National Academy, after furnishing the army with officers, can no longer supply the demand for practical scientific men."[27] Whereas West Point trained engineers who had to serve in the U.S. Army, military institutions like GMI promoted civil engineering with the same scientific education as at West Point.

The continued viability and success of southern military academies between 1839 and 1860 demonstrate their significance in the southern promotion of progress and science in the antebellum period. Engineering programs were rare nationwide; as a major site of engineering education, military schools merit more historiographic attention.[28] Until

---

[26] Trescot, *Address*, 17 (first quotation), 12 (second quotation); Hill, "Remarks of Major D. H. Hill, of the N. C. Military Institute at Charlotte, Before the Committee on Education of the North Carolina Legislature" (n.p., [1860]) (third and fourth quotations).

[27] *Report by the Board of Visitors of the Georgia Military Institute*, 13. Rudolph, *Curriculum*, 62, explains that science found its best position in new schools. The connection between West Pointers and engineering is often discussed; e.g., James R. Endler, *Other Leaders, Other Heroes: West Point's Legacy to America Beyond the Field of Battle* (Westport, CT: Praeger, 1998).

[28] Terry Reynolds notes military schools as the first in a pattern of practical, engineering schools but presents neither the breadth of the movement nor its southern focus; Reynolds, "Education of Engineers," 470–71.

the mid-1830s, West Point remained the nation's first and premier engineering school; Rensselaer Polytechnic Institute officially commenced its engineering curriculum in 1835 and its polytechnic designation in 1850 and became the second engineering school for the nation. In the early 1830s, the state universities in Alabama and Virginia joined a few northern private colleges in creating engineering programs or schools. These programs failed in the years following the Panic of 1837, however, when even Rensselaer dropped to fewer than ten students in 1845. During this difficult period, VMI and other military higher schools with engineering in their curricula started to open; in 1845, VMI admitted thirty new cadets. After 1839, then, military schools offered one of the few sustained programs for engineering training in the antebellum nation. Overall, just less than 10 percent of all antebellum military academy matriculates and 14 percent of the graduates became engineers. As a historian of engineering education at the University of Virginia stated, "VMI educated career engineers."[29]

As a result of such educational priorities, southern military education successfully led non-elite alumni into "practical professions," as described by a speaker at the Virginia state academy. In addition to the alumni who entered engineering, military schools funneled 19 percent of their alumni into law, 17 percent into medicine (including dentistry, reflecting the moderate status of antebellum doctors), and nearly 30 percent into teaching. In fact, sixty-two alumni in the sample were recorded as working for railroads, both before and after the Civil War. This tendency reflected an increase from the small number of southern cadets' fathers, brothers, or grandfathers (only ten with recorded connections) who were associated with railroads in the antebellum years. A small number of alumni also worked as surveyors, an occupation for which they had also been educated.[30]

[29] Norrell, *Promising Field*, 20; O. Allan Gianniny Jr., "The Overlooked Southern Approach to Engineering Education: One and a Half Centuries at the University of Virginia, 1836–1986" in *Proceedings of the 150th Anniversary Symposium on Technology and Society* (Tuscaloosa: University of Alabama, 1988), 157 (quotation); James Gregory McGivern, *First Hundred Years of Engineering Education in the United States (1807–1907)* (Spokane: Gonzaga University Press, 1960); Guralnick, *Science and the Ante-bellum College*; Reynolds, "Education of Engineers," 466; James, "Engineering an Environment for Change."
[30] Thirteen members of the sample and no fathers of alumni were recorded as having been surveyors.

Even in nontechnical careers, military alumni could use their practical education to their advantage. Alumni teachers could specialize in math, science, and military science, as their education focused on these practical subjects. They had more preparation than college students did. Thirty-five percent of alumni teachers worked in a scientific field or at a military program; this percentage may actually have been higher because many men did not record the specific subjects they taught. Whatever the field, alumni found professional careers that paid sufficiently well in the antebellum South.[31]

Young men knew the vocational nature of military schools, and some left the institutions when they were uninterested in those career benefits. Timothy Thorp, for example, explained that the $600 he would spend at VMI over four years could be better invested for his future as he did not want to become an engineer. During his first year in 1841, this orphan resigned and eventually became a doctor. Other cadets expressed their interest in agriculture and therefore felt a practical education unnecessary.[32] Military education held men focused on the scientific vocations of its practical progress.

Practical Progress: Educating the Emerging Middle Class

Military educators and speakers espoused the expansion of schooling for young men needing careers – members of the emerging southern middle class. Heriot's 1850 speech at the Citadel on "The Best System of Practical Education" extolled SCMA as a place to educate "the mass, – the working classes, – the more exclusively industrial portion of the people." He further praised the military education that SCMA professors had received at the Kentucky and Mississippi Military Institutes. He used a class-based argument to compliment the practical and progressive education that military programs offered. Continuing a conscious acknowledgement of class and the practical skills required by its students,

---

[31] Lawrence Massillion Keitt, *Address Before the Two Literary Societies of the Virginia Military Institute* (Richmond: MacFarlane and Fergusson, 1856), 17 (quotation). For example, Charles Derby to Francis H. Smith, 9 May 1855, and T. F. Johnson to Francis H. Smith, 11 February 1851, VMI Archives.

[32] Timothy Thorp to Francis H. Smith, 28 March 1841; William Meredith to Francis H. Smith, David Meredith student file, 6 June 1844, VMI Archives.

the charter of Jefferson College in Mississippi declared that its military component led to the "acquisition of scientific and practical knowledge, which had recommended it to the *mass* of the community."[33] In a variety of ways, people connected with military schools advocated the advances of practical education for the Old South's emerging middle class.

Administrators would alternately stress that the cream of society attended (in an effort to entice elite enrollment) or that they sponsored the indigent (in order to appear philanthropic). While addressing their constituents, school administrators might present their young charges as the aristocracy of southern society. For example, in an article endorsing the Western Military Institute, *Gleason's Pictorial Drawing-Room Companion* declared that the sons of prominent men and Revolutionary veterans attended the school.[34] At the other extreme, in applications to the legislatures for funding, state military institutes clearly declared that they provided the only educational opportunity for poor students, and this was what legislators wanted to hear. The North Carolina legislature specified that only a cadet "who is unable to obtain an education in any other way" could receive tuition remission. Georgia, likewise, stipulated that any state cadet who was found to have "pecuniary means [that] are sufficient to defray his own expenses" would lose his eligibility for tuition payments from the state.[35] Although the term "indigent" was used, it was most likely an exaggeration. VMI accepted a significant number of orphans, but the poor probably could not have afforded the expenses even with a scholarship.

Most often, and most accurately, school administrators located their enrollment in the developing middle class, and the scientific curricula combined with increased public funding meant that state and private military institutions offered educational opportunity for young men with

[33] Heriot, *The Polytechnic School*, 5 (quotation). *The Charter and Statutes of Jefferson College* (Natchez: Book and Job Office, 1840), 89 (italics in original).
[34] For specific use of the term "indigent," see John P. Thomas, "Origin of the State Military Academies," *Russell's Magazine* (December 1858), 7; Brockenbrough, *Corner Stone*, 6–7; "Military Institute," *Gleason's Pictorial Drawing-Room Companion*, 4 (1 January 1853), 16. Only 12 percent of cadets had relatives who are documented as having served in the Revolutionary war.
[35] House Document 32, 8 December 1854 (first quotation), North Carolina Legislature, North Carolina State Archives; Act Number 3, 21 January 1852 (second quotation), Georgia Legislature, Georgia Archives.

limited wealth. Practical education meant that a cadet did not have to pay for the tutoring in classical languages that would have otherwise been necessary, that his family did not lose his labor during such preparation, that he could afford the expenses, and that he would be trained for a career, especially in teaching or engineering. Thus, men with fewer resources and more interest in professional occupations could employ southern military schools to start themselves in careers. Progress and career were thus the significant outcomes of the practical education.

In *College Reform*, VMI superintendent Francis H. Smith, the most prominent southern military educator in the antebellum years, described the advantage of the military system as having funding that allowed non-elite young men to attain secondary education and enter careers. Requiring a vocation excluded the elite; southern planters inherited land and slaves sufficient for their livelihoods (or enough cash and connections to obviate practical education). Three years later, in an 1854 report on VMI's enrollment, Smith made overt correlations between the middle-rank students and the curriculum's emphasis on career placement: "The large number of cadets admitted from among those who were not blessed with much of this world's goods, at once suggested to the authorities of this institute, that when these should graduate, they must be prepared for the active calls of life; and hence drawing, civil engineering and other practical branches were introduced."[36] As the other sources indicated, the "mass" of people required careers.

At the NCMI, Superintendent D. H. Hill identified his constituency as "the poor" but connected them to industry and entrepreneurship. "Since our school is essentially a school of science, intended for the fostering and cultivation of the mechanic arts, it becomes a matter of the highest importance that we should have the sons of the poor." Hill described those youths as possessing "the mechanical talent more fully developed than the more favored classes" because the poor were required to use tools for their livelihood. "We may reasonably hope our school to be the nursery of [industrialists:] Arkwrights, Fultons, Whitneys, &c.," he continued, emphasizing science and technology occupations for his students

[36] Francis H. Smith, *College Reform* (Philadelphia: Thomas, Cowperthwait and Co., 1851). *Report of the Board of Visitors of the VMI* (1854), 42.

(and excluding the scientifically minded agriculturalist).[37] Hill's "poor" was the same group as Smith's "those who were not blessed with much of this world's goods," Heriot's "working classes," and Jefferson College's "mass" (as the poor could not, in reality, have afforded the costs of such schools). In similar ways, military schools reflected the progress of scientific education and of educational opportunity for the middle class.

All these illustrations show that the practical component of the military school curricula directly addressed the cadets' need for careers, what VMI superintendent Smith and others labeled the "active calls of life."[38] KMI, in a similar vein, "offer[ed] rare advantage to those seeking an education eminently scientific and practical . . . adding Book-Keeping for the business man." With these additional course offerings, KMI wanted to assure that its graduates could attain whichever practical occupation they chose. This military school implemented a practical curriculum with courses in both science and business, another developing facet of useful education in the antebellum years. One father explicitly wanted his son to learn to handle money (and not to be "thoughtless" with it) so that "he would be fitted for the active duties of life."[39] Employing nearly identical phrasing the year before his son's superintendent used it, this father illustrates that the call for activity in careers was ubiquitous.

The curriculum, alongside the funding and disciplinary system, of military education created an entrée for middle-class youths into higher schooling throughout the Old South. The institutions used practical progress – science and vocational education – to replicate the national development of science curricula in antebellum academies and colleges. More importantly, the success of military education demonstrates how schooling became available to a larger and more diverse population in the last decades of the Old South. Interest in and demand for practical education grew, as did the middle class throughout the late antebellum

[37] D. H. Hill, "Remarks of Major D. H. Hill, of the N. C. Military Institute at Charlotte."

[38] The same phrase is found in *Catalogue of the Officers and Cadets, Together with the Prospectus and Internal Regulations of The American Literary, Scientific and Military Academy* (Middletown: E and H Clark, 1826), 43.

[39] Kentucky Military Institute broadside (n.p., n.d.) (first quotation), Special Collections, University of Kentucky. At the same time, KMI maintained Greek as a supplementary course for cadets who might aim for a college education. Henry Jones to Francis H. Smith, 26 March 1853 (second quotation), William Jones student file, VMI Archives.

years. The growing number of men in the middle social position and of alumni (especially alumni having their own sons) increased the number of people encouraging curricular reforms and educational expansion. It followed that schools with practical programs increased in each decade.

Focusing on practical education, military schools offered a specific opportunity to men who desired professional occupations. The institutes' practical curricula and career preparation separated them from the classical colleges and preparatory academies that served the southern elite. Young men with less time and fewer resources than were required for classical training entered military schools. With that education, alumni could then find employment in professional careers, especially those connected to scientific pursuits, such as engineering or science education. Middle-class southerners grasped these options, reflecting their view of progress as connected to modern developments, technology, and their own careers. They echoed the educational changes and expansion ongoing in the North but did so in distinctly southern institutions and ways. The practical curriculum promoted progress in the South, preparing young men of the emerging middle class for active, professional lives.

6

Professions and Status
Middle-class Alumni Stability and Mobility

"The next two years will tell a great deal for me and if I don't seize and improve each moment which presents itself to me for improvements I will regret as long as I live and therefore I will make good use my time and try to make a man of myself," Americus Cartwright promised while a student at Kentucky Military Institute (KMI) in 1858. He decided to pursue the practical course and add Latin "if Pa wants me to study Law I will do it [but] I think by that time I will be qualified to take hold of Pa's business which I have always desired." Writing to his elder brother, this young man weighed the law career his father chose for him and the family wholesale and retail merchant business. He worked out these choices at "college," as he dubbed the military school, deciding between the lucrative and professional careers for which his practical education tailored him. This cadet probably considered occupations along the same lines as did his older brother, who became a rancher after also attending KMI.[1]

A young man's choice of occupation was, of course, important for his future. After leaving military schools, alumni pursued the best careers they could. As with any individual decision, some alumni gave preference to their interests, whereas the majority probably sought to fit those interests to either the most prestigious or the most lucrative occupation possible (or the best of both worlds when they could get it). The question remains, beyond individual proclivities, how would a middle-class

---

[1] Americus Cartwright to Brother, 16 September 1856 (quotations), Cartwright Papers, The Center for American History, University of Texas at Austin. Biographical data from "Robert Lane Cartwright," in B. B. Paddock, *History of Central and Western Texas* (Lewis Publishing Co., 1911), II:867.

southerner in the 1850s decide what career would bring him the most money or prestige?

As in any place and period, young men never chose jobs for the good of their social class or because of complex analyses of social mobility in their given social structure. However, young men could only select occupations they could access and must have generally understood social mobility in their society. A military institute graduate would seek the best career he could enter, unless an interest or option called him into a specific occupation. Education and social class shaped the occupations and opportunities available to all young men, military alumni included. Alumni's choices bring middle-class mobility into focus in the antebellum South. This chapter argues that young middle-class southerners entered professional careers (via military education) to maintain or improve their social status and that this professional concentration aided class formation because it redefined status in its own image. The chapter explores the emerging southern middle class's use of education to enter professions for social stability (and the potential for upward mobility). Next, the dominance of professional and nonagricultural careers in military alumni occupations is detailed and correlated to that of those of their fathers. Multigenerational information confirms the stability and upward mobility that military education granted to the developing southern middle class.

Social Status and Mobility in the Old South

Social mobility describes a rise in an individual's or group's social position.[2] The most common scholarly consideration of the issue in the antebellum United States has privileged the northern market economy, which at least rhetorically encouraged upward mobility. Scholars describe the Old South as a time and place with limited mobility in

---

[2]Stephan Thernstrom, *Poverty and Progress: Social Mobility in a Nineteenth Century City* (Cambridge: Harvard University Press, 1964), 83–84, states that examining an increase in status (prestige) is extremely problematic for the historian. He indicates that the clearest mode of analysis is occupation, but Michael B. Katz argues that occupation does not fully equal status. Katz, "Occupational Classification in History," *Journal of Interdisciplinary History*, 3 (Summer 1972), 63–88.

comparison to northern expectations. This refrain, even in texts that perhaps overemphasize the capitalist orientation of planters, says that few men entered professions and the only path to upward mobility was ownership of plantations and increasing numbers of slaves.[3] Although accurately reflecting elite expectations, this model too rigidly defines social position, which varies across time and region. Given the shifting definitions, historians need to reconstruct the meanings of social position to a given population, recognizing that at all times it was under flux, especially so in the antebellum years. Focusing on the last decades of the Old South, how, then, did men define that elusive quality of social position on which mobility is based? The Citadel speaker who equated "happiness and success" with "honor and prosperous fortune" illustrated the necessity of combining monetary gain with community valuation.[4] Certainly, the crux of social position in the South rested in status and secondarily in wealth.

Status is probably the best way to measure an antebellum southerner's social position. Planters possessed both wealth and status, but even when they lacked cash in hand, they had status. Wealth aided in status but did not create it. Whereas in the North, "American status depended upon economic position," as one scholar declared, southerners relied more on community-centered prestige. Members of the planter aristocracy, for example, could maintain social appearances while in debt, and no amount of wealth could give an African American equal status to whites. Status reflected the outwardly directed nature of southern elite culture. Honor and reputation were based on the community's estimation of a man's worth, and status similarly represented the community's valuation of a man. The emerging southern middle class's goals for stability and mobility rested in the basic ideas of status and wealth that surrounded them. Similar to their modification of the ideals of southern honor and

---

[3] For example, Laurence Shore, *Southern Capitalists: The Ideological Leadership of an Elite, 1832–1885* (Chapel Hill: University of North Carolina Press, 1986); William Kauffman Scarborough, *Masters of the Big House: Elite Slaveholders of the Mid-Nineteenth-Century South* (Baton Rouge: Louisiana State University Press, 2003).

[4] James D. Tradewell, *Address on the Study of the Federal Constitution Delivered Before the Polytechnic and Calliopean Societies of the Citadel Academy* (Charleston: Walker, Evans and Co., 1857), 33.

manhood, the group realigned the prevalent social dictates with their expectations.[5]

The redefinition of status allowed mobility for nonplanters. In the Old South, planters dominated the social structure, and that domination privileged land and slave ownership in the valuation of status. Men of the emerging middle class, although they may have wanted such property, began to redefine status into professional, nonagricultural occupations and standards that they could achieve. The redefinition was meant to instill those occupations and standards with prestige so that they gave those men status and increasing social position. It privileged nonagricultural, professional careers that could best be achieved through nonclassical education, indeed in the distinctly southern institution of military education. Also, it encouraged young men to work for the maintenance of their (or their families') social positions as much as upward mobility. They sought status in non-elite ways.

A central component in the emerging southern middle class's redefinition of status entailed their support for and encouragement of professionalization. The beginning stirrings of professionalization, in which the national middle class of the late antebellum period engaged, entailed both the legitimation of professional careers and focus on professional status.[6] Considering the latter, privileging professionalism was not just a private matter. As members of the southern middle class solidified a class ideal around that value – much as the northern middle class had already begun to do – the younger members who filled the ranks of the developing class changed the ethos of a portion of the Old South. Indeed, they replaced the basis of elite social position with goals they could attain. If elite reputation encompassed land and slave ownership, kin relations, classical education, honor, and mastery, men of the southern middle rank could claim to possess only the intangible last two and, perhaps, important relatives. Thus, replacing the aristocracy of plantations, first

---

[5] See Kenneth S. Greenberg, *Honor and Slavery* (Princeton: Princeton University Press, 1996); Bertram Wyatt-Brown, *Southern Honor: Ethics and Behavior in the Old South* (New York: Oxford University Press, 1982); Richard Walsh, "The Revolutionary Charleston Mechanic," in *Small Business in American Life*, ed. Stuart W. Bruchey (New York: Columbia University Press, 1980), 64 (quotation).

[6] On professions, also see Arno J. Mayer, "The Lower Middle Class as Historical Problem," *Journal of Modern History*, 47 (September 1975), 429.

families, and university education with professions, impersonal relationships, and higher schooling (including military education), the emerging middle class could build on northern and internal industrial impulses.

The connection of the middle class with professionalism has been well established by historians. According to Burton Bledstein and others, the argument that professionalization coincided with the middle class is prevalent in every profession.[7] The progression of middle-class men obtaining education, entering professional callings, and working to legitimate those professions is the accepted development for northerners. Southerners, without public school systems and within a hierarchical agricultural society, have previously been exempted from this "American" model. In actuality, middle-class southerners possessed goals and started professional development similar to northerners. The study of men at military schools helps to answer the neglect of southern professionalism and to refocus the development of a professional middle class on the antebellum period, rather than the 1870s or 1880s.

The southern middle class felt that another vital component in its formation and mobility was education, the same as in the North.[8] Their expansion of military education demonstrates that connection, using public funding and practical education. At the same time these young men redefined social position so they could attain higher status, they expanded the emerging southern middle class. Striving for individual social mobility, alumni encouraged the expansion of a southern middle

---

[7] On professionalization in occupations, see Burton J. Bledstein, *The Culture of Professionalism: The Middle Class and the Development of Higher Education in America* (New York: W. W. Norton, 1976); Robert H. Wiebe, *The Search for Order, 1877–1920* (New York: Hill & Wang, 1967); Daniel H. Calhoun, *Professional Lives in America: Structure and Aspiration, 1750–1850* (Cambridge: Harvard University Press, 1965); James W. Gordon, *Lawyers in Politics: Mid-Nineteenth Century Kentucky as a Case Study* (New York: Garland Publishers Inc., 1990); Samuel Haber, *The Quest for Authority and Honor in the American Professions, 1750–1900* (Chicago: University of Chicago Press, 1991); Thomas Haskell, *The Emergence of Professional Social Science: The American Social Science Association and the Nineteenth-Century Crisis of Authority* (Urbana: University of Illinois Press, 1977); Roscoe Pound, *The Lawyer from Antiquity to Modern Times* (St. Paul: West Publishing Co., 1953); Beth Barton Schweiger, *The Gospel Working Up: Progress and Pulpit in Nineteenth-Century Virginia* (New York: Oxford University Press, 2000); Steven M. Stowe, *Doctoring the South: Southern Physicians and Everyday Medicine in the Mid-Nineteenth Century* (Chapel Hill: University of North Carolina Press, 2004).

[8] Jonathan Daniel Wells, *The Origins of the Southern Middle Class, 1800–1860* (Chapel Hill: University of North Carolina Press, 2004), 135.

class in nonagricultural occupations. By the 1840s, young men in a social position below the plantation elite sought mobility both through entering the elite as they knew it and, increasingly as the middle class developed, through creating more accessible definitions.

When entering the occupational world, alumni selected their careers from occupations available to them and their judgment on which they could succeed in. They had to balance their own personal advancement with social expectations. The hope of young men coming to maturity in the late antebellum years did not always conform to the dominant model of plantations. If cadet members of the southern middle class aspired to be plantation owners, very few expressed it in their writing. They identified themselves with professional aspiration and standing. "Every prof[ession] is open to me and I can choose any," Henry Burgwyn told his father. "An Engineer's life would not suit me, I think a [doctor's] still less." His first choice would be to teach in a "Southern Military Institute," specifically either the University of Alabama's cadet corps or the Louisiana State Seminary and Military Academy; otherwise, Burgwyn would follow in his father's footsteps as a planter.[9] This young man considered professional occupations before agriculture, confirming that even a planter's son investigated careers outside of planting. Furthermore, even cadets with limited means expressed the same ability to choose their occupations. For example, Cadet William Lee, whose widowed mother had an uncle pay his costs above the state-paid tuition, said that he thought of being an engineer; Lee's uncle, however, wanted him to be a lawyer. Thus, he thought of studying law while he taught the two required years.[10]

Unlike planters' sons, who could expect the wealth and prestige of land and slaves as their inheritance, sons of the middle rank like Cadet Lee found themselves in precarious positions. A concise description of

[9] Henry Burgwyn Jr. to Henry Burgwyn Sr., 14 March 1861, Burgwyn Family Papers, Southern Historical Collection, Wilson Library, University of North Carolina at Chapel Hill (hereafter SHC). Also see, Archie K. Davis, *The Boy Colonel of the Confederacy: The Life and Times of Henry King Burgwyn, Jr.* (Chapel Hill: University of North Carolina Press, 1985).

[10] William Lee to Francis H. Smith, 15 July 1853, Preston Library, Virginia Military Institute Archives (hereafter VMI Archives). Within six months of graduation, Lee worked for a railroad but found himself unemployed within the year and unable to find a teaching situation paying more than $300/year; Lee to Francis H. Smith, 16 January 1854, 23 March 1854, VMI Archives.

the cadets' definition of professional success showed in the benefits that Lee's mother felt a teaching assistantship would give her son: "Industry and advancement."[11] Hard work, that much praised middle-class and masculine trait, led to upward mobility; in terms of advancement, monetary prosperity played a role, but only in conjunction with status, good character, and professional standing.

Young men without landed estates had to worry that they would find themselves with less autonomy and status than their fathers enjoyed. Studies of social mobility in the North suggest that the antebellum era was a time in which young men were as likely to face downward mobility as success. Historians have described the hindrances to mobility that middle-class men confronted in the North, particularly in urban areas. For example, Stephan Thernstrom, in his seminal study, admonishes that downward mobility was common among the working class in Massachusetts, 1840–1880. Clyde and Sally Griffen concur that rates of failure increased in New York, 1850–1880.[12] The applicability of such northern or postbellum studies vexes southern historians because of mobility's contested existence in the historiography of the Old South.

Thernstrom's evidence suggests a tenuous social situation for military alumni who were trying to maintain or improve their social position in the late antebellum years. They feared downward mobility and struggled for upward mobility in a hierarchical southern system focused on the elevation of planters, yet patterns of military school attendance – specifically the socioeconomic status of fathers and of sons – reveal a trend opposite that of Thernstrom's northerners. Military alumni provide a group to study antebellum mobility in depth, answering Mary Ryan's call, "To put it in the rather graceless language of social science history, we still need mobility studies and cohort analysis."[13]

The resilience of southern middle-class youth, moreover, suggests a success in using military education that was not prevalent in the North

---

[11] Mary Lee to Francis H. Smith, 4 December 1852, William Lee student file, VMI Archives.

[12] Thernstrom, *Poverty and Progress*, esp. 152–54; Clyde and Sally Griffen, "Small Business and Occupational Mobility in Mid-Nineteenth-Century Poughkeepsie," in *Small Business in American Life*, ed. Stuart W. Bruchey (New York: Columbia University Press, 1980), 140; Howard P. Chudacoff, "Success and Security: The Meaning of Social Mobility in America," *Reviews in American History*, 10 (December 1982), 101–12.

[13] Mary P. Ryan, "Thinking Class," *American Quarterly*, 37 (Spring 1985), 145.

or in a later period. Just as alumni demonstrated significantly more upward mobility than Thernstrom's laborers, those southerners appear to have democratized education more than other northern or postbellum studies indicate. A study of nineteenth-century Ontario, Canada, found that education offered only "marginal advantage" and even then only for elites; similarly, students at the postbellum, land-grant Illinois Industrial University came primarily from the top tiers of the "industrial classes." A cross-regional study suggests that students at small colleges "had to work their way through the occupational hierarchies," relegated to nonurban areas; this conclusion coincides more with the military alumni working in multiple careers for social mobility. That survey also concludes that liberal arts colleges provided mobility and probably did so for middle-rank southerners, but its lack of evidence on student backgrounds in the South "was disappointing." In contrast, this study's data demonstrate that members of the emerging southern middle class successfully used military education to promote a redefinition of status and mobility into professional, nonagricultural careers.[14]

Rethinking mobility in this way suggests cross-regional, national definitions of the middle class and of mobility. Some southerners feared this occurrence as "Yankeeification," but the implication that northern ideals washed over the southern middle class does not reflect the process of cultural adaptation. Middle-class southerners, even when they valued traits already prevalent among their northern counterparts, possessed their own regional views. Whereas northerners entered evangelical reform to promote abolition and individualism, southerners supported a hierarchical and slave-based system. Southerners accepted and developed values that reflected their cultural surroundings. The emerging middle class in that region redefined mobility, allowing themselves better access to the near top of the hierarchy. They did not, however, want to destroy the plantation system, nor did they necessarily perceive a disjunction

---

[14]Maris A. Vinovskis, "Quantification and the Analysis of American Antebellum Education," *Journal of Interdisciplinary History*, 13 (Spring 1983), 769 (first quotation), 776; J. Gregory Behle and William Edgar Maxwell, "The Social Origins of Students at the Illinois Industrial University, 1868–1894," *History of Higher Education Annual*, 18 (1998), 94 (second quotation); Colin B. Burke, *American Collegiate Populations: A Test of the Traditional View* (New York: New York University Press, 1982), 96, 126 (fourth quotation), 203 (third quotation).

between professionalism and the slave aristocracy.[15] Thus, the emerging middle class engaged in a process to create alternative status to, but not challenging, elites.

Alumni Occupations

In their choices for success and social stability, young men demonstrated their preference for professional careers. In his memoir, 1857 Citadel alumnus Henry Moore listed the careers of 160 South Carolina Military Academy (SCMA) antebellum graduates: "48 were teachers, 27 physicians, 20 lawyers, 16 civil engineers and architects, 15 farmers, 12 merchants, 9 ministers of the Gospel, 2 city officials, 3 editors, 1 railroad official, [and] 7 were dead." His calculations generally coincide with an examination of the careers of alumni at all antebellum military schools. Alumni were predominantly nonagricultural and consisted of large numbers of professionals. Less than 25 percent of them found employment in agriculture whereas more than 66 percent chose professional occupations, including law, medicine, and engineering.[16] Teaching, as Moore stated, proved to be the preferred field, although alumni teachers, as analyzed later, often used the career as a means of advancement.

Military educators stressed that their students entered "all the learned professions."[17] The cadets themselves described wanting to be in a variety of different occupations, mostly professional, after leaving school. KMI graduate Americus Cartwright vacillated between law and business as his brother entered commercial agriculture as a rancher. In their highest-achieved status, alumni were 64.4 percent professional as shown in

---

[15] Wells, *Origins of the Southern Middle Class*; Chad Morgan, *Planters' Progress: Modernizing Confederate Georgia* (Gainesville: University Press of Florida, 2005).

[16] Henry Moore, unpublished memoir, typescript, 1899, The Citadel Archives and Museum (hereafter CIT), 3. Moore's figures have not been included in the tables of this work because he did not indicate if these careers were the ones that the alumni engaged in before or after the Civil War. See Appendix 2, Tables 4 and 5.

[17] John W. Brockenbrough, *On Laying the Corner Stone of the New Barracks of the Virginia Military Institute* (New York: John Wiley, 1850), 12. Henry A. Wise, *Drawing Out the Man: The VMI Story* (Charlottesville: University of Virginia Press, 1978), 25, lists the occupations of VMI graduates from 1842 through 1862 as teacher, lawyer, doctor, and engineer in order.

Table 6.1. *Alumni occupations: highest-achieved occupational status*

Occupation	Number of alumni	Percentage
Professional	453	64.4
Agriculturalists	148	21.0
Proprietors	67	9.5
Public Service	15	2.1
White-collar Employees	20	2.8
Skilled Trades	1	0.1
$N = 704$ individuals		

Note: Data represent the highest achieved status based on the same hierarchy as the fathers exhibited in Table 1.1; they combine men with single and multiple occupations. Students and alumni without careers were excluded. Published figures from the South Carolina Military Academy register were excluded.
Source: See Appendix 2, Table 1.

Table 6.1. Teachers, physicians, and attorneys far exceeded every other nonagricultural choice for young men who remained in a single occupation in the antebellum years. When the occupations of alumni who pursued multiple jobs are added, teaching, law, and medicine rank in order.[18]

Law was the most chosen career in those learned professions. Not needing further schooling made the occupation of law attractive, and it required less formal study than did medicine. Graduate degrees in law were rare in the antebellum years; most lawyers apprenticed under a practicing attorney or studied to pass the bar exam on their own time. For some future lawyers, teaching provided a few years (and funds) to prepare for the bar. Practicing lawyers revealed great variety in experience and success. Some of the more esthetic ones worked with "the science of law" and examined constitutional issues. They spent their time researching and writing briefs. Other attorneys practiced criminal law, which required presentations before juries and less academic case work. Any trial lawyer might find himself in a courtroom brawl, but by the time the alumni entered the profession, most lawyers were not circuit riders. These men could, however, have acted as debt collectors. They entered a profession in which attorneys were beginning to specialize and might

[18] See Appendix 2, Tables 4 and 5.

have had to work to solicit clients away from the consolidating partner-
ships. They lived when lawyers were seen to "spring from the people,"
but more easily sprang from the emerging southern middle class.[19]

Young lawyers did not necessarily lead lives of luxury; most of them
owned no land and may have had to accept livestock in payment from
their farming clients. In the late antebellum period, attorneys had a varying status, as might be the case even today, yet young men entering law
felt themselves able to earn prestige. They could gain social prominence,
demonstrate mastery of oratory, and enter legislative service. Successful
lawyers could accumulate wealth and status.[20]

Two military alumni stated the general perception that law was the
"chief road to preferment and distinction." "The prof. of Law however is
the only one by which a man in this country can rise to power," echoed a
cadet from another school. Although neither of these young men entered
law, 19 percent of their peers did.[21] These southerners calculated that a
career in law was the best route for upward mobility. Their desire for
prestige led them into a professional career they thought both had value
in itself and offered mobility. Certainly some of these young men may
have sought ascension to the plantation elite via the law, as James Henry
Hammond had done in an earlier generation, or even to the presidency,
as Kentucky-born Abraham Lincoln. Of course, as the majority of men
could not achieve such a leap, they would seek to improve the status and
prestige in the career of law itself. Achieving an improved community
valuation of the career meant that an alumnus lawyer could achieve
monetary security and enter a profession with occupational mobility.

---

[19] North Carolina was the only southern state in the antebellum period that maintained even
nominal requirements for the education and professional training of lawyers. This loosening
of regulation was part of a national trend in the antebellum period; Pound, *The Lawyer from
Antiquity to Modern Times*, 227–28; Gordon, *Lawyers in Politics*, 45.

[20] Gordon, *Lawyers in Politics*, 231, describes Kentucky lawyers as young (71 percent younger
than 40 years), with moderate resources (61 percent had less than $5,000 in wealth), and
landless (47.6 percent owned no land); Haber, *Quest for Authority and Honor in the American Professions*, 124–32; Calhoun, *Professional Lives in America*, 59–87, states that the law
profession aided a man's social mobility. Haber and Calhoun focus on lawyers in Tennessee;
Gordon, on Kentucky.

[21] Daniel Trueheart to Francis H. Smith, 10 July 1859 (first quotation), VMI Archives. Henry
Burgwyn Jr. to Henry Burgwyn Sr., 14 March 1861 (second quotation), SHC. See Appendix 2,
Tables 4 and 5.

Akin to interest in the law, cadets wrote that they wanted to become doctors. The number of alumni doctors was high, especially among SCMA graduates; 16.8 percent of all military academy and 22 percent of Citadel alumni became doctors. Becoming a doctor often meant additional schooling, which alumni commonly sought at the University of Virginia or Jefferson Medical College in Philadelphia. During the antebellum period, however, medical school was not yet a necessity. Doctors attended patients, diagnosed them, and occasionally dispensed medicines. The career was not necessarily an easy path to respectability as many people distrusted conventional medicine, especially in the 1830s and 1840s.[22] Of course, some doctors earned prestige in their communities and enjoyed the fraternity of their colleagues, particularly in urban areas; in Memphis, for example, they formed a medical society in 1851 following the national organization of the American Medical Association in 1847.[23]

Alumni were clearly part of the wave of new practitioners working to professionalize; nationally, antebellum physicians' desire for status created their advancement of medical schools and professional organizations. Alumni doctors also reflected the increase in medical professionals during the 1850s, when the number of men entering medicine grew at a greater rate than those selecting other professions. By 1860, there were two doctors for every lawyer and clergyman in the South.[24] Individual physicians probably hoped that, with perseverance, they would establish a large clientele, be well compensated, and increase their status.

The two careers that military education specifically fostered were teaching and engineering. The curriculum and administrators explicitly promoted those occupations. Cadets noticed the changes in their environment and understood the development of railroads, surveying, and engineering as opportunities. A reasonable number of engineers came

[22] Most alumni recorded as doctors received some advanced training; it is unclear if the physicians attended medical school in 14 percent of cases, but alumni also attended schools in many other states, including Kentucky, Maryland, New York, and Louisiana; Stowe, *Doctoring the South*. For example, C. Irvine Walker, "Reminiscences of Days in the Citadel," unpublished memoir, CIT; Edmund Pendleton to Philip Winn, 20 March 1842, VMI Archives.

[23] Haber, *Quest for Authority and Honor in the American Professions*, 142–53; Gerald N. Grob, *Edward Jarvis and the Medical World of Nineteenth-Century America* (Knoxville: University of Tennessee Press, 1978), esp. 29; John Harley Warner, "A Southern Medical Reform" in *Science and Medicine in the Old South*, ed. Ronald L. Numbers and Todd L. Savitt (Baton Rouge: Louisiana State University Press, 1989), 206–25.

[24] Stowe, *Doctoring the South*, 8–9, 22.

out of military academies; 11.7 percent of all surveyed alumni became engineers or worked for the railroads. Even a man who was to inherit land might have attended a military school to be trained as a civil engineer to be "of great service to himself and his neighbors." Indeed, one alumnus felt that too many of his peers "drop[ped] the individuality which their education has given them and pursue[d] some calling for which they are not fitted."[25] Military education molded youths into professional engineers.

Engineers developed urban areas, including streets, but more than half of them built railroads or canals. They generally worked their way up through the ranks, similar to an apprenticeship. Attending an engineering program, such as one at Rensselaer Polytechnic Institute or a military school, allowed a young man to bypass the lowest positions and thereby increase the speed of his ascent in the profession. As an assistant, a beginning engineer would survey, draft, or perform computations. As a professional, engineers inspected the land, supervised construction of the project, built necessary machinery, and monitored the costs. In general, engineers were well respected and well compensated. During times of economic depressions, however, these positions could be expendable; in Virginia, state engineer salaries were halved from $1,500 to $666 during the hard times between 1837 and 1843. Whatever the salary, engineering offered alumni a career with status. The words "respectable" and "gentlemen" applied to young engineers suggest that Americans valued the career.[26] The respectability coincided with the increased appreciation of science and expertise. Thus, these conditions contributed to the fact that significantly more men worked as engineers as one part of their career rather than as a sole occupation; an apprenticeship or sporadic periods of unemployment could be funded with teaching, for example.

Many military graduates turned to teaching for their careers because they had been prepared for that field. As the number of scientific

---

[25] Robert H. Simpson to Francis H. Smith, 12 December 1853; Robert M. Marshall to Col. Charles Dorman, 5 October 1839 (first quotation), John Marshall student file; Daniel Trueheart to Francis H. Smith, 10 July 1859 (second quotation), VMI Archives.

[26] Daniel H. Calhoun, *The American Civil Engineer: Origins and Conflicts* (Cambridge: Harvard University Press, 1960), ix, 46–47, 141–44, 193 (quotations); Terry Mark Aldrich, *Rates of Return on Investment in Technical Education in the Ante-Bellum American Economy* (New York: Arno Press, 1975), 52, 69.

positions at schools increased, the demand for mathematics and chemistry teachers certainly grew, and alumni filled those positions. One young man attended the military programs at Fleetwood Academy, Rumford Academy, and then the alma mater of his teachers, the Virginia Military Institute (VMI). He was willing to incur debt for his education because he was "encouraged by the fact that the graduates of the Institute have established a reputation which has created a demand for their services particularly as teachers."[27] Young men such as this VMI alumnus would be trained for the professional careers of teaching and engineering or would be in a position to enter law or medicine.

Whereas professional careers in law, medicine, engineering, and education predominated, other cadets ended up in proprietorships. The most common proprietary alumni occupations were divided almost equally between merchants and unspecified businessmen. Eleven percent of alumni found their ways into business or mercantile employment; just less than 10 percent of the men worked in proprietorships as their highest-achieved status, as Table 6.1 shows. A few cadets started interesting enterprises – the Pony Express and a steamboat business, among others. These entrepreneurial men seemed to be in the minority, however. The cadets who preferred entering business to graduating primarily just wanted to quit school; an exception was Americus Cartwright's goal of taking over his father's business that opened this chapter. Their parents usually encouraged staying the course in school. One father thought that business was a dangerous profession in the economic climate of the 1840s. "I fear it is a bad time for a young man to set out in business," he wrote to his son. "He must however be diligent and industrious for some time before he can establish himself in any business."[28] Members of the emerging southern middle class seeking businesses would not have had plantations to fall back on and relied on hard work as the key to gaining stability or upward mobility over time. This was also true of

[27] R. S. Smith to Francis H. Smith, 21 February 1851, VMI Archives.
[28] John Winn to Philip Winn, 8 January 1841, Winn Family Papers, Rare Book, Manuscript and Special Collections Library, Duke University (hereafter Duke). Other boys described troubles finding work, including Augustus Powell to Francis H. Smith, 10 December 1845, VMI Archives; Robert P. Carson, unpublished memoir, Virginia Historical Society (hereafter VHS). Also, E. Montague Grimke to Father, 1 July 1852, CIT.

other southern college graduates; as Colin Burke notes, "business did not offer a great opportunity for mobility to liberal arts students."[29] Perhaps the middle-class alumni, lacking family connections, had to prove their worth in a career, such as teaching, before an established businessman would accept their partnership.

Proprietorships could have been riskier enterprises, or more difficult to enter, than professional occupations. Because many alumni required monetary security in addition to any altruistic goals they expressed, the sure career paths dominated. A much higher percentage of alumni chose proprietorships as one of their multiple occupations than remained solely in that occupation before the war broke out. Only 7 percent of alumni worked in proprietorships for their only career, whereas 26.3 percent engaged in them as one part of their career lives.[30] Successful men, including SCMA graduate Micah Jenkins, combined careers to find stability through dual careers, and other men countered the uncertainty of the times through employment in professional occupations.

Young men leaving military higher schooling did not enter public service in large numbers. Indeed, the percentage of the highest-achieved status in public service is a low 2.1 percent (see Table 6.1). Poor advancement in the antebellum army surely contributed to alumni avoiding the U.S. Army. At least one father felt that entering the armed forces meant the end of his son's education and a poor career, as "cousin Charly" discovered in the seven years after he graduated from West Point. A few cadets did resign to serve their country in the Mexican War, but otherwise cadets did not enter the armed services in significant numbers.[31] Only 5.1 percent of alumni joined the army or navy before the Civil War; some of these men, however, entered as doctors or engineers, relying on professional identity. Their choices reflected the ability to succeed more

---

[29] Burke, *American Collegiate Populations*, 135 (quotation).
[30] Appendix 2, Tables 4 and 5.
[31] R. Kingsbury to Theodore Kingsbury, 11 February 1847, Theodore Kingsbury Correspondence, SHC. At least twenty-three military academy alumni were involved in the Mexican War: W. J. Magill, C. O. LaMotte, F. T. Bryan, R. H. Burks, I. W. Smith, W. A. Scott, L. T. Menefee, A. C. Layne, R. H. Keeling, W. H. Williamson, D. S. Lee, G. A. Porterfield, C. R. Munford, T. S. Garnett, A. C. Cummings, E. C. Carrington, R. C. W. Radford, A. M. McCorkle, B. D. Fry, J. B. Dorman, J. L. Bryan, H. L. Shields, and C. E. Carter.

easily in other careers. It is unknown whether more of these men would have entered public service as they and their careers matured.

The younger generation diverged from their fathers' status by being less likely to enter public service than white-collar jobs. Some alumni became clerks and the white-collar ranks, as they represented the entry to professional positions. There was not a great deal of status attached to white-collar employees, but a clerk had hopes of moving into better professional or proprietary careers. It was most commonly in the position of clerk, either for a court or a business, that these white-collar men found employment.[32] What is striking is that the number of white-collar employees is relatively low; less than 4 percent of alumni did not rise above white-collar positions and 3 percent of alumni found their highest status careers in white-collar occupations (see Table 6.1). Their education and middle-class rank allowed alumni to enter professions rather than starting or stalling at the lower status of white-collar employees.

As the list of careers indicates, alumni rooted in the developing southern middle class emerged from military education and preferred professional occupations. They selected nonagricultural occupations in even greater numbers than they chose professional careers. Fully 78.8 percent of men with a single occupation remained outside of agriculture; all alumni, regardless of single or multiple careers, maintained a high nonagricultural rate of 76.6 percent.

As a singly chosen occupation, however, agriculture was most frequently selected; 140 alumni became agriculturalists whereas 134 maintained teaching careers. However, including alumni with multiple careers, the rate of agriculture slips below that of teaching. Only 23 percent of all the surveyed alumni engaged in an agricultural profession (as their sole career or as one of multiple occupations). This amount compares to 50 or greater percent (depending on location) of the southern population engaged in agriculture. Even when alumni became agriculturists, men felt that military education helped planters. "The same method, and discipline, and promptness which military education promotes and exacts, is equally advantageous in every department of business," the Honorable

---

[32] For a discussion on northern clerks' journal writing, see Thomas Augst, *A Clerk's Tale: Young Men and Moral Life in Nineteenth-Century America* (Chicago: University of Chicago Press, 2003).

S. W. Trotti declared, as it is for "the most successful planters."[33] The Meredith brothers probably accepted this view because they attended VMI before receiving farms from their father. Although they did farm, former military school cadets did so at a much lower rate than their southern peers and their fathers.

Cadets' nonagricultural and scientific tendencies appear to have set them apart from the graduates of southern state universities and small liberal arts colleges. Southern small colleges were four times as likely to produce agriculturalists as were northern schools. Although more than 25 percent of the elite university matriculates were "planters or large farmers" and still more must have possessed small farms, only 21 percent of military alumni were solely agricultural and rarely planters. The overall low occurrence of secondary education in the Old South encouraged alumni into professional occupations, so that some professions exhibited similar rates between college and military school graduates. The practical progress stressed in military education, however, moved young men into engineering and teaching, both of which were neglected fields among the graduates of other southern institutions of higher education. Whereas less than 3 percent of southern college students entered engineering, almost 12 percent of military school alumni enjoyed that vocation. "I think it probable that the Virginia Military Institute has turned out more civil Engineers than any ten of our Southern Colleges united," Military educator D. H. Hill calculated; "in fact, the Colleges both North and South have done but little in this respect." With teaching as the most common nonagricultural career choice among military alumni, the differences are even greater; Colin Burke's raw data indicate that only 8 percent of southern college and university graduates became teachers in 1850 as compared to 27 percent of military education matriculates (and a much higher 39 percent among graduates).[34] Middle-class cadets

---

[33] S. W. Trotti, *An Address Delivered before the Calliopean and Polytechnic Societies of the State Military Academy* (Charleston: Burges, James and Paxton, 1847), 19 (quotation). William Meredith to Francis H. Smith, 6 June 1844, VMI Archives. James L. Morrison, "*The Best School in the World*": *West Point, the Pre-Civil War Years, 1833–1866* (Kent: Kent State University Press, 1998), 158.

[34] Burke, *American Collegiate Populations*, 184–90, 188 (first quotation), Table 4.3. See Appendix 2, Tables 4 and 5. Hill, "Remarks of Major D. H. Hill, of the N. C. Military Institute at Charlotte, Before the Committee on Education of the North Carolina Legislature" (n.p., [1860]; second quotation).

used the specific qualities of military education to enter professional and nonagricultural careers, especially ones for which their schooling most qualified them.

The Citadel graduating classes showed an interesting divide between students who performed well and those who became planters. SCMA honor graduates (the cadets ranked numbers one and two in class standing) for every antebellum year, except 1855, produced a teacher. In contrast, the 10 percent of graduates who became planters or farmers remained predominately in the lower half of their classes. Their placement suggests that young men with the economic capital to become planters did not feel the need to perform as well as their classmates. The cadets who relied on the military education for their future careers and success worked to achieve a good standing (and thus a good recommendation after graduation). It is also unsurprising that state-funded cadets were more likely to graduate from VMI than were tuition-paying cadets. Twenty-nine percent of the paying cadets graduated compared to 44 percent of state cadets.[35] Of course, it would also not be surprising that the top students from each class were more desirable to the schools hiring teachers; becoming an agriculturist, however, depended on one's family and not on outside hiring.

The high percentage of cadets entering and maintaining professional careers and status demonstrates their success in finding social stability. Comparing alumni to their fathers shows, in addition, that military education fostered upward mobility. Cadets' biographies and correspondence provide two sets of occupational data that show their social mobility relative to their fathers' positions. At the most comprehensive level, the careers of 704 alumni and 368 fathers illustrate the overall trend; the professions and the highest-achieved status of each group offer a picture of the occupational shift of late antebellum southern middle class. Nonagricultural careers dominated among men who sent their sons into military education and likewise among alumni. The data on all available military school men demonstrate that approximately 70 percent of all military academy fathers worked entirely in nonagricultural occupations. As a group, alumni increased the nonagricultural propensity of the fathers to 76.6 percent working outside of agriculture.

[35] *Semi-Annual Examination* (n.p., July 1860), American Antiquarian Society.

A more direct correlation between the professions of 294 cadets (including brothers) and their 282 fathers shows the social mobility of those individuals, one-third of the sample. The comparison of fathers to their sons concludes that alumni benefited by maintaining their fathers' status or by earning upward mobility. Directly correlating individual fathers' occupations to those of their alumni sons confirms the nonagricultural reliance of the emerging middle class. Among nonagricultural fathers, 82 percent of their sons remained outside agricultural life. Among alumni whose fathers held nonagricultural or mixed careers, the total rises to 89 percent of alumni being occupied in nonagricultural callings. Finally, the careers of their grandparents and kin confirm the increasing nonagricultural and professional concentration of the alumni in the emerging southern middle class.

The movement into nonagricultural careers is stark when the occupations of fathers and their sons are correlated. Given the inheritance of land within families, agricultural continuity would be expected; however, cadets were often younger sons and without expectation of inheriting, even in agricultural families. Thus, among solely agricultural fathers, only 50 percent had sons who went into farming; most of these sons combined careers in and out of agriculture. One such young man, teacher and law student Robert P. Carson, describes his farming father "while not having the advantage of an education, and a poor man."[36] Only one-third of the sons with farming fathers remained solely agricultural. Fathers with mixed professions produced sons who worked nonagriculturally at the rate of 58 percent. Alumni participated in the increasing acceptance and prevalence of professionals in the Old South.

Social Stability and Mobility: Occupation and Status

Comparing the alumni and fathers either as entire groups or in direct comparison as individuals, the second generation also demonstrated significant gains in professional occupations. In the highest-achieved status for the entire data set, alumni were 64 percent professional compared to 53 percent of fathers (see Tables 6.1 and 1.1). Alumni were more concentrated in the professions, as their highest-achieved status reflects; young

---

[36] Carson, unpublished memoir, VHS.

men sought that type of career above all others. Youths left military school specifically prepared for professional occupations, and two-thirds of alumni enjoyed them. Furthermore, it is important to remember that some alumni had not fully established themselves in their career by the time they headed off to war. Cadets who continued their education after a military academy graduation were mostly likely heading for careers in law or medicine. Alumni working as both teachers and clerks may have moved into the professions later in life (or might have done so had the Civil War not intervened). An even higher proportion of alumni might have transitioned into professions as the middle class developed.

Because the proportion of professionals among the alumni increased greatly from the previous generation, decreases in all other occupational categories are unsurprising. The fathers represented a more balanced cross-section of occupations than did their sons. The alumni exhibited a striking absence in careers ranked below proprietors; 5 percent of alumni versus 13 percent of their fathers worked in the three lowest categories. Alumni's ability to avoid the lowest level of employment is also noticeable. Whereas a low 2.2 percent of fathers labored in the skilled trades, an almost negligible 0.1 percent of their sons so toiled. Only one individual among the 855 cadets for whom occupational data are available (archival sources and SCMA register) worked solely in a skilled trade. A young man like William Gordon, whose father was reportedly a blacksmith and who became a civil engineer, illustrates the professional status granted by military education.

Among military school alumni, the rates of upward mobility are staggering. An analysis comparing father and son highest achieved occupational status shows the gains that military education offered. Table 6.2 suggests that an extremely low number of alumni exhibited downward mobility. Only 14.3 percent of alumni found themselves in a lower social position than that of their fathers. Two-thirds of those alumni entered agriculture, however, and only eleven exhibited actual downward mobility; even there, most of those eleven alumni worked in proprietorships, which may have flourished into higher-status careers later in their lives. Because professional status was the largest category of downward mobility, it is suggestive of how difficult attaining the position must have been. No alumni with fathers in the lowest three ranks fell below that status.

Table 6.2. *Alumni mobility correlated to fathers' occupation*

Fathers' occupation	Sons in same category, %	Sons having upward mobility, %	Sons having downward mobility, %
Professional	78.4	–	21.6
Agriculturalists	41.3	47.8	10.9
Proprietors	26.8	68.3	4.9
Public Service	9.1	90.9	–
White-collar Employees*	–	100.0	–
Skilled Trades*	33.3	66.7	–
Total	56.5	29.2	14.3

$N = 282$ fathers, 294 sons

Note: These categories represent only three fathers in skilled trades and white-collar careers.
Source: See Appendix 2, Table 1.

Thus, even the alumni who might be labeled marginally successful must be seen as maintaining the social position of their birth.

Cadets worried about losing status and not finding professional success. "There is scarcely an opening for a young man in the professional line of business, so I hardly know what profession to follow and even after I have determined upon one I would have to go somewhere else to derive any profit from it," fretted a VMI senior in 1850; he knew the career he would enter to avoid failure, writing to his brother, "I have some idea of studying law."[37] Despite such fears, and in opposition to Thernstrom's northern findings, downward mobility was not prevalent among military alumni.

It is important to note that sons primarily continued in the same occupational position as their fathers. Table 6.2 shows that the majority of alumni, 56.5 percent, maintained their fathers' highest-achieved status. More than three-quarters of the alumni, the largest category within the data set, were professional sons of professional fathers, and nearly 200 cadets fall under this description. For example, Edmund Pendleton, member of VMI's first graduating class and son of a doctor, moved into Ohio and Louisiana to practice law; John Wylie was another physician's son who entered law, following graduation from the SCMA; and Daniel

[37] Henry Carrington to William Carrington, 6 October 1850, VMI Archives.

Lindsey followed in his father's career path as a lawyer after his KMI commencement.

Finally, more than 29 percent of alumni demonstrated a direct increase in social position, as Table 6.2 suggests. Removing the top category in which professional fathers produced similar heirs, the upward mobility of alumni increases to 59 percent. Other than professional and agricultural occupations, alumni in the other categories exhibited a two-thirds or greater rate of increased status. This finding suggests that alumni valued professional occupations more than any other. Even agricultural fathers produced a higher percentage of professional sons than agricultural sons. Fathers with proprietorships educated their sons into their position or one above at the very high rate of 95 percent. Across-the-board maintenance or increase in social position confirms the benefit of military education in social mobility between alumni and their parents.

Unfortunately the small sample size at the bottom of the social ranking, reflective of the middle class (not yeoman, plain folk, or laborer) constituency of military schools, makes analysis in those categories difficult. All three of the alumni with fathers in white-collar positions exhibited upward mobility, as did two of the three men with fathers in skilled trades. Only VMI cadet John Hill, who did not graduate, remained in his father's social position and occupation when he became a carpenter. Men with fathers in the lower middle class and the few in the lower ranks who gained access to higher schooling used it for mobility.

In order to move into professional careers, alumni often switched between occupations. They worked in multiple careers, as their fathers had, as one component of gaining higher social position. James Oakes suggested that combining agricultural and professional careers was a significant path to mobility, at least for small planters. Reaching a similar conclusion on that point, William K. Scarborough found that 21.3 percent of elite planters used nonagricultural pursuits to add wealth to their plantation income; removing those men involved in land speculation, certainly a career tied to agriculture, drops the number to 20.2 percent.[38] The results among military school men reflect a somewhat greater usage of more than one career. A quarter of the fathers had multiple occupations

[38] James Oakes, *The Ruling Race: A History of American Slaveowners* (New York: Vantage Books, 1982), 11, 58. Scarborough, *Masters of the Big House*, 219.

(25.8 percent), whereas a slightly smaller percentage of their sons (22.3 percent) had more than one profession.

Fathers of military school alumni, however, did not pursue multiple occupations in the same way as planters. The 20 percent of planters with a second occupation pursued dual careers, which meant two occupations simultaneously; combining agricultural and nonagricultural jobs appeared more often among military school fathers than alumni. Among fathers with several occupations, 38 percent had some connection to agriculture. In the alumni cohort, even fewer southern middle-class men had farming associations; 31 percent of the second generation had such work histories.[39] The high percentage of military school men in nonagricultural professions stands in stark contrast to that of the plantation elite. Even when they established a career alongside agricultural pursuits, alumni moved away from the agricultural norm; their pattern with multiple occupations was more often to combine nonagricultural professions.

The middle class engaged in sequential careers more than in dual careers. For example, a young man could work as a clerk as he studied to become a lawyer; James Coles did just that, working in his uncle's store before passing the bar in 1860. Coles's experience indicates how men in the middle social position used occupations differently from planters. Alumni moved between jobs more often than they operated in them concurrently. What appeared to happen in most cases was that alumni taught for a few years to gain footing in the legal profession; education and law was the most common combination for alumni with multiple careers.

Not surprisingly, among fathers and sons with multiple careers, all the examples of white-collar employees combined that job with a higher-status one. Only one father worked at multiple occupations with a public service career and nothing higher. Fathers combined a legal career with legislative work as their most common dual profession. They exhibited a greater range of multiple careers than did their sons. This could reflect the sons' short period of career development or can be attributed to the fathers' generation having to work harder for mobility in the early stages of the formation of the middle class.

A more clearly accessed avenue to mobility across the nation was geographical relocation; southerners moved west to find new plantations and

---

[39] See Appendix 2, Tables 2 and 5.

new areas of opportunity, and young men like KMI alumnus Americus Cartwright did the same. Some men wanted to move west into the newer southern states or, in general, described moving around to different positions. Among alumni who recorded working out of state, the South was the most popular region for relocation; Cartwright and his brother both settled in Texas after attending military school in Kentucky.[40] Charles Derby's movement among five teaching positions in four states over a period of seven years illustrated the extreme case. The alumni movement showed that occasionally physical mobility helped social mobility. As a friend told a VMI student, "I shall go down South and try my fortune down there and see what I can make as there is no chance in Old Virginia for a young man. Unless he has got plenty of means to go upon."[41] Unlike this writer, most military school graduates used their educations as their "means" to find professional positions, whether in their home states or further west.

Alumnus Gabriel Jordan wrote that the west was the place to be. After teaching at Rappahannock Military Institute in Virginia, John R. Jones relocated to Florida. Having established an academy there, Jones wanted a teacher of military tactics, who would receive a good salary of $600. In another representative letter, VMI alumnus James Murfee gave Smith a long explanation about the school he was opening, while confessing that he really wanted a professorship at the University of Tennessee because the salary would help his family. The not-very-subtle implication was that Murfee wanted a recommendation to teach tactics, math, or natural philosophy (the subjects specific to his military education).[42] Murfee, however, remained a teacher, ultimately achieving the rank of commandant of the University of Alabama's cadet corps in 1860. Clearly,

---

[40] See John R. Jones to Francis H. Smith, 28 January 1849 [1850]; Gabriel Jordan to William Dabney Stuart, 22 November 1854, VMI Archives. KMI cadets who moved south include A. Eugene Erwin, Charles Martin, and William Word; see James Darwin Stephens, *Reflections: A Portrait – Biography of the Kentucky Military Institute, 1845–1971* (Georgetown, KY: Kentucky Military Institute, 1991). The idea of moving south for better wages coincided with the fact that salaries generally were higher in the newer southern states; Robert A. Margo, *Wages and Labor Markets in the United States, 1820–1860* (Chicago: University of Chicago Press, 2000), 45.

[41] William B. Barnes to William McAllister, December 1861, Duke.

[42] Gabriel Jordan to William D. Stuart, 22 November 1854, VMI Archives. R. D. Powell to Francis H. Smith, 16 August 1845; John R. Jones to Francis H. Smith, 29 November 1859; James Murfee to Francis H. Smith, 27 August 1855, VMI Archives.

mobility was on this young man's mind as he moved west from Virginia to Tennessee and Alabama.

Whatever state in which cadets lived, the upward mobility of someone like John Moomau, a lawyer with a hatter father, is obvious. Fortunately, data on 142 relations (66 maternal and 76 paternal or unspecified kin) allow analysis of mobility across three generations within the same family. Mobility and career change across three generations demonstrate that families generally exhibited similar occupational patterns. In a similar proportion to fathers, the majority of grandparents and kin held professional occupations: 56 percent held professional positions, and only 12 percent worked agriculturally.[43] Alumni found considerable stability and upward social mobility from the positions of their grandparents.

Professionals dominated among the kin, with doctors and lawyers in almost equal representations (thirteen to fifteen individuals reporting in each job). The other occupations with comparable figures are twelve maternal grandparents who were agricultural and fourteen nonmaternal or unspecified kin legislators. The same as the alumni's fathers, their grandparents were primarily nonagricultural. Interestingly, three times as many maternal kin were in agriculture than were paternal kin.[44] This may illuminate the gradual development of the middle class as nonagricultural; in some cases, planter daughters or cousins married professional men, which accounts for the high number of maternal kin, in comparison to paternal grandparents, who were farmers or planters.

Some specific examples illustrate the three-generation mobility of military school alumni. Young men with agricultural grandparents found their ways into professions. The turn away from agriculture developed unevenly, as it did in Hervey McDowell's life. His maternal grandfather was an Irish immigrant farmer, and his father followed that agricultural path also, despite his own father being a judge. McDowell established himself as a doctor after attending the Western Military Institute and graduating from KMI. VMI cadets, including the Ross and the Steptoe brothers, headed for professional careers rather than going with the agricultural side of their families. Similarly, cadet Caleb Boggess became an attorney like his maternal grandfather and not a farmer like his father.

---

[43] See Appendix 2, Table 3.
[44] See Appendix 2, Table 3.

Indeed, examples of alumni who found agricultural careers when their fathers and grandfathers were nonagricultural are intriguing. It suggests that the prevalence of the planter as the pinnacle of social status drew a few alumni into careers with land and slaves rather than into professions. It also suggests that young men could obtain land even when their fathers were not planters. Overall, however, these young men were in the minority among their peers. Alumni and their relatives maintained a nonagricultural continuity. More than half of all kin, fathers, and alumni in a family were all nonagricultural. Without considering the occupations of the fathers' generation, alumni whose kin were nonagricultural maintained that focus about 70 percent of the time.

Other cadets lacked agricultural backgrounds and continued the professional calling of their grandparents or fathers. Victor Manget followed in his father's footsteps; Mr. Manget Senior was an educator who taught at Amherst College and then at the Georgia Military Institute as his son attended the Citadel. Victor, graduating second in his class of 1857, taught at two male academies and certainly achieved some upward mobility from his maternal grandfather, a grocer. Likewise, William Mahone used VMI to enter professional occupations, first military education and then engineering, rising above his father's proprietorship in a country store and hotel and at least meeting the status of his maternal grandfather's tobacco merchant business. KMI, as a bachelor's degree–granting institution, may have attracted professionals even more than did other military schools. KMI cadets Benjamin Helm and Thomas Monroe Jr. represent descendents of Kentucky governors; Helm's father and maternal grandfather were attorneys, and Monroe's father was a lawyer and military educator, whereas his mother's father had been governor. Both young men (one with eleven siblings and the other a fourth son) used KMI to become attorneys.

By far, professionalism is the dominant outcome in kin career development. No matter the categories of grandparents' highest-achieved careers, their grandchildren achieved professional careers more than three-quarters of the time (77.6 percent). The maintenance of professional status, although high, is unsurprising because a cadet's move from a family of professionals into a white-collar career (true of only three alumni) would exhibit an unfortunate downward mobility. (In addition, the striking absence of kin in the skilled trades and only one white-collar representation prevented a high rate of declining social position.) An overwhelming upward mobility – direct increase in social position and status over three generations – is seen in all but seventeen cases (14.7 percent). This finding suggests the fathers' role in the ascension of their families, in part through placing their sons in military education. More than half of the families continued a professional standing, anchoring themselves in the emerging southern middle class dedicated to professional, nonagricultural careers. Thus, military education appears to have directly created stability for the southern middle class.

Social Stability and Mobility: Wealth

Alumni found status in their professions and, in those careers, also worked for wealth, that secondary component of position in the Old South. Planters possessed wealth and displayed it in their homes, clothing, and entertainment. Although such conspicuous display may have been desired, cadets most often described establishing a career with moderate salaries, those comparable to average white-collar earnings. Even a professorship – a coveted position along alumni educators – earned them between $600 and $2,500 a year. Their salaries could not compare with the thousands or tens of thousands that elites accumulated through their investments.[45] Those salaries, however, provided an adequate middle-class income, above that of the yeomanry, plain folk, and working class.

Alumni appeared more concerned with the acquisition of wealth for the maintenance of social position than for excessive accumulation. They generally did not describe their futures strictly in monetary terms. For example, a Citadel cadet turned down an engineering position that paid $1,200 (more than twice a starting teacher's salary) because it required him to leave school before graduation. Clearly, money was not the sole measure of success, and in general, alumni earned enough to support themselves well. Four years into running his own military academy, Micah Jenkins hoped to earn between $400 and $800 per year. This

---

[45] Scarborough, *Masters of the Big House*, ch. 6. Using college and university data, Burke calculates that professors' salaries ranged between $500 and $2,500 per year in the South in 1850; *American Collegiate Populations*, 48.

sum would have been a moderate income when compared to the $623 that an average white-collar worker in the South annually earned; in the South Atlantic states, the same average salary was $515.[46] Thus, Jenkins's earnings were about average or slightly above average for all southern white-collar workers. Many of Jenkins's military academy alumni peers earned comparably good salaries.

Antebellum professionals earned salaries that offered them suffi-cient wealth. Doctors generally earned less than wealthy merchants and lawyers, but more on average than the total population, especially if practicing in an urban area. Similarly, across the United States, a begin-ning engineer earned approximately $750 per year and could expect that amount to triple as he rose in the ranks.[47] The alumni's first salaries equaled that average white-collar salary of $515; teachers secured the low end of the range, and engineers obtained more. The alumni put them-selves into careers that would grow with them and increase their status over the years.

Alumni sought sufficient wealth in professional careers to establish themselves, relying on the status the occupations granted rather than solely on the monetary benefits. Some youths appeared to earn $500 or less per annum. Although most graduates did not object to their salaries, one alumnus complained that the military academy promised him that he would earn $500 upon graduation. He found himself, how-ever, advertising for a teaching position at $300 a year. Other alumni accepted teaching jobs for as little as $200 per year. Poor William Stith wanted a position at his alma mater because he had taught his two years

---

[46] Moore, unpublished memoir, CIT, 4. Micah Jenkins to John Jenkins, 29 August 1859, John Jenkins Papers, SCL. Margo, *Wages and Labor Markets in the United States*, 45. Margo uses the designation "white-collar labor." The South Central region (Arkansas, Kentucky, Tennessee, Alabama, Mississippi, and Louisiana) had income averages significantly higher than the rest of the United States. Income in the South Atlantic region (Maryland, Virginia, the Carolinas, Georgia, and Florida) was slightly less than that of the North and Midwest.

[47] E. Brooks Holifield, "The Wealth of Nineteenth-Century American Physicians," *Bulletin of the History of Medicine*, 64 (Spring 1990), 79–85. Holifield calculates that southern doctors earned more than their northern counterparts. Grob, *Edward Jarvis and the Medical World of Nineteen-Century America*, 30, 45, describes a nonmilitary school–educated doctor who earned $131.20 in his six months in practice in Massachusetts; the next year, he earned $600; and six years later in Louisville, Kentucky, he billed $2,400 (although he could not collect much of it). Aldrich, *Rates of Return on Investment in Technical Education in the Ante-Bellum American Economy*, 249–52.

to meet the state scholarship requirement but had earned only $100 for five months as that was all he could recoup from his students.[48] Reality must have been similarly hard for another young man. "All of [VMI's] graduates are getting very profitable employment as teachers Engineers etc.," Cadet Henry Carrington wrote to his brother in 1850; "most of them get on an average $1000 per annum which is not to be grinned at these hard times."[49] A few alumni earned this amount after years of working in teaching or other occupations. Whereas the Georgia Military Institute paid its superintendent $2,000 per annum and a VMI graduate recorded a $1,000-per-year teaching offer, the Western Military Institute in Kentucky paid its professors only $400 per year. Most alumni, like Carrington, had to wait for years to receive a salary of $1,000.[50] Annual salaries appear to have varied considerably, from $200 to $1,200; men with more years in a career earned the higher end of the range. Most of the alumni with low salaries appear to have been those with monetary resources to supplement their meager incomes; their economic status is

---

[48] Young men entering their first teaching positions often mentioned their salaries. Most cadets indicated no problems with their salaries; Briscoe Baldwin to Francis H. Smith, 27 November 1849; William Lee to Francis H. Smith, 23 March 1854, VMI Archives. Other letters listed a similar $500-per-year salary: Charles Derby to Father, 26 February 1847; George S. Patton to Francis H. Smith, 9 July 1854; Robert H. Simpson to Francis H. Smith, 24 June 1853, VMI Archives. Other alumni concentrated on jobs paying $400 per year: James C. Hiden to Francis H. Smith, 7 September 1857; Stephen T. Pendleton to Francis H. Smith, 14 September 1849, VMI Archives. E. A. Fristoe to Francis H. Smith, 4 April 1850; Gabriel C. Wharton to Francis H. Smith, 6 June 1848, VMI Archives, offered a position at $250 per year. William Stith to General W. H. Richardson, 1 December 1847, VMI Archives.

[49] Henry Carrington to William Carrington, 11 February 1850, VMI Archives. Carrington probably earned more than most of his peers after he inherited his family plantation at his brother's death. Prior to his brother's death, Carrington was a younger son in need of a career to support himself.

[50] The Western Military Institute superintendent stated that the nominal salary of $400 in Kentucky was the equivalent of a real salary of $600 in Virginia. T. F. Johnson to Francis H. Smith, 11 February 1851; Daniel Trueheart to Francis H. Smith, May 1856, VMI Archives. The most recent analysis of wages in the antebellum South does not present earnings by specific profession; Margo, *Wages and Labor Markets in the United States*, 45. Thus, in comparison to white-collar salaries in the South Central region, $400 was below average. Charles Derby to Francis H. Smith, 9 May 1855; Daniel Trueheart to Francis H. Smith, May 1856, VMI Archives. David Rodes to Francis H. Smith, 23 May 1848, VMI Archives, described another teacher receiving a $1,000 salary for continuing at a local academy. George Patton to Francis H. Smith, 16 January 1855, VMI Archives, said that he would earn $700 as a teacher three years after graduation; Wilford Downs quickly became a Principal and earned $600, student file, VMI Archives. Another man described a $60 monthly salary; this placed him two-thirds above the average white-collar salary for his region; Carson, unpublished memoir, VHS.

unsurprising because they would not rely on their earnings to support themselves or their families. Alumni, then, found sufficient salaries from their careers to be successful in terms of standard of living. In that facet of social position, they achieved success. With regard to the more important part of social position – prestige – alumni entered professional careers to achieve success, stability, and mobility.

Although he came from a "humble" background according to one of his classmates, William Gordon was a successful VMI man. Following in the professional tradition of his peers, he worked as a civil engineer and became a military educator at the Hillsboro Military Academy during the Civil War.[51] Young men such as Gordon emerged from military education into professional careers. Entering professions (in part via military education) accomplished more than individual maintenance or mobility of social position, however. It aided in the formation of the middle class and started to redefine social position.

In addition to mirroring and expanding the nonagricultural and professional status of their fathers, southern young men who entered military education received the direct benefit of social stability or upward social mobility from their schooling. Certainly a portion of their success came from the salaries they earned, but the more important facet of their continued support of military education rested in the prestige it began to grant the expanding middle class in the Old South. The prestige of the schools increased as members prospered, and the value of education concurrently rose. Individual members of that class found nonagricultural, professional training and careers that increased their social position relative to those of their fathers.

Members of the southern middle class increasingly moved into nonagricultural and professional careers, as seen from fathers' to alumni's generations. By professionalizing status, they allowed more men to access mobility, especially using education and, in particular, military schools. In some men's minds, the move to privilege professionalism may have rivaled the plantation elite. For the most part, however, this was an ideology based in the developing southern middle class that did not challenge the elite (from either group's point of view). The elite would not have

---

[51] Thomas Munford to Joseph R. Anderson, 23 August 1912, VMI Archives; Stephen A. Ross, "Hillsboro Military Academy," *Bennett Place Quarterly* (Summer 1999), 2.

been bothered by the career choices of 15 percent of the population below them; and some of the members of the emerging middle class were less successful relatives of the first families. That these men supported the slave system should not be surprising; proslavery ideology led industrialists to suggest the best continuation of the slave system in industrial labor.[52] As with southern industrialists, the middle class developed not an antagonism to the plantation but saw itself as a corrective to some social problems associated with it. The southern middle class was inherently attempting to clarify the boundary between its members and those beneath them – access to schooling and professional careers separated them from the yeomanry, plain folk, and any developing urban working class. The change in ideology and increase in mobility among the emerging southern middle class suggest that alternatives to the southern planter elite were beginning to bubble to the smooth surface of planter domination in the late antebellum years.

[52] For example, see George Fitzhugh, *Cannibals All! Or, Slaves without Masters* (Richmond: A. Morris, 1857); Shore, *Southern Capitalists*; Morgan, *Planters' Progress*; Wells, *Origins of the Southern Middle Class*, ch. 8.

7

Networks of Military Educators

On the Fourth of July 1845, nineteen-year-old Robert H. Simpson received his diploma from the Virginia Military Institute (VMI). Though Simpson was surely happy to have been released from the academic toil and military discipline, graduation did not sever his connection with the school. In fact, Simpson had already written to VMI's superintendent for help locating a suitable teaching position.[1] With his diploma and with this petition, Simpson, like many of his peers, accessed what has been an overlooked function of the late antebellum South's military schools: their role as a launching pad for the professional careers of nonagricultural, non-elite southerners.

In the years following his graduation, Simpson found himself in the situation of many young southern men. Simpson's middle-rank status as the son of a teacher left him without connections to a plantation or apprenticeship. His pursuit of a higher social position returned him time and again to his alma mater. Almost yearly missives, commencing with the 1845 letter, asked the VMI superintendent for recommendations or placement in openings of which the professor knew. "You will doubtless receive applications for teachers from various quarters of the State and perhaps of the Union. You have done me the kindness to offer me several such situations which circumstances have prevented me from accepting," Simpson declared in 1849, "and now I trust I shall not be troublesome for soliciting another such offer from you." Throughout the years, Simpson

---

[1] Robert Simpson to Francis H. Smith (hereafter FHS), 1 July 1845, 23 December 1845, 4 December 1848, 4 June 1849, 19 January 1850, Preston Library, The Virginia Military Institute Archives (hereafter VMI Archives).

received references and returned the favors by encouraging his students to enroll at VMI. He also dreamed of higher-status occupations, first college professorships and then the more lucrative career of engineering; as he was ready to move up, he repeatedly contacted his former professor for help. In exchange for assistance in securing an engineering job, for example, Simpson proffered his current teaching post, with a decent salary of $500, to a VMI graduate of the superintendent's choosing.[2] Such exchanges, in which alumni requested jobs, offered soon-to-be-vacant positions, and sent students to their alma maters, illustrate the career networks in which alumni and military educators forged social mobility in the tenuous antebellum world of the emerging southern middle class.

This chapter argues that military school networks facilitated, primarily, social stability and mobility for individual members of the southern middle class and, secondarily, the southern middle class's redefinition of social mobility as achieved through the professions, not plantations. It demonstrates the operations of military educators' networks that helped to create the social mobility discussed in the previous chapter. Former cadets such as Robert Simpson created and used active networks to locate stable nonagricultural careers, move into more profitable or respected professions, help professionalize the most commonly selected occupation of teaching, and thereby enhance the status of these middle-class young men. The chapter examines the two levels of the networks' results: success for the southern middle class's individual members and the elevation of its professional status, particularly in teaching, in the Old South.[3] Working in education tended to give alumni secure positions and status as teaching professionals, safeguarding them in an unreliable educational marketplace. The positions produced individual advantage in careers, income, and social mobility. Alongside these personal results, the networks provided for the professionalization of teaching and military education, particularly through its expansion in numbers and locations. Finally, the analysis locates the military school networks among

---

[2] Simpson to FHS, 23 December 1845, 4 June 1849 (quotation), 3 October [1851], 24 June 1853, 12 December 1853, 21 December 1853, VMI Archives.

[3] On this development in the North, see Burton J. Bledstein, *The Culture of Professionalism: The Middle Class and the Development of Higher Education in America* (New York: W. W. Norton and Company, 1976).

the myriad social institutions through which alumni fostered status and mobility.

Professional Networks at Military Schools

Cadet Simpson's correspondence with his alma mater reveals the military school alumni networks, and an exchange of letters about an 1849 vacancy at Rappahannock Military Institute demonstrates how jobs came into the networks. When VMI superintendent Francis Henney Smith heard that a teacher was leaving Rappahannock, he wrote to the school's superintendent to inquire if that were true. Rappahannock's superintendent confirmed that he needed a new teacher and asked about a VMI graduate who had already applied. Smith recommended that man in two separate letters. When the alumnus did not take the position, Smith suggested two other alumni. Separately, yet another VMI graduate applied for the job and wrote to Smith for a recommendation, which he sent. This final alumnus ended up with the job, but he wanted to leave it within three months. By January 1850, the original VMI graduate after whom the Rappahannock superintendent had inquired started teaching at the school. Over the course of six months, the VMI superintendent had proposed four alumni for one military school position, and the two graduates who used his recommendations left after two years or less. All this fuss was for $350 a year and a furnished room.[4]

As in the Simpson and Rappahannock examples, the most visible networks were among alumni teachers. Although graduates entered other professions, teaching proves to be the clearest example of the networks because, before the Civil War, more military school alumni found opportunities in education than in any other single career (including farming); 28 percent of the alumni whose careers are known taught for some period. That percentage increases to 39 percent in the pool of graduates, rather than matriculates. It is striking that, by 1850, VMI, the first and largest state-funded military school, had educated the equivalent of 12.3 percent of all Virginia's college and academy teachers. Superintendent Smith

---

[4] FHS to George Butler, 25 May 1849, 5 June 1849, 20 June 1849, 18 July 1849; Butler to FHS, 1 June 1849; Briscoe Baldwin to FHS, 24 July 1849, 24 November 1849, 12 March 1850; Charles Derby to FHS, 6 August 1849, VMI Archives.

explicitly compared VMI to the antebellum schools for training teachers that were more common in the North. "It has become an object with most of the graduates," he described, "to seek employment in the profession of teaching." In 1848 Smith reported to the Virginia General Assembly that "of eighty-four graduates, forty-five have been, and thirty-three are now actually engaged in teaching."[5] His figure of 54 percent is much greater than the 39 percent from the information currently available on alumni career choices. A decade later, educator D. H. Hill calculated that nearly 50 percent of VMI graduates became teachers and explicitly wanted his military school in North Carolina to "serve as a Central Normal School for the training of suitable instructors of youth."[6] More likely than both Smith's and Hill's being in error, the larger percentage probably more accurately represents alumni who have not been recorded as educators but who taught for short periods before entering other careers.

Indeed, private and state military institutions as closely resembled normal schools with military discipline as they did West Point. Consistent with calculations for alumni of VMI, those for alumni of the South Carolina Military Academy (SCMA) indicate that teaching was a significant career choice. An 1857 SCMA graduate recorded approximately 30 percent of antebellum graduates of his alma mater as having entered the teaching profession.[7] Military schools advanced teaching as

[5] Career information is available for 855 of the total sample; 27.7 percent of all matriculates, 38.8 percent of all schools' graduates, and 40.2 percent of VMI graduates taught at some point before the Civil War. The census identified 73 professors and 547 academy teachers, and VMI had produced 76 teachers by 1850. FHS, *Introductory Address to the Corps of Cadets of the Virginia Military Institute* (Richmond: MacFarlane and Fergusson, 1856); FHS, *The Regulations of Military Institutions, Applied to the Conduct of Common Schools* (New York: John Wiley, 1849), 5 (quotation); *Semi-Annual Report of the Virginia Military Institute*, 14 January 1848, American Antiquarian Society. Colin B. Burke, *American Collegiate Populations: A Test of the Traditional View* (New York: New York University Press, 1982), 188–89, notes "perhaps a majority" of northern college students taught at some point. He also contends that many southern colleges focused on teacher training, confirming military education's part in regional and national trends.

[6] Hill, "Remarks of Major D. H. Hill, of the N. C. Military Institute at Charlotte, Before the Committee on Education of the NC Legislature" (n.p., [1860]).

[7] Henry Moore, unpublished memoir, typescript, 1899, The Citadel Archives and Museum (hereafter CIT), 3. Moore does not specify whether his number of 31.4 percent indicates antebellum or postbellum careers and appears to omit early years of teaching. Published sources similarly put the number at 29.1 percent; John P. Thomas, *The History of the South Carolina Military Academy* (Charleston: Walker, Evans and Cogswell Co., 1893), 258–69; *Alumni Register*, CIT.

a worthy career after graduation and as a prize for good performance during school. Simply put, the Citadel, VMI, Kentucky Military Institute (KMI), and other academies rewarded cadets by making them teachers' assistants or assistant professors. After graduation, many alumni at those state schools taught as required by their funding. Led by administrators like Smith, teachers created status and social stability for their middle rank by establishing career networks.

The grease on the wheels of these networks was information and correspondence. Alumni reinforced their connections to their military alma maters in order to receive recommendations and positions; as they did so, they reinforced ties that forged career networks through the schools they had attended. Even five years after commencement, teacher Robert Simpson updated Smith on his life and position (including salary). When sociologist Mark Granovetter explored communication between members of a cohort, he showed that weak ties, those of acquaintanceship rather than of close friendship, better facilitated communication across a network. This works the same as six degrees of separation – people can be connected to and share information with others whom they do not personally know. In this way, a graduate writing to his alma mater connected all the alumni he knew, but who did not themselves write, to a career network. One former cadet could contribute the information of available teachers and open positions without the candidates even being aware of the information exchange.[8] In this cohort of antebellum matriculates of a specific type of southern school, alumni only vaguely aware of each other could spread job information and positions via the direct and/or repeated communication of one or two men to their former superintendent. Thus, more than one alumni network may have grown out of a military school, and each school most likely spawned its own networks.

The central agent in these career networks was, indeed, the principal of the military academy. Akin to Horace Mann's dispensing advice throughout the developing common school movement in the North,

---

[8] Mark Granovetter, "The Strength of Weak Ties," *American Journal of Sociology*, 78 (1973), 1360–80. For a methodological discussion of network studies, see Peter V. Madsen, "Network Data and Measurement," *Annual Review of Sociology*, 16 (1990), 435–63; Peggy G. Hargis, "For the Love of Place: Paternalism and Patronage in the Georgia Lowcountry, 1865–1898," *Journal of Southern History*, 70 (November 2004), 825–64. For example, Stephen Pendleton to FHS, 25 May 1845; Daniel Trueheart to FHS, 10 July 1859, VMI Archives.

Smith received letters from school board representatives and principals looking for teachers. For example, William Terrill, father of a VMI graduate with another son enrolled, asked Smith to locate a teacher for a local school. Principals often hired VMI graduates as teachers on Smith's recommendation alone and even allowed him to complete the deal with the cadets. One VMI alumnus wrote that the superintendent of the Western Military Institute (WMI) "says that a recommendation from you will suffice" to secure him the situation. "As other openings are presenting themselves it is important that I should know your wishes," Smith wrote, in an attempt to secure future openings from one employer, "and at what time his [an alumni teacher's] services would be required."[9] In turn, dozens of young men wrote to their schools because the administrators knew of jobs through a variety of means and placed alumni in those positions.

Although Smith had particular influence as a longstanding and successful superintendent, professors also received requests from cadets. At VMI, Professors J. T. L. Preston of Modern Languages and T. H. Williamson of Engineering and the Board of Visitors president General W. H. Richardson also acted as connections in networks.[10] VMI's records and the correspondence of its superintendent from 1839 to 1889, Francis H. Smith, thus provide scholars with the best evidence of a well-developed network. Comprehensive data from all extant correspondence at all southern military schools confirm as much as possible the circumstances of VMI networks. Evidence verifies that, at SCMA, Superintendent Charles Courtenay Tew advised at least two alumni educators and probably engaged in networking similar to Smith's; unfortunately because the SCMA records burned with Columbia, South Carolina, in 1865, reconstructing career networks there remains problematic.[11]

---

[9] William Terrill to FHS, 8 February 1855; Charles Derby to FHS, 11 June 1851 (first quotation); FHS to Hilary Harris, 1 June 1859 (second quotation), 20 June 1859; FHS to Philip Slaughter, 1 June 1859, VMI Archives. Jonathan Daniel Wells, *The Origins of the Southern Middle Class, 1800–1861* (Chapel Hill: University of North Carolina Press, 2004), 142–45.

[10] William H. Stith to Gen. W. H. Richardson, 1 December 1847; James Ashton to Maj. J. Preston, 20 July 1858; FHS to Philip St. George Cocke, 2 June 1859, VMI Archives.

[11] Micah Jenkins to Brother, March 22, [1855], Micah Jenkins Papers, Rare Book, Manuscript, and Special Collections Library, Duke University (hereafter Duke). Bruce Allardice, "West Points of the Confederacy: Southern Military Schools and the Confederate Army," *Civil War History*, 43 (December 1997), 315, mentions Smith's "teacher-placement service."

Alumni Teaching Careers

The networks' first result was placing individuals in the most commonly selected career – teaching.[12] "I am much oblige[d] to you for your kindness," recent graduate Charles Steptoe thanked Smith, "in proposing me to Mr. Catlett as an applicant of the school at Mr. Taliaferro's." The position had been offered not only to Steptoe but was contained in a longer list of options to another 1859 graduate. "There are several vacancies now opening and I will mention them to you," began Smith; the list included a $500-per-year math and tactics position at the Norfolk Male Institute, a replacement for another graduate at Norfolk Academy, and the Taliaferro situation Steptoe had been offered. Smith made sure that one of the men filled the openings, telling the second young man, "In the event of [Steptoe's] not going there, it would be a good situation for you, otherwise you might entertain either of the places at Norfolk."[13] Just as this valedictorian accepted a position (the first mentioned), the networks proved successful in securing alumni positions. "I am afraid I shall not be able to supply you with a teacher at this time," Smith explained in 1859 to a graduate requesting an assistant; "The demand has been such that all whom I could recommend, are now engaged."[14]

Lacking access to head-hunting firms, young southern men without kin connections relied on school networks. One VMI alumnus, two years out of school and desperate to leave the poorly paid "drudgery" of his teaching position, offered his former superintendent "six per cent on a year's salary if you will secure me a situation in any College or academy that will pay from $500.00 to $1000."[15] The archives do not provide Smith's response, as he must have answered the letter privately and not through official correspondence. Although this offer of monetary compensation is unique in the correspondence, the teacher's desperation

[12] Even though they desired engineering positions, alumni requested recommendations for engineering much less often than they did for teaching. L. W. Reid to Major Preston, 29 July 1858, 3 August 1858; Daniel Trueheart to FHS, 3 June 1851, 22 June 1859, VMI Archives.

[13] Charles Y. Steptoe to FHS, 18 August 1859 (first and second quotations); FHS to William Clarke, 17 August 1859 (third and fourth quotations), VMI Archives. To speculate on the larger connections within the network, it is probably no coincidence that a Catlett and two Taliaferro cadets attended VMI. Charles Derby to Father, 26 February 1847, VMI Archives.

[14] FHS to John R. Jones, 14 December 1859, VMI Archives.

[15] Levin W. Means to FHS, 14 January 1861, VMI Archives.

was echoed by other missives. Young men often needed positions, and this pledge suggests the reasonable salaries these middle-rank men sought (a $500 salary seems a modest goal). Cadets such as 1848 VMI graduate George Robertson, whose uncle could only help him find a position that fell through, returned to the alumni career network without other options.[16]

The networks allowed cadets to enter teaching positions as other alumni departed them. When leaving a situation, alumni informed their former administrators, often requesting other VMI graduates to take their places. "I shall retire from the school at the end of this session (15th of July) and would like to procure some suitable person to take my place as Associate Principal," alumnus George Patton, ancestor of the World War II general, explained to Smith, "if you can aid me by pointing out a proper person, you will oblige me."[17] Smith consciously staffed and re-staffed schools, especially ones with military components. "I would recommend to you as a successor to Mr. Edmonds [VMI '58], Mr. Wm Keiter of the graduating Class," he informed the principal of Hampton Academy in 1859; Keiter "of course expects to get the same salary &c. as Mr. Edmonds."[18]

WMI's superintendent made sure of always having at least one VMI graduate working at his school and, in 1851, told of the happy circumstances of the last VMI man at Western: "You will recollect having kindly procured for us the assistance of Wm. A. Forbes a graduate of VMI. The result to him, was a beautiful wife with $10,000 in cash, and the Presidency of a Southern College at $1200 per an[num]." He continued, "We now need the services of a good mathematician, who can also render efficient aid in Tactics." Superintendent Smith followed up on the request; after having recommended Forbes for the original position, Smith also found a replacement for Forbes at Western and eventually placed another alumnus with Forbes at the new college. Forbes' decision to remain an

---

[16] George W. Robertson to FHS, 28 August 1851, VMI Archives.

[17] George Patton to FHS, 16 January 1855 (quotations), VMI Archives. Also, William Finney to FHS, 2 September 1848, 20 November 1849; Briscoe Baldwin to FHS, 27 November 1849; Gabriel C. Wharton to FHS, 6 June 1848, VMI Archives.

[18] Three weeks later, the exchange continued when Smith explained that Keiter and another VMI applicant accepted better positions and he suggested a third alumnus for the position; FHS to J. B. Cary, 1 June 1859 (quotation), 26 June 1859, VMI Archives.

educator must have reflected his economic success and an evaluation of its prestige as within the range of the law (the profession of his father and maternal grandfather) and of an agricultural life with his wife's money.[19] Forbes shows the flexibility of such networks as he not only gained social mobility from his introduction into a network but also facilitated two younger graduates' careers.

Not only did superintendents replace alumni in the same positions, they situated young men in jobs created by alumni educators. The ties of successful teachers back to their alma maters built the networks. Micah Jenkins, the 1854 valedictorian of SCMA, exemplifies alumni patterns of teaching – six years before the Civil War for Jenkins – and of networking to foster others' careers. Even before graduation, Jenkins started teaching at the Citadel as an assistant professor during his senior year. Then, the January following commencement, Jenkins and Citadel classmate Asbury Coward opened Kings Mountain Military Academy as a preparatory school for their alma mater. The school at Kings Mountain enrolled more than 100 cadets each year and annually sent a few students into the state military academy of South Carolina. As the school successfully developed, Jenkins also considered opening a pharmacy and studying law, but he continued teaching at Kings Mountain until entering the Confederate army.[20] In the meantime, Jenkins and Coward employed an 1857 Citadel graduate as a Kings Mountain teacher. (In fact, the teacher's brother was an 1851 Citadel alumnus and also a military educator.) They acted as both recipients of their network and as perpetuators of or employers in it.

Similarly within a VMI network, alumni teachers wrote to Superintendent Smith specifically to ask for assistants from the VMI inventory of graduates. John R. Jones, John Pitts, and George Patton wanted assistants in their schools, especially teachers who could enforce military discipline. "He would be expected to be a thoroughly qualified graduate,"

---

[19] T. F. Johnson to FHS, 11 February 1851 (quotations); FHS to William A. Forbes, December 21, 1850, VMI Archives.

[20] Micah Jenkins to John Jenkins, 24 February 1856, 27 February 1856, 21 July 1857, 4 July 1859, John Jenkins Papers; Asbury Coward and Micah Jenkins, Articles of Agreement, 5 January 1855, Micah Jenkins Papers, The South Caroliniana Library, University of South Carolina (hereafter SCL); Jenkins to Brother, 22 March [1855], Duke. See E. T. Crowson, "Jenkins, Coward, and the Yorkville Boys," *Alumni News* (Winter 1974–5), CIT.

Jones explained, "to teach 6 hours a day and to assist in carrying out the military feature."[21] Through these letters and in a variety of ways, alumni aided other graduates of their schools to find employment.

The networks even provided a certain stability for men who proved (repeatedly) unsuccessful; it could not garner them upward social mobility but could ensure maintenance of social position. Indeed, over months or years, the same young men repeatedly wrote back to Smith about situations, as Simpson had.[22] Whereas Simpson's recurring requests came out of ambition – looking for a more profitable position or career – some men found themselves without jobs and seem to have hung on to employment via the networks. Certainly VMI alumnus Charles Derby was the extreme case of networking; he was an unsuccessful teacher who constantly needed new positions. During the seven years that he spent as a teacher, Derby had at least five different positions and vied for another five. He moved between jobs, staying at no position for longer than two years. Despite his volatility, Derby remained continually employed using a career network out of VMI to find new positions when his personality (or possible drinking problem) caused him to move. Letters spanning the 1840s and 1850s between Derby and Superintendent Smith contained Derby's repeated requests for positions. "If there will not be a vacancy in the Institute, I would willingly accept one of the many good situations which the application to you for teachers place at your disposal," an early letter qualified, "provided I should not interfere with the [prospects of the] present graduating class."[23] Even with a problematic man such as Derby, the security of a teaching career proved itself, in that such a man remained employed by using his military school ties. The stability of teaching careers provided these young men with a middle social position; moreover, the networks maintained, even augmented, educators'

---

[21] John R. Jones to FHS, 28 January 1859, 29 November 1859 (quotation); John H. Pitts to FHS, 15 July 1848; George Patton to FHS, 9 July 1854; Norborne Berkeley to FHS, 25 November 1852; Stephen Pendleton to FHS, 15 December 1855, VMI Archives.

[22] Robert H. Simpson to FHS, 23 December 1845, 9 January 1850; Daniel Trueheart to FHS, 28 September 1850, 3 June 1851; Alexander C. Jones to FHS, 1 December 1850; Henry Whiting to FHS, 1 August 1853, 23 August 1856; Augustus Powell to FHS, 10 December 1845; Robert Rodes to FHS, 20 June 1859, VMI Archives.

[23] Charles Derby to FHS, 4 May 1849 (quotation), 27 October 1849, 21 May 1851, 11 June 1851, 21 July 1851, 24 October 1851, 13 January 1852, 25 November 1853, 27 December 1854, 7 March 1855, 17 September 1855, 2 December 1855; Robert Rhodes to FHS, 8 October 1859, VMI Archives.

professional status and hopefully granted individuals mobility through better placement.

Not only could the stability of a career result from participating in a network, alumni could also increase their income, that second component of social position and success. Some men specified salaries they would accept; Robert Simpson, for example, complained about the moderate annual compensation that teaching provided, $400 to $500 yearly, as a reason to leave the profession (which, in the end, he did not do). Henry Whiting asked for positions Smith knew that paid more than $400 annually. (Two weeks later, Whiting thanked Smith for the posting he accepted.) Indeed, another former cadet refused a tutoring situation Smith offered because it provided insufficient funds for him to live; he, in addition, wanted to study medicine while teaching.[24] Alumni then benefited from realistic salaries that the networks almost assured upon graduation or from a later request.

As some alumni educators earned satisfactory salaries, such as George Patton's $700 or William Forbes's $1200, the goal to increase income could be attained through new positions. One of the men in the 1849 exchange told Smith that he moved to Rappahannock Military Institute specifically because it paid more than his previous school. "I then was at the age of 19 appointed teacher in the [Norfolk] Academy where I had received so much of my previous education. I remained there two years till August 1851. The first year my pay was $400 – the second it was $500," another 1849 VMI alumnus explained in his diary his rising salary in conjunction with his moves; "in the May previous to my leaving I had received the appointment of Adjunct Prof. of Math at this [William and Mary] College, and I removed here in October. The pay guaranteed is $700." Another alumnus showed a slower increase in pay, but in three years, his earnings increased from $425 to $500 per year.[25] Indeed, most alumni advanced after they entered the professional world.

---

[24]These starting teachers' salaries compared favorably to the average annual salary for clerks in southern states, approximately $600; Robert A. Margo, *Wages and Labor Markets in the United States, 1820–1860* (Chicago: University of Chicago Press, 2000). Simpson to FHS, 1 December 1846, VMI Archives. Whiting to FHS, 18 July 1853, 1 August 1853; also William Lee to FHS, 23 March 1854, VMI Archives.

[25]Robert Gatewood, unpublished diary (quotation); William Finney to FHS, 20 November 1848; John R. Jones to FHS, 28 January 1849; George Patton to FHS, 16 January 1855; George Robertson to FHS, 7 December 1850; Robert H. Simpson to FHS, 9 January 1850, 24 June 1853,

In addition to salaries, alumni's accumulation of wealth or possessions over their lifetimes indicates their success. Some men eventually inherited wealth or land, after a father's or brother's death. For example, Owen Mortimer Roberts, Jr., graduated from the Citadel in 1859 and went home to care for his dying father (who passed away the following year). Roberts Senior was a dentist, a middle-class status occupation, but owned three slaves that the Citadel alumnus inherited on the eve of the Civil War. From VMI, Robert Rodes taught for two years (probably to fulfill his scholarship requirement) and then became a civil engineer. His 1861 will described a professional who achieved much in the thirteen years since graduation. His estate included five slaves and a value of $2,250. Rodes's younger brother also attended VMI to work as a commission merchant and then gained enough land to farm.[26]

Additionally, the networks could offer more than just references for steady incomes; alumni occasionally received direct monetary benefits. Some youths thanked Smith for the loans he made to them. In the days of paternal discipline, that a superintendent (or the institutions) loaned enough money (the amount usually specified was ten to twenty dollars) to young men to start themselves in careers is unsurprising. Furthermore, some youths, whether graduates or not, retained their connections to VMI by explaining their inability to pay off their school accounts. Some alumni's incapacity to repay debts (often expenses in excess of their state scholarships) meant a period of interest-free loan while young men began their careers. Edward Edmonds, whose father committed suicide during Edward's first year at VMI, explained that he had paid off some of the loans he took out to remain in school and "yours shall be the next debt attended to, I hope you will excuse me, but I am doing all in my power to do your recommendation and the Inst. the fullest Justice." Another young man claimed that he had never heard of Superintendent Smith, presumably as a representative of VMI, refusing to loan money to cadets.[27] All this correspondence meant, beyond the cash, that matriculates

---

VMI Archives. These salaries fall on the low end of the income range for college professors in 1850; Burke, *American Collegiate Populations*, 48.

[26] Sams Family Papers, SCL; Rodes student file, VMI Archives.

[27] Edward C. Edmonds to FHS, 18 May 1859; Francis Suddoth to FHS, 18 July 1856; VMI Archives. Also see, George Patton to FHS, 26 January 1852; Edward Fristoe to FHS, 9 July 1846; James Ashton to Maj. J. Preston, 20 July 1858, VMI Archives.

could offer information into a network or attempt to access it themselves.

In their attempts at mobility, young men wanted to move from uncertain futures into secure careers and financial success. People of the middle class had to defend their position – particularly as that above the yeomen, plain folk, and working class – and aspired to more status. Young middle-class men by the late antebellum era viewed teaching both as a reputable profession and as a stepping-stone to more lucrative and higher status occupations, such as law. Tutoring usually did not receive the same approbation.[28] Military teaching gained added respect through military status, bestowing at least military rank on southern youths. Some military academy men happily found that success in teaching before (and after) the Civil War, whereas others sought upward mobility in professions with more status and rewards than teaching had. Alumni of the latter bent could seek mobility specifically by preparing for a better career as they taught.

In 1848 Superintendent Smith stated that 54 percent of VMI graduates became teachers and, further, that 73 percent of the men who became teachers remained so during the first seven years the school produced graduates. More comprehensive data for the period 1840 to 1860 show that 51 percent of alumni educators remained faithful to the profession (see Table 7.1). Simpson and other members of the networks helped professionalize the career and simultaneously benefited from its rising status. Throughout the 1840s and 1850s, alumni turned educators used their growing professional acceptance to legitimate the occupation itself.

In contrast, slightly less than half of alumni teachers used it as a temporary career. Table 7.1 shows that one-third of alumni began their careers as teachers and then moved to another occupation (and the number may be as high as 44 percent if the men with unspecified career orders are added); a low 4 percent of alumni teachers turned to education after working another job. In one way, the high percentage of men who

---

[28] Bertram Wyatt-Brown, *Southern Honor: Ethics and Behavior in the Old South* (New York: Oxford University Press, 1982), 186–87, describes tutoring positions in the early nineteenth century as filled by Princeton and Yale graduates. Military alumni accepted some tutoring but looked for more prestigious placements, especially in military education as the field expanded.

Table 7.1. *Military school alumni teachers, 1840–1860*

Order of occupation	Number of alumni	Percentage
Teachers only	116	51.1
Teachers first and then one occupation	58	25.6
Teachers first and then two occupations	17	7.9
Teachers with one other occupation (order unspecified)	19	8.4
Teachers with two occupations (order unspecified)	5	2.2
Other occupation and then teacher	7	3.1
Teacher and concurrent occupation	3	1.3
Other occupation, then teacher, then other occupation	2	0.9
$N = 227$ individuals		

Note: Service in the Mexican War was not included as an occupation.
Source: See Appendix 2, Table 1.

left the education field reflects the funding structure of the state military academies. During most years, half of the cadets at VMI and one-fourth of those at the Citadel were obligated to teach as a condition of their scholarships. Similar to West Point graduates' leaving the army, some alumni served their required time and tried for professional success after their service. This is a specific reason why military alumni could use teaching as a launching pad. For example, brothers George and Waller Patton, the family's fourth and fifth sons, taught for a few years before following in their father's footsteps in law.[29]

Not unusual in the teaching profession, North or South, this attempt to improve one's status indicates the less-than-preeminent status (and salary) of antebellum teachers. Robert Simpson, for example, tried learning Greek, a subject omitted in his military academy education and one required for his goal of college professorship, while teaching. Likewise, young men similar to Micah Jenkins prepared for law in a time when individual study was the primary requirement for passing the bar. Cadets made this type of career goal explicit in their letters. "I have much to say to you in my next in regard to your proposition," a Citadel cadet John Wylie told his younger cousin Lafayette Strait, also at SCMA, "to take a

[29] On the Patton brothers, see their student files, VMI Archives.

school while you are studying medicine."[30] "I am solely dependent upon my salary," a VMI graduate complained, "not only temporarily but as the means whereby I may be able to prosecute my studies and carry out my intention of becoming a physician." Needing money was inherent to the middle class (though not exclusively so, of course); young alumni of the middle social position were clearly not men without resources nor were they elites. These cadets often lacked the wealth to sustain medical apprenticeships without an income, unlike the elites at the University of Pennsylvania examined by Daniel Kilbride.[31] A majority of military school alumni started their professional lives by teaching, and some strove to become part of the 33 to 44 percent of educators who left it for another profession.

The development of new careers must be seen as a facet of social mobility in the Old South. Similar to James Oakes's identification of the typical slaveowner's adopting dual careers as an attempt at mobility, military academy men who switched careers do not contradict this part of his argument. Men predominately opted for educational positions as their first choice in their series of multiple careers rather than selecting it as a later career choice; alumni taught as a first job six times more often than they worked in education later in their antebellum occupational lives. Even including the men whose order of careers was unspecified in the number of men who taught as a second career, the ratio of teaching as a first job rather than as a later career remained high at 3:1. Table 7.1 also highlights the rarity of men who shifted between more than two occupations after teaching; less than 10 percent had more than two different professions.[32] Teaching could serve as a launching pad into

[30]John D. Wylie to Lafayette Strait, 4 January 1854 (quotations), SCL. Similarly, Charles Y. Steptoe to FHS, 14 July 1859; William Lee to FHS, 15 July 1853; Briscoe G. Baldwin to FHS, 27 November 1849; William Finney to FHS, 2 September 1848, VMI Archives. Edward Fristoe also wanted to learn Greek to enter a professorship; Fristoe to FHS, 4 April 1850, 24 May 1852, VMI Archives. Other cadets teaching while studying to become lawyers include Robert P. Carson, William Clarke, Giles B. Cooke, Joseph Hambrick, Charles Hurt, Alexander C. Jones, James Kincheloe, and Craig McDonald.
[31]Instead, young William Finney went into the Pony Express; Finney to FHS, 20 November 1848 (quotation), VMI Archives. Daniel Kilbride, "Southern Medical Students in Philadelphia, 1800–1860: Science and Sociability in the 'Republic of Medicine,'" *Journal of Southern History*, 65 (November 1999), 697–732.
[32]On multiple careers, James Oakes, *The Ruling Race: A History of American Slaveowners* (New York: Vantage Books, 1982), esp. 58–59.

a (hopefully) higher-status career. Whether seeking careers, incomes, or mobility, military school educators found assistance through their networks.

Professionalization and Status

Concurrent to promoting individual advancement, the networks served to professionalize teaching and military education so that its practitioners increased their status. Status – that ever-important quality in the antebellum South – reflected a man's social position as perceived by his community and its evaluation of his reputation. Certainly planters, the elite of society who set the tone of much of the white community, based their lives on status and honor.[33] Young men in military academies entered professions to raise themselves in their status-conscious society. They wanted prestige, but they also challenged the preeminent definition of it. Their vision of success did not fully align with the planter model – slave and plantation ownership – but was accessible by less well-to-do cadets. They desired "industry and advancement" through professional status. Perpetuating the system of military education was one way in which the middle class began to assert a nonagricultural mobility.

One of its members' best paths to status was to obtain a professional teaching career, achieved though military school networks, and then to improve the society's estimation of that career. This path equaled professionalization, the elaboration of the career, and the resultant increase in status of those professions. Lawyers, physicians, dentists, and teachers pursued professionalization in the nineteenth century through control of exclusive knowledge, creation of organizations, and eventually legislation regulating the profession. The first stage in the professionalization of military teaching made specialized education a prerequisite for the

---

[33] For extended discussions of honor, see Wyatt-Brown, *Southern Honor*; Kenneth S. Greenberg, *Honor & Slavery: Lies, Duels, Noses, Masks, Dressing as a Woman, Gifts, Strangers, Humanitarianism, Death, Slave Rebellions, The Proslavery Argument, Baseball, Hunting, and Gambling in the Old South* (Princeton: Princeton University Press, 1996); Craig Thompson Friend and Lorri Glover, eds., *Southern Manhood: Perspectives on Masculinity in the Old South* (Athens: University of Georgia Press, 2004); Robert F. Pace, *Halls of Honor: College Men in the Old South* (Baton Rouge: Louisiana State University Press, 2004).

career, just as other professionalizing fields at the time demanded.[34] Military education acted for teacher training and certainly offered specialized curricula with military and scientific content. In the antebellum years, the second phase of professionalization began with the creation of professional organizations. Historians present the professionalization of teachers through the associations and publications of common school educators, but the increasing use of specialized knowledge to explore the professionalization of private school educators expands our understanding of the middle class and social class formation.[35] Although they did not form their own organizations, military educators and their charges relied on their extrainstitutional career networks, which acted as protoprofessional organizations. Before 1860, state legislatures incorporated schools but did not regulate military (or any) educators; however, the establishment of academies strictly adhering to the models of West Point and VMI created some de facto standards.

The processes of professionalization in the Old South illuminate class formation and interaction. Beth Barton Schweiger and Steven M. Stowe have examined southern ministers and doctors beginning the process in the 1840s. Their studies indicate regional distinctiveness and national

---

[34]Bledstein, *Culture of Professionalism*, esp. 84; Thomas Haskell, *The Emergence of Professional Social Science: The American Social Science Association and the Nineteenth-Century Crisis of Authority* (Urbana: University of Illinois Press, 1977); Samuel Haber, *The Quest for Authority and Honor in the American Professions, 1750–1900* (Chicago: University of Chicago Press, 1991); Steven M. Stowe, *Doctoring the South: Southern Physicians and Everyday Medicine in the Mid-nineteenth Century* (Chapel Hill: University of North Carolina Press, 2004); Paul H. Mattingly, *The Classless Profession: American Schoolmen in the Nineteenth Century* (New York: New York University Press, 1975). Beth Barton Schweiger presents the professionalization of Virginia ministers beginning in full force in the 1840s, focusing on education; *The Gospel Working Up: Progress and Pulpit in Nineteenth-Century Virginia* (New York: Oxford University Press, 2000), ch. 3.

[35]Wells, *Origins of the Southern Middle Class,* 148, states, "After 1840, a growing subculture of teachers emerged"; he cites professional journals (mostly for common school teachers) in the South but describes mostly female teachers. The feminization of teachers started in this era in elementary, public, and northern schools; in the South, in particular, teaching professionalized as a male career. Studies outside of the northeast remain to be done, as notes Kim Tolley and Margaret A. Nash, "Leaving Home to Teach," in *Chartered Schools: Two-Hundred Years of Independent Academies in the United States, 1727–1925,* ed. Nancy Beadie and Kim Tolley (New York: RoutledgeFalmer, 2002), 162, 180 n. 4; Carl Kaestle, *Pillars of the Republic: Common Schools and American Society, 1780–1860* (New York, 1983), ch. 6; Christie Ann Farnham, *The Education of the Southern Belle: Higher Education and Student Socialization in the Antebellum South* (New York: New York University Press, 1994), ch. 4.

similarities. Stowe's "country orthodoxy" of southern physicians and Schweiger's 123-person source base describe no networking comparable to the military educator networks.[36] Military alumni, but neither doctors nor ministers, began networks, perhaps because teaching provided the best opportunity for such social change. Studies on professions, such as military education, must be incorporated into the larger scope of the ways professionalization occurred in the Old South. Military alumni increased the status of teaching in part through their participation in its professionalization. Their success with this amorphous mobility can be seen in networking's results: Over twenty years, professionalization brought about the growth in numbers of military educators, of military institutions, and in the prestige of both teachers and schools.

After cadets graduated from the earliest academies, they entered and developed the field of military education. From the early to late antebellum period, a shift occurred in the founders of and teachers at private and state military academies. Just as Yale and Princeton graduates established the earliest southern universities, West Pointers such as Francis H. Smith started and staffed the first generation of military institutions. Because the antebellum army lacked opportunities for advancement and necessitated postings in often undesirable locations, antebellum West Point graduates frequently resigned their commissions, and some of those men started military schools.[37] By the 1850s, however, the private and state military institutes, with their teaching networks, had produced a sufficient number of alumni to take over military education. Former soldiers still worked at military schools, including William T. Sherman accepting the superintendence of the Louisiana state military institute in 1859, but their representation dropped greatly as other military educators became available.

---

[36] Schweiger, *Gospel Working Up*; Stowe, *Doctoring the South*; Steven Stowe, "H-South Review: Stowe Replies to Emberton's Review," H-South posting, 2 March 2006.

[37] They also taught at seven of the eight technical colleges, which possessed curricula similar to military schools but lacked the disciplinary structure; the exception was Rensselaer Polytechnic Institute in New York. William Baumer Jr., *Not all Warriors: Portraits of Nineteenth-Century West Pointers Who Gained Fame in Other Than Military Fields* (Freeport, NY: Books for Libraries, 1971); James R. Endler, *Other Leaders, Other Heroes: West Point's Legacy to America Beyond the Field of Battle* (Westport, CT: Praeger, 1998), 58, ch. 4; Dean Paul Baker, "The Partridge Connection: Alden Partridge and Southern Military Education" (Ph.D. diss., University of North Carolina, 1986).

The new military institutions alumni founded meant more positions for their peers and their students. The growth of military schools followed the national trend in college and academy growth; eighteen new military academies started in the 1840s and thirty-five in the 1850s, compared to at least double each number for new colleges nationwide.[38] More than one-fourth of alumni teachers made the transition from military education to military educator. A case in point, 1846 Citadel alumnus W. J. Magill went on to teach at KMI and advanced to the Commandant of the Georgia Military Institute (GMI) by 1860. Also, Thomas Rowe Thornton attended two military academies, Rappahannock Military Institute and Virginia's state military academy, before teaching math and becoming the principal at Rappahannock. He replaced John R. Jones, also a VMI alumnus, at Rappahannock after Jones resigned to establish a new military academy in Florida.

Like Jones, military alumni started military schools throughout the South. William Morrissett, for example, graduated from Hampton Academy (with a cadet corps) and VMI, taught at Hampton, and then founded Williamsburg Military School in 1852. The networks encouraged and staffed alumni schools, including Abingdon Male Academy, Albemarle Military Institute, Chuckatuck Military Institute, Culpeper Military Academy, Fleetwood Academy (with a cadet corps), Petersburg Military Academy, and academies in Tazewell County, Onancock, and Petersburg in Virginia; Military and Scientific Institute at Baton Rouge, Louisiana; Columbus Military Academy, Mississippi; Quincy Military Academy in Florida; a military program at Central Masonic Institute in Selma, Alabama; a military school in Lexington, Missouri; Hillsboro Military Academy (HMA) and Raleigh Military Academy in North Carolina; and Kings Mountain Military Academy in South Carolina. These examples indicate that military school alumni created employment

---

[38] Donald G. Tewksbury, *The Founding of American Colleges and Universities Before the Civil War, With Particular Reference to the Religious Influences Bearing Upon the College Movement* (1932; reprint, Archon Books, 1965), 16, calculates the number of colleges founded 1840–49 as 32 to 42 and those started in 1850–61 as 66 to 92. Tewksbury used some restrictive qualifications collecting his data (especially in counting only colleges that continued to exist into the twentieth century); the number of new schools therefore may have been greater than his figures; see, for example, Natalie A. Naylor, "The Antebellum College Movement: A Reappraisal of Tewksbury's *Founding of American Colleges and Universities*," *History of Education Quarterly*, 13 (Fall 1973), 261–74.

opportunities within the system of military education that their networks perpetuated.

To increase the success of their professional niche and their specialized knowledge, every military institution attempted to secure at least one West Point or VMI graduate – thus legitimating the martial side of the equation. The educational background of military institute professors is often difficult to ascertain, but of those whose schooling is known, the majority attended military schools themselves. According to their catalogues, for example, three of five professors at KMI in 1853, four of five at HMA in 1860, and four of five at WMI in 1853 came from military programs.[39] Alumni then hired other men from the networks, as Jenkins and Coward did at Kings Mountain. An interesting example is the founder of KMI, West Point graduate R. T. P. Allen. He started Bastrop Military Institute in Texas with his son, creating a career for the young man as a military educator. When Allen quit Kentucky in 1856, he sold KMI to a teacher at WMI.[40] Thus, the ownership of KMI rotated between military educators, and more than half of Kentucky's faculty remained private and state military academy graduates.

The networks also recommended alumni schools, continuing to promote individual careers and the vocation of teaching. Endorsements for alumni-founded schools and pedagogical advice supported young teachers. New principals hoped for the additional aid that Smith's approval might bring: "It gives me pleasure to recommend the male Academy under the charge of Mr. J. Calvin Councill [VMI '48]. Mr. Councill is a distinguished graduate of this Institution and discharged with great credit the duties of Ass't Prof. of Mathematics for one year." Publishing such a testimonial from the era's leading military educator was intended to increase enrollments and longevity at Councill's new school. This type

[39] Professors at military institutes, when not military school alumni, generally held bachelor's degrees. *Catalogue of the Officers and Cadets of the Kentucky Military Institute, Six Miles from Frankfort Kentucky* (Frankfort, 1853); *Semi-Annual Register, of the Officers and Cadets, of the Hillsboro' Military Academy* (Raleigh: Jon. W. Syme Printer, 1860); *Rules and Regulations of the Western Military Institute at Tyree Springs* (Nashville: John F. Morgan, 1854). Allardice, "West Points of the Confederacy," 314, agrees.

[40] On the history of KMI, see James Darwin Stephens, *Reflections: A Portrait-Biography of the Kentucky Military Institute, 1845–1971* (Georgetown, KY: Kentucky Military Institute, 1991). Cadet Leeland Hathaway followed Edwin Morgan from Western to Kentucky; unpublished memoir, c. 1890, Leeland Hathaway Recollections #2954, Southern Historical Collection, Wilson Library, University of North Carolina at Chapel Hill (hereafter SHC).

of recommendation and the smattering of pedagogical advice that the networks provided aided alumni's educational careers, but more significantly they encouraged military educators to instruct more cadets as the years progressed. They aided the continuance of schools in areas with high failure rates.[41] Still, the addition of more schools and more young men who entered and professionalized the teaching profession raised all of them. The professionalization of military education resulted in increased status and in stability and mobility for members of the emerging southern middle class.

The specialized curricula of the academies offered alumni the best advantage teaching mathematics or military tactics. Augustus Powell found this advantage to be true, as he boasted of opening the only school in his area of Mississippi to teach mathematics. "Every day of my life I see the tremendous advantages the VM Inst. Graduates have over all others in our profession," an 1848 alumnus exclaimed.[42] This young man worked first as a teacher and later as an engineer, so the comment could refer to either prominent career. Significantly, college curricula deemphasized training in these fields, so cadets encountered less competition to teach or specialize in them. Most colleges and universities followed the 1828 Yale Report's prescription of classical curriculum with supplementary courses in mathematics. Before the Civil War, the study of math increased but never predominated in universities, and military higher school graduates received more exposure to math and engineering than did most college students. As college and military academy alumni competed for jobs, more training in specialized fields provided advantages in hiring to military graduates. Also, increasing the number of programs in tactics and math, such as Powell's school in Mississippi, allowed alumni enhanced opportunity in gaining those positions for which their military and scientific education specifically prepared them.

Benefiting from the networks and the specialized curricula, military academy alumni could teach as a stable career. "I should prefer

---

[41] FHS to J. C. Councill, 20 June 1859, VMI Archives. Also, FHS to G. M. Edgar, 16 June 1859, VMI Archives. Burke concludes that failure rates for liberal arts colleges in the South were significantly higher than those in other regions; for example, Kentucky exhibited a 50 percent failure rate compared to 14 to 20 percent nationwide; *American Collegiate Populations*, 14–15.

[42] Augustus Powell to FHS, 4 November 1846; Robert Rodes to FHS, 27 November 1856 (quotation), VMI Archives.

permanency to lucrativeness," a graduate clarified to Smith as he asked for a new posting in 1851. As a teacher, this young man entered the same profession as his maternal grandfather. Indeed, when recent graduate William Clarke could not get an engineering position, he immediately turned to Smith: "I desire a place [teaching], and would put you to the trouble to secure me one if in your power."[43] Clarke chose the security of a teaching career in 1859 when, one month after graduation, the more profitable one of engineering did not develop. He would continue teaching at Norfolk Academy, organized with its own cadet corps, into the years after the Civil War. Just over half of the alumni who chose education remained in that career until the war.

Educators' new schools expanded military education into the newer states, including the twelve state military academies, dubbed the "West Points of the South." Many southerners moved west to find new plantations and new areas of opportunity, and teachers did the same, locating stable careers and professional status further afield. They spread the web of connections across the lower South from Florida to Texas.[44] VMI provided the model for at least WMI, Louisiana State Seminary and Military Academy, University of Alabama cadet corps, and Missouri Military Institute. The founders of the Western, Alabama, and Louisiana military academies, furthermore, turned to the VMI networks for teachers. By 1851, an alumnus of the state school in Virginia reported that military education had taken off in Alabama and that some residents wanted to start a state military institute, indicating in part the networks' success. Unfortunately, financing limited attempts to found a program, but they succeeded in 1860 when L. C. Garland implemented a cadet corps at the University of Alabama, using Smith's advice. Moreover, VMI's network of military educators acted to staff the new military course. James Murfee, an 1853 VMI alumnus who had been teaching in Virginia since graduation but sought a better salary, relocated to Alabama, as did two 1860 VMI graduates who went directly to the military program. Similarly, president of the Louisiana State Seminary and Military Academy

[43] Daniel Trueheart to FHS, 3 June 1851 (first quotation); William Clarke to FHS, 11 August 1859 (second quotation), VMI Archives.
[44] Gabriel Jordan to William D. Stuart, November 22, 1854, William Dabney Stuart Papers; John R. Jones to FHS, 29 November 1859; R. D. Powell to FHS, 16 August 1845, VMI Archives; Robert Oswald Sams, unpublished memoir, CIT.

Board of Trustees George Mason Graham received six recommendations for teachers from Smith. Smith ended up negotiating among alumni – the candidates – about whom to locate in the new institution. In the end, Louisiana appointed only one VMI alumnus, but the negotiations showed the prevalence of the military educator networks.[45]

At the same time as military education took hold in newer states, older schools expanded to enroll more cadets into the system. Modeled on VMI as providing both good supervision of the state armory and practical education, the second state military institute, SCMA, also provided schooling for the emerging middle class. SCMA developed as two separate academies, the Arsenal in Columbia and the Citadel in Charleston; the first-year program relocated to the Arsenal Academy, thus boosting the number of cadets that would matriculate and propagate its networks as they ventured throughout the region. A postwar superintendent described how the antebellum SCMA's "steady increasing demand for the admission of pupils" led to the Citadel adding a third story and two new wings and to the Arsenal adding two additional buildings. In other states, VMI built new barracks in 1850 to house more cadets; KMI moved locations in part to augment its facilities; and WMI joined with the University of Nashville to increase resources and enrollment.[46] See the images of KMI (Figure 1) and VMI (Figure 8) to appreciate a sense of their size in the 1850s.

[45] Graham selected William T. Sherman, an 1846 West Point graduate, as superintendent. George M. Graham to FHS, 30 May 1859, 4 August 1859; FHS to George M. Graham, 18 August 1859; FHS to William T. Sherman, 30 September 1859; FHS to Robert Rodes, 20 June 1859; Rodes to FHS, 4 July 1859; Daniel Trueheart to FHS, 10 July 1859, VMI Archives. John Hope Franklin, *The Militant South, 1800–1860* (Boston: Beacon Press, 1956), ch. 8; Allardice, "West Points of the Confederacy"; Edwin L. Dooley, " 'A fine college from this time forward': The Influence of VMI on the Militarization of the University of Alabama" (n.p., 19 April 1997).

[46] Ashbury Coward, "The Sketch of the South Carolina Military Academy," *Year Book* (1892), 2 (quotation); Royster Lyle Jr. and Matthew W. Paxton Jr., "The VMI Barracks," *Virginia Cavalcade*, 23 (1974), 14–29; Western Military Institute, *Order Book*, 1848–1855, Jean and Alexander Heard Library, Vanderbilt University Archives. KMI increased its average enrollment from 72 to 150 cadets in the early 1850s; see KMI, *Circular of Information on Ante-bellum and Post-bellum Professors and Officers of the Institute* (Frankfort, 1878), Rare Pamphlet Collection, Special Collections Department, The Filson Historical Society. A large college had 100 or more students in the antebellum South, especially in western states; Burke, *American Collegiate Populations*, 49.

At a very basic level, the networks resulted in more men teaching at more military programs throughout the late antebellum years. In a reciprocal relationship, military institutions increased their attendance by accepting the pupils of their graduates; Simpson, Jenkins, and their peers used that advantage in the competitive world of private schooling. Alumni teachers at preparatory academies often had cadets from their schools apply to the military higher schools, and especially to their alma maters. While using the networks to aid his own career, Simpson also increased the networks by enrolling students at VMI. Similarly, VMI alumni John H. Pitts at Fleetwood Academy and James Phillips at Chuckatuck Military Institute fed their students into established military schools. SCMA essentially guaranteed entrance every year for two cadets from Jenkins's and Coward's military institute.[47] Other alumni teachers also used their connections to assure entrance for their students.

As superintendents represented their schools, their reputations grew alongside the professional standing of military education. VMI's Francis Smith was an excellent example of stature gained through the military education profession. By the age of 27, when he started at VMI, the native Virginian had graduated West Point, instructed there, resigned the army, and taught at Hampden-Sidney College. Over the next two decades, Smith spoke to the Virginia legislature, published on military education, served a year as president of West Point's Board of Visitors, and helped develop other schools. Alumni educators used Smith's textbooks, such as *An Elementary Treatise on Algebra*, and demonstrations with their own students. The four editions each of Smith's two *Treatises* published prior to the Civil War suggest their popularity.[48] Likewise, C. C. Tew of SCMA,

---

[47] Rod Andrew Jr., *Long Gray Lines: The Southern Military School Tradition, 1839–1915* (Chapel Hill: University of North Carolina Press, 2001), 20–21, partially attributes the success of military education to the growing number of alumni. Examples include Robert H. Simpson to FHS, 11 December 1851; Charles Derby to FHS, 23 August 1852; James J. Phillips to FHS, 13 December [1846], 24 December 1846; Stephen Pendleton to FHS, 25 May 1845; John H. Pitts to FHS, 15 July 1845; James J. Phillips to FHS, 12 August 1856; John R. Jones to FHS, 28 January 1849 [1850], Charles Urquhart student file, VMI Archives.

[48] Charles Derby to FHS, 27 November 1849, 21 July 1851; Augustus Powell, 4 November 1846, VMI Archives. Not surprisingly, the teachers who complimented Smith on his texts were also men who relied on the network and Smith's recommendations. FHS, *An Elementary Treatise on Analytical Geometry: Translated from the French of J.B. Biot* (New York: Wiley and Putnam, 1840); FHS, *An Elementary Treatise on Algebra: Prepared for the Use of the Cadets of the*

a merchant's son who taught at his alma mater after his 1846 graduation, raised himself to superintendent of Arsenal Academy, published articles on military education, and started HMA in North Carolina; he probably gained status analogous to Smith's among his former students.[49] Thus, as superintendents advanced their graduates and academies, they enhanced their own status.

Authors and speakers increasingly praised military education's scientific curriculum and practical education, and advocates promulgated institutions throughout the South. Even some elites began to recognize military education as southerners came to terms with modern and industrial ideas; in 1853, South Carolina College president James H. Thornwell defended the usefulness of military education, despite its status below that of colleges.[50] Military education, particularly in the 1850s, received praise and respect as valuable schooling, but antebellum contemporaries never equated its status with that of collegiate education in the way military educators occasionally wished. People recognized it as a southern institution and as such, it shows the development of southern thought distinct from the northern middle class and the southern elite. The increase in military teachers' status becomes evident, however, in the 1862 Morrill Land Grant Act, which provided for instruction in practical education and military tactics; the inclusion of military teachers as professors indicated the increased legitimacy and professionalization of the occupation in the prewar years.[51]

Virginia Military Institute, and Adapted to the Present State of Mathematical Instruction in the Schools, Academies, and Colleges, of the United States (Philadelphia: Thomas, Cowperthwait and Co., 1848); FHS, *The American Statistical Arithmetic: Designed for Academies and Schools* (Philadelphia: Thomas, Cowperthwait and Co., 1845).

[49] Careers such as J. M. Richardson's teaching for Tew at HMA seven years after leaving SCMA endorse that connection. C. C. T., "Art. IX. South-Carolina Military Academies." Tew is briefly discussed in "Family Losses in the Civil War," *The Confederate Veteran*, 10 (February 1902), 79–80; Steven A. Ross, "To 'Prepare Our Sons for all the Duties that May Lie before Them': The Hillsborough Military Academy and Military Education in Antebellum North Carolina," *North Carolina Historical Review*, 79 (January 2002), 1–27.

[50] Edwin Heriot, *The Polytechnic School, the Best System of Practical Education* (Charleston: Walker and James, 1850); D. H. Hill, *Essay on Military Education, delivered at Wilmington NC, November 14, 1860 Before the State Educational Convention* (Charlotte: Daily Bulletin Office, 1860); FHS, *The Regulations of Military Institutions*; FHS, *College Reform* (Philadelphia: Thomas, Cowperthwait and Co., 1851). Thornwell, *Letter to His Excellency Governor Manning on Public Instruction in South Carolina*, November 1853.

[51] Obviously, the Morrill Act did not apply to the Confederate states when enacted, but schools started under it after the war. Its passage in the United States reflected both wartime concerns

Reflective of new professional leanings in the Old South, military teaching, a specialization within the nationwide process, earned additional respect with military status. Educators at the twelve state schools received rank with their hire; Superintendents Smith and Tew, for example, were granted the rank of colonel. A GMI cadet's father felt that his son's position as cadet Captain gave the young man "a higher standing in the School and also among the citizens." Certainly rank and title offered markers of prestige and respectability.[52] Professionalization increased the number of military teachers, number of schools, status of educators, and public approval of military education.

As professionalization developed during the antebellum years, teaching became a profession requiring skills and education rather than an informal job for youths as it had been previously considered. Teaching slowly changed from a respectable but lowly occupation to one that young men made increasingly acceptable; this process has been traced among northern teachers, described well by Burton Bledstein as starting in the mid-nineteenth century. The fact that military school alumni taught at rates far greater than that of their fathers (2.5 percent of fathers were educators versus 27.7 percent of alumni) suggests the increased status of the career in one generation. The results of early professionalization brought young middle-class men to view teaching both as a reputable occupation and as a stepping-stone to what they perceived as more lucrative and higher status professions, particularly law.

Networks in the Southern Context

The career networks aided middle-class stability within the larger social, regional, and educational communities that historians of the South

and a valuation of military education that supports their increased presence and status in the 1850s. Michael O'Brien, *Conjectures of Order: Intellectual Life and the Antebellum South, 1810–1860* (Chapel Hill: University of North Carolina Press, 2004), 392, notes that mathematical education did not equate to a gentleman's status but it clearly raised those men above the "common mass," and I am arguing that that ranking reflected middle-class stability.

[52] R. H. Kingsbury to Theodore Kingsbury, 26 August 1846, SHC. Andrew, *Long Gray Lines*; Kilbride, "Southern Medical Students in Philadelphia." VMI professors were given rank, but not in the state militia, while HMA professors did receive commissions in their state milita; Henry Wise, *Drawing Out the Man: The VMI Story* (Charlottesville: University of Virginia Press, 1978) and Ross, "To 'Prepare Our Sons for All the Duties that May Lie before Them,'" 16.

study.[53] In the paradoxical and uneven way that social change occurs, the networks were based in and even mirrored patronage at the same time as they integrated a more modern system into traditional southern expectations. This analysis demonstrates that military alumni networks were not patronage because elites more often accessed their community associations whereas middle-class cadets relied on networks; alumni friendships acted as connections for the networks, and non-elite teachers staffed the quasi-bureaucratic networks. The associations, moreover, show that the developing southern middle class possessed southern values – not only because of the institutions' southernness – but because they were built on the community expectations of the Old South. They complement the historiographic assertion that the South maintained premodern relationships but incorporated into the model a developing southern middle class based on education and professional status.

As layers of social and cultural networks coexisted, military educators' career networks did not preclude others.[54] Because the networks replicated other relationships within society, their existence is unsurprising. Similar networks among college students rested in the many options that the elite possessed: kin, patronage, classical education, land, or money. Of course, relatives in any era and region acted as career networks. Kin relationships smoothed entry into professional careers, as families promoted sons and attempted to locate them the best positions possible. Graduates of southern universities ran their states; South Carolina College, the most elite southern university, produced a large number of governors and legislators, as did the University of Virginia. Alumni of those institutions, primarily planters' sons, certainly engaged in some type of student–professor networking, although more likely they relied on kin connections or their wealth to enter careers; in general, southern

[53] Many historians accept and discuss southern community expectations; see, for example, Wyatt-Brown, *Southern Honor*, and Greenberg, *Honor & Slavery*; Jennings L. Wagoner Jr., "Honor and Dishonor at Mr. Jefferson's University: The Antebellum Years," *History of Education Quarterly*, 26 (Summer 1986), 157–63.

[54] Gregg D. Kimball pointed out that voluntary associations did not prevent other layers of connection; Southern Historical Association Conference, Memphis, Tenn., November 4, 2004. See also John Gordon Deal, "The Forgotten Southerner: Middle-Class Associationalism in Antebellum Norfolk, Virginia" (Ph.D. diss., University of Florida, 2003).

elites did not require school-based networks.[55] Friendship, kinship, literary societies, Greek letter societies, alumni associations, marriage, and militia membership provided those ties that brought information into the networks of military educators.

Maintaining community connections was important in the Old South, so military school matriculates built networks as they maintained friendships. Amity brought alumni together, but it simultaneously formed them into career networks. The loose connections of their acquaintances – correspondence over miles and years – brought information into networks. Specifically, they provided connections that encouraged the bureaucratic networks of military educators. Friendships, such as the one between VMI alumni Gabriel Jordan Jr. and William D. Stuart, helped bring information into the networks but did not act as job locators. These young Virginians probably met in the barracks and corresponded after their 1850 graduation. A letter between them is the only example of a direct job offer. Four years after graduating together, Jordan told Stuart that he would help track down an engineering post for Stuart if the man chose to quit teaching; Jordan suggested, however, that the switch was unlikely because teaching gave Stuart "a comfortable competency, and something besides." Indeed, Stuart's father suffered from a nervous condition that ended his law practice, so the son's education was left partially to the state and his career to the networks.[56] These young men gave each other friendship and informal career information, which must have been unremarkable between associates. The same as Jordan and Stuart, some cadets kept in touch with each other, and these ties passed knowledge of job openings and teachers into the networks. A cadet drawing from 1855 suggests the friendship formed between roommates in Figure 5. The more

---

[55] It should be noted that similar networks probably existed at nonmilitary schools, though without the dominance of one career their success and depth may not have been as great. Schweiger, *Gospel Working Up*, esp. appendix. Also, Kilbride, "Southern Medical Students in Philadelphia"; Michael Sugrue, "South Carolina College; The Education of an Antebellum Elite" (Ph.D. diss., Columbia University, 1992); Lorri Glover, *Southern Sons: Becoming Men in the New Nation* (Baltimore: The Johns Hopkins University Press, 2007), 56.

[56] Jordan to Stuart, November 22, 1854 (quotation); A. H. Stuart to FHS, 6 May 1847, VMI Archives. For a more common example of alumni exchanges see: Edmund Pendleton to Philip Winn, 28 March 1845, VMI Archives; T. H. Blount to Columbus Cartwright, 12 April 1855, Americus Cartwright Papers, Center for American History, University of Texas; Tom Lucas to Lafayette Strait, 6 May 1855, SCL.

typical friendship circle probably more closely resembled the intellectuals in the Old South who supported each other as isolated, educated men but who never extended their connections into career advancement. Alumni letters confirm Granovetter's "The Strength of Weak Ties" argument that strong friendships did not help career placement as well as did weak ties among men who connected into networks.[57]

As they pursued friendships and what may have had the appearance of patronage, military academy alumni actually started networks that were institutional and quasi-bureaucratic. Continuing acquaintance among alumni was important so that one man could inform the other networks of openings and available professors. Especially good aids to information exchange were the men with friends at different military schools, so more data would enter any given network. Whereas kin may have attended the same school – the Otey brothers at VMI or cousins John Wylie and Lafayette Strait at SCMA – other youths were at different schools, such as cousins Archibald Govan Hill at VMI and William Govan at Rumford Academy (with a military program run by a VMI graduate). In North Carolina, a doctor's son at HMA noted that he was friends with a North Carolina Military Institute cadet.[58] School-based career networks better aided middle-class young men who lacked patronage in the late antebellum society that was negotiating modernizing influences.

The networks applied the understood values of the Old South to a new system outside of the established power elite of the plantation class, but without opposing the elite. In one of his many letters back to his alma mater, Simpson explained the power of a superintendent in the alumnus–professor relationship: "He is frequently applied to for Teachers & he knows what each one is suited for and can be of material assistance. He can confine his recommendations for high or low situations to the most recent Graduate or let the latter gradually rise and not take the prominent positions whilst a mere boy." Simpson's description

---

[57] Granovetter, "The Strength of Weak Ties." Michael Sugrue states that South Carolina College alumni, including James Henry Hammond who was also studied by Drew Gilpin Faust [*A Sacred Circle* (Baltimore, 1977)], corresponded but not for occupational aid; Sugrue, " 'We Desire our Future Rulers to be Educated Men': South Carolina College, the Defense of Slavery, and the Development of Secessionist Politics," in *The American College in the Nineteenth Century*, ed. Roger Geiger (Nashville: Vanderbilt University Press, 2000), 93.

[58] Egbert Ross to Emma Ross, 20 April 1860, Egbert A. Ross Papers, SHC.

indicates that alumni had to remain on good terms to get the best positions, but he also described an alumnus's "reciprocal duties," specifically
"refuting slanders against" the school and its professors.[59] Certainly, this
echoes the language of southern honor. Relationships in the networks,
however, modified the reciprocal duties of honor with more institutional
expectations. Even as elucidated by Simpson, the networks worked within
southern culture but did not duplicate the duties of southern community
or patronage relationships. Professors surely recognized the demands of
southern honor, but they acted as administrators in a developing bureaucracy. This networking, in the transitional period of the antebellum years,
was part of both a developing career-placement bureaucracy and the creation of a patronage-like system for the middle class within a southern
society so reliant on those types of connections.

Friendship, literary societies, Greek letter societies, and alumni associations all brought alumni into social contact, but none of these groups
enhanced status or mobility as the networks did. Educational organizations served middle-class southern youths as bureaucratic examples
encouraging the second stage of professionalization, the creation of professional organizations. Literary or debating societies, organizations that
most antebellum colleges and large military academies enjoyed, helped
cement the networks. Cadets in those groups debated each other, com-
posed speeches, and produced stories and poetry, which were occasionally published in the *Kentucky Military Institute Magazine*, for example.
See the poem reproduced from a North Carolina cadet (Figure 9). The
first debating society at VMI started within one month of the school's
opening, according to a cadet's letter home. Cadets in VMI's Society of
Cadets and Dialectic Society, the Citadel's Calliopean and Polytechnic
Societies, WMI's Arathenian and Addisonian Societies, or KMI's Philo-
mathean Society encouraged friendships that supported the networks.
Historians describe literary societies as extracurricular expressions of
friendship, student life, imagination, and well-rounded collegiate education.[60] The clubs helped boys grow into men, negotiating military

---

[59] Simpson to FHS, 21 December 1853, VMI Archives.
[60] Robert F. Pace describes them as having "near absolute" influence and being the site in which
students' honor ethic developed; *Halls of Honor*, 73. Frederick Rudolph, *The American
College and University: A History* (New York: Alfred A. Knopf, 1962), ch. 7, esp. 143–46,
and *Curriculum: A History of the American Undergraduate Course of Study Since 1636* (San

discipline and instilling the southern-valued trait of oratory through their debate and speeches.

Some men would maintain friendships in their postgraduate years, whereas others lost contact with their former classmates; even though some friendships grew out of them, however, the purpose and activities of the societies necessarily meant that the organizations remained internal to particular campuses and that most bonds dissipated outside the barracks' confines. Literary societies created stability within the institutions; as can be seen in poems and songs passed down across the years, an institutional memory resided within the student body. Throughout the 1850s, VMI cadets copied at least three of the same poems into their journals. (The most interesting was an ode which caricatured "The Faculty," calling the Commandant a "bullfrog" and another professor vain and fat.)[61] Of course, literary societies, being institution-specific as were networks, encouraged friendships, which supported the networks.

Networks built on the friendships of literary societies, and the same connections existed with the few Greek letter societies in the Old South. Fraternities, subsequent to the Civil War, evolved into centers for social life during school and for alumni networking after graduation. Before 1865, however, the rudimentary forms of fraternities, individual chapters of intrauniversity organizations, gained inroads in northern universities but were not emphasized in the South. The lack of developed bureaucratic and of reform organizations led to relatively low interest in the region. Greek letter societies began asserting preeminence over literary societies in the North in the 1840s and 1850s, but few fraternities existed at southern universities by 1856.[62] The state military institutes in Kentucky

Francisco: Jossey-Bass Publishers, 1978), 98; James McLachlin, "The *Choice of Hercules*: American Student Societies in the Early 19th Century" in *The University in Society*, ed. Lawrence Stone (Princeton: Princeton University Press, 1974), 2:449–94; Wells, *Origins of the Southern Middle Class*, 101–02.

[61] Diaries with poetry include those of William E. Arnold, Thomas Barksdale, Charles Barton, Joseph Carpenter, John Fletcher Early, Philip Gibbs, Edward C. Shepherd, and William O. Yager, VMI Archives. For a similar example from West Point, see Gary Gallagher, "A North Carolinian at West Point: Stephen Dodson Ramseur, 1855–60," *North Carolina Historical Review*, 62 (January 1985), 14 n. 39.

[62] McLachlin, *ibid.*, examines Princeton College and omits regional analysis. Clyde Sanfred Johnson, *Fraternities in Our Colleges* (New York: National Interfraternity Foundation, 1972), ch. 1–3; Stephens, *Reflections*; Francis W. Shepardson, ed., *Baird's Manual of American College Fraternities* (Menasha, WI: George Banta Publishing Co., 1930), 3.

and Georgia started small Greek societies in the late 1850s, but otherwise military schools followed the southern pattern. In the antebellum era, fraternities never provided career networking similar to that of military school networks.

Formal alumni associations likewise did not act explicitly for career placement but helped establish friendships that in turn aided the networks. Career networking may have been a by-product of the associations, but it was never an intended result. Rather, the career networks in evidence at the antebellum military institutes essentially functioned as precursors to modern alumni associations. The day after graduation, the first VMI graduates founded the Alumni Military Association in 1842; likewise, alumni at the state military institutes in South Carolina and Kentucky formed associations before the Civil War. Operationally the groups mirrored college literary or debating societies; they offered speeches by graduates and encouraged social gatherings, joining men by alma mater rather than adolescent affinities. Speakers before VMI in 1850 and Rappahannock Military Institute in 1851 assumed that alumni networks would start "a kind of pigmy republic," as the Rappahannock orator labeled such a system. Wearing a VMI or Citadel ring today may have tangible career results, but this was not necessarily so before the Civil War. That alumni networks occurred in the prewar South highlights the need for more research into the neglected field of men's collective activity in furthering professional careers. Fraternal societies that alumni might join, such as the Freemasons or Odd Fellows, could also have acted as friendship and network creation points. Literature about alumni associations now, however, focuses on the organizations' fund-raising component, which of course takes them very far from their nineteenth-century origins.[63] Institutionally, then, other organizations promoted neither middle-class stability nor professional status but encouraged friendships, which in turn created better networks.

Another way in which connections were created between alumni was through marriage. In addition to having career patterns similar to that of

[63] Heriot, *The Polytechnic School*, 17; G. W. Lewis, *Address Delivered Before the Literary Society and Students Generally of the Rappahannock Academy and Military Institute, July 30, 1851* (Washington: Gideon and Co., 1852), 11 (quotation). Wise, *Drawing Out the Man*, 474–75. A comprehensive study of alumni organizations still needs to be done; most texts are institution specific.

his peers, the successful Citadel graduate and Kings Mountain founder, Micah Jenkins, also participated in that other common bonding and mobility network: marriage. Jenkins's family relations highlight the interwoven nature of military school graduates. After leaving the Citadel, he married the daughter of General D. F. Jamison, the state senator who had introduced the bill to create SCMA.[64] Jenkins not only married a woman with a prominent father, but he married a woman with a connection to his military academy milieu. Marriages such as Jenkins's indicated women's contribution to social lives at the academies and in the alumni networks. These marriages cemented the class and ideological ties that began at the academies; they fostered kin networks that aided in middle-class stability.

Despite their complaints to the contrary, cadets found opportunities to meet young women. The young men, like students in nonmilitary schools, placed great importance on female society outside of school. They wanted to visit with local women, either at neighboring female academies or in homes. Thus, cadets sought passes to get off campus and reasons to bring ladies onto campus. On a weekly basis, cadets could see women at church, at relatives' houses, or in town. Women attended annual cadet balls, examinations, special lectures, and more frequently, dress parades. (Figure 10 shows a WMI invitation to a military ball sent to a lady.) Not surprisingly, the subject of women was a common one in the letters between adolescent boys or young men. "I have become quite a beau since I have been a Cadet," one young man told his brother.[65] A student at Wake Forest College teased his friend at Raleigh Military

[64]Jenkins to Brother, 22 March [1855], Duke. For Jamison's endorsement of SCMA, see the Committee on the Military, "Report on the Governor's Message," c. 1844, South Carolina Division of Archives and History. General Jamison's son and Jenkins's brother-in-law continued the military academy connection by becoming a professor at SCMA's Arsenal Academy during the Civil War; see, Claudius Fike to Parents, 7 January 1862, Claudius Lucian Fike papers, SCL.

[65]Henry Carrington to William Carrington, 1 December 1849 (quotation), VMI Archives. Similar subjects were discussed in letters dated 6 October 1850 and 29 January 1851. Tom Lucas to Lafayette Strait, 6 May 1855, SCL; James Saunders to Johnny, 24 November 1842; William Green to Capt. Duff Green, 10 September 1843; Dabney Atherton to Cordelia Atherton, 5 September 1852, VMI Archives; Archibald Govan Hill to B. H. Goodloe, 14 September 1858, Jones Family Papers, VHS; C. Irvine Walker, "Reminiscences of Days in the Citadel," unpublished memoir, CIT. Thomas Carey, unpublished diary, February 1863–May 1863, SCL, recorded meeting women numerous times including 10 February, 13 February, 7 March, 8 May 1863.

Academy for being suspended for dancing. This punishment did not, however, decrease the cadet's interest in women.[66] The Raleigh cadet continued to write to his friends about his flirtations.

Beyond being part of an academy's social scene, women at local schools found suitors at the nearby institutions. The journal that Cadet Thomas H. Law kept during his three years at the Citadel described the numerous visits that he and his peers made. Of the women that he met on these visits, two married Citadel cadets. Law himself would marry the niece of a local minister whose sermons he found "dry."[67] Cadets were not the only local students to become husbands of local women; students at Washington College, located next door to VMI, for example, also married local girls. A cadet at the Citadel, however, claimed in what may have been accurate or wishful thinking that local girls were more "partial" to cadets than to college students. So, on some level, military education brought many cadets into marriageable situations. Definitely, a few cadets married women from the area around their schools.[68]

The alumni certainly tried to maintain their middle-class status or to rise above it with marriage to women of their rank or slightly above it. Cadets' letters rarely indicated what the young men looked for in women, other than beauty (and accessibility). Thus, the backgrounds of their sweethearts and wives were rarely described. In the thirty-one cases that accounted for wives' origins, slightly more than 50 percent were the daughters of doctors. Like the professional tendencies of the alumni and their families, their wives appear to have come from similar

---

[66] William H. Whitfield to Theodore Kingsbury, 11 February 1845, 15 May 1845, SHC. Kingsbury had other discussions with friends about women, including W. D. Hiflin to Theodore Kingsbury, 11 July 1845; R. H. Bugg to Theodore Kingsbury, 11 July 1845, SHC; similarly, Tom Lucas to Lafayette Strait, 6 May 1855, SCL; Moses Custis Jr. to John Custis, 28 January 1861, SHC.

[67] For example, Law went to three separate outings in his first month at school; Thomas Hart Law, *Citadel Cadets: The Journal of Cadet Tom Law* (Clinton, SC: PC Press, 1941), 5 January, 25 January, 26 January 1856. John Adger Law, the editor of *Citadel Cadets*, wrote that Ida Hunter married George W. Dargan (at the Citadel 1858–59) and Emma Wilson married James F. Pressley, an 1855 graduate; Law, 94 n. 3, 101 n. 1, 220 n. 2. Egbert Ross to Emma Ross, 20 April 1860, SHC, said that another cadet was dating a local resident.

[68] John Pressley to Thomas, 5 November 1849, CIT. Edmund Pendleton to Philip Winn, 20 March 1842, 9 June 1842, VMI Archives. Richard Duke married a local woman a year after graduating from VMI. Professors at VMI also married local women; Beverly Stanard, *Letters of a New Market Cadet*, ed. John G. Barrett and Robert K. Turner Jr. (Chapel Hill: University of North Carolina Press, 1961), 13.

professional backgrounds.[69] Of course, wealth often attracted marriage partners; marrying widows could also indicate a desire to marry a woman with established wealth or status. Alumni usually waited to marry at least six years after leaving school, so that they would have been in their mid- to late twenties and more established in their careers.[70]

Strikingly, only two wives were recorded as having agricultural back- grounds: One was the daughter of a "retired cotton planter" and the other's father gave her a farm (possibly upon marriage). Alumni did not record attempting to marry planters' daughters, which could have vaulted them into the elite (despite the difficulties James Henry Hammond found). The omission suggests their strong professional tendencies, even in marriage.

More often, however, military alumni wed women related to the men around them, as did Micah Jenkins. Through marriage, former school- mates or teaching colleagues found themselves related to each other. William Porcher DuBose's cousin, attending a local school, married DuBose's Citadel classmate Samuel Gaillard. Likewise, Walter Bowen's sister married a man the year behind her brother at VMI; Thomas Baber's sister wed his classmate as Charles D. Rice's sister married her brother's classmate; William Silvester's sister Lydia married a young man who graduated the year after her brother; James Meem married a classmate's sister; John Wylie married a woman whose family knew his classmate at the Citadel; and Edwin Harvie and Hodijah Meade were brothers-in- law as they had been classmates at VMI.[71] Edward Gwathmey and his cousin attended Albemarle Military Institute in Charlottesville, run by John B. Strange, a graduate of the first VMI class; Gwathmey explained his teacher's relationship to the cadets as "His wife was our cousin, Miss Agnes Gaines of Petersburg Va."[72] Additionally, Citadel professor Peter

---

[69] Student files, VMI Archives. Information on other wives showed that alumni married eight of their cousins, six widows, one former student, two wealthy women, and four women distantly related to important men.

[70] Jane Turner Censer, *North Carolina Planters and their Children, 1800–1860* (Baton Rouge: Louisiana State University Press, 1984), 93, states that the average age for marriage in North Carolina and Alabama was twenty-five. The median age of marriage for North Carolina elite planters' sons was twenty-four.

[71] William P. DuBose, "Soldier, Philosopher, Friend, Awakener of the Undying Good in Men," unpublished memoir, typescript 1946, SCL. Student files, VMI Archives.

[72] Edward Garlick Gwathmey, unpublished autobiography, c. 1928, VHS, 3.

F. Stevens married the superintendent's sister, and Nellie Hawkins, the daughter of KMI's Latin professor, wed Superintendent E. W. Morgan.[73] The same occupation implied both a similar class background and social sphere between the families. These men's marriages show that almost every year at least one marital connection further elaborated the military alumni networks and deepened those connections into kinship.

In other cases, the relationships indicated a longer connection between similarly educated men. Women married men who attended the same military schools as their brothers or cousins, even if the men were not at the institution concurrently. For example, VMI alumnus James A. Madison's sister married Thomas D. Taliaferro (despite being in the same class year, the men do not appear to have shared the barracks: Madison attended one semester in 1846 and Taliaferro attended in 1849–1850); Henry Coleman married the sister of a cadet, who was at VMI two years before Coleman attended; Thomas Burke wed a relative of John H. Pitts, who had graduated from VMI four years before Burke arrived; and James Saunders's sister married a man who graduated five years after his future brother-in-law left VMI.[74] Marriages of this pattern suggest either that alumni had social relationships outside of the schools or that alumni networks brought men of different years together.

In a few cases, the age differences appeared large enough to indicate that one man influenced his relative by marriage to attend his alma mater (or his wife did so). John Strange, the Albemarle teacher who wed two students' cousin, may have encouraged one of those young men to enroll in VMI thirteen years after himself. Similarly, another cadet, who stayed at VMI for the 1840–1841 school year, helped to get his wife's nephew into the school in 1861 (perhaps to avoid serving in the war). Scott Shipp married the sister of a cadet graduated six years before his future brother-in-law. The relatives of VMI superintendent Smith's wife found their way into VMI; her brother resigned after a year in February 1842, but her cousin was the valedictorian of the graduating class of that year. Another of her nephews attended in 1848. Nepotism itself was nothing

[73] John D Wylie to Lafayette Strait, 2 March 1854, SCL. Stevens had also been a cadet under Francis W. Capers before becoming a professor at the Citadel and marrying Mary Capers. Also, William Gordon McCabe wed the daughter of his principal at Hampton Academy (which had an antebellum cadet corps) in 1915.

[74] James Saunders to Johnny, 24 November 1842, VMI Archives.

new, but marriage and women here forged the connections that built networks and stabilized middle-class status.

Finally, alumni networks continued through local militias. By the late antebellum period, militias were no longer the vital institutions that they had been in the colonial years. Especially after the volunteer frenzy of the Mexican War, militia numbers and service declined, more prominently in the North but also in the South. Of the militias that remained active, some had both formal and informal connections to local military schools. In practice, a few schools made functional connections with them. For example, the three Savannah volunteer corps donated tents to GMI when it opened. GMI, despite accepting supplies, made its superiority to the militia system clear: "Our militia system is a failure; the people are sick of it; and some other must be devised, 'if in time of peace we would prepare for war.'" The school also successfully petitioned to have its students exempted from militia duty. Like the Savannah militia, the Washington Light Infantry had a close relationship with the Citadel.[75]

Despite the few official connections and general lack of institutional interest, cadets exhibited some personal attraction to the militia. Cadet diaries and letters described attending militia parades and musters. Their interest in the militia dovetailed with their appreciation of military spectacle and was a component of their ideal of manhood. After graduation, some cadets completed the circle and took positions as officers in the militias. Certainly this offered increased prestige and fulfillment of any citizen–soldier drives.[76] Men like Charles Crump became captains

[75] R. M. Smith to Governor James McDowell, 24 November 1843, SHC; Act 183, 8 December 1851, Georgia Legislature, Georgia Archives, exempted professors and cadets. On the decline of the militia, see James Whisker, *The Rise and Decline of the American Militia System* (Cranbury, NJ: Associated University Presses, 1999), ch. 7. Military academies often portrayed themselves as a better alternative to the militia system; William A. Graham, *General Joseph Graham and his Papers on North Carolina Revolutionary History* (Raleigh, NC: Edwards and Broughton, 1904), 124–34; *Report by the Board of Visitors of the Georgia Military Institute, To his Excellency, Howell Cobb, Governor of the State of Georgia For 1853* (1853), Duke, 11 (quotation). Lynwood Holland, "Georgia Military Institute, The West Point of Georgia, 1851–64," *Georgia Historical Quarterly*, 43 (1959), 227; Bowling C. Yates, *History of the Georgia Military Institute* (Marietta, GA: [Author], 1968), 2. Law, *Citadel Cadets*, illustrated the repeated interactions between the militia and cadets.

[76] See, for example, Law, *Citadel Cadets*, 21 February 1858, 5 May 1858, 197, 232–33. Micah Jenkins wanted to get his cadets into his brother's militia; Micah Jenkins to John Jenkins, 25 May 1856, SCL. A speaker at the Citadel suggested that the sons of the Palmetto Regiment would be provided with a good education at the military academy; Trotti, *Address*, 24. The WMI

in the Nottoway militia or, like William Tennent, were elected to the Washington Lights. Anecdotal evidence indicates that fifty of the 1,057 alumni, 5 percent, joined militias before the Civil War.

Conclusion

The networks that military school alumni actively constructed in the decades before the Civil War were unique among other social structures in the antebellum South in that they located employment and redefined mobility for middle-class southern men. The existence and elaboration of the networks created a self-perpetuating niche for military educators. In response to military schools' encouragement of teaching and the alumni's desire for careers, graduates involved themselves in social and career networks and received personal benefits. Individuals informed each other of positions, created new positions, found employment at more than one school, and improved their salary or career stability. These networks resulted in an educational community that improved careers and status. They facilitated the high rate of alumni upward social mobility seen in the previous chapter. The networks, and the niche they perpetuated, offered military school graduates professional stability in the antebellum South – a time and place ruled by the agricultural elite.

In addition to individual status, the networks encouraged middle-class mobility by professionalizing teaching and military education; young southern military alumni could improve the status of similarly educated men and of the teaching profession, in which the middle class invested many of its hopes. Increasing the number of schools and the prestige accrued to them helped the members of that rank. Former cadets such as Robert Simpson created and used active networks to locate stable non-agricultural careers, move into more profitable or respected professions, help professionalize the most commonly selected occupation of teaching, and thereby enhance the status of middle-class young men. Military higher schools spread throughout the South, legitimating the career and attracting more cadets as the years passed. Networks helped men of the

and KMI both allowed commissioned militia officers to attend ten months of classes without cost; ch. 69, 20 January 1847, ch. 60, 19 January 1848, Kentucky Legislature; Lester Austin Webb, "The Origin of Military Academies in the United States Founded in the Nineteenth Century" (Ph.D. diss., University of North Carolina, 1958), 67. Andrew, *Long Gray Lines*.

emerging middle class hold themselves above the yeoman and plain folk ranks, an important aspect in creating class stability. This professionalization raised the status of military alumni and all other southerners who taught and fostered the process of class formation.

Military educational networks had a distinctly southern cultural aspect in their location in military education, more pronounced in the South, and their paradoxical continuation of community-based culture as they created impersonal paths of professional mobility. The networks were a movement toward modernization in the Old South; they were, however contradictory it may now seem, built on (and even built to mimic) the region's premodern community and patronage expectations. The student–professor networks, in fact, depended on the maintenance of community connections, albeit not connections of kin or neighborhood, but those of school and professional identity. Although John Hardin Best and Lawrence Cremin assert that much of southern education occurred outside formal institutions, these data suggest that middle-class networking derived from formal education.[77] Career networks among military academy matriculates in the prewar South performed functions analogous to those of postbellum bureaucratic organizations; career placement and development organizations, for example, functioned more formally and impersonally than the networks but produced similar results. Middle-class development occurred alongside the antebellum articulation of social, cultural, political, and economic institutions, the increase in military schools, and professionalization; these processes resulted in more complex bureaucratic development in some locations and less in others.

Military educator networks demonstrate the developing social stability of nonagricultural professionals; they also suggest that these men's attempts at upward social mobility, driven by the networks, proceeded at the individual career level and with the professionalization of teaching. Mobility, with its contested existence in the historiography of the Old South, has been passed over for the emerging middle class because the field has focused on both ends of the social spectrum. Nonagricultural

---

[77] Best, "Education in the Forming of the American South," *History of Education Quarterly*, 36 (Spring 1996), esp. 44, 48; Cremin, *American Education: The National Experience, 1783–1876* (New York: Harper and Row, 1980), 465.

professionals in the middle social position worked to increase their access to higher schooling and to ensure its benefits; specifically, professionalization improved status. Almost equally, antebellum military teachers maintained the occupation and strove for more prestigious and lucrative careers; thus, stability was the certain result of their actions, but upward mobility was their hope. Indeed, the southern middle class and their views of status show that the group participated in the modernizing and cultural shifts of the late antebellum years. This period's professionalization and legitimation of professional status encourage the examination of mobility outside of land and slaves, for professionals in the middle class as well as for the master class. Although it solidified class distinctions, unlike class formation in the North, this system was not necessarily derivative of the emerging capitalist market. Military educator networks, overall, acted concurrently with numerous social organizations but represented one path to stability for a particular segment of southern society.

8

Classifying the Middle Class

Historians' treatment of the northern experience as normative has influenced our definitional model of the American middle class. Although this model is excellent, to be sure, it has often, unfortunately, omitted or negated the southern experience. Southern historians exploring the middle social position of white society must confront the problem of the content and formation of a *southern* middle class in order to improve their understanding of antebellum social structure, both regionally and nationally.[1] Definitions of southern social groups, unfortunately, have often been vague enough to include virtually every white man in the Old South. Sharpening definitional boundaries across the field will help historians to strengthen important research on the elite and lower ends of the economic spectrum, to examine the characteristics of the southern middle class, and to place that group further within the model of the American middle class. This chapter assesses the antebellum American middle class, including southerners. It suggests definitional categories for

[1]Michele Gillespie, *Free Labor in an Unfree World: White Artisans in Georgia, 1789–1860* (Athens: University of Georgia Press, 2000), xix, examines the middle rank of southern society into white artisans. Gillespie, Comment, American Historical Association, Washington DC (January 6, 2007); Jonathan Daniel Wells, *The Origins of the Southern Middle Class, 1800–1861* (Chapel Hill: University of North Carolina Press, 2004); Frank J. Byrne, *Becoming Bourgeois: Merchant Culture in the South, 1820–1865* (Lexington: University of Kentucky Press, 2006); Frank L. Owsley, *Plain Folk of the Old South* (1949; reprint, Baton Rouge: Louisiana State University Press, 1982); Eugene Genovese, "Yeomen Farmers in a Slaveholders' Democracy," *Agricultural History*, 49 (April 1975), 331–42; Stephanie McCurry, *Masters of Small Worlds: Yeoman Households, Gender Relations, and the Political Culture of the Antebellum South Carolina Low Country* (New York: Oxford University Press, 1995); Joan E. Cashin, *A Family Venture: Men and Women on the Southern Frontier* (New York: Oxford University Press, 1991).

the national middle class, indicates how the emerging southern middle class matched those criteria, and then considers the unique qualities of the group's southern regionalism.

Economic Development and Context

Economic differentiation between classes produced different relationships to people and goods and even different aspirations and values. It created the environment for the "middle class," a group whose middle economic and occupational position, and the status conferred by that position, defined it in the nation. This study places the emerging professional middle class within the antebellum southern social structure and suggests class definitions that encompass more than an urban, industrial middle class.

It is easiest to understand the northern and southern middle classes as a single entity if they can both be understood as inherently capitalist, but as Eugene Genovese has argued, the southern master class exhibited a prebourgeois mentalité within which it began to incorporate beliefs in progress and industry. The ever-present historiographic question regarding planters' capitalist or premodern tendencies focuses the issue. Another historian adeptly presents the master class and southern slaveowners socially and culturally oriented towards them as "forced to remain merely *in* not *of* the capitalist Atlantic system." Unlike the northern middle class, southerners were not necessarily capitalists or industrialists. Moreover, they could be industrialists without being capitalists as Marx understood the term.[2]

Economic changes and the ideological trends they brought with them transcended north–south boundaries in the antebellum United

---

[2] Genovese, *The Slaveholders' Dilemma: Freedom and Progress in Southern Conservative Thought, 1820–1860* (Columbia: University of South Carolina Press, 1992); also, Elizabeth Fox-Genovese and Eugene D. Genovese, *Mind of the Master Class: History and Faith in the Southern Slaveholders' Worldview* (New York: Cambridge University Press, 2005); Mark M. Smith, *Mastered by the Clock: Time, Slavery and Freedom in the American South* (Chapel Hill: University of North Carolina Press, 1997), 9 (quotation, italics in original). The debate about the capitalist nature of the South continues; see, for example, Laurence Shore, *Southern Capitalists: The Ideological Leadership of an Elite, 1832–1885* (Chapel Hill: University of North Carolina Press, 1986); William Kauffman Scarborough, *Masters of the Big House: Elite Slaveholders of the Mid-Nineteenth-Century South* (Baton Rouge: Louisiana State University Press, 2003); Chad Morgan, *Planters' Progress: Modernizing Confederate Georgia* (Gainesville: University Press of Florida, 2005).

States. It should be unsurprising, then, that nonagricultural southerners exhibited greater involvement with modern economic and social systems than did others in the Old South. Emerging middle-class men were a segment of southern society not so focused on the slave- and landholding that nurtured premodern concerns with honor and status. Developing capitalism, market presence, impersonal exchanges, and bureaucratization filtered into the region but never completely dominated it in the antebellum period.

The nonindustrial emerging middle class and the industrial "bourgeoisie" ought not to be equated as groups with the same definitional characteristics. This study focuses its attention on the former.[3] During the late antebellum decades, southern culture and modernizing trends shaped the ongoing process of the forming middle class. That the emerging southern middle class was not a class "for itself" does not negate the fact that its members behaved in certain ways that benefited the group, however; for example, middle-class men encouraged the professionalization of teaching so that teachers could gain status and improve their social stability, which made the class as a whole more stable.[4] The members of the emerging southern middle class shared some values and ideas, even the beginnings of class awareness, though they did not possess class consciousness. Some segments of the emerging group, especially in urban areas, demonstrated class coherence, but across the South, no ideological or social glue held the majority of this forming class together. Middle-class formation was, certainly, a process: Absent class consciousness, the group came together and acted in similar, more recognized (and self-aware) ways as the antebellum years advanced.[5] The process increased

[3] Writing about nineteenth-century Britain, historian David Cannadine argues, "The sort of classes for which Marxists searched never existed as they hoped to find them"; *The Rise and Fall of Class in Britain* (New York: Columbia University Pres, 1999), 17. This is accurate for the United States and, more so, for the Old South. Robert H. Wiebe, *The Search for Order, 1877–1920* (New York: Hill & Wang, 1967), 13–4, asserts that classes did not form in the prewar period. Peter N. Stearns, "The Middle Class: Toward a Precise Definition," *Comparative Studies of Society and History*, 21 (July 1979), 377–96; Arno J. Mayer, "The Lower Middle Class as Historical Problem," *Journal of Modern History*, 47 (September 1975), 409–36.

[4] Max Weber, *From Max Weber: Essays in Sociology*, ed. H. H. Gerth and C. Wright Mills (New York: Oxford University Press, 1958), 191–93. Mayer, "The Lower Middle Class as Historical Problem," 410–11, 425.

[5] Stuart M. Blumin, *The Emergence of the Middle Class: Social Experience in the American City, 1760–1900* (New York: Cambridge University Press, 1989).

the class's legitimacy and its numerical and monetary resources from the 1830s through the 1850s.

In order for "class action" (and class consciousness) to develop, members needed to recognize first, the economic structure and second, that their situation resulted from it. In the American context, the second realization was often delayed; many antebellum southern youths believed geographic mobility or slave ownership would raise their position in the economic structure, thus counteracting the hierarchy. The national middle class performed some collective actions, most notably on behalf of reform. Lobbying efforts for education, including state-funded military schools, represented not just a form of social altruism but also a means of offering personal assistance for the class; its southern segment was successful with state military institutes as was the northern portion with public education. Class consciousness for the middle ranks of the South, both middle and working class, did not develop until after the war. But there is clear evidence of professionalization, an especially pertinent process to the formation of the middle class, in the antebellum years – earlier than other studies often locate it.[6]

Within the diversifying antebellum economy, then, lay the seeds of the emerging middle class in America. The beginnings of capitalist economic development and the general growth of the society provided space in which a middle group could develop. Identifying that central rank and the status conferred by it allows us to define the middle class – hence its name. Within that middle social position, the development of economic demographics denotes the group.

Social Hierarchy

The basic definition of "middle class" centers on the rank and status that members of the class derived from their middle social position in society. Regardless of region, the middle class was socially and economically

---

[6] Weber, *From Max Weber*, esp. 84; Stearns, "The Middle Class," 388; Ira Katznelson, "Working-Class Formation: Constructing Cases and Comparison," in *Working-Class Formation: Nineteenth-Century Patterns in Western Europe and the United States*, ed. Ira Katznelson and Aristide R. Zolberg (Princeton: Princeton University Press, 1986); Sean Wilentz, *Chants Democratic: New York City and the Rise of the American Working Class, 1788–1850* (New York: Oxford University Press, 1984), 15–18; Owsley, *Plain Folk of the Old South*, 133.

above the lower ranks of white people. Members tended to self-identify as middle class or middle rank; although self-reporting should never be the sole determinant of a man's social position, it can be confirmed by other criteria here suggested.

The emerging southern middle class's characteristics and choices indicated and reflected its position in the social hierarchy between the elite and the yeomen. In the Old South, middle-class status meant separation from the plain folk, the yeomanry, and laborers. Keeping in mind the fluidity of social boundaries, the lower limits of the middle class and the upper range of plain folk may have been blurred. Samuel C. Hyde attempted to remove the "definitional imprecision" from the term "plain folk" in 2005, stating, "In short, *plain folk* is not synonymous with *middle class*, but, instead, plain folk are those among the middle class who farmed."[7] Agriculturalists may have entered the emerging southern middle class, but separating the plain folk from the middle class makes both analytical categories more useful.

The middle class was also not the yeomanry. The yeomanry fell at the low end of the land-owning economic spectrum, owning less than 100 acres and as many as five slaves. Historians have distinguished between upcountry and lowcountry yeomen and between slaveholding and nonslaveholding yeomen.[8] Middle-class men lacked the resources and influence of the elites, but their economic position offered them more opportunities than were available to yeomen, who generally lived close to the subsistence level. The middle class's demonstrated interest in education and in the opportunity to acquire it illustrated the extent to which their social position and wealth placed them above their yeomen counterparts; their redefinition of status as outside agriculture confirmed it.

---

[7] Gillespie, *Free Labor in an Unfree World*; Wells, *Origins of the Southern Middle Class*; Samuel C. Hyde Jr., ed., *Plain Folk of the South Revisited* (Baton Rouge: Louisiana State University Press, 1997), x (first quotation), 7 (second quotation); Samuel C. Hyde Jr., "*Plain Folk* Reconsidered: Historiographical Ambiguity in Search of Definition," *Journal of Southern History*, 71 (November 2005), 813 (third quotation). Owsley, *Plain Folk of the Old South*, 7–8.
[8] They may have been as much as 30 to 40 percent of the antebellum white population. McCurry, *Masters of Small Worlds*, 47–51, 54; James Oakes, *The Ruling Race: A History of American Slaveowners* (New York: Vantage Books, 1982), 37–41. Genovese, "Yeomen Farmers in a Slaveholders' Democracy"; Steven Hahn, *The Roots of Southern Populism: Yeoman Farmers and the Transformation of the Georgia Upcountry, 1850–1890* (New York: Oxford University Press, 1983); Lacy K. Ford Jr., *Origins of Southern Radicalism* (New York: Oxford University Press, 1988); Cashin, *A Family Venture*.

In the category of working class, artisans lived in the lower strata of southern society unless they became entrepreneurial or accumulated enough wealth to purchase a few slaves later in life (or through generational mobility). Their situation and status often necessitated the use of their manual labor to maintain or increase their social position. Because antebellum southern laborers were often African American, enslaved, or immigrant, as a group they had little mobility or access to higher schooling. They do not appear to have used education, or specifically to have used military schools, to advance their position. Successful artisans who became proprietors could have moved their sons into the emerging middle class by the 1850s; the intergenerational mobility demonstrated in this study suggests that that was the case.[9] The frequency with which working-class laborers managed to improve their social position in the Old South is yet to be determined, but that group is fairly easily distinguished from the emerging middle class by its members' occupations, status, resources, and values. Likewise, those criteria separate the emerging southern middle class from the agricultural plain folk and yeomanry.

Within the developing middle class, a category of lower-middle-class men can be identified. Historians of Europe describe the "petit bourgeoisie," but this term has not made the transition to America (and is not applicable in the same way in this period). Those men designated "white-collar" were subordinate to professionals in status as they were in income. Nonetheless, men of the lower middle class, such as clerks, still possessed the potential for upward mobility, and as such this study locates them in the middle class.[10] Again, separating the middle class from the plain folk and working class increases the definitional specificity to consider the existence of a lower middle class.

Cadets did not represent the lowest economic strata among whites. Only one alumnus earned no status higher than skilled trades (matching

---

[9] Gillespie, *Free Labor in an Unfree World*, xviii, 101–03, 111.

[10] Further examination of the lower middle class may help clarify the differences between the American middle class and the Marxist bourgeoisie as owners or as managers in an incompletely industrialized antebellum United States. Mayer, "The Lower Middle Class as Historical Problem," 411, 424 (quotation); Clyde and Sally Griffen, "Small Business and Occupational Mobility in Mid-Nineteenth Century Poughkeepsie," in *Small Business in American Life*, ed. Stuart W. Bruchey (New York: Columbia University Press, 1980), 124.

his father's social position). This absence is unsurprising, given that the urban working class of the Old South, small compared to the North and located in the few metropolitan areas of the South, was primarily foreign-born or African American.[11] Young middle-class southerners tried to raise themselves above the poor and particularly wanted to access stability and mobility to separate themselves further.

Young men of the emerging middle class tried to differentiate themselves from the lower classes. In the case of cadets, this resulted in the young men rarely representing themselves as poor; indeed, young men from a middle economic position worked to distance themselves from those of the lower ranks. One Rappahannock Military Institute student succinctly told his mother, for example, "I hate poor people more than you." Seventy percent of the 1860 Citadel class submitted written resignations after obeying a professor's command to march out of the room – a command they believed classed them with charity school children and thereby dishonored them. Recognizing their place as middling – aggressively not poor, but also not wealthy – was a trait of the middle class across the nation.[12]

Military educators acknowledged their students' status as middle class. They promoted the idea that "the laboring man" or "working class," but not "manual labor[ers]," attended their schools. *Harper's New Monthly*, in an article about the city of Charleston, stated that "the graduates of [the Citadel] have mostly been working-men." The practical curriculum and free tuition allowed state-funded military cadets to escape a life of limited education and of being "bound to a trade." These young men had to rely on themselves rather than "preferment" for their upward mobility.[13] They

---

[11] Ira Berlin and Herbert G. Gutman, "Natives and Immigrants, Free Men and Slaves," *American Historical Review*, 88 (December 1983), 1175–1200. See Appendix 2, Table 1; Table 6.1; Table 6.2.

[12] John Scott to Lucinda Henry, July 16, 1850 (quotation), Ball Family Papers, Virginia Historical Society (hereafter VHS). Thomas Hart Law, *Citadel Cadets: The Journal of Cadet Tom Law* (Clinton, SC: PC Press, 1941), 38–39, 191–93.

[13] Quotations taken, in order, from: Edwin Heriot, *The Polytechnic School, the Best System of Practical Education* (Charleston: Walker and James, 1850), 11; George F. Holmes, *Inaugural Address* (Memphis: Franklin Book and Job Office, 1849); *Harper's New Monthly*, n.d., 11, Citadel File, South Carolina Historical Society; Francis H. Smith, *Introductory Address to the Corps of Cadets of the Virginia Military Institute* (Richmond: MacFarlane and Fergusson, 1856); F. W. Capers, *State Military Academies* (Charleston: Tenhet and Corley, 1846), 21.

had limited opportunities for social advancement based on their birth, and the ideology of military school advocates suggested that the path out of drudgery started with education, and more specifically with the scientific education offered by military schools.

Because middle position defined the class and its members wished not to be equated to those below them, the more complex connections existed not between middle-class southerners and their social inferiors but between them and elite southerners. Middle-class northerners, despite their wealth, chafed at their exclusion from elite society. Southern men of the emerging middle class, in contrast, probably relied more on the elite planters than their northern counterparts did on the northern elite. Both groups could emulate the exclusive lifestyles of those above them in the social hierarchy. Elites possessed many tangible and intangible benefits that middle-class men did not, including wealth, time to pursue a classical education, and prestige in the Old South. Planters who owned hundreds of acres of improved land and more than fifty slaves represented the pinnacle of southern society. As planters' views altered over the period, their influence continued. Individuals were, however, conflicted about the changes they lived through.[14] Although the members of the emerging middle class were not antagonistic to the elite, they were also neither of the elite nor ideologically identical to them. The existence of an emerging middle class that began to act for its own benefit and to develop its own values could, but need not, have challenged the idea of planter hegemony. Hegemonies require the consent of the governed, and it is not a leap to believe that the middle class worked within the system.[15] Yet although a cadet could "hate poor people," he needed connections

[14] Robert Tracy McKenzie, *One South or Many?: Plantation Belt and Upcountry in Civil War-Era Tennessee* (New York: Cambridge University Press, 1994), ch. 1; Owsley, *Plain Folk of the Old South*, 7–8. Also see, Hyde, "*Plain Folk* Reconsidered," 819; Berlin and Gutman, "Natives and Immigrants, Free Men and Slaves"; Genovese, *The Slaveholders' Dilemma*. Of course, men labeled small or middling planters would have owned fewer slaves by definition.

[15] T. J. Jackson Lears, "The Concept of Cultural Hegemony: Problems and Possibilities," *American Historical Review*, 90 (1985), 567–93. Peter S. Carmichael, *The Last Generation: Young Virginians in Peace, War and Reunion* (Chapel Hill: University of North Carolina Press, 2005), 30, presents young southerners as approving of slavery, progress, and bourgeois ideas without attempting to overthrow planters.

to those above him in the hierarchy and was likely to have also admired their wealth and lifestyle.

Thus, the basic definition of the "middle-class" is derived from its members' position in the social hierarchy, which reflected economic position, occupation, and status. Self-identification confirmed by analysis of the social hierarchy suggests the composition of the group. Participants in military education identify one segment of the emerging southern middle-class in this way.

Demographic Characteristics

In addition to middle social and economic position, demographic characteristics and similar values united the middle rank. As historians have built models for the national middle-class, objective criteria to identify the middle-class position include occupation and prestige, access to sufficient resources and goods (income, wealth, and possessions – in the South, this could have included the ownership of human labor), social organization (especially associations), and cultural values (education, professional identity, and others centered on self-discipline).[16] This analysis focuses on those definitional characteristics and choices and encourages continuing exploration of additional ones. It demonstrates the characteristics of the emerging southern middle class and its connection to the national middle class.

OCCUPATION AND PRESTIGE

Middle-class northerners and southerners worked in nonmanual occupations, especially professional or entry-level white-collar jobs. Being primarily nonagricultural in the agricultural United States, they gained status from their nonmanual and professional employment. Men with agricultural pursuits could also be considered middle class in the Old South. To qualify for this definition probably entailed having connections to the market economy; yeomen and plain folk had some, but more often limited, interactions with its modernizing influences. Middle-class

---

[16] Mayer, "The Lower Middle Class as Historical Problem," 424; Katznelson, "Working-Class Formation"; Stuart M. Blumin, "The Hypothesis of the Middle-Class Formation in Nineteenth-Century America: A Critique and Some Proposals," *American Historical Review*, 90 (1985), 299–338; Blumin, *Emergence of the Middle Class*.

agriculturalists would have possessed wealth equivalent to middle economic resources and, to receive comparable status from agriculture, would probably have had to be slaveowners. Sharing the same social organization and values would also place them among the emerging middle class. Thus, economic realities centrally defined the middle social position, which primarily consisted of nonagricultural and professional men.

The occupational structure of military academy families confirms their middle-class position. The careers of military school alumni and their fathers were strikingly less agricultural than those of the rest of southern society, with the large portions of both generations (and a majority of the alumni) in professional employment. These professionals' place in the occupational structure exhibited their emerging middle-class position by occupation and by the prestige that that occupation provided. In 1860, ministers, professors, editors, physicians, lawyers, and scientific occupations made up only 2 percent of the U.S. workforce.[17] Southern military education, in contrast, illustrates a concentration of men in those occupations. Recommendation letters often described fathers by their occupations; this designation served to connect the man to his labor and indicated that he worked for a living rather than resided as a gentleman planter. Military alumni were more likely to be nonagricultural and professional than southerners who were not in the emerging middle class; they showed a great deal of social mobility based on their occupations. Their generational mobility based on occupation also suggests that middle social and economic position.

Occupational structure and mobility, two distinct analyses, demonstrate middle-class position and status. Status was significant in the North, but it was probably even more significant for southerners, surrounded as they were by a more status-driven society.[18] Thus, participants in southern military education can highlight the occupations, their mobility (in part through professionalization), and the concurrent reevaluation and improvement in status among the emerging middle class in the Old South.

---

[17] Colin B. Burke, *American Collegiate Populations: A Test of the Traditional View* (New York: New York University Press, 1982), 55, 143.

[18] Michael B. Katz, "Occupational Classification in History," *Journal of Interdisciplinary History*, 3 (Summer 1972), 63–88.

To properly define "class," we want to be sure that the group is accurate – defined both sufficiently narrowly and sufficiently broadly. The connection of members of single professions to the larger emerging southern middle class and the national group still needs further analysis; applying the terminology "class" to a professional group does not reflect the way Marx, Weber, Thompson, or this study would identify it.[19] As historians continue to explore the national middle class, including southerners, our usage of terms and creation of group boundaries should become clearer. It is necessary to consider more than occupation and status as the determinants of class.

ACCESS TO SUFFICIENT RESOURCES AND GOODS

Young men of the middle class possessed resources sufficient to reflect their place in the social hierarchy and their demographic characteristics. As the theorists agree, access to goods partially defined the middle class. Members' ability to buy consumer goods (along with their consumption patterns) and to spend money on education helped to identify them as members of the middle class. Similar access to goods, then, should be consistent across the group. Yet access to goods varied by location, not only by region but also within regions, as an assortment of factors, including banking, monetary development, stores, and transport, influence consumption patterns. In the South, members of the emerging middle class were neither sons of yeomen nor laborers without cash. The majority of them also were neither elite nor planters' offspring with classical educations and the potential for college education. They possessed adequate resources – either sufficient assets or access to patronage – to mark them as middle class.

Most cadets' parents described their economic situations as representative of their middle social status. Calling themselves families of "limited means," for example, often reflected the large number of children they had to educate. After Philip Winn was unable to obtain state cadet status, his father lamented the family situation. Philip's three older brothers had received an English education, which itself cost less than a classical one and excluded these boys from the elite world of college education. Yet Mr. Winn's finances left little for Philip and his eleven younger siblings

---

[19] Byrne, *Becoming Bourgeois*.

to obtain even an education of this type. Mr. Winn clearly wanted his children to be educated, even if a classical education was impossible. He needed the tuition remission offered at a state military academy to accomplish that goal.[20] Having sufficient resources to provide only his eldest three sons with limited educational opportunities, Mr. Winn identified himself as being in a tenuous economic position. His situation is one of many evidenced in this study that show the high cost of education relative to middle-class resources.

Parents and independent young men apparently sacrificed to provide or receive military education. Many cadets entered with state scholarships, and as many complained about having to pay their way through. Even cadets who inherited money may have had only a small amount. One guardian informed a school that his ward's expenses as a state-funded cadet would "pretty smartly exceed the interest of all his patrimony." Another guardian described his ward's income as less than 100 dollars and stated that the cadet had "had the misfortune to lose his parents." Though he was "not left entirely destitute of means," these means were "totally inadequate" to pay for a "liberal education."[21] Thus, many cadets themselves or their families had inadequate resources to pay for a long and expensive education.

The state scholarship system particularly helped cadets pay for school who entered from apprenticeships; although this was only a small number of cadets, their situation indicates their non-elite status and the possibility that education would have improved their career prospects. In cadet Henry Smyth's senior year, his father inquired about placing a younger son at VMI who had been a printer for two and a half years. The family evidently arranged for the older brother to attend a higher school while the younger son went into a trade. Although his father and friends agreed to pay for the young man's education, he never enrolled. Smyth's father, formerly in the U.S. Army, worked as a lawyer and the editor of the *Wytheville Republican*; he appears to have wanted his sons to

[20] John Winn to Philip Winn, 4 May 1840, 11 December, 1840 (quotation), Winn Family Papers, Duke.
[21] Gabriel Jordan to Francis H. Smith, 5 September 5, 1851 (first quotation), Hiram Strickler student file; Alfred Moss to Board of Visitors, 12 May 1847 (remaining quotations), John T. Moss student file, Preston Library, Virginia Military Institute Archives (hereafter VMI Archives).

maintain his middle-class status, and he seems also to have had access to money or patronage. Another youth, apparently the son of a bricklayer, was described as "early accustomed to manual labor." Yet another young man had clerked in a store for two years before entering a military higher school.[22]

Clearly some men were, as Edward Shepherd's father presented himself, "unable to enter" their sons as tuition-paying cadets. Rather than characterizing themselves as poor, however, more parents portrayed themselves as being outside the elite. No cadets' fathers described themselves or were discussed as lower class (though some were described as working in skilled trades), even in a situation in which underestimating the family's income might have helped them to obtain money from the state. Unsurprisingly, families preferred to describe themselves as "not <u>Rich</u>" or of "limited means" rather than mark themselves as indigent. "I don't feel able to educate him as I would wish, as I have a large family of children (eight in number), and they motherless," a father wrote in clarifying his economic responsibilities. Another father was said to be "not <u>rich</u>," though he was "very well off for a preacher at any rate." Such statements echo the antebellum West Point survey, in which the majority of cadets ranked themselves in the "moderate" income level, rejecting the "affluent" and "indigent" extremes.[23]

Although many young men in a middle economic situation needed funding, only a few unfairly characterized themselves as destitute. One young man remembered his father as "a poor man" without an education himself who borrowed money so that the son could attend the state

[22] Harrold Smyth to Judge Brockenbrough, 14 July 1846, Alexander Smyth student file; J. Griffins to Board of Visitors, 19 August 1839 (first quotation), Charles Deyerle student file; Charles A. Swarm to Board of Visitors, 21 June 1847 (second quotation), Philip Gibbs student file, VMI Archives.

[23] James Shepherd to Francis H. Smith, 13 August 1849 (first quotation), Edward Shepherd student file, VMI Archives; John D. Wylie to Lafayette Strait, 19 August 1852; Father to E. Montague Grimke, [July 1852] (second quotation), The South Caroliniana Library, University of South Carolina, (hereafter SCL); Edmund Taylor to Francis H. Smith, 11 May 1846 (third quotation), William Battaile student file; John Stephenson to Francis H. Smith, n.d. (fourth quotation), Robert Stephenson student file, VMI Archives (emphasis in original). James L. Morrison, *"The Best School in the World": West Point, the Pre-Civil War Years, 1833–1866* (Kent: Kent State University Press, 1986), 60–61, 159. The West Point survey indicated that most cadets self-identified with the median income category: 2 percent indigent, 11 percent reduced, 83 percent moderate, and 4 percent affluent.

military institute with funding. The young man then explained that all his siblings received collegiate training, his older brothers at the University of Virginia, Emory and Henry, and Hampden-Sidney. In a time when female education was certainly not expected, his sister also received a formal education.[24] This cadet's family was clearly not poor, despite his description of himself as such in his memoir. Similarly, John Moomau's parents were "in ordinary circumstances, his father being a hatter with a large family to maintain and educate." The author of a letter recommending Moomau for scholarship undercut his assertion of the family's poverty by stating that the young man would pay his own way if he was unable to attain state funding.[25] The truly poor would have been unable to enroll their children at a collegiate institution: Student beneficiaries in the state selection process received free tuition, but the required expenses at VMI or the Citadel amounted to 100 to 200 dollars per year, more than or most of a laborer's yearly salary. This echoed the increase in tuition across the nation – from one-third of a skilled manual laborer's salary in 1800 to 60 percent of it in 1860.[26]

Given the middle class's monetary resources, the usefulness of being connected to a source of patronage becomes glaringly evident. Use of patronage, credit, and employment reflected middle-class resources and status. A VMI alumnus recommended a student to his alma mater, describing the father as "extremely poor" but explaining that friends would pay for the boy's last three years at school. Edward Shepherd's father may have been unable to pay the young man's tuition, but two years later he explained that the boy's grandmother and a family friend would cover Edward's expenses. Someone provided money for a photograph of Edward in his uniform (Figure 4).[27] Such situations suggest that students who requested funding were not entirely destitute of resources, and furthermore that some of their resources were nonmonetary.

[24] Robert P. Carson, unpublished memoir, VHS. All the sons attended schools in Virginia, possibly to limit travel costs.
[25] Recommendation letter, John Moomau student file; recommendation, John Wildman student file, VMI Archives.
[26] Burke, *American Collegiate Populations*, 50.
[27] Robert H. Simpson to Francis H. Smith, 24 June 1853 (first quotation); James Shepherd to Francis H. Smith, 9 June 1851 (second quotation), VMI Archives.

Economic distinctions created a specific relationship to goods (or the possibility of attaining goods or a level of lifestyle). With sufficient resources, middle-class men could purchase luxury goods, although not at the same level as wealthy elites. Rather than credit-based transactions of the sort common in agriculture, professional middle-class men would have had some money to spend on goods, working as they more often did in a cash economy. White-collar workers were often paid a wage, whereas professionals received direct payment for their work (if they could collect their bills). Some of the emerging middle class were merchants, and men in that occupation clearly had better-than-average access to merchandise.[28] In the Old South, cadets had possessions, read newspapers, and purchased clothing, although all in moderation. Most telling, they attended higher schooling. The sufficient resources of the class, illustrated among military alumni, created the ability and limits of consumption among the emerging middle class.

Social Organization

The American middle class sought and demonstrated its economic success and lifestyle through various aspects of social organization. Stuart M. Blumin identifies these aspects as consumption patterns, residence, voluntary associations, and family structure.[29] Thus, patterns of social organization, specifically ones derived from the class's position in the economic and social structure, define the national middle class.

Urban residence was a cross-regional characteristic of large portions of the middle class. Antebellum middle-class Americans can most easily be identified in urban areas; Jonathan Daniel Wells describes southern middle-class professionals in these areas. Studies of the Old South suggest that urban dwellers tended to be more involved in the market economy and thus had more similarities to northerners than did rural southerners. The "embourgeoisement" of urban southerners made the location of the emerging southern middle class in urban areas unsurprising. Had they

---

[28] On merchants, see Byrne, *Becoming Bourgeois.*

[29] Blumin, "The Hypothesis of the Middle-Class Formation in Nineteenth-Century America" and *Emergence of the Middle Class.*

been solely located there, however, the group would have been severely limited, because the region exhibited restricted urban development.[30]

There was even a symbiotic relationship between professionals and urban areas: Professional men attracted schools to their areas, because they valued and could afford schooling. As the number of professionals increased in an area, educators located schools where professional men might engage their services; for example, Charles C. Tew left a military institution in South Carolina to found the Hillsboro Military Academy among a large population of attorneys in North Carolina. Thus, for historians, new schools and developing education systems potentially mark areas, especially in the South and West, where the middle class lived. Considering alongside this proposition James Oakes's image of the socially mobile small slaveholder located primarily on the frontier suggests that middle-class traits could have extended into the rural South.[31] Professionals in rural areas and small towns exhibited enough of the characteristics of the middle class to locate them among its members, so that urban residence appears not to have been a decisive factor; this is certainly true for the emerging southern middle class and potentially so for the national group. Those professionals may, in fact, have had more individual influence in their communities than their urban peers had.[32] Rural professionals should be included in the national middle class, as they exhibited the same qualities as southern men in military education.

Family structure, with nuclear families and specific gender relations, is another type of social organization that marked the middle class. Northern society entered a cult of domesticity in a way that southern wives of planters and yeomen did not; northern patterns of domestic relations, however, were more prevalent in nonagricultural southern households.[33]

---

[30] Elizabeth Fox-Genovese, *Within the Plantation Household: Black and White Women in the Old South* (Chapel Hill: University of North Carolina Press, 1988), 70 (quotation). Robert C. Kenzer, *Kinship and Neighborhood in a Southern Community: Orange County, North Carolina, 1849–1881* (Knoxville: University of Tennessee Press, 1987), 33; Wells, *Origins of the Southern Middle Class.*

[31] Both James Oakes and Frank Owsley suggest increased social mobility on the southern frontier. Oakes, *Ruling Race;* Owsley, *Plain Folk of the South,* 142.

[32] Mayer, "The Lower Middle Class as Historical Problem," 429.

[33] Nancy Cott, *The Bonds of Womanhood: "Women's Sphere" in New England, 1780–1835* (New Haven: Yale University Press, 1977); Fox-Genovese, *Within the Plantation Household;* McCurry, *Masters of Small Worlds;* Cashin, *A Family Venture;* Joan Turner Censer,

Women's roles in the emerging southern middle class were closer to the northern middle-class norm than to that of southerners connected to agricultural labor. The cult of domesticity, however, may have marked northern society more than it did southern middle-class social organization. Middle-class men had similarities across regions; restrained manhood was more common in the middle class of both regions than were other models. Southern middle-class manhood demanded occupational expectations similar to those of northern professionals but also retained southern traits. Although American middle-class men and women shared traits, southern men and southern women, regardless of class, also possessed traits that separated them from northerners.

Middle-class families nationwide sacrificed to promote their children's success and social stability (or mobility). In both the North and the South, they relied on extended families for help with their children's education and placement in careers, although perhaps even more so in the South, with its strong community ideology. Social networking through families perpetuated middle-class values and relationships; for example, young men and women of the emerging middle class could marry to cement economic standing and status.

Outside of its members' homes, the middle class organized itself into voluntary associations and organizations that reflected its values and demographics. Scholarship on voluntary associations makes connections between associations and middle-class status. Members of the emerging southern middle class participated in lodges and meetings, and among military alumni groups could create friendships that became the seeds of military educator networks. Military alumni joined Masonic lodges: although records mention only thirteen, those few men probably found themselves among others of their class.[34] Occupational organizations,

North Carolina Planters and Their Children, 1800–1860 (Baton Rouge: Louisiana State University, 1984); Byrne, *Becoming Bourgeois*; Wells, *Origins of the Southern Middle Class.*

[34] Mark C. Carnes, *Secret Ritual and Manhood in Victorian America* (New Haven: Yale University Press, 1989), 3 n. 9; Samuel Haber, *The Quest for Authority and Honor in the American Professions* (Chicago: University of Chicago Press, 1991), 123; John Gordon Deal, "The Forgotten Southerner: Middle-Class Associationalism in Antebellum Norfolk, Virginia" (Ph.D. diss., University of Florida, 2003); Ami Pflugrad-Jackisch, "A Host of Shameless Imposters: Fraternal Orders and the Urban Confidence Man in Antebellum Virginia," presented at Southern Historical Association Conference, Memphis (4 November 2004); Wells, *Origins of the Southern Middle Class*, ch. 4.

such as those for common school teachers, similarly brought members of the class together.

Cultural Values

"The key point in analyzing the middle stratum of society," Peter Stearns asserts, "is to isolate distinct, sometimes partially contradictory cultures of values." The particulars of economic situation, social hierarchy, demographics, and values began to make the emerging middle class distinct from other groups. Separate, but not completely different, from other groups, the emerging middle class displayed both national and southern traits.

EDUCATION

Members of the American middle class promoted education, and their sufficient resources allowed them to pursue it. Education in and of itself offered opportunities for personal improvement, both moral and intellectual. It enriched a man's life, helped him maintain his moral standards, and connected him to his peers. It made him better and gave him a foundation for respect and prosperity. Not surprisingly, many nonelite educational institutions implied or explicitly stated a connection among education, career, and success. The emerging southern middle class promoted education as did its northern counterparts. "Remember that education is the business of life," a speaker instructed VMI cadets.[35]

Middle-rank southerners, like their northern counterparts, sought education. Professionals in two Tennessee counties enrolled their children in schools more often than did fathers with other occupations, despite only 10 to 11 percent of school children coming from nonagricultural homes.[36] Because their economic situation limited their access to secondary education, middle-class men who sent their sons to military schools usually had not benefited from higher education themselves. It was common for cadets' fathers to express their desire to have their sons

---

[35] Willoughby Newton, *Virginia and The Union* (Richmond: MacFarlane and Fergusson, 1858), 31 (quotation); Rossiter Taylor, *Ante-bellum South Carolina* (1942; reprint, New York: Da Capo Press, 1970), 112.

[36] Keith Whitescarver, "Political Economic, Schooling, and Literacy in the South" (Ed. D. diss., Harvard University, 1995), 73–4.

schooled because they had not been able to attend college themselves. "Never having an opportunity myself to get an education," a father wrote of his disappointment about his two sons' decision to leave VMI, "I determined to give my sons one, but I have failed, I shall now learn them to work."[37] This man made a conscious effort to give his sons the advantage that he lacked.

The emerging southern middle class enrolled the younger generation in antebellum universities less frequently than did either southern elites or middle-class northerners. Middle-class southerners encountered difficulty affording university education for their children. As all middle-class youth needed to pursue careers, moreover, their fathers living in both regions were less likely to support the ideals of classical education. In some cases, middle-class families sent their oldest sons to a college and their younger son or sons to military institutions – a cheaper alternative that offered more vocational training. Middle-class southerners also took advantage of higher schools and smaller colleges, which proliferated as part of national reforms to curriculum and to lower college admission standards and costs.[38] Given their economic demographics, resources, and place in southern society, middle-class southerners lacked access to, and the benefits of, classical education in ways that elites did not.

PROFESSIONAL IDENTITY

Middle-class Americans employed education to maintain their nonmanual, primarily professional status. Education helped to create formal systems for young men's entry into professional careers in a variety of ways. In addition to the quasi-bureaucratic networking explored in Chapter 7, educators would guide their charges into professional careers. Charles Mason Sr., a farmer and legislator, placed his son "under [the VMI Superintendent's] sole and special protection...Although I have no personal acquaintance with you, I take the liberty and hope, as I do not doubt you will find, the charge both easy and agreeable to manage." When his son graduated four years later, Mason clarified, "I should like

[37] William Meredith to Francis H. Smith, 24 June 1844, VMI Archives. Similarly, Carson, memoir, VHS.

[38] Robert F. Pace, *Halls of Honor: College Men in the Old South* (Baton Rouge: Louisiana State University Press, 2004); Frederick Rudolph, *Curriculum: A History of the American Undergraduate Course of Study Since 1636* (San Francisco: Jossey-Bass Publishers, 1977), ch. 3.

extremely to consult you in regard to what calling or profession he should follow. You have had a better oppertunity [*sic*] recently, to form a correct estimate of what his mind is fitted for, and in what capacity he would most likely to succeed best."[39] The preference for professional careers and even the manageable behavior necessary for them showed in the father's choices, directed by the military school; young Charles became a civil engineer.

One benefit of education was the opportunity it created for networking. We have seen how using military education to create career networks aided the development of the southern middle class; this same dynamic may well have been at work at other types of schools across the nation. Networking, in turn, increased professionalization, which reinforced the middle class's central economic differentiation.

Professional status also led to certain ideas about professional lifestyle. Men identified with their careers rather than with the land. It was this central reason that middle-class men sought education for their sons. As professionals themselves, they identified their success with their careers and wanted the advantage of education to improve the career possibilities for their sons. "I am really dependent upon my daily labour for a support," one father began. He continued to explain that his son's graduation would "recompense me for" the expense and effort of the education.[40] This man described himself as working for a living, and his hopes for his son entailed both monetary and career compensation.

OTHER CULTURAL VALUES

The national middle class shared cultural values. Theorists have identified the values in place in the mid-nineteenth-century middle class as entrepreneurship, professionalization, venerating private property, individualism, industry, self-discipline, self-regulation, self-improvement, professional identity, evangelicalism, and restrained manhood.[41] In the

[39] Charles Mason to Francis H. Smith, 23 July 1848 (first quotation), 10 June 1852 (second quotation), VMI Archives.
[40] J. R. Bridges to Francis H. Smith, 3 March 1849, Edward Bridges student file, VMI Archives.
[41] Stearns, "The Middle Class," 394 (quotation). The vast historiography on the northern middle class describes that group's qualities; Wells, Carmichael, and Byrne ascribe many of those traits to middle-class southerners. Mayer, "The Lower Middle Class as Historical Problem."

1840s and 1850s, an emerging southern middle class drew its values from its southern environment and from its occupational similarity to the northern middle class. Thus, the values shared by the northern and southern middle classes represented national values of the class.

Many values of the middle class derived from its economic situation. Middle-class men exhibited ambition and, in the South, a developing drive for a specific vision of mobility that coincided with the established one in the North. Of course, aspirations may be found in any class (just as fears of downward mobility can) yet they appear to be especially prevalent among middle-class men, whose tenuous position was reflected by them.[42] Although the fear of downward mobility existed for all of the middling ranks, established middle-class men often worried about their children's failure while hoping anxiously for their success. A portion of middle-class men's professional identity validated education as a means to advantage, career, and mobility. Such a desire for self-improvement was another value of a national middle class. Self-discipline, clear in southern military education, also benefited all middle-class men.

The centrality of self-discipline in national middle-class ideals filtered into the acceptance of restrained manhood and values associated with northern evangelicals. The middle class, regardless of location, worked for its improvement, and men came to value traits that embodied improvement and hard work. Whether cadets in the Old South or students in the North, young men learned what it meant to be a man as they grew up. They incorporated traits from the society around them and from their class position.

Middle-class southerners did not adopt northern middle-class ideas wholesale, although some middle-class values were accepted nationally.[43] This study stresses cultural convergence but maintains regional distinctiveness. Nineteenth-century Americans, the same as Britons, saw themselves in a hierarchy with both economic and cultural components. Gentility and refinement separated classes, seen in the North and among elite southerners educated in Pennsylvania.[44] Although military education

---

[42] Mayer, "The Lower Middle Class as Historical Problem," 424; Carmichael, *Last Generation*, 11.

[43] Wells, *Origins of the Southern Middle Class*, e.g. 13. Carmichael, *Last Generation*.

[44] Cannadine, *Rise and Fall of Class in Britain*; Richard Bushman, *The Refinement of America: Persons, Houses, Cities* (New York: Alfred A. Knopf, 1992); Daniel Kilbride, "Southern Medical

may have comprised a more modern, progressive, and professional segment of the Old South, scholarship suggests that similar trends occurred
among other groups. The distinctiveness of the middle social position is
revealed in military education, but it clearly reflects larger changes in the
South and the nation. Cadets also demonstrate that national middle-class
values existed.

Southern Regionalism

The southern middle class arose, in part, for reasons specific to southern regionalism. The members of the emerging southern middle class
understandably displayed regional traits, as did northerners. What the
southern experience particularly contributes to the definitional model is
the necessity of weighing status, especially the status of professionals.
Occupation, though it is certainly important to any evaluation of class
difference, is not the sole determinant of that difference. Prestige is as
significant as occupation (and certainly, for many antebellum men, the
two would have been integrally connected). Nonmanual labor – the sort
that was done by the middle class – did not have the same cultural meaning in the North as it did in the South. Agriculturalists (who perhaps
owned a few slaves) with professional careers, for example, still engaged
in farm labor, and land ownership in fact conferred status in the Old
South. Nonmanual labor, then, marked the middle class, and historians
can focus on nonagricultural work, the professions, and the status that
came along with such occupational choices as they attempt to define that
class. It must be the presence of that nonmanual, usually professional
career with its resultant status, social organization, and values that distinguish the emerging southern middle class from plain folk or planters
sons. Within a region, whether the North, the South, or even the West,
status, consumption patterns, social organization, and values all varied
to some degree.

The middle class and its particular social status developed out of new
relationships in America during the transitioning years of the 1840s and
1850s. Southern merchants, Frank Byrne argues, saw themselves in a
middle social position because of their occupational existence between

planters and yeomen (more money and status than yeomen, less of both than planters).[45] Other professionals were similarly in that middle-class status. Planters' younger sons might move into professions, not in opposition to slavery but as better personal choices for success. Some southerners turned to industrial solutions to modernize the slave state. The economic order, with the help of the emerging middle class and other pro-industry southerners, was changing. The rank and file of the developing class, however, never accumulated the economic resources to enter the upper range of the social order. They could raise themselves above the lower economic and social classes (plain folk, yeomen, laborers, and obviously African Americans). For middle-class southerners, however, there was a great necessity to alter the definition of success. In order to develop the group and individual success, then, nonagricultural professional members of the developing southern middle class looked to institutions and models of success different from those of the elite. Military schooling was one avenue in cultural reorientations.[46] Similar processes of professionalization and networking, however, occurred across the nation.

In the Old South, industrialists and some members of the emerging middle class sought to enter the existing social order with slaves and plantations. Middle-class military school enrollees felt the pull of southern ideology. Some of the alumni purchased farms and accepted the dominant model of success – that is, the plantation economy. John Brockenbrough, to give one example, taught for two years after his 1850 VMI graduation and then, rather than follow in his father's footsteps as a legislator, became a farmer. By 1860, he had acquired 281 acres and eight slaves – not enough to qualify as a planter, but certainly enough to indicate that he leaned toward the planter ideal. That said, Brockenbrough did not represent the majority of his peers, who chose professional paths and thus refigured the southern basis for success.

Using military education, the emerging southern middle class demonstrated little outright opposition between the classes, which would have aided in the development of class consciousness. Certainly, the middle-class members were explicit in their antagonism toward the lower classes – an antagonism that may have denoted their fear of downward mobility.

---

[45] Byrne, *Becoming Bourgeois*.
[46] See Owsley, *Plain Folk of the Old South*, 142–49.

Many in the emerging middle class, however, sought to enter the planter elite if they could, even as they changed the standards of mobility. There were tensions between groups and especially between individuals in different places and at different times, but these tensions never led to class warfare. The middle class acted more to change its own members' ideology and society's estimation of them than to attack the planter elite;[47] after all, planters could not provide better wages or working conditions, as the middle class–planter relationship was vastly different from the employee–employer relationship that drove much of northern and European class formation. Also, the centrality of community in the Old South created close cross-class connections, including connections of patronage and kin assistance.

The emerging southern middle class, in short, was *southern*, and as such, it shared values with the southern master class that it did not share with the northern middle class. Imbibing southern values included imbibing a positive attitude toward slavery, but southern values meant more than that; the partial adherence of the emerging southern middle class to the values of southern honor and rugged masculinity, for example, also showed the persistence of southernness in this group. Self-discipline was a national middle-class value, but the drive for mastery and the insistence on hierarchy of the southern middle class resonated with traditional southern culture. That the members of the southern middle class maintained community relationships in new ways, such as the networks of military school educators that replaced kin connections with proto-bureaucratic systems, reflected their acceptance of elements of southern culture. The southernness of the emerging middle class in the region can also be seen in values that northerners possessed that southerners less frequently accepted: The southern middle class embraced educational reform, for example, but not more widespread reform in the guise of abolition or women's rights. A more detailed differentiation between the national middle class and the emerging southern middle class still remains to be made.

---

[47] This conclusion differs from Wells's interpretation in *Origins of the Southern Middle Class*, esp. ch. 8. In part because this study denies class consciousness to the emerging middle class, it does not assert class antagonism. The middle rank certainly distinguished itself from those below it, but the middle-class population in military education did not demonstrate enmity toward the elite.

Conclusion

In creating a definitional model of the antebellum American middle class, the group's middle social rank must take precedence. This position derives from its economic situation – their place in the economic structure and development of early nineteenth-century America. Secondary characteristics – demographics, social organization, and values – also help to categorize members of the national middle class. The national middle class demonstrated the demographic criteria of occupations in nonmanual and nonagricultural work, occupational status, access to goods, sufficient resources, gender definitions, associations, belief in and use of education, and professional occupation and identity. They shared values centered in self-discipline and in professionally helpful qualities.

These characteristics encouraged a particular segment of the developing southern middle class to pursue military education. The educational experiences they had and the values that they imbibed began to separate them from the elite. Southern military schools provide a window into the class component of southern schooling, and especially its support of the emergence of a southern middle class. Because of the schools' institutional characteristics, young men at military schools were often non-elite, with inadequate kin connections or wealth to include them among the elite.

This study argues that the emerging middle class was an economic class that was developing as a status group based on its members' lifestyles and occupations (specifically, their professional occupations). Of course, class and status groups overlap. An emerging middle class with nationwide traits developed in the late antebellum years. The disparities between men of that social rank illustrate the problems of identifying the national middle class as a class "for itself." Although men in the developing southern middle class (who shared national middle-class characteristics while maintaining some southern traditions) began acting and thinking in similar ways, they did not exhibit complete class consciousness.

Conclusion

In his last year at Raleigh Military Academy, Cadet Theodore Kingsbury pled with his father to let him go off to war. The young man's father doused his son's enthusiasm, telling the young man that the army experience would be temporary and detrimental to his long-term career. Young Kingsbury agreed that the Mexican War would not be his fight.[1] His petition illustrated cadet interest in the Mexican War, which would be surpassed fifteen years later by cadet and alumni involvement in the Civil War. That war would shatter the lives of individual men and families, whereas military schools and the emerging southern middle class would rise from the ashes, albeit in different form than their antebellum counterparts.

Throughout the 1850s, cadets occasionally remarked on political happenings. They followed newspapers and debated issues of the day. In 1840, a Virginia Military Institute (VMI) cadet claimed that all but three or four of his peers supported the Whig Party. Fifteen years later, another Virginian worried that the Know Nothings, of whom he disapproved, would defeat the Democrats within the state. Certainly more southerners supported the Democratic Party by the mid-1850s than had earlier, but Joel Scott at the Western Military Institute (WMI) remained a steadfast Whig. Still, support for secession when it came ruled the day, possibly founded on state-based allegiance.[2]

---

[1] R. Kingsbury to Theodore Kingsbury, 11 February 1847, Theodore Kingsbury Correspondence, Southern Historical Collection, Wilson Library, University of North Carolina at Chapel Hill (hereafter SHC).

[2] Philip James to John Winn, 20 March 1840, Winn Family Papers, Rare Book, Manuscript and Special Collections Library, Duke University (hereafter Duke); J. F. Neff to Parents, 14

The majority of cadets followed their states into the Confederacy, as did the larger stream of the emerging southern middle class. Following disunion, cadets at VMI and WMI hung secession flags (which the administrations made them take down). Cadets who were unionist, including the one described by a WMI fellow cadet in Tennessee in February 1861, probably kept quiet in the pro-southern atmosphere. A few cadets served in the Union army, but an even larger number than that did not serve for either side. Most alumni of southern military schools, however, became a trained fighting force for the Confederate States of America (CSA). Young men on both sides were caught up in war fever and patriotism in the early years. Southern cadets possessed the same motivations that caused other young men to enlist. The graduates filled the officer ranks of the CSA; approximately 90 percent of the South Carolina Military Academy (SCMA) alumni ranked from lieutenant to brigadier-general in the Civil War. More than 10,000 military alumni served in the Confederate army.[3]

Cadets who remained at school during the war wrote about their readiness for the fight. For example, Gratz Cohen at the Georgia Military Institute (GMI) told his father in 1862 that he paid particular attention to drill so that he would be prepared when he entered the war. Likewise, Cadet Beverly Stanard wanted to see the elephant. He obeyed his mother by remaining at VMI until the cadets marched out of the institute in May

April 1855, Preston Library, Virginia Military Institute Archives (hereafter VMI Archives); Frederick Bryan to Isabel Bryan, 16 March 1861, John Heritage Bryan Papers, Department of Archives and History, North Carolina State Archives (hereafter NCSA). Peter S. Carmichael, *The Last Generation: Young Virginians in Peace, War and Reunion* (Chapel Hill: University of North Carolina Press, 2005), ch. 4–5. The cadets' general silence on politics is unsurprising because of their youth.

[3] On the connection of middle-class southerners to secession, see Jonathan Daniel Wells, *The Origins of the Southern Middle Class, 1800–1861* (Chapel Hill: University of North Carolina Press, 2004), ch. 9; Carmichael, *ibid.*; Frank J. Byrne, *Becoming Bourgeois: Merchant Culture in the South, 1820–1865* (Lexington, KY: University Press of Kentucky, 2006), ch. 4–5. Charles Copeland Wight, unpublished memoir, Virginia Historical Society (hereafter VHS); C. O. Bailey to Charley Bailey, 24 February 1860 [1861], John B. Bailey Papers; Lewis Edwin Harvie, unpublished memoir, SHC; Henry Hendrick to Mary A. Hendrick, 19 April 1861, Duke. Bruce Allardice, "West Points of the Confederacy: Southern Military Schools and the Confederate Army," *Civil War History*, 43 (December 1997), 310–31, suggests the number is 12,000 men. James Lee Conrad, *Young Lions: Confederate Cadets at War* (Mechanicsburg, PA: Stackpole Books, 1997); Rod Andrew Jr., *Long Gray Lines: The Southern Military School Tradition, 1839–1915* (Chapel Hill: University of North Carolina Press, 2001), 26–28; Gary R. Baker, *Cadets in Gray: The Story of the Cadets of the South Carolina Military Academy and the Cadet Rangers in the Civil War* (Columbia: Palmetto Bookworks, 1989).

1864. At the Battle of New Market, Stanard got his wish to fight. He would be one of ten cadets to die from wounds inflicted in combat.[4] Overall, cadets spoke about their interest in battle, and educators described the academies' service to the state in the war effort.

The situation of Cadets Cohen and Stanard indicates the paradox of the military school situation. When troops began mustering, two conflicting impulses hit the institutions and their students. Cadets could wax eloquent about wanting to fight – yet, they were young men who had not enlisted in the Confederate Army. Some cadets in the 1860s were younger than seventeen years old and too young to enter; older cadets, however, followed the wartime influence that kept them in schools and out of active service. Institutionally, military academies directed cadets out of active service so that the schools would maintain a large enough student body to remain open. Although some closed, the larger state military schools stayed open when the war began and continued to run, if on irregular schedules, through the first years of the war. The SCMA, VMI, GMI, University of Alabama, West Florida Seminary, and Hillsboro Military Academy (HMA) remained open into 1864 or 1865. The largest four of these institutions enrolled about 2,000 youths during the war.

Military programs in fact increased enrollments; the number of cadets entering VMI during the Civil War doubled from most antebellum years and rose over 100 for the first time. In April 1862, GMI had a cadet contingent of 125 able-bodied young men. Throughout the war, CSA officials had a mixed regard for the state military schools. President Jefferson Davis, a West Point graduate himself, began naming cadets for a proposed CSA military academy in April 1861. It never succeeded. Instead, the southern state military institutes drilled volunteers and recruits, similar to the national academy. The government called on the Alabama cadets, for example, in March 1862 to train 12,000 soldiers.[5]

---

[4] Gratz Cohen to Solomon Cohen, 10 June 1862, SHC. Beverly Stanard, *Letters of a New Market Cadet*, ed. John G. Barrett and Robert K. Turner Jr. (Chapel Hill: University of North Carolina Press, 1961), 50, 55. On enlistment, see James M. McPherson, *For Cause and Comrades: Why Men Fought in the Civil War* (New York: Oxford University Press, 2007). James Gindlesperger, *Seed Corn of the Confederacy* (Shippensburg, PA: Burd Street Press, 1997), creates historical fiction to describe the battle.
[5] Andrew, *Long Gray Lines*, 28–29; Conrad, *Young Lions*, 53, 87–89, 153, 156; Lori A. Lisowksi, "The Future of West Point: Senate Debates on the Military Academy During the Civil War," *Civil War History*, 34 (March 1988), 5–21.

In contrast to military schools remaining open, many other educational institutions in the South closed immediately or lost their students by 1862. The elite South Carolina College, for example, closed in 1861 so that the student body could enlist. Military schools might have had trouble retaining their upperclassmen, who often left to join up. From 1861 through 1865, VMI graduated only 100 of the 529 matriculates and the University of Alabama's cadet corps graduated less than 200 of 624. Overall, however, military higher schools created a unique opportunity for men to avoid temporarily active battle and still serve the Confederacy by training volunteer corps. The open institutions benefited monetarily from these high enrollments and from government funding. For example, the CSA appeared to have provided VMI with shoes, because the cadets served the army as drillmasters. Thus, schools and educators must have found it advantageous for many reasons (including patriotism) to protect the schools' functions.

The desire to preserve the programs, however, changed the institutions. At least one military school altered the way it presented honor. The superintendent of Alabama's cadet corps, L. C. Garland, sent a form letter to cadets' parents in February 1863. He explained that it was neither an honor nor a duty for the cadets to join the CSA. He wanted "parental authority" to keep the young men at school (and thus paying tuition).[6] Garland reversed the parental role in military discipline; before the war, the institutions superseded parents, yet the war increased parental influence – the choice between life or potential death was clearly more significant than school discipline. Perhaps Garland and other military educators felt the need to maintain institutional power (using parental authority) over the pull of enlistment.

Under General Order No. 23, the CSA exempted military school faculty but left cadets open to the draft. The CSA exempted military professors so that they could continue to train new soldiers and engineers for wartime construction. State governors appealed to President Davis, but the government refused to exempt cadets. For all practical purposes, however, the exemption existed. In Virginia, Governor William Smith apparently took it upon himself to refuse the VMI cadets' enlistment.[7]

---

[6] L. C. Garland, 9 February 1863, Mayre Dabney collection, SHC.

[7] The decision to exempt military professors followed antebellum exemptions for cadets and teachers from militia, road, and jury duty; Lynwood M. Holland, "Georgia Military Institute, The West Point of Georgia, 1851–64," *Georgia Historical Quarterly*, 43 (1959), 225–47. James

The regulation allowed some military alumni, because a large proportion of them were already teachers and military educators, to avoid enlistment (and conscription). Two alumni from the Citadel, for example, taught "under Mr. Ford, at the Military Academy of Montgomery Ala." Robert Oswald Sams explained, "I was head of the Military Department." He used this career to avoid military service in the Civil War. After writing to his parents that he wanted to fight but could not break his obligation to Ford, Sams switched positions to teach at the Arsenal Academy rather than enlist right away. The friend who went with him to Mr. Ford's was not so lucky; he quit teaching at the military school and died in the war. Similar to Sams, James Murfee and Digges Poynor, VMI graduates from 1845 and 1860 respectively, taught the cadet corps at the University of Alabama throughout the Civil War and only entered battle twice when they marched out with the cadets. William Gordon, that unpopular 1852 VMI alumnus, taught at HMA in 1862.[8] Faculty at all the institutions remained inside school walls and supplied trained men for many of the bloody battles.

On an individual level, wartime military schools could protect young men from battle. Although most cadets described wanting to go into combat, some certainly did not want to risk their lives. It was rare that young men wrote explicitly that they wanted to avoid the war. Arthur D. Cowles, however, was one such cadet at HMA in 1864. Cowles wrote to his father, "I see that they [Congress] have passed a bill conscripting from 17 to 50 it would have gotten me if I had but only remained at home. As it is they cannot touch me. No cadets have ever been conscripted from this institution – therefore I am safe." Suggesting that he was not the only young man gloating over being in school, he continued, "There is

---

Conrad, "Training for Treason," *Civil War Times Illustrated*, 30 (September/October 1991), 23–6. Governor Smith's action spurred angry letters from CSA Secretary of War George Randolph. See *The War of the Rebellion* (Washington DC: Government Printing Office, 1880–1901), Ser. IV, 1:1080–5, 1121, 2:123, 154, 3:722–3. Stanard, *Letters of a New Market Cadet,* 32.

[8] Robert Oswald Sams, unpublished memoir (quotations); R. O. Sams to Ma, 17 November 1861; Caroline Sams to Marion Sams, 2 December 1861, Sams Family Papers, The South Caroliniana Library, University of South Carolina (hereafter SCL). Claudius Fike reported twenty-two-year-old Sams's teaching at SCMA; Fike to G. A. Fike, 23 August 1862, Claudius Lucian Fike papers, SCL. Conrad, *Young Lions,* 52–53; Edwin L. Dooley, "'A fine College from this time forward': The Influence of VMI on the Militarization of the University of Alabama" (n.p., 1997), 15–16.

[*sic*] at least 25 boys here that are from 19 to 23. I am progressing with my studies very well."⁹ Cowles then calmly reported his grades, after having explained that he had shirked military service. His letter implied that at least twenty-five young men avoided the army by attending this particular military school in North Carolina.

Indeed, the educator networks worked so well that alumni used them for a new purpose after 1861. Rather than for professional positions, alumni could use their relationships to secure their sons and relatives places at their alma maters and, thus, off the battlefields. For example, the brother-in-law of an 1843 VMI graduate wrote to the VMI superintendent hoping to enroll his seventeen-year-old son rather than send him to the army. The superintendent apparently participated in the cadet's desire to avoid service and remain at VMI.¹⁰ The alumnus and his family used the same networks that existed before the war, but to a very different end.

By October 1864, the Confederate Secretary of War issued Special Order No. 102 that drafted all males seventeen years old or older. Cadets who had avoided active service before this point would begin to serve under that order. Thus, not before 1864 were cadets at military schools called into active battle. Their duty as combat troops was effective but limited. Two of the fifty-four University of Alabama cadets fighting at Beasley's farm were killed, and the others only saw combat as a unit at River Hill in April 1865. Similarly, the faculty commanded GMI cadets at the Battle of Resaca in May 1864, the same month that Stanard and his VMI peers fought at the Battle of New Market, and the cadets of SCMA marched into action in December 1864 at Tulifinny Creek. Studies have detailed cadet service.¹¹ For most of the war, at least partially, enrolling in a military academy allowed young men to avoid or postpone active service in the CSA.

Wartime cadets recorded their lives at school with banal stories similar to those of antebellum cadets. For example, Cadet Claudius Fike

---

⁹ Arthur Cowles to Calvin Cowles, 3 July 1864, Calvin J. Cowles Collection, NCSA.

¹⁰ R. L. Patterson to Francis H. Smith, 22 May 1863, William Warden student file, VMI Archives. Other letters such as this one very likely existed. Samuel B. Hannah to John Hannah, 18 February 1861, Hannah Family Papers, VHS.

¹¹ Conrad, *Young Lions*, 53, 87–90, 113, 119–20, 145–47. Allardice, "West Points of the Confederacy"; Andrew, *Long Gray Lines*; Baker, *Cadets in Gray*; Keith Bohannon, "Cadets, Drillmasters, Draft Dodgers, and Soldiers: The Georgia Military Institute During the Civil War," *Georgia Historical Quarterly*, 79 (1995), 5–29.

paid to attend SCMA from January 1861 through at least August 1864. In the thirteen existent letters that he wrote home during the war, seven included no reference to the war and the other six generally recorded factual information rather than personal impressions of war. He listed his course schedule and grades, repeatedly reported the demerits he received, described his clothing with great interest, even comparing uniform buttons with palmettos to those with eagles, and thanked his father for borrowing the money to purchase him those uniforms.[12] In fact, Fike wrote that he wanted to spend an extra year at the Arsenal Academy, lengthening his schooling to a five-year program. Was he wondering if the war would last until 1866?

Cadets more often described themselves as serving their country and facing danger. When Seaborn Montgomery wrote to his father in 1864, he had been in school, including GMI, throughout the entire Civil War. Montgomery, however, qualified his need for new shoes with the phrasing "if I live." Whatever the young man's perception of his position, Montgomery and his peers enjoyed little risk. In reality, at most military schools, cadets acted as drillmasters, which entailed little physical jeopardy. Even performing nonlife-threatening military duty could be regarded negatively; a cadet's father disapproved of the HMA cadets' guarding prisoners of war, telling his son, "we were glad to hear of your return to school for I did not like to pay ten dollars a day and you out on duty that others should do."[13]

Thus, the war created an environment in which some cadets sought the experience that others avoided. It would, however, be anachronistic to say that southern state and private military schools had been preparing for their wartime role since their inception or new funding system in the South in 1839. The schools provided the Civil War with men accustomed

---

[12] Claudius Fike to Parents, 4 January, 7 January, 20 April 1862; Claudius Fike to G. A. Fike, 12 February, 1 May, 15 May, 20 May, 6 July, 23 August, 12 September, 21 December 1862, 20 December 1863, 5 August 1864, SCL. Similarly, other cadets took little notice of the ongoing war; see, John Boinst, unpublished diary, 1862, The Citadel Archives (hereafter CIT); J. P. Cromartie to Grandmother, c. 1863, NCSA; Carey Thomas, unpublished diary, 5 February 1863–15 May 1863, SCL.

[13] Seaborn Montgomery Jr. to Seaborn Montgomery Sr., 8 May 1864 (first quotation), Duke; Beverly Jones quoted in Stephen A. Ross, "To 'Prepare Our Sons for All the Duties That May Lie before Them': The Hillsborough Military Academy and Military Education in Antebellum North Carolina," *North Carolina Historical Review*, 79 (January 2002), 25 (second quotation).

to (or accepting of) the privations of military life. In most ways, though, the wartime and postwar changes in southern society altered the significance of antebellum military education. Those institutions existed in an almost completely different social and educational environment than what the war wrought.

The significance of antebellum military education is, first, that it illuminates the emerging southern middle class, a group difficult to locate and differentiate; second, it indicates that southern education offered social stability or mobility; finally, it explicitly linked middle-class stability or mobility to the ongoing national professionalization of teachers, more advanced and bureaucratic in the North but also visible in the Old South. Military schools in the 1840s and 1850s possessed institutional qualities that gave them a special role in the society. In particular, public funding and nonclassical curriculum allowed an increased number of non-elite young men to attend higher schooling. The ability to enter military schools with an English education negated the need for tutors in the classics. Thus, the sufficient funds that men of the emerging middle class possessed allowed them to utilize military programs for scientific, vocational, and practical education. Public funding at the twelve state military institutes encouraged young men of the emerging middle class to enroll, and military education meant schooling at reduced cost. In addition to monetary advantage, the curriculum attracted families interested in the changing times – particularly science and technology – and needing vocations.

Parents who wanted advantage for their sons self-identified as middle rank, and their economic demographics confirmed their judgment. The cadets' fathers shared similar work characteristics, including nonmanual, nonagricultural, and professional occupations. They enjoyed the status conferred by those professions. Their economic situation separated them from the elite and lower classes, providing them with sufficient resources for education but also causing them to rely on patronage and debt. Yeomen and laborers at the subsistence level could not afford these schools, and most men in the middle economic position lacked the wealth for universities (and preparatory classical training). Military school families appear to have manifested those qualities and to have represented the characteristics of the growing southern middle class and of the national middle class.

At schools and after graduation, alumni embodied traits of men in their social position. Because they lived within the military institutions, within their families, and within southern society, cadets blended portions of southern honor and military discipline.[14] In some instances, such as cadet scuffles, their actions appeared to conform to the code of southern honor but actually reflected a move away from it as they negotiated between the contradicting impulses. Cadets illustrated that a diversity of thought and beliefs existed beyond elite ideals. They did not reject southern honor but neither did they entirely embrace it. They particularly imbibed southern hierarchy and, to a lesser extent, mastery. Their views of honor, duty, and manhood centered on obedience and self-discipline. The centrality of self-regulation reflected the emerging middle class's general adoption of restrained manhood. Fostering an inner sense of duty, they blended submission and independence in their vision of manhood. Their fathers' and their own professional identities also probably fostered self-discipline; religious impulses emphasized the same values. The male culture at the academies led them to accept traits that flourished in the North, including industry, fortitude, religiosity, temperance, and frugality. These traits placed their values in line with those of the northern middle class. Within the schools, middle-class southerners maintained some regional traits as they connected to national ones of their class.

Military educator networks, and the niche they perpetuated, offered military school graduates professional careers in the antebellum South. Military educators improved the status of similarly educated men and of the teaching profession, in which the emerging middle class invested many of its hopes for stability and growth. In addition to commonplace social networks, military teachers participated in the development of quasi-bureaucratic, non-elite options to mobility. They assisted in professionalization, a nationwide trend. Most alumni entered teaching and worked for the professional status of that career, succeeding in increasing its presence, visibility, and prestige. In the generation before the Civil War, cadets exhibited the traits of the developing southern middle class.

The economic and occupational structure, combined with values, suggests the development of new paths for social mobility, as seen in military

---

[14] While at school, the youths may have lived in an intermediary place of adolescence and of secondary education, but some of those beliefs surely stayed with them in adulthood.

educator networks. Across the nation, the growing middle class found opportunity in education, and the southern part of the group could access schooling and, through it, try for social stability and mobility. Cadets and their families used practical curricula, funding arrangements, and vocational networks to encourage further mobility in professional occupations, and military alumni created social networks to assist each other. The emerging middle class supported an alternative career trajectory to planting and even to marrying planters' daughters. Women of the emerging middle class probably cemented their husbands' position and certainly created more network connections. Military education promoted occupations outside of the agricultural system. The new concept of and avenue to mobility emerged as part of the professionals' developing cultural beliefs. The redefinition of status into qualities attainable by middle-class men centered on professionalization and values.

Alumni were an important segment of the emerging southern middle class and also of the national middle class. In the study of these young men, class appears to have been as influential a determinant of culture as region.[15] Similar middle-class traits and ideals arose nationally. The characteristics of socioeconomic position, economic demographics, social organization, and values can define the antebellum American middle class. The primary defining characteristic was existence in the middle social position, thus the "middle class" between elite and poor. However, their location in the occupational structure, predominately nonmanual and nonagricultural work, is significant to describe that position. This socioeconomic location encouraged the development of social arrangements (especially family and associations) and values in many members of the group; middle-class men promoted education, professionalism, and self-discipline whether they lived in the North or the South. The antebellum middle class changed with the times across the nation, as both ideology and classes are constantly in flux. This study considers the process of middle-class formation in the 1840s and 1850s, examining one group in depth as it illuminates the middle class regionally and nationally.

The evidence from antebellum military education suggests that an elite hegemony did not control southern culture even though it influenced

<hr>

[15] See Daniel Kilbride, "Southern Medical Students in Philadelphia, 1800–1860: Science and Sociability in the 'Republic of Medicine,'" *Journal of Southern History*, 65 (November 1999), 697–732.

regional values; however, even as the emerging middle class encouraged a desirable alternative to elite culture, it was not antagonistic.[16] Military alumni point to a widening separation between the traditional elite worldview and an emerging professional middle class in the generation before the Civil War. This developing middle class's professional orientation began to alter men's vision of social mobility and created accompanying cultural changes. As more youth entered this type of schooling, the language of honor may have begun to shift (had the war not come). In this transitional period, some of its members would have used professional careers and bureaucratic networks, hoping to earn enough for plantation and slave ownership.

It is, of course, impossible to say how the southern middle class would have developed had the war not come. The Morrill Land Grant Act of 1862 represented the United States's attempt to legislate both military and practical education. Section 4 provided for "maintenance of at least one college where the leading object shall be, without excluding other scientific and classical studies and *including military tactics*, to teach such branches of learning as are related to agriculture and the mechanic arts, in such manner as the legislatures of the States may respectively prescribe, in order to promote the liberal and *practical education* of the industrial classes on the several pursuits and *professions* in life." This phrasing echoed what southern military schools had been saying for the previous twenty years. Schools such as Texas A & M and Virginia Tech opened in the 1870s and 1880s, with science-based curricula and military components.[17]

Antebellum military schools taught comparatively little about military arts; the Civil War changed the focus of their curricula to one of wartime necessity. The Morrill Act further altered this balance. Of course, following the war, pedagogical changes and curricular reform made the significance of the military schools' practical education out-of-date anyway. Military schools that reopened generally reorganized as colleges.

---

[16] Carmichael *Last Generation*, 7, suggests that all southerners, no matter the class or number of slaves owned, shared the same worldview (which was the "intellectual framework of the dominant slaveholding class"). Rather than Carmichael's generational study, this text uses class analysis and thus identifies differences among groups.

[17] Http://www.higher-ed.org/resources/morrill1.htm (italics added). See Andrew, *Long Gray Lines*, ch. 2; John A. Adams Jr., *Keepers of the Spirit: The Corps of Cadets at Texas A&M University, 1876–2001* (College Station: Texas A&M University Press, 2001).

For example, the Arsenal Academy in Columbia, South Carolina, burned in February 1865 and was never reopened; its sister school, the Citadel, would reopen with alumni help in 1882, under the leadership of an 1851 alumnus and former military educator. Superintendent Francis H. Smith resurrected VMI.[18] Other schools, especially state military institutes, collapsed into state universities; this was true in Florida, Georgia, and Louisiana, and WMI connected with what has become Vanderbilt University.

Some military alumni who had devoted their antebellum professional lives to military teaching at those schools did not return home. Robert Simpson, C. C. Tew, and Micah Jenkins did not survive the Civil War; the war may, however, have encouraged middle-class mobility, a resurrection of the antebellum social significance of the networks in which they had participated. The networks or similar associations seem to have been revived in the postbellum years, bringing other Confederates into teaching.[19] Next-door to VMI, Washington College would be renamed Washington and Lee, honoring its postwar president Robert E. Lee. Jenkins's former partner Asbury Coward returned to Kings Mountain Military Academy and later to the superintendence of their alma mater, the Citadel, in a new educational and social environment.

Military education is a proxy for the study of the emerging southern middle class. To answer the ever-present historiographic question of continuity or change across the Civil War, military education offered no continuity for the middle class after the war. Public education, and later the Reserve Officers' Training Corps (ROTC), completely negated the class-based position of military schools after 1865. The identification of the emerging middle class, their values, professional occupations, and promotion of progress certainly created a foundation for the postwar

---

[18] See institutional histories for details, including Henry A. Wise, *Drawing Out the Man: The VMI Story* (Charlottesville: University of Virginia Press, 1978); O. J. Bond, *The Story of the Citadel* (Richmond: Garrett and Massie, 1936). Kurt Allen Sanftleben, "A Different Drum: The Forgotten Tradition of the Military Academy in American Education" (Ed. D. diss., College of William and Mary, 1993) focuses on Kemper Military School and its connection to junior college development.

[19] Dan R. Frost, *Thinking Confederates: Academia and the Idea of Progress in the New South* (Knoxville: University of Tennessee Press, 2000). Robert F. Pace aptly describes how the Civil War ended the educational culture at antebellum southern colleges in *Halls of Honor: College Men in the Old South* (Baton Rouge: Louisiana State University Press, 2004), ch. 5.

rise of the middle class, however. Historians have identified specific ways in which Confederate soldiers entered academia and promoted the Lost Cause ideology, the citizen–soldier ideal continued in pre- to postwar military schools, and the antebellum middle class formed the basis of the group in the New South.[20] This study illuminates military education's role in the ongoing development of a professional middle class, including the professionalization of teaching.

After the war, a middle class did emerge in the New South.[21] In that context, military schools began again, but public funding and the standardization of public school curricula meant that military academies no longer functioned as the same forward-looking educational institutions. Former military institutions either dropped their military focus, like the University of Alabama, or retrenched, such as VMI. Other new military schools developed out of World War I preparedness, although the twentieth-century images often figured them as reformatories. The late nineteenth and early twentieth centuries saw the foundations of what would be attacked in the 1990s as backward looking, but which contradicted the educational opportunity and role in class formation of antebellum military education.

---

[20] Frost, *Thinking Confederates*; Andrew, *Long Gray Lines*; Wells, *Origins of the Southern Middle Class*.

[21] There are excellent studies of the postwar South; see, for example, Edward L. Ayers, *The Promise of the New South* (New York: Oxford University Press, 1992); C. Vann Woodward, *The Origins of the New South, 1877–1913* (Baton Rouge: Louisiana State University, 1951), esp. ch. 1.

Military Schools and Schools with Cadet Corps Founded Before 1861

Abingdon Male Academy (Abingdon, VA)

Alabama Military and Scientific Institute (Eufaula, AL)

Alachua Military Institute (Newnansville, FL)

Albemarle Military Institute (Charlottesville, VA)

Alexander Institute (Tulip, AR)

American Classical and Military Lyceum (Mount Airy, PA)

American Literary, Scientific and Military Academy (Norwich, VT)

Arkansas Military Institute (Tulip, AR)

Bastrop Military Institute (Bastrop, TX)

Betts Military Academy (Stamford, CT)

Bingham's Military School (Oxford/Fayette, NC)

Bowden Collegiate and Military Institute (Carroll Co., GA)

Brandon State Military Institute (MS)

Caldwell Institute (NC)

Central Masonic Institute (Selma, AL)

Collegiate and Military School (Boston, MA)

Columbus Military Academy (Columbus, MS)

Culpeper Military Academy (Culpeper, VA)

Danville Military Institute (Danville, VA)

Delaware Military Academy (Wilmington, DE)

Eagleswood Military Academy (Perth Amboy, NJ)

Episcopal High School (Alexandria, VA)

Erskine College (Erskine, SC)

Fleetwood Academy (Walkerton, VA)

Florida Collegiate and Military Institute (Tallahassee, FL)

Florida Seminary (FL)

Franklin Military School (Duplin, NC)

Front Royal Academy (Front Royal, VA)

Georgia Military Institute (Marietta, GA)

Gibson F. Hill's Military Academy (AL)

Glenville Male Collegiate and Military Institute (Glenville, AL)

Hampton Military Academy (Hampton, VA)

Henderson Military and Female Institute (Henderson, NC)

Hillsboro Military Academy (Hillsboro, NC)

Jefferson College (Washington, MS)

Jones Military School (Wilmington, NC)

Kemper Military Junior College (Boonville, MO)

Kentucky Military Institute (Drennon Springs, KY)

Kings Mountain Military Academy (Yorkville, SC)

La Grange Military Academy (La Grange, AL)

Lenoir County Military School (Smithfield, NC)

Louisiana State Seminary and Military Academy (Alexandria, LA)

Mantua Classical and Military Academy (Philadelphia, PA)

Marion Military College (Marion, AL)

Maryland Military Academy (Oxford, MD)

Metropolitan Academy and Gymnasium (New York, NY)

Military Academy at Middleburg (Middleburg, VA)

Military Academy at Tazewell Co. (Jeffersonville, VA)

Military and Scientific Institute (Baton Rouge, LA)

Military School (Onancock, VA)

Military School at Lexington (Lexington, MO)

Mississippi Military Academy (MS)

Missouri Literary, Scientific and Military Academy (St. Louis, MO)

National Scientific and Military College (Brandywine, DE)

Norfolk Academy (Norfolk, VA)

North Carolina Class, Math and Military Academy (Raleigh, NC)

North Carolina Literary, Scientific and Military Academy (Raleigh, NC)

North Carolina Military Academy (Raleigh, NC)

North Carolina Military Institute (Charlotte, NC)

Oak Hill Military Academy (Granville, NC)

Pennsylvania Literary, Scientific and Military Collegiate Institute (Harrisburg, PA)

Pennsylvania Military Academy (Chester, PA)

Petersburg Military Academy (Petersburg, VA)

Portsmouth Academy (Portsmouth, VA)

Quincy Military Academy (Quincy, FL)

Raleigh Military Academy (Raleigh, NC)

Rappahannock Academy and Military Institute (Rappahannock, VA)

Rice Creek Spring Military Academy (Rice Creek Spring, SC)

Rumford Academy (King William Co., VA)

Shelby Military Institute (Shelby Co., TN)

South Carolina Military Academy (the Arsenal) (Columbia, SC)

South Carolina Military Academy (the Citadel) (Charleston, SC)

Southern Military Academy (Wetumpka, AL)

Southern Polytechnic Institute (AL)

St. Thomas's Hall (MS)

Sumterville Male Academy (Sumterville, AL)

Texas Military Institute (Bastrop, TX)

Texas Military Institute (Galveston, TX)

Texas Monumental and Military Institute (La Grange, TX)

Tuskegee Classical and Scientific Institute (Tuskegee, AL)

United States Military Academy at West Point (West Point, NY)

United States Naval Academy at Annapolis (Annapolis, MD)

Unity Scientific and Military Academy (Claremont, NH)

University of Alabama (Tuscaloosa, AL)

University of Mississippi (Oxford, MS)

Virginia Literary, Scientific and Military Academy (Portsmouth, VA)

Virginia Military Institute (Lexington, VA)

Wake Forest College (Winston-Salem, NC)

West Alabama Institute (Sumterville, AL)

West Florida Seminary (Tallahassee, FL)

Western Military Institute (Georgetown, KY)

Westover Military Academy (Lynchburg, VA)

Williamsburg Military School (Williamsburg, VA)

Wisewell's Yonkers Collegiate and Military Institute (Yonkers, NY)

Tables

Table 1. *Fathers' occupations: single occupations*

Occupation	Profession	Percentage
Professional	125	45.8
Clergy	11	
Doctor	56	
Engineer	2	
Lawyer or judge	36	
Teacher	2	
Agricultural	69	25.3
Planter	48	
Farmer	21	
Proprietors	32	11.7
Banker	3	
Businessman	7	
Dentist	2	
Merchant	17	
Shopkeeper	3	
Public Service	26	9.5
Legislator	17	
U.S. Armed Forces member	4	
Government employee	5	
White-collar Employees	15	5.5
Artist	1	
County, city, or court clerk	10	
Editor/Author	2	
Rent or tax collector	2	

(continued)

Table 1 *(continued)*

Occupation	Profession	Percentage
Skilled Trades	6	2.2
Blacksmith	1	
Bricklayer	1	
Carpenter	1	
Hatter	1	
Mechanic	1	
Upholsterer	1	
$N = 273$ individuals		

Note: Unspecified agricultural men have been recorded as farmers; when information on land and slave ownership is available, men with more than one-hundred acres or ten slaves have been placed in the planter category. The ninety-five fathers with multiple careers are not included (See Table 2).

Sources for all tables: Archival research conducted at: The Citadel Archives and Museum; Rare Book, Manuscript, and Special Collections Library, Duke University; Department of Special Collections, Richard Woodruff Library, Emory University; The Filson Historical Society; Georgia Department of Archives and History; The Library of Virginia; Department of Archives and History, North Carolina State Archives; South Carolina Department of Archives and History; South Carolina Historical Society; The South Caroliniana Library, University of South Carolina; Southern Historical Collection, Wilson Library, University of North Carolina at Chapel Hill; Tennessee State Library and Archives; Special Collections, University of Kentucky; University of Texas at Austin; Jean and Alexander Heard Library, Vanderbilt University; Virginia Historical Society; Preston Library, The Virginia Military Institute Archives; Department of Library Special Collections, Manuscripts, Western Kentucky University.

Table 2. *Fathers' occupations: multiple occupations*

Occupation(s)	Number of fathers
Lawyers	
Lawyer & Legislator	23
Lawyer & Legislator & Editor	1
Lawyer & Legislator & Teacher	2
Lawyer & Legislator & Agriculturalist & Editor	1
Lawyer & Legislator & Public Servant	1
Lawyer & Legislator & Agriculturalist	2
Lawyer & Agriculturalist	8
Lawyer & Agriculturalist & Manufacturer & Public Servant	1
Lawyer & Merchant & Clerk	1
Lawyer & Merchant & Public Servant	1
Lawyer & Businessman	1
Lawyer & Banker	1
Lawyer & Armed Services Member & Editor	1
Lawyer & Public Servant	1
Lawyer & Clerk	1
Doctors	
Doctor & Agriculturalist	6
Doctor & Legislator	1
Doctor & Legislator & Agriculturalist & Businessman	1
Doctor & Legislator & Businessman	1
Doctor & Teacher	1
Doctor & Businessman & Armed Services Member	1
Agriculturalists	
Agriculturalist & Merchant	4
Agriculturalist & Merchant & Legislator	2
Agriculturalist & Businessman	4
Agriculturalist & Businessman & Public Servant	1
Agriculturalist & Public Servant	2
Agriculturalist & Editor	1
Agriculturalist & Legislator	1
Agriculturalist & Skilled Tradesman	2
Armed Services	
Armed Services Member & Editor	1
Armed Services Member & Engineer	3
Teachers	
Teacher & Lawyer	1
Teacher & Agriculturalist	2
Teacher & Agriculturalist & Businessman	1
Teacher & Clergy	2
Teacher & Legislator & Businessman	1

(continued)

Table 2 *(continued)*

Occupation(s)	Number of fathers
Merchants	
Merchant & Legislator & Banker	1
Merchant & Legislator & Businessman	1
Merchant & Banker	3
Merchant & Businessman	1
Merchant & Businessman & Public Servant	1
Merchant & Public Servant	1
Clergy	
Clergy & Banker & Author	1
Businessman & Banker	1

$N = 95$ individuals

Table 3. *Kin occupations*

Occupation	Maternal relatives	Nonmaternal relatives	Guardians
Professional	34	48	4
Clergy	4	5	0
Doctor	14	15	4
Editor/Author	0	1	0
Engineer/Railroad industry	1	4	0
Lawyer/Judge	14	13	0
Lawyer & Legislator	0	1	0
Teacher	1	1	0
Agricultural	12	5	0
Planter or Farmer	12	4	0
Farmer & Legislator	0	1	0
Proprietor	6	5	0
Banker	0	1	0
Businessman/Merchant	5	4	0
Manufacturer	1	0	0
Public Service	14	18	1
Clerk or government employee	3	3	0
Legislator	9	14	1
U.S. Armed Forces Member	2	1	0

$N = 147$ individuals

Note: Kin are grandfathers and uncles. All nonspecified grandparents have been placed with nonmaternal kin. All kin acting as guardians have been placed within their respective kin categories. Guardians whose kinship relationship was unspecified have been placed in the guardian category.

Table 4. *Alumni occupations: single occupation*

Occupation	Profession	Percentage
Professional	406	61.4
Clergy	11	
Doctor	113	
Engineer	49	
Lawyer or judge	99	
Teacher	134	
Agricultural	140	21.2
Planter	36	
Farmer	104	
Proprietors	46	7.0
Architect	1	
Banker	3	
Builder	2	
Businessman	28	
Dentist	4	
Merchant	21	
Miner	6	
Pharmacist	1	
Public Service	18	2.7
U.S. Armed Forces member	13	
Government employee	5	
White-collar Employees	26	3.9
Accountant	5	
Artist	1	
County, city, or court clerk	4	
Clerk (business)	10	
Editor	5	
Librarian	1	
Skilled Trades	1	0.2
Carpenter	1	
Students	24	3.6
$N = 661$ individuals		

Note: Alumni refers to both graduates and attendees of military schools. The 194 alumni with multiple careers (see Table 5) are not included.

Table 5. *Alumni occupations: multiple occupations*

Occupation	Number of Alumni
Teachers	93
Teacher & Lawyer	23
Teacher & Lawyer & Engineer	3
Teacher & Lawyer & Editor	2
Teacher & Lawyer & Clergy	2
Teacher & Lawyer & Legislator	2
Teacher & Lawyer & Legislator & Editor	1
Teacher & Doctor	8
Teacher & Agriculturalist	11
Teacher & Agriculturalist & Editor	1
Teacher & Agriculturalist & Clerk (civil)	1
Teacher & Engineer	16
Teacher & Engineer & Public Servant	4
Teacher & Engineer & Miner	1
Teacher & Merchant	4
Teacher & Merchant & Legislator	4
Teacher & Businessman	1
Teacher & Clerk (civil)	1
Teacher & Clerk (civil) & Editor	1
Teacher & Builder	1
Teacher & Armed Services Member	1
Teacher & Armed Services Member & Doctor	1
Teacher & Armed Services Member & Clerk (civil)	1
Teacher & Miner	1
Teacher & Public Servant	2
Lawyers	67
Lawyer & Agriculturalist	6
Lawyer & Agriculturalist & Businessman	1
Lawyer & Agriculturalist & Legislator	1
Lawyer & Legislator	4
Lawyer & Legislator & Businessman	1
Lawyer & Legislator & Editor	2
Lawyer & Merchant	1
Lawyer & Businessman	1
Lawyer & Editor	1
Lawyer & Engineer	1
Lawyer & Engineer & Public Servant	1
Lawyer & Banker	1
Lawyer & Clerk (business)	2
Lawyer & Clerk (civil)	1
Lawyer & Clerk (civil) & Public Servant	1
Lawyer & Public Servant	4
Lawyer & Armed Services Member & Agriculturalist	1
Lawyer & Legislator & Armed Services Member	4

Occupation	Number of Alumni
Doctors	21
Doctor & Engineer	2
Doctor & Agriculturalist	7
Doctor in Armed Services & Public Servant	1
Doctor in Armed Services	1
Doctor & Businessman	1
Agriculturalists	60
Agriculturalist & Businessman	8
Agriculturalist & Merchant	5
Agriculturalist & Merchant & Businessman	1
Agriculturalist & Clergy	1
Agriculturalist & Clerk (civil)	1
Agriculturalist & Clerk (business)	1
Agriculturalist & Miner	1
Agriculturalist & Public Servant	2
Agriculturalist & Engineer	8
Agriculturalist & Engineer & Legislator	1
Agriculturalist & Fisherman	1
Agriculturalist & Armed Services Member	1
Engineers	51
Engineer & Miner	2
Engineer & Merchant	3
Engineer & Businessman	4
Engineer & Armed Services Member	2
Engineer & Public Servant	3
Merchants	20
Merchant & Businessman	1
Merchant & Editor	1
Editors	11
Editor & Miner	1
Editor & Clergy	1
Clerks	13
Clerk (business) & Miner	1
Clerk (civil) & Miner	1
Clerk (civil) & Businessman	1
Bankers	3
Banker & Armed Services Member	1
Banker & Accountant	1
Businessmen	22
Businessman & Legislator	1

$N = 194$ individuals

Bibliography

MANUSCRIPT COLLECTIONS

American Antiquarian Society, Worcester, Massachusetts (AAS)
    Academy Catalogs
    College and University Catalogs

The Citadel Archives and Museum, Charleston, South Carolina (CIT)
    John Boinest Diary
    Walter S. Brewster Papers
    Citadel Speeches, 1846–1952
    Asbury Coward Papers
    Richard Dwight Addresses
    E. Montague Grimke Correspondence
    Thomas A. Huguenin Papers
    Micah Jenkins Correspondence
    John Kershaw Papers
    Thomas Hart Law Addresses
    Victor Manget Papers
    Henry Moore Autobiography
    John Patrick Papers
    John C. Pressley Correspondence
    William Tennent Addresses
    C. Irvine Walker Papers

Duke University, Rare Books, Manuscript and Special Collections Library, Durham, North Carolina (Duke)
    Anonymous Personal Notebook
    William Calder Diary
    John J. Chadick Poem
    William F. Collins Notebook
    Eugene Cordill Papers
    Charles Duffy Papers
    James Erwin Papers

Henderson Military and Female Institute Speech
Micah Jenkins Papers
Robert E. Johnson Correspondence
John R. Jones Scrapbook
W. Robert Leckie Papers
Louis Marks Autograph Book
William Miller McAllister Papers
Seaborn Montgomery Jr. Papers
Adeline Osborne Palmer Papers
Alden Partridge Correspondence
Portsmouth Academy Proceedings of Trustees, 1825–47
Lyndon Swaim Papers
Tillinghast Family Papers
Pierce Manning Butler Young Papers
Winn Family Papers

Emory University, Department of Special Collections, Richard Woodruff Library,
    Atlanta, Georgia (Emory)
Theodore T. Fogle Papers
Graves Family Papers
Joseph B. Jones Papers

The Filson Historical Society, Louisville, Kentucky
Bodley Family Papers
Florian O. Cornay Papers
Dabney-Joyes Family Papers
Fenley-Williams Family Papers
Foote Family Papers
Lillard Family Papers
Rare Pamphlet Collection
Jacob F. Weller Papers
C. Williams Papers

Georgia Archives, Morrow

The Library of Virginia, Richmond
George A. Goodman Correspondence
Charles Green Expense Book
Thomas Munford Certificate
William D. Stuart Certificate
Tazewell Papers
Virginia Military Institute Demerit Book, 1959

North Carolina State Archives, Department of Archives and History, Raleigh
    (NCSA)
John Heritage Bryan Papers
Calvin J. Cowles Collection

Daniel Harvey Hill Papers
William Andrew Jeffries Papers
Albert Moses Luria Papers
Tew Papers

South Carolina Department of Archives and History, Columbia (SCDAH)
Reports of Committee on Military Affairs

South Carolina Historical Society, Charleston (SCHS)
William Carson Papers
Citadel Addresses
Benjamin Perry Papers

South Caroliniana Library, University of South Carolina, Columbia (SCL)
Dreher-Duncan Papers
William Porcher DuBose Speech
Gaston, Strait, Wylie and Baskin Families Papers
Edward Montague Grimke Correspondence
John Jenkins Correspondence
Micah Jenkins Correspondence
McGee and Charles Families Papers
Nance-Newberry Papers
Obear Family Papers
William Renwick Correspondence
Sams Family Papers
Carey Thomas Diary
William Tennent Correspondence

Southern Historical Collection, Wilson Library, University of North Carolina at
Chapel Hill (SHC)
James B. Bailey Papers
Burgwyn Family Papers
Calder Family Papers
Thomas Casey Correspondence
Raleigh Edward Colston Papers
Mayre Dabney Correspondence
Laurent Dupre Correspondence
George M. Edgar Papers
Philip Fitzhugh Correspondence
Emma Ross Harty Correspondence
Lewis Harvie Papers
Leland Hathaway Correspondence
Theodore Kingsbury Correspondence
Edgar W. Knight Papers
Miriam G. Moses Papers
Egbert A. Ross Papers

Tennessee State Library and Archives, Nashville (TSLA)
  Dyas Collection – John Coffee Papers
  Marion Institute Foundation Papers
  Shelby Military Institute Acts
  University of Nashville Register
  Western Military Institute Acts

University of Kentucky, Special Collections, Louisville
  Kentucky Military Institute Archives

University of Mississippi Archives and Special Collections, J. D. Williams Library,
    Oxford
  Bledsoe Address
  Clayton Address
  Holmes Address
  Thompson Address

Center for American History, University of Texas, Austin
  Americus Cartwright Papers

Vanderbilt University, Jean and Alexander Heard Library, Nashville, Tennessee
  Western Military Institute and University of Nashville Records

Virginia Historical Society, Richmond (VHS)
  James Coles Bruce Correspondence
  Robert Preston Carson Memoir
  Joseph Hart Chenoweth Correspondence
  Catlett Fitzhugh Conway Manuscript
  Crutchfield Speech
  Dunn Family Papers
  Edmundson Family Papers
  Flowerree Family Papers
  Garland Family Papers
  Gooch Family Papers
  Graham Family Papers
  Hugh B. Grigsby Papers
  Guerrant Family Papers
  Edward Garlick Gwathmey Autobiography
  Hankins Family Papers
  Hannah Family Papers
  Harrison Family Papers
  Holliday Family Papers
  Hundley Family Papers
  Jones Family Papers
  Majette Family Papers
  Craig McDonald Poem
  Pollard Family Papers

Robert Beverly Randolph Correspondence
Francis Williamson Smith Papers
Sara Smith Papers
Wight Family Papers

The Virginia Military Institute Archives, Preston Library, Lexington (VMI Archives)
William Elisha Arnold Notebook
Thomas F. Barksdale Papers
Barton Family Papers
John M. Cary Papers
Joseph H. Chenoweth Papers
Charles Derby Papers
John Fletcher Early Diary
Philip A. Fitzhugh Papers
Robert Gatewood Diary
Philip C. Gibbs Notebook
R. M. T. Hunter Papers
Edward Sixtus Hutter Papers
Thomas T. Munford Collection
Order Books
Rumbough Papers
James Saunders Correspondence
Valentine C. Saunders Correspondence
Edward Clarence Shepherd Collection
J. Strange Correspondence
Student Files, 1842–1860
Superintendent's Outgoing Correspondence
Richard C. Taylor Correspondence
James Henry Waddell Papers
Walter W. Williams Diary
William O. Yager Journal

Western Kentucky University, Department of Library Special Collections, Manuscripts, Bowling Green (WKU)
Rosa (Praigg) Dickerson Collection
Green Collection
Temple Collection

PUBLISHED PRIMARY SOURCES

Annual Announcement of the Law, Literary, and Medical Departments of the University of Nashville. Nashville: John T. S. Fall, 1854.
"A Bill to Provide for the Education of State Cadets at the North Carolina Military Institute, and for Other Purposes." North Carolina Senate Bill No. 25. Raleigh: John Spelman, 1861.

Barbour, Benjamin Johnson. *Address Delivered Before the Literary Societies of the Virginia Military Institute at Lexington.* Richmond: MacFarlane and Fergusson, 1854.

Barnard, Frederick A. P. *Letter to the Honorable the Board of Trustees of the University of Mississippi.* Oxford: University of Mississippi, 1858.

———. *Report on the Organization of Military Schools, Made to the Trustees of the University of Mississippi, November 1861.* Jackson: Cooper and Kimball, 1861.

Bledsoe, Albert Taylor. *Address Delivered at the University of Mississippi by the Request of the Trustees and the Societies of the University.* Oxford: Board of Trustees of the University of Mississippi, 1849.

Bond, Natalie Jenkins and Osmun Latrobe Coward, eds. *The South Carolinians: Colonel Asbury Coward's Memoirs.* New York: Vantage Press, 1968.

Brockenbrough, John W. *Address Delivered on Laying the Corner Stone of the New Barracks of the Virginia Military Institute.* New York: John Wiley, 1850.

Brooks, Aubrey Lee and Hugh Talmage Lefler, eds. *The Papers of Walter Clark.* Vol. 1. Chapel Hill: The University of North Carolina Press, 1948.

Capers, F. W. *State Military Academies. An Address Delivered Before the Calliopean Society of the Citadel Academy, Charleston.* Charleston: Tenhet and Corley, 1846.

Carroll, Bartholomew R. *The Claims of Historical Studies upon the Youth of Our Country.* Charleston: Walker, Evans and Co., 1859.

Catalogue and Regulation of the Western Military Institute at Georgetown, Kentucky. Cincinnati: Herald of Truth Printers, 1848.

Catalogue, Course of Study, Address to the Patrons, &c. of Williamsburg Military School. Richmond: Charles A. Wynne, 1853.

Catalogue of the Hampton Male and Female Academy. Richmond: H. K. Ellyson, 1856.

Catalogue of the Hampton Male and Female Academy. Richmond: H. K. Ellyson, 1858.

Catalogue of the Officers and Cadets of The American Literary, Scientific and Military Academy. Hanover, NH: Ridley Bannister, 1821.

Catalogue of the Officers and Cadets of the Kentucky Military Institute, Located near Frankfort, Franklin County, Kentucky. Frankfort: A. G. Hodges and Co., 1848.

Catalogue of the Officers and Cadets of the Kentucky Military Institute, Six Miles from Frankfort Kentucky. Frankfort: A. G. Hodges and Co., 1851.

Catalogue of the Officers and Cadets of the Kentucky Military Institute, Six Miles from Frankfort Kentucky. Frankfort: A. G. Hodges and Co., 1852.

Catalogue of the Officers and Cadets of the Kentucky Military Institute, Six Miles from Frankfort Kentucky. Frankfort: A. G. Hodges and Co., 1853.

Catalogue of the Officers and Cadets of the Kentucky Military Institute, Six Miles from Frankfort Kentucky. Frankfort: A. G. Hodges and Co., 1855.

Catalogue of the Officers and Cadets of the Kentucky Military Institute, Six Miles from Frankfort Kentucky. Cincinnati: Moore, Wilstach, Keys and Co., 1856.

Catalogue of the Officers and Cadets of the Kentucky Military Institute, Six Miles from Frankfort Kentucky. Frankfort: S. I. M. Major and Company, 1859.

Catalogue of the Officers and Cadets of the North Carolina Military Institute, Charlotte North Carolina. First Session, 1859–1860. Charlotte: N.p., 1860.

Catalogue of the Officers and Cadets of the Western Military Institute. Cincinnati: C. Clark, 1851.

Catalogue of the Officers and Cadets, Together with the Prospectus and Internal Regulations of The American Literary, Scientific and Military Academy, at Middletown, Connecticut. Middletown: E. and H. Clark, 1826.

Catalogue of the Officers and Cadets, Together with the Prospectus and Internal Regulations of The American Literary, Scientific and Military Academy, at Middletown, Connecticut. Middletown: E. and H. Clark, 1827.

Catalogue of the Officers and Graduates of the University of Nashville. Nashville: A. Nelson and Co., 1850.

Catalogue of the Officers and Students of the Rappahannock Academy and Military Institute, Caroline County, Virginia. Baltimore: John Murphy and Co., 1851.

A Catalogue of the Officers and Students of Unity Scientific and Military Academy. Claremont, NH: National Eagle Press, 1836.

A Catalogue of the Officers and Students of Unity Scientific and Military Academy. Claremont, NH: Book Office by N. W. Goddard, 1837.

A Catalogue of the Officers and Students of Unity Scientific and Military Academy. Claremont, NH: Book Office by N. W. Goddard, 1838.

The Charter and Statutes of Jefferson College, Washington Mississippi, as Revised and Amended. Natchez: Book and Job Office, 1840.

Clayton, Alexander M. *Address Delivered at the First Annual Commencement of the University of Mississippi.* Oxford: Board of Trustees of the University of Mississippi, 1849.

Coward, Ashbury. "The Sketch of the South Carolina Military Academy." *Year Book* (1892).

Fox, C. J. "Memorial of the North-Carolina Military Institute." North Carolina Senate Memo No. 5. 1860.

Graham, William A. *General Joseph Graham and his Papers on North Carolina Revolutionary History.* Raleigh: Edwards and Broughton, 1904.

Heriot, Edwin. *The Polytechnic School, the Best System of Practical Education. An Address Delivered before the Cadet Polytechnic Society, State Military Academy. June 14, 1850.* Charleston: Walker and James, 1850.

Hill, D. H. *College Discipline: An Inaugural Address delivered at Davidson College North Carolina. December 28, 1855.* Salisbury: Watchman Office, 1855.

———. *Essay on Military Education, delivered at Wilmington NC, November 14, 1860 Before the State Educational Convention.* Charlotte: Daily Bulletin Office, 1860.

———. "Remarks of Major D. H. Hill, of the N. C. Military Institute at Charlotte, Before the Committee on Education of the North Carolina Legislature." Broadside. N.p., [1860].

Holmes, George F. *Inaugural Address.* Memphis: Franklin Book and Job Office, 1849.

Jacob, Diane B. and Judith Moreland Arnold, eds. *A Virginia Military Institute Album, 1839–1910*. Charlottesville: University of Virginia Press, 1982.

Keitt, Lawrence Massillion. *Address Before the Two Literary Societies of the Virginia Military Institute*. Richmond: MacFarlane and Fergusson, 1856.

Kendrick, Rev. J. R. *Reason and Faith. Or, A Caution Against Trusting the Human Understanding*. Charleston: A. J. Burke, 1855.

Knight, Edgar W. *A Documentary History of the South before 1860*. Vol. 5. Chapel Hill: University of North Carolina Press, 1949–1953.

Law, Thomas Hart. *Citadel Cadets: The Journal of Cadet Tom Law*. Clinton, SC: PC Press, 1941.

"A Letter Concerning 'The Virginia, Literary, Scientific and Military Academy.'" Annotated by Marshall W. Butt. *Virginia Magazine of History and Biography*, 52 (April 1944): 97–103.

Lewis, G. W. *Address Delivered Before the Literary Society and Students Generally of the Rappahannock Academy and Military Institute, July 30, 1851*. Washington: Gideon and Co., 1852.

Lossing, Benson J. *Cadet Life at West Point*. Boston: T. O. H. P. Burnham, 1862.

Magill, William J. *The Development of Truth Dependent Upon Education*. Charleston: Walker, Evans and Co., 1858.

Massie, James W. *An Address Delivered Before the Society of Alumni of the Virginia Military Institute*. Richmond: MacFarlane and Fergusson, 1857.

McCrea, Tully. *Dear Belle: Letters from a Cadet and Officer to His Sweetheart, 1858–1865*. Edited by Catherine S. Crary. Chapel Hill: University of North Carolina Press, 1965.

McGowen, Samuel. *An Address Delivered before the Polytechnic and Calliopean Societies of the State Military Academy, at the Annual Commencement, November 22, 1850*. Charleston: Edward C. Councell, 1851.

Military Academy Commission. *Report*. U.S. Senate Miscellaneous Document No. 3. 13 December 1860.

"Military Institute." *Gleason's Pictorial Drawing-Room Companion*, 4 (1 January 1853): 16.

Newton, Hon. Willoughby. *Virginia and The Union. An Address, Delivered Before The Literary Societies of the Virginia Military Institute*. Richmond: MacFarlane and Fergusson, 1858.

North Carolina General Assembly. "A Bill to Create a Scientific and Military School and a State Arsenal." House Doc. No. 32. Raleigh: W. W. Holden, 1854.

Official Register of the Officers and Cadets of the Georgia Military Institute, Marietta, Georgia. N.p., June 1853.

Official Register of the Officers and Cadets of the Georgia Military Institute, Marietta, Georgia. Atlanta: J. I. Miller and Co. Printers, July 1858.

Official Register of the Officers and Cadets at the South Carolina Military Academies. Charleston: J. B. Nixon, 1850.

Official Register of the Officers and Cadets at the South Carolina Military Academies. Charleston: J. B. Nixon, 1853.

Official Register of the Officers and Cadets at the South Carolina Military Academies. Charleston: J. B. Nixon, 1854.

Official Register of the South Carolina Military Academy. Charleston: R. W. Gibbes, 1860.

Patterson, Giles. *Journal of a Southern Student, 1846–68, with Letters from a Later Period*. Edited by Robert Croom Beatty. Nashville: University of Tennessee Press, 1944.

Pinckney, Henry L. *The Necessity of Popular Enlightenment to the Honor and Welfare of the State. An Oration delivered before the Literary Societies of the South Carolina College*. Columbia: I. C. Morgan's Letter Press, 1845.

Pike, Albert. *An Address Delivered by Albert Pike, Esq., to the Young Ladies of the Tulip Female Seminary and Cadets of the Arkansas Military Institute at Tulip, on 4th June, 1852*. Little Rock: William E. Woodruff, 1852.

Porter, William D. *State Pride. An Oration Delivered before the Calliopean and Polytechnic Societies of the State Military School, at Charleston*. Charleston: Walker, Evans and Co., 1860.

Prospectus of the Mantua Classical and Military Academy, Two and a half Miles West of Philadelphia, under the direction of Victor Value. Philadelphia: P. M. Lafourcade Printer, 1828.

Register of Cadets and Regulations of the Western Military Institute at Georgetown Kentucky. Georgetown: N.P., 1849.

Register of Former Cadets: Virginia Military Institute. Centennial Edition. Roanoke, VA: Roanoke Printing Co., 1939.

Register of the Officers and Cadets of the Virginia Military Institute. Philadelphia: Crissy and Markley, 1847.

Register of the Officers and Cadets of the Virginia Military Institute. Philadelphia: Thomas, Cowperthwait and Co., 1851.

Register of the Officers and Cadets of the Virginia Military Institute. Philadelphia: Thomas, Cowperthwait and Co., 1852.

Regulations of the Citadel Academy at Charleston, and Arsenal Academy at Columbia. Columbia: A. S. Johnston, 1849.

Regulations of the Georgia Military Institute, Marietta, Georgia. N.p., January, 1853.

Regulations of the Georgia Military Institute, Marietta, Georgia. Atlanta: C. R. Hanleiter, 1857.

Regulations of the Kentucky Military Institute, Six Miles from Frankfort, Kentucky. Frankfort: A. G. Hodges & Co., 1851.

Regulations of the Military Academies of South Carolina: With a list of the Board of Visitors. Columbia: R. W. Gibbes, 1850.

Regulations of the Military Academies of South Carolina. Columbia: R. W. Gibbes, 1858.

Regulations for the North Carolina Military Institute at Charlotte North Carolina. Charlotte: Bulletin Office Print, 1860.

Regulations of the United States Military Academy at West Point. New York: John F. Trow, 1857.

Report by the Board of Visitors of the Georgia Military Institute, To his Excellency, Howell Cobb, Governor of the State of Georgia for 1853. [Anonymous]: 1853.

Report of the Board of Visitors of the Virginia Military Institute. Richmond: Ritchies and Dunnavant Printers, 1852.

Riley, Agnes Graham, ed. "Letters of a V.M.I. Cadet, 1857–1858." *Wythe County Historical Review*, 4 (January 1973): 13–23.

Rules and Regulations of the Western Military Institute at Tyree Springs, Sumner County, TN, and the Official Register of Officers and Cadets for the Collegiate Year 1853–54. Nashville: John F. Morgan, 1854.

Semi-Annual Register, of the Officers and Cadets, of the Hillsboro Military Academy. Raleigh: Jno. W. Syme Printer, 1860.

Shaw, Arthur Marvin. "Student Life at Western Military Institute: William Preston Johnston's Journal, 1847–1848." *Filson Club History Quarterly*, 18 (1944): 78–108.

Smith, Francis H. *College Reform.* Philadelphia: Thomas, Cowperthwait and Co., 1851.

————. *Introductory Address to the Corps of Cadets of the Virginia Military Institute.* Richmond: MacFarlane and Fergusson, 1856.

————. *The Regulations of Military Institutions, Applied to the Conduct of Common Schools.* New York: John Wiley, 1849.

————. *The Virginia Military Institute: Its Building and Rebuilding.* Lynchburg: J. P. Bell Publishers, 1912.

Stanard, Beverly. *Letters of a New Market Cadet.* Edited by John G. Barrett and Robert K. Turner Jr. Chapel Hill: University of North Carolina Press, 1961.

Thomas, John P. *On the Profession of Arms. The Annual Address Delivered before the Association of Graduates of the State Military Academy of South-Carolina, in Charleston, SC, April 9, 1859.* Charleston: Walker, Evans, and Company, 1859.

————. "Origin of the State Military Academies." *Russell's Magazine* (December 1858): 3–12.

Tradewell, James D. *Address on the Study of the Federal Constitution Delivered Before the Polytechnic and Calliopean Societies of the Citadel Academy, Charleston, SC.* Charleston: Walker, Evans and Co., 1857.

Trescot, William Henry. *The Annual Address Before the Calliopean and Polytechnic Societies of the Citadel Academy, Charleston, SC.* Charleston: Walker and Evans, 1856.

Trotti, S.W. *An Address Delivered before the Calliopean and Polytechnic Societies of the State Military Academy, at the Annual Commencement, November 18, 1847.* Charleston: Burges, James and Paxton, 1847.

Tucker, Stephen, ed. "West Point Letters of Cadet Milo S. Hascall, 1848–1850." *Indiana Magazine of History* (September 1994) 90: 278–94.

Turner, Charles W., ed. "The Education of Col. David Bullock Harris, C.S.A., Using his West Point Letters, 1829–1835." *West Virginia History*, 46 (1985/6): 45–57.

University of Nashville, Collegiate Department, Western Military Institute. *The Official Register of Officers and Cadets for the Collegiate Year 1854–5, and Rules and Regulations, with Annual Announcement of Faculty and Officers for 1855–6.* Nashville: Cameron and Fall and Book and Job Printers, 1855.

University of Nashville, Collegiate Department, Western Military Institute. *The Official Register of Officers and Cadets for the Collegiate Year 1855–6, and Rules and Regulations, with Annual Announcement of Faculty and Officers for 1856–7.* Nashville: Cameron and Fall, 1856.

University of Nashville, Collegiate Department, Western Military Institute. *Register of Cadets for the Collegiate Year 1857–8, and Announcement of Officers for 1857–8.* Nashville: Cameron and Fall, 1857.

The War of the Rebellion: Compilation of Records of the United States and Confederate Governments. Vol. 5. Washington, DC: Government Printing Office, 1880–1901.

"Western Military Academy." *Nashville Union and American* (14 February 1855): 2.

Williams, Robert W., Jr. and Ralph A. Wooster, eds. "A Cadet at Bastrop Military Institute: The Letters of Isaac Dunbar Affleck." *Texas Military History,* 6 (Spring 1967): 89–106.

Yeadon, Richard. *Address, on the Necessity of Subordination, in our Academies and Colleges, Civil and Military; before the Calliopean and Polytechnic Societies of the Citadel Academy.* Charleston: Walker and James, 1854.

BOOKS, PAMPHLETS, AND DISSERTATIONS

Aldrich, Terry Mark. *Rates of Return on Investment in Technical Education in the Ante-Bellum American Economy.* New York: Arno Press, 1975.

Allmendinger, David F., Jr. *Paupers and Scholars: The Transformation of Student Life in Nineteenth-Century New England.* New York: St. Martin's Press, 1975.

Ambrose, Stephen E. *Duty, Honor, Country: A History of West Point.* Baltimore: Johns Hopkins University Press, 1966.

Andrew, Rod, Jr. *Long Gray Lines: The Southern Military School Tradition, 1839–1915.* Chapel Hill: University of North Carolina Press, 2001.

Augst, Thomas. *A Clerk's Tale: Young Men and Moral Life in Nineteenth-century America.* Chicago: University of Chicago Press, 2003.

Ayers, Edward L. *Vengeance and Justice: Crime and Punishment in the Nineteen-century American South.* New York: Oxford University Press, 1994.

Bailyn, Bernard. *Education in the Formation of American Society: Needs and Opportunities for Study.* Chapel Hill: University of North Carolina, 1960.

Baker, Dean Paul. "The Partridge Connection: Alden Partridge and Southern Military Education." Ph.D. dissertation, University of North Carolina, 1986.

Baker, Gary R. *Cadets in Gray: The Story of the Cadets of the South Carolina Military Academy and the Cadet Rangers in the Civil War.* Columbia: Palmetto Bookworks, 1989.

Baumer, William, Jr. *Not All Warriors: Portraits of Nineteenth-Century West Pointers Who Gained Fame in Other Than Military Fields.* Freeport, NY: Books for Libraries, 1971.

Beadie, Nancy and Kim Tolley, eds. *Chartered Schools: Two Hundred Years of Independent Academies in the United States, 1727–1925.* New York: Routledge-Farmer, 2002.

Beller, Susan Provost. *Cadets at War.* White Hall, VA: Shoe Tree Press, 1991.

Bledstein, Burton J. *The Culture of Professionalism: The Middle Class and the Development of Higher Education in America.* New York: W. W. Norton and Company, 1976.

———— and Robert D. Johnson, eds. *The Middling Sort: Explorations in the History of the American Middle Class.* New York: Routledge, 2001.

Blumin, Stuart M. *The Emergence of the Middle Class: Social Experience in the American City, 1760–1900.* New York: Cambridge University Press, 1989.

Bond, O. J. *The Story of the Citadel.* Richmond: Garrett and Massie, 1936.

Boogher, Elbert. *Secondary Education in Georgia, 1732–1858.* Philadelphia: N.P., 1933.

Breen, T. H. *Tobacco Culture.* Princeton: Princeton University Press, 1985.

Brodie, Laura Fairchild. *Breaking Out: VMI and the Coming of Women.* New York: Pantheon Books, 2000.

Bruce, Dickson D., Jr. *Violence and Crime in the Antebellum South.* Austin: University of Texas Press, 1979.

Bruchey, Stuart W., ed. *Small Business in American Life.* New York: Columbia University Press, 1980.

Burke, Colin B. *American Collegiate Populations: A Test of the Traditional View.* New York: New York University Press, 1982.

Bushman, Richard L. *The Refinement of America: Persons, Houses, Cities.* New York: Alfred A. Knopf, 1992.

Byrne, Frank J. *Becoming Bourgeois: Merchant Culture in the South, 1820–1865.* Lexington, KY: University Press of Kentucky, 2006.

Calhoun, Daniel H. *The American Civil Engineer: Origins and Conflicts.* Cambridge: Harvard University Press, 1960.

————. *Professional Lives in America: Structure and Aspiration, 1750–1850.* Cambridge: Harvard University Press, 1965.

Cannadine, David. *The Rise and Fall of Class in Britain.* New York: Columbia University Press, 1999.

Carmichael, Peter S. *The Last Generation: Young Virginians in Peace, War and Reunion.* Chapel Hill: University of North Carolina Press, 2005.

Carnes, Mark C. *Secret Ritual and Manhood in Victorian America.* New Haven: Yale University Press, 1989.

———— and Clyde Griffen, eds. *Meanings for Manhood: Constructions of Masculinity in Victorian America.* Chicago: University of Chicago Press, 1990.

Cash, W. J. *The Mind of the South.* New York: Vantage Books, 1941.

Cashin, Joan E. *A Family Venture: Men and Women on the Southern Frontier.* New York: Oxford University Press, 1991.

Censer, Jane Turner. *North Carolina Planters and Their Children, 1800–1860.* Baton Rouge: Louisiana State University, 1984.

Conrad, James Lee. *The Young Lions: Confederate Cadets at War.* Mechanicsburg, PA: Stackpole Books, 1997.

Coon, Charles L. *North Carolina Schools and Academies, 1790–1840: A Documentary History.* Raleigh: Edwards and Broughton, 1915.

Coulter, E. Merton. *College Life in the Old South.* 1928. Reprint, Athens: University of Georgia Press, 1951.

Couper, William. *One Hundred Years at V.M.I.* Vol. 4. Richmond: Garrett and Massie, Inc., 1939.

Cremin, Lawrence A. *American Education: The National Experience, 1783–1876.* New York: Harper and Row Publishers, 1980.

Cunliffe, Marcus. *Soldiers and Civilians: The Martial Spirit in America, 1776–1865.* Boston: Little, Brown and Company, 1968.

Dabney, Charles William. *Universal Education in the South.* Vol. 1. 1936. Reprint, New York: Arno Press and the New York Times, 1969.

Davis, Archie K. *The Boy Colonel of the Confederacy: The Life and Times of Henry King Burgwyn, Jr.* Chapel Hill: University of North Carolina Press, 1985.

Deal, John Gordon. "The Forgotten Southerner: Middle-Class Associationalism in Antebellum Norfolk, Virginia." Ph.D. dissertation, University of Florida, 2003.

Degler, Carl N. *Place over Time: The Continuity of Southern Distinctiveness.* Baton Rouge: Louisiana State University Press, 1977.

Downey, Tom. *Planting a Capitalist South: Masters, Merchants, and Manufacturers in the Southern Interior, 1790–1860.* Baton Rouge: Louisiana State University Press, 2006.

Duncan, John Donald. "Pages from Froissart: The Ante-Bellum Career of Micah Jenkins." M.A. thesis, University of South Carolina, 1961.

Easterby, J. H. *College of Charleston.* Charleston: College of Charleston, 1935.

Endler, James R. *Other Leaders, Other Heroes: West Point's Legacy to America Beyond the Field of Battle.* Westport, CT: Praeger, 1998.

Faludi, Susan. *Stiffed: The Betrayal of the American Man.* New York: William Morrow and Company, 1999.

Farnham, Christie Anne. *The Education of the Southern Belle: Higher Education and Student Socialization in the Antebellum South.* New York: New York University Press, 1994.

Faust, Drew Gilpin. *James Henry Hammond and the Old South: A Design for Mastery.* Baton Rouge: Louisiana State University Press, 1982.

————. *A Sacred Circle: The Dilemma of the Intellectual in the Old South, 1840-1860.* Baltimore: The Johns Hopkins University Press, 1977.

Fogel, R. W. and S. L. Engerman. *Time on the Cross: The Economics of American Negro Slavery.* Boston: Little, Brown and Company, 1974.

Ford, Lacy K., Jr. *Origins of Southern Radicalism.* New York: Oxford University Press, 1988.

Forman, Sidney. *West Point: A History of the United States Military Academy.* New York: Columbia University Press, 1950.

Fox-Genovese, Elizabeth. *Within the Plantation Household: Black and White Women in the Old South.* Chapel Hill: University of North Carolina Press, 1988.

———— and Eugene D. Genovese. *Mind of the Master Class: History and Faith in the Southern Slaveholders' Worldview.* New York: Cambridge University Press, 2005.

Frank, Stephen M. *Life with Father: Parenthood and Masculinity in the Nineteenth-century American North.* Baltimore: The Johns Hopkins University Press, 1998.

Franklin, John Hope. *The Militant South, 1800–1860.* Boston: Beacon Press, 1956.

————. *A Southern Odyssey: Travelers in the Antebellum North.* Baton Rouge: Louisiana State University, 1976.

Friend, Craig Thompson and Lorri Glover, eds. *Southern Manhood: Perspectives on Masculinity in the Old South.* Athens: University of Georgia Press, 2004.

Frost, Dan R. *Thinking Confederates: Academia and the Idea of Progress in the New South.* Knoxville: University of Tennessee Press, 2000.

Geiger, Roger L., ed. *The American College in the Nineteenth Century.* Nashville: Vanderbilt University Press, 2000.

Genovese, Eugene. *The Slaveholders' Dilemma: Freedom and Progress in Southern Conservative Thought, 1820–1860.* Columbia: University of South Carolina Press, 1992.

Gillespie, Michele. *Free Labor in an Unfree World: White Artisans in the Slave-holding Georgia, 1789–1860.* Athens: University of Georgia Press, 2000.

Gilmore, David D. *Manhood in the Making: Cultural Concepts of Masculinity.* New Haven: Yale University Press, 1990.

Gindlesperger, James. *Seed Corn of the Confederacy.* Shippensburg, PA: Burd Street Press, 1997.

Glover, Lorri. *Southern Sons: Becoming Men in the New Nation.* Baltimore: The Johns Hopkins University Press, 2007.

Gordon, James W. *Lawyers in Politics: Mid-nineteenth-century Kentucky as a Case Study.* New York: Garland Publishing, Inc., 1990.

Greenberg, Amy S. *Manifest Manhood and the Antebellum American Empire.* New York: Cambridge University Press, 2005.

Greenberg, Kenneth S. *Honor and Slavery: Lies, Duels, Noses, Masks, Dressing as a Woman, Gifts, Strangers, Humanitarianism, Death, Slave Rebellions, the Proslavery Argument, Baseball, Hunting, and Gambling in the Old South.* Princeton: Princeton University Press, 1996.

Grob, Gerald N. *Edward Jarvis and the Medical World of Nineteen-Century America.* Knoxville: University of Tennessee Press, 1978.

Guralnick, Stanley M. *Science and the Ante-bellum College.* Philadelphia: American Philosophical Society, 1975.

Haber, Samuel. *The Quest for Authority and Honor in the American Professions, 1750–1900.* Chicago: University of Chicago Press, 1991.

Hahn, Steven. *The Roots of Southern Populism: Yeoman Farmers and the Transformation of the Georgia Upcountry, 1850–1890.* New York: Oxford University Press, 1983.

Haskell, Thomas. *The Emergence of Professional Social Science: The American Social Science Association and the Nineteenth-century Crisis of Authority.* Urbana: University of Illinois Press, 1977.

Heatwole, Cornelius J. *A History of Education in Virginia.* New York: Macmillan Co., 1916.

Heyrman, Christine Leigh. *Southern Cross: The Beginnings of the Bible Belt.* New York: Alfred A. Knopf, 1997.

Hollis, Daniel Walker. *South Carolina College.* Vol. 1. Columbia: University of South Carolina Press, 1951.

Holman, Andrew C. *A Sense of Their Duty: Middle-class Formation in Victorian Ontario Towns.* Montreal: McGill-Queen's University Press, 2000.

Horowitz, Helen Lefkowitz. *Campus Life: Undergraduate Cultures from the End of the Nineteenth Century to the Present.* New York: Alfred A. Knopf, 1987.

Hyde, Samuel C., Jr., ed. *Plain Folk of the South Revisited.* Baton Rouge: Louisiana State University Press, 1997.

Johansen, Shawn. *Family Men: Middle-class Fatherhood in Early Industrializing America.* New York: Routledge, 2001.

Johnson, Clyde Sanfred. *Fraternities in Our Colleges.* New York: National Interfraternity Foundation, 1972.

Johnson, Paul E. *A Shopkeeper's Millennium: Society and Revivals in Rochester, New York, 1815–1837.* New York: Hill and Wang, 1978.

Johnson, Thomas, Jr. *Scientific Interests in the Old South.* New York: D. Appleton-Century, 1936.

Kaestle, Carl F. *Pillars of the Republic: Common Schools and American Society, 1780–1860.* New York: Hill and Wang, 1983.

Karsten, Peter. *The Military in America.* 2nd Ed. New York: Free Press, 1986.

Kenzer, Robert C. *Kinship and Neighborhood in a Southern Community: Orange County, North Carolina, 1849–1881.* Knoxville: University of Tennessee Press, 1987.

Kett, Joseph F. *Rites of Passage: Adolescence in America 1790 to the Present.* New York: Basic Books, 1977.

Kimmel, Michael. *Manhood in America: A Cultural History.* New York: Free Press, 1996.

Knight, Edgar W. *The Academy Movement.* Chapel Hill: N.p., 1919.

———. *A Documentary History of Education in the South before 1860.* Vol. 5. Chapel Hill: University of North Carolina Press, 1953.

———. *Public School Education in North Carolina.* Boston: Houghton Mifflin Co., 1916.

Long, Barbara. *United States v. Virginia: The Virginia Military Institute Accepts Women.* Berkeley Heights, NJ: Enslow Publishers, 2000.

Madsen, David. *Early National Education, 1776–1830.* New York: John Wiley & Sons, Inc., 1974.

Mahon, John K. *History of the Militia and the National Guard.* New York: Macmillian, 1983.

Manegold, Catherine S. *In Glory's Shadow: Shannon Faulkner, the Citadel, and a Changing America.* New York: Alfred A. Knopf, 1999.

Margo, Robert A. *Wages and Labor Markets in the United States, 1820–1860.* Chicago: University of Chicago Press, 2000.

Mattingly, Paul H. *The Classless Profession: American Schoolmen in the Nineteenth Century.* New York: New York University Press, 1975.

McCurry, Stephanie. *Masters of Small Worlds: Yeoman Households, Gender Relations, and the Political Culture of the Antebellum South Carolina Low Country.* New York: Oxford University Press, 1995.

McGivern, James Gregory. *First Hundred Years of Engineering Education in the United States (1807–1907).* Spokane: Gonzaga University Press, 1960.

McGregor, A. A. *History of LaGrange College.* N.p., n.d.

McKenzie, Robert Tracy. *One South or Many?: Plantation Belt and Upcountry in Civil War-Era Tennessee.* New York: Cambridge University Press, 1994.

Meriwether, Colyer. *Higher Education in South Carolina with a Sketch of the Free School System.* 1889. Reprint, Spartanburg: The Reprint Co., 1972.

Morgan, Chad. *Planters' Progress: Modernizing Confederate Georgia.* Gainesville: University Press of Florida, 2005.

Morrison, James L. *"The Best School in the World": West Point, the Pre-Civil War Years, 1833–1866.* Kent: Kent State University Press, 1986.

Noble, M. S. C. *A History of Public Schools in North Carolina.* Chapel Hill: University of North Carolina Press, 1930.

Norrell, Robert J. *A Promising Field: Engineering at Alabama, 1837–1987.* Tuscaloosa: University of Alabama Press, 1990.

Oakes, James. *Slavery and Freedom: An Interpretation of the Old South.* New York: Alfred A. Knopf, 1990.

———. *The Ruling Race: A History of American Slaveowners.* New York: Vantage Books, 1982.

O'Brien, Michael and David Moltke-Hansen, eds. *Intellectual Life in Antebellum Charleston.* Knoxville: University of Tennessee Press, 1986.

Olsen, Christopher J. *Political Culture and Secession in Mississippi: Masculinity, Honor, and the Antiparty Tradition, 1830–1860.* New York: Oxford University Press, 2000.

Owsley, Frank L. *Plain Folk of the Old South.* 1949. Reprint, Baton Rouge: Louisiana State University Press, 1982.

Pace, Robert F. *Halls of Honor: College Men in the Old South.* Baton Rouge: Louisiana State University Press, 2004.

Pappas, George S. *To the Point: The United States Military Academy, 1802–1902.* Westport, CT: Praeger Publishers, 1993.

Pippin, Kathryn A. "The Common School Movement in the South, 1840–1860." Ph.D. dissertation, University of North Carolina, 1977.

Pound, Roscoe. *The Lawyer from Antiquity to Modern Times.* St. Paul: West Publishing Co., 1953.

Proctor, Nicolas W. *Bathed in Blood: Hunting and Mastery in the Old South.* Charlottesville: University of Virginia Press, 2002.

Pugh, David. *Sons of Liberty: The Masculine Mind in Nineteenth-century America.* Westport, CT: Greenwood Press, 1983.

Pusey, William W., III. *The Interrupted Dream: The Educational Program at Washington College (Washington and Lee University), 1850–1880.* Lexington: Washington and Lee University, 1976.

Robertson, James I., Jr. *Stonewall Jackson: The Man, the Soldier, the Legend.* New York: Macmillan, 1997.

Robinson, Dale Greenwood. *The Academies of Virginia, 1776–1861.* Richmond: The Dietz Press, 1977.

Rodgers, Robert L. "An Historical Sketch of the Georgia Military Institute, Marietta, Georgia." 1890. Reprint, Atlanta: Kimsey's Book Shop, 1956.

Rotundo, E. Anthony. *American Manhood: Transformation in Masculinity from the Revolution to the Modern Era.* New York: Basic Books, 1993.

Rudolph, Frederick. *The American College and University: A History.* Athens: University of Georgia Press, 1990.

———. *Curriculum: A History of the American Undergraduate Course of Study Since 1636.* San Francisco: Jossey-Bass Publishers, 1977.

Ryan, Mary P. *Cradle of the Middle Class: The Family in Oneida County, New York, 1790–1865.* New York: Cambridge University Press, 1981.

Sanftleben, Kurt Allen. "A Different Drum: The Forgotten Tradition of the Military Academy in American Education." Ed.D. dissertation, College of William and Mary, 1993.

Scarborough, William Kauffman, ed. *The Diary of Edmund Ruffin.* Vol. 1. Baton Rouge: Louisiana State University Press, 1972.

———. *Masters of the Big House: Elite Slaveholders of the Mid-nineteenth-century South.* Baton Rouge: Louisiana State University Press, 2003.

Schmidt, George P. *The Liberal Arts College: A Chapter in American Cultural History.* New Brunswick: Rutgers University Press, 1957.

Schweiger, Beth Barton. *The Gospel Working Up: Progress and Pulpit in Nineteenth-century Virginia.* New York: Oxford University Press, 2000.

Shifflet, Crandall A. *Patronage and Poverty in the Tobacco South: Louisa County, Virginia, 1860–1900.* Knoxville: University of Tennessee Press, 1982.

Shore, Laurence. *Southern Capitalists: The Ideological Leadership of an Elite, 1832–1885.* Chapel Hill: University of North Carolina Press, 1986.

Sizer, Theodore. *The Age of Academies.* New York: Teachers College, 1964.

Smith, Mark M. *Mastered by the Clock: Time, Slavery and Freedom in the American South.* Chapel Hill: University of North Carolina Press, 1997.

Stephens, James Darwin. *Reflections: A Portrait – Biography of the Kentucky Military Institute, 1845–1971.* Georgetown: Kentucky Military Institute, 1991.

Stowe, Steven M. *Doctoring the South: Southern Physicians and Everyday Medicine in the Mid-nineteenth Century.* Chapel Hill: University of North Carolina Press, 2004.

————. *Intimacy and Power in the Old South: Ritual in the Lives of the Planters.* Baltimore: The Johns Hopkins University Press, 1987.

Strum, Philippa. *Women in the Barracks: The VMI Case and Equal Rights.* Lawrence: University of Kansas Press, 2002.

Sugrue, Michael. "South Carolina College: The Education of an Antebellum Elite." Ph.D. dissertation, Columbia University, 1992.

Taylor, Rosser H. *Ante-bellum South Carolina: A Social and Cultural History.* 1942. Reprint, New York: Da Capo Press, 1970.

Tewksbury, Donald G. *The Founding of American Colleges and Universities Before the Civil War, With Particular Reference to the Religious Influences Bearing Upon the College Movement.* 1932. Reprint, Archon Books, 1965.

Thernstrom, Stephen. *Poverty and Progress: Social Mobility in a Nineteenth-century City.* Cambridge: Harvard University Press, 1964.

Thomas, John Peyre. *The History of the South Carolina Military Academy.* Charleston: Walker, Evans and Cogswell Co., 1893.

Thompson, E. P. *The Making of the English Working Class.* New York: Vintage Press, 1963.

Wagers, Margaret Newman. *The Education of a Gentleman: Jefferson Davis at Transylvania, 1821–1824.* Lexington: Buckley and Reading, 1943.

Waugh, John C. *The Class of 1846: West Point to Appomattox: Stonewall Jackson, George McClellan and Their Brothers.* New York: Warner Books, 1994.

Webb, Lester Austin. "The Origin of Military Schools in the United States Founded in the Nineteenth Century." Ph.D. dissertation, University of North Carolina, 1958.

Weber, Max. *From Max Weber: Essays in Sociology.* Edited by H. H. Gerth and C. Wright Mills. New York: Oxford University Press, 1958.

Wells, Jonathan Daniel. *The Origins of the Southern Middle Class, 1800–1861.* Chapel Hill: University of North Carolina Press, 2004.

Whisker, James B. *The Rise and Decline of the American Militia System.* Cranbury, NJ: Associated University Presses Inc., 1999.

Whitescarver, Keith. "Political Economics, Schooling, and Literacy in the South." Ed.D. dissertation, Harvard University, 1995.

Wiebe, Robert H. *The Search for Order, 1877–1920.* New York: Hill & Wang, 1967.

Wilentz, Sean. *Chants Democratic: New York City and the Rise of the American Working Class, 1788–1850.* New York: Oxford University Press, 1984.

Wise, Henry A. *Drawing Out the Man: The VMI Story.* Charlottesville: University of Virginia Press, 1978.

Wise, Jennings C. *Personal Memoir of the Life and Services of Scott Shipp.* Lexington, VA [?]: N.p., 1915.

Wyatt-Brown, Bertram. *The Shaping of Southern Culture: Honor, Grace, and War, 1760s–1880s.* Chapel Hill: University of North Carolina Press, 2001.

————. *Southern Honor: Ethics and Behavior in the Old South.* New York: Oxford University Press, 1982.

Wyeth, John Allan. *The History of LaGrange Military Academy and the Cadet Corps.* New York: The Brewster Press, 1907.
Yates, Bowling C. *History of the Georgia Military Institute, Marietta, Georgia, Including the Confederate Military Service of the Cadet Battalion.* Marietta, GA: [The Author], 1968.

ARTICLES AND PAPERS

Acree, Mary Evelyn Turpin. "Fleetwood Academy." *The Bulletin of the King & Queen County,* 6 (January 1959): 1–2.
Agnew, James B. "Hellions From Marion Square." *Civil War Times Illustrated,* 21 (May 1982): 34–39.
Allardice, Bruce. "West Points of the Confederacy: Southern Military Schools and the Confederate Army." *Civil War History,* 43 (December 1997): 310–31.
Behle, J. Gregory and William Edgar Maxwell. "The Social Origins of Students at the Illinois Industrial University, 1868–1894." *History of Higher Education Annual,* 18 (1998): 93–109.
Benson, T. Lloyd. "The Plain Folk of Orange: Land, Work, and Society on the Eve of the Civil War." In *The Edge of the South: Life in Nineteenth-century Virginia,* edited by Edward L. Ayers and John C. Willis. Charlottesville: University Press of Virginia, 1991.
Berlin, Ira and Herbert G. Gutman. "Natives and Immigrants, Free Men and Slaves." *American Historical Review,* 88 (1983): 1175–1200.
Best, John Hardin. "Education in the Forming of the American South." *History of Education Quarterly,* 36 (Spring 1996): 39–51.
Blumin, Stuart M. "The Hypothesis of the Middle-class Formation in Nineteenth-century America: A Critique and Some Proposals." *American Historical Review,* 90 (1985): 299–338.
Bohannon, Keith. "Cadets, Drillmasters, Draft Dodgers, and Soldiers: The Georgia Military Institute During the Civil War." *Georgia Historical Quarterly,* 79 (1995): 5–29.
Boyd, David French. "General W. T. Sherman as a College President." *The American College,* 2 (April 1910): 1–8.
Bridges, Amy. "Becoming American: The Working Classes in the United States before the Civil War." In *Working-Class Formation: Nineteenth-century Patterns in Western Europe and the United States,* edited by Ira Katznelson and Aristide R. Zolberg. Princeton: Princeton University Press, 1986.
Brown, David. "Attacking Slavery from Within: The Making of *The Impending Crisis of the South.*" *Journal of Southern History,* 70 (August 2004): 541–76.
Campbell, Edward D. C., Jr. "Major Thomas J. Jackson and the Trial of Cadet Walker." *Virginia Military Institute Alumni Review* (Winter 1976): 19–21.
Chudacoff, Howard P. "Success and Security: The Meaning of Social Mobility in America." *Reviews in American History,* 10 (December 1982): 101–12.

Cline Cohen, Patricia. "Unregulated Youth: Masculinity and Murder in the 1830s City." *Radical History Review*, 52 (1992): 33–52.

Conrad, James L. "The Katydid Cadets." *Civil War Times Illustrated*, 21 (May 1982): 18–25.

———. "Training for Treason." *Civil War Times Illustrated*, 30 (September/October 1991): 23–64.

Cooling, B. Franklin, III. "Delaware Military Academy, 1859–1862." *Delaware History*, 14 (1971): 177–87.

Couper, William. "The V.M.I. Diploma." *The VMI Alumni News*, 6 (June 1930): 4.

Crowson, E. T. "Jenkins, Coward, and the Yorkville Boys." *Alumni News* (Winter 1974–5): 1–4.

Daniels, George H. "Business, Industry, and Politics in the Antebellum South: The View from Tuscaloosa, Alabama." *Proceedings of the 150th Anniversary Symposium on Technology and Society.* Tuscaloosa: University of Alabama, 1988.

Davis, O. L., Jr. "The Educational Association of the C.S.A." *Civil War History*, 10 (March 1964): 67–79.

Dodd, William G. "Early Education in Tallahassee and the West Florida Seminary, Now Florida State University." *The Florida Historical Quarterly*, 27 (1948): 172–88.

Dooley, Edwin L., Jr. "'A fine college from this time forward': The Influence of VMI on the Militarization of the University of Alabama." N.p., 19 April 1997.

———. "Gilt Buttons and the Collegiate Way: Francis H. Smith as Antebellum Schoolmaster." *Virginia Cavalcade*, 36 (1986): 30–9.

Drinkwater, L. Ray. "Honor and Student Misconduct in Southern Antebellum Colleges." *Southern Humanities Review*, 27 (Fall 1993): 323–44.

Durrill, Wayne K. "The Power of Ancient Words: Classical Teaching and Social Change at South Carolina College, 1804–1860." *Journal of Southern History*, 65 (August 1999): 469–98.

Easterlin, Richard A. "Regional Income Trends, 1840–1950." In *The Reinterpretation of American Economic History*, edited by Robert William Fogel and Stanley L. Engerman. New York: Harper and Row, 1971.

Eelman, Bruce W. "'An Educated and Intelligent People Cannot Be Enslaved': The Struggle for Common Schools in Antebellum Spartanburg, South Carolina." *History of Education Quarterly*, 44 (Summer 2004): 250–70.

Elson, Ruth Miller. "American Schoolbooks and 'Culture' in the Nineteenth Century." *Mississippi Valley Historical Review*, 46 (December 1959): 411–34.

Faludi, Susan. "The Naked Citadel." *New Yorker* (5 September 1994): 62–81.

"Family Losses in the Civil War." *The Confederate Veteran*, 10 (February 1902): 79–80.

Fishlow, Albert. "The American Common School Revival: Fact or Fancy." In *Industrialization in Two Systems*, edited by Henry Rosovksy. New York: John Wiley, 1966.

Flynt, Wayne. "Southern Higher Education and the Civil War." *Civil War History*, 14 (June 1968): 211–25.

Fox-Genovese, Elizabeth. "Strict Scrutiny, VMI, and Women's Lives." *Seton Hall Law School Constitutional Law Journal*, 6 (Summer 1996): 987–90.

Fraser, Cadet J. W. "First Cadet Finals Are Called to Mind." N.p., *c.* 1940.

Gallagher, Gary W. "A North Carolinian at West Point: Stephen Dodson Ramseur, 1855–60." *North Carolina Historical Review*, 62 (January 1985): 1–28.

Geiger, Roger. "The Rise and Fall of Useful Knowledge: Higher Education for Science, Agriculture and the Mechanics Arts, 1850–1875." *History of Higher Education Annual*, 18 (1998): 47–65.

Genovese, Eugene D. "Yeomen Farmers in a Slaveholders' Democracy." *Agricultural History*, 49 (April 1975): 331–42.

Gershenberg, Irving. "Southern Values and Public Education: A Revision." *History of Education Quarterly*, 10 (Winter 1970): 413–22.

Gianniny, O. Allan, Jr. "The Overlooked Southern Approach to Engineering Education: One and a Half Centuries at the University of Virginia, 1836–1986." *Proceedings of the 150th Anniversary Symposium on Technology and Society.* Tuscaloosa: University of Alabama, 1988.

Gorn, Elliott J. " 'Gouge and Bite, Pull Hair and Scratch': The Social Significance of Fighting in the Southern Backcountry." *American Historical Review*, 90 (February 1985): 18–43.

Granovetter, Mark. "The Strength of Weak Ties." *American Journal of Sociology*, 78 (1973): 1360–80.

Greenough, Jan Price. "Forgive Us Our Transgressions: Rule and Misrule in Antebellum Southern Schools." *Southern Historian*, 21 (2000): 5–24.

Guralnick, Stanley M. "Sources of Misconception of the Role of Science in the Nineteenth-century American College." In *Science in America Since 1820*, edited by Nathan Reingold. New York: Science History Publications, 1976.

Holifield, E. Brooks. "The Wealth of Nineteenth-Century American Physicians." *Bulletin of the History of Medicine*, 64 (Spring 1990): 79–85.

Holland, Lynwood M. "Georgia Military Institute, The West Point of Georgia, 1851–64." *Georgia Historical Quarterly*, 43 (1959): 225–47.

Hutson, Charles W. "The South Carolina College in the 1850s." *The Sewanee Review* (1910): 333–43.

Hyde, Samuel C., Jr. "*Plain Folk* Reconsidered: Historiographical Ambiguity in Search of Definition." *Journal of Southern History*, 71 (November 2005): 803–830.

Jabour, Anya. "Masculinity and Adolescence in Antebellum America: Robert Wirt at West Point, 1820–1821." *Journal of Family History*, 23 (October 1998): 393–416.

James, Mary Ann. "Engineering an Environment for Change: Bigelow, Peirce, and Early Nineteenth-Century Practical Education at Harvard." In *Science at Harvard: Historical Perspectives*, edited by Clark A. Elliott and Margaret W. Rossiter. Bethlehem: Lehigh University Press, 1992.

Johnson, Dudley S. "William Harris Garland: Mechanic of the Old South." *Georgia Historical Quarterly*, 53 (1969): 41–56.

Katz, Michael B. "Occupational Classification in History." *Journal of Interdisciplinary History*, 3 (Summer 1972): 63–88.

Katznelson, Ira. "Working-class Formation: Constructing Cases and Comparison." In *Working-Class Formation: Nineteenth-Century Patterns in Western Europe and the United States*, edited by Ira Katznelson and Aristide R. Zolberg. Princeton: Princeton University Press, 1986.

Kilbride, Daniel. "Southern Medical Students in Philadelphia, 1800–1860: Science and Sociability in the 'Republic of Medicine.'" *Journal of Southern History*, 65 (November 1999): 697–732.

Knapp, John W. "Designed to be Permanent." N.p., n.d.

Lears, T. J. Jackson. "The Concept of Cultural Hegemony: Problems and Possibilities," *American Historical Review*, 90 (1985): 567–593.

Lisowksi, Lori A. "The Future of West Point: Senate Debates on the Military Academy During the Civil War." *Civil War History*, 34 (March 1988): 5–21.

London, Lena. "The Military Fine, 1830–1860." *Military Affairs*, 15 (Fall 1951): 133–44.

Lord, Gary Thomas. "Alden Partridge's Proposal for a National System of Education: A Model for the Morrill Land-Grant Act." *History of Higher Education Annual*, 18 (1998): 11–24.

Lyle, Royster, Jr. and Matthew W. Paxton Jr. "The VMI Barracks." *Virginia Cavalcade*, 23 (1974): 14–29.

Mayer, Arno J. "The Lower Middle Class as Historical Problem." *Journal of Modern History*, 47 (September 1975): 409–36.

Mayfield, John. "'The Soul of a Man': William Gilmore Simms and the Myth of Southern Manhood." *Journal of the Early Republic*, 15 (Fall 1995): 477–500.

McLachlin, James. "The *Choice of Hercules*: American Student Societies in the Early 19th Century." In *The University in Society*, edited by Lawrence Stone. Vol. 2. Princeton: Princeton University Press, 1974.

Morrison, James L., Jr. "Educating the Civil War General: West Point, 1833–1861." *Military Affairs*, 38 (October 1974): 108–11.

———. "Getting through West Point: The Cadet Memoirs of John C. Tidball, Class of 1848." *Civil War History*, 26 (December 1980): 304–25.

Naylor, Natalie A. "The Antebellum College Movement: A Reappraisal of Tewksbury's *Founding of American Colleges and Universities*." *History of Education Quarterly*, 13 (Fall 1973): 261–74.

Oakes, James. "The Politics of Economic Development in the Antebellum South." *Journal of Interdisciplinary History*, 15 (Autumn 1984): 305–16.

O'Boyle, Lenore. "The Classless Society: Comment on Stearns." *Comparative Studies of Society and History*, 21 (July 1979): 397–413.

Pace, Robert F. and Christopher A. Bjornsen. "Adolescent Honor and College Student Behavior in the Old South." *Southern Cultures*, 6 (Fall 2000): 9–28.

Pearson, Alden B., Jr. "A Middle-class, Border-state Family During the Civil War." In *The Southern Common People: Studies in Nineteenth-century Social*

History, edited by Edward Magdol and Jon L. Wakelyn. Westport, CT: Greenwood Press, 1980.

Pflugrad-Jackisch, Ami. "A Host of Shameless Imposters: Fraternal Orders and the Urban Confidence Man in Antebellum Virginia." Presented at Southern Historical Association Conference, Memphis, TN, November 4, 2004.

Posey, Walter Brownlow. "LaGrange: Alabama's Earliest College." *Birmingham-Southern College Bulletin*, 26 (November 1933): 3–23.

Reynolds, Terry S. "The Education of Engineers in America Before the Morrill Act of 1862." *History of Education Quarterly*, 32 (Winter 1992): 459–82.

Ross, Stephen A. "Hillsboro Military Academy." *Bennett Place Quarterly* (Summer 1999): 1–2.

_____. "To 'Prepare Our Sons for all the Duties that May Lie before Them': The Hillsborough Military Academy and Military Education in Antebellum North Carolina." *North Carolina Historical Review*, 79 (January 2002): 1–27.

Ryan, Mary P. "Thinking Class." *American Quarterly*, 37 (Spring 1985): 140–45.

Skelton, William B. "The Army in the Age of the Common Man, 1815–1845." In *Against All Enemies*, edited by Kenneth J. Hagan and William R. Roberts. Westport, CT: Greenwood Press, 1986.

Smith, Peter Tincher. "The Militia of the United States, 1846–1860." *New York Review*, 15 (1919): 21–47.

Stearns, Peter N. "The Effort at Continuity in Working-class Culture." *Journal of Modern History*, 52 (December 1980): 626–55.

_____. "The Middle Class: Toward a Precise Definition." *Comparative Studies in Society and History*, 21 (July 1979): 377–96.

"Symposium: Reappraisals of the Academy Movement." *History of Education Quarterly*, 41 (Summer 2001): 216–70.

Thornton, J. Mills, III. "Fiscal Policy and the Failure of Radical Reconstruction in the Lower South." In *Region, Race, and Reconstruction: Essays in Honor of C. Vann Woodward*, edited by J. Morgan Kousser and James M. McPherson. New York: Oxford University Press, 1982.

Tolley, Kim. "Science for Ladies, Classics for Gentlemen: A Comparative Analysis of Scientific Subjects in the Curricula of Boys' and Girls' Secondary Schools in the United States, 1794–1850." *History of Education Quarterly*, 36 (Summer 1996): 129–154.

Urban, Wayne J. "History of Education: Southern Exposure." *History of Education Quarterly*, 21 (Summer 1981): 131–45.

Vinovskis, Maris A. "Have We Underestimated the Extent of Antebellum High School Attendance?" *History of Education Quarterly*, 28 (Winter 1988): 551–68.

_____. "Quantification and the Analysis of American Antebellum Education." *Journal of Interdisciplinary History*, 13 (Spring 1983): 761–86.

Wagoner, Jennings L., Jr. "Honor and Dishonor at Mr. Jefferson's University: The Antebellum Years." *History of Education Quarterly*, 26 (Summer 1986): 154–79.

Warner, John Harley. "A Southern Medical Reform." In *Science and Medicine in the Old South*, edited by Ronald L. Numbers and Todd L. Savitt. Baton Rouge: Louisiana State University Press, 1989.

Zuckerman, Michael. "Penmanship Exercises for Saucy Sons: Some Thoughts on the Colonial Southern Family." *South Carolina Historical Magazine*, 84 (1983): 152–66.

Index

middle-class constituency, 75–76, 131,
146–49, 228, 246
regulations, 44, 54, 63–68, 70, 92, 99, 112,
136, 138
the poor unable to afford, 138, 254
Military service (antebellum), 3, 165
Militias, 218–19
Modernizing trends, *See* Economic and
social change
Morrill Land Grant Act, 206, 257

Normal schools, *See* Teachers: training

Oakes, James, 17, 27, 172, 196
Orphans, 55, 147. *See also* Cadets: family
position (birth order)

Panic of 1837, 50, 54, 145, 163
Parents/parenting, 44, 60, 70–72, 81, 90, 98,
102, 109, 113, 115, 124, 127, 23–34, 247, 250,
254. *See also* Discipline: parental
expectations; Education: family
aspirations; Women. Professionalization; Chapter 7
concern about money, 43–51, 52–54
fathers' occupations, 21–26, 145, 265–68
guardians, 50, 55–56, 57, 233, 268
Partridge, Alden, 3, 41, 68
Patronage, 52–54, 57, 72, 235
Physicians, 25, 57, 145, 159, 162, 175, 178,
197–99, 215
Plain folk, 17, 226
Planters, 17, 20–21, 22, 26, 27, 31–32, 74, 105–6,
153, 167, 168, 172–73, 180, 197, 208–9, 229,
245
Politics, 247
Practical, *See* Curriculum: practical
nineteenth-century definition of,
131
Professionalization, 12, 154, 155, 162, 183,
197–99, 202, 206–7, 211, 220, 254
Progress
19th-century definition of, 131
acceptance of, 20, 130, 223, 258
as science and technology, 138–40
as vocation, 142–44
Proprietors, 19, 25, 164, 165, 172, 227
Public service careers, 22, 25, 165–66

Rappahannock Military Institute, 64, 93, 174,
184, 192, 213

Refinement, 50, 109, 242
Religion, 105, 117–19, 125, 140
Ruffin, Edmund, 26, 32, 54

Schedules, *See* Military education:
regulations
Scholarships, 36, 42, 147, 233
at military schools vs. state universities, 8,
39–40
recipients' requirement to teach, 3, 85, 101,
179, 195
Science education, *See* Curriculum: practical
Secession, 247–48
Self-discipline, 9, 76, 78, 81, 96, 104, 105, 117,
121, 128, 242, 255. *See also* Chapter 4
Shepherd, Edward C., 43, 235
Sherman, William T., 199, 204
Simpson, Robert H., 124, 130, 182, 192, 195,
205, 210, 258
Slave ownership, 12, 26–28, 102,
229
Slaves, *See* African Americans: enslaved
Smith, Francis H., 11, 38, 42, 45, 47, 53, 69, 72,
82, 89, 93, 111, 130, 139, 148–49, 174, 182,
184–85, 187, 194, 199, 201, 204, 205, 252,
258
Social mobility, 11, 19, 152–53, 156–58, 161, 180,
194, 196, 227, 231, 255
alumni compared to family, 25, 169–72,
175–77, 233
and stability, 177, 183, 214, 219–21
fear of downward mobility, 157,
242
South Carolina College, 8, 31, 60, 63, 114,
133–34, 208, 250
South Carolina Military Academy, 8, 22, 38,
40, 43, 54, 55, 89, 120, 138, 139, 159, 162,
168, 185, 195, 204, 211, 228, 248, 252,
258
Southern community expectations, 12, 31, 72,
79, 92, 104, 153, 208, 220, 245
Status, 20, 22, 25, 34, 53, 77, 107, 109, 142, 152,
153–54, 168, 177, 180, 194, 196, 197, 215,
219–20, 225, 230, 231, 241, 243–44, 255.
See also Social mobility
alumni occupational status, 159, 160,
164–66, 177–78, 190
defined, 16
of teachers, 192, 195, 199, 206, 224
redefinition by middle class, 102, 105,
107–8, 154–56, 256

For EU product safety concerns, contact us at Calle de José Abascal, 56–1°,
28003 Madrid, Spain or eugpsr@cambridge.org.